Martin,

Stop ....

years before buying

my next book!

To my wonderful father,
who I know will read this
book cover to cover, but
not understand it.

"Yesterday is gone. Tomorrow has not yet come. We have only today. Let us begin." -

Mother Theresa.

Published in English in 2019 by TPub Ltd copyright © Twisted Studios Ltd, trading as TPub Comics. All rights reserved.

T Pub

Publisher/ Creative Director: Neil Gibson
Head of Operations: Linda Canton
Digital Distributor: Staci Sherman
Team Manager: Jodie Denton
Editorial Assistance: Sarah Meeks
Head of Social Media: Leon Othenin-Girard
Secret Weapons: Eli Morgan, Kush Gorasia, and Ian Assang
Friend: Jennifer Yi

Neil Gibson's Twisted Sci-fi

The Theory

Volume 1

Written by: David Court, Forrest Helvie, and Neil Gibson

Illustrated by: Amrit Birdi, Atula Siriwardane, Cem Iroz, Davide Puppo, Jake Elphick, Jim Terry, Phil Buckenham, and V.V. Glass

Covers: Abigail Harding and Vince Sunico

Additional artwork: Chelsea Ambrose, Rob Banbury and Cornelia Abfalter

Coloured by: Liezl Buenaventura

Lettered by: Justin Birch

Edited by: Sarah Meeks with Neil Gibson

Additional story edits and special thanks to: Nieros

Graphic Design by: Jed McPherson and Sarah Meeks

Accidental Financier: A.C.: DMWH

Intentional Investor: M.V.H.

Deal Maker: Kenny Diack

Science Advice: Kian Momtahan and Mark Maslin

Neil Gibson is an odd guy.

I know this, because I know him. I mean, I really know the guy. We've shared the stage, sleeping spaces, meals, and one time his toothbrush (but, don't tell him that, he'd freak out.) We've stayed at each others homes, played with the others' kids, and I may or may not have let a certain Mr. Gibson sleep in my lap while TTC'ing it home after a particularly eventful post Fan Expo evening.

So, take it from me when I say this oddness is a feature, not a bug. You see, the way Neil thinks about the world is wholly unique. I've never met someone who is so logical, who can so effortlessly and completely think things through, who also is so wildly creative.

I've also never met someone who is so easy to fool.

"...this oddness is a feature not a bug."

Seriously, if you have a wild and outlandish story that you can say with a straight face, Neil James Gibson will buy it. Hook. Line. And Sinker. And then, after he realizes you've been putting him on, his eyes will get wide, and he'll get ready to swear at you before breaking into a big laugh. Then he'll offer you a gin and tonic, made with some impossibly good old British gin, and try to get you very drunk so he can plot his revenge while you're insensible.

And it will be a kind, and very funny revenge, except you won't fall for it, because for all his gifts, Neil is REALLY bad at lying or pretending. But he'll laugh at that too, because there is nothing Neil likes better in life than a good joke. Even if he is the butt of it.

That's as long as you admit you've taken the piss. Neil does NOT like people holding on to the joke too long. He sees it as being cruel. It's one thing to trick someone so that everyone, including the person tricked, has had a laugh. It's another for that person to feel like they've been targeted.

"Neil has started another incredible journey with this book."

I haven't mentioned this part yet, but in addition to being odd, Neil is an incredibly kind human being. You see it in how he treats his family. You see it in the way he works with his team at TPub, and you especially see it at conventions. If you've never met Neil in person, I BEG you to do so. Go up to him at a convention and I promise you, you'll leave his presence feeling better about yourself, and the world in general.

I bring all this up to really underscore how outright bizarre it is that someone so logical, so kind, so uplifting, can write so many fucked up stories.

I apologize for cursing, but there isn't any other way to describe his work. It all started back with Twisted Dark, which is how I first met Neil – being pulled in by THE classic image of the series. An evilly-grinning mouth, blood staining the teeth. If you haven't read any of Neil's magnus opus – a sprawling series of very nasty stories which seem completely separate yet somehow all begin to entwine – then you're missing out.

Think of it as The Twilight Zone, but in a shared universe, and written by the illegitimate child Steven King never knew he had. It's brilliant, and I am mad at him that it has taken him as long as it has to get out as much as he has.

I guess his excuse is that in addition to being a writer, Neil also RUNS TPub, which he has built into one of the most interesting and thriving independents out there. Neil's goal with TPub isn't just to entreating comic fans with his stories, its to convert the world into seeing the power of the comics medium for storytelling and communication. (it also may be that, hilariously for a guy running a freaking media empire, Neil is an awful multi-tasker. Seriously, when you do meet Neil at a convention, buy a book and ask him to sign it, then ask him a question about his process. The results will be adorable.)

TPub is the best publishing house you've (probably) never heard of, and also a great hub for launching new talent. A huge chunk of Britain's best young, and deranged, creators – I like to call them New Gonzo – started with Neil. People like Ryan O'Sullivan, Caspar Wijngaard, and Dan Watters all cut their teeth at TPub. If you've bought this book and are an aspiring comic creator, I highly recommend you take Neil's webinars on how to make it in the industry. Better yet, use those to create the perfect pitch and bring your book to Neil. He'll treat it like it's own. I should know. I've done that myself.

So this is all a long road to get to the book you're holding in your hands now. Twisted Sci-Fi/The Theory. It has all the hallmarks of a classic Gibson yarn. Several, seemingly unrelated storylines. Gotcha twists. A shocking amount of emotional resonance in so few pages. And, new to the broth, is Neil's incredible grasp of what makes science fiction awesome. From giant mechs with hidden secrets, ill-fated quests to conquer death, to a time-travelling visitor you'd never want to meet, but just have to say hello to, Neil has started another incredible journey with this book.

It makes me kind of hate the man, actually. Why does he get to be so good at inventing totally unique worlds in multiple genres no less, while I'm barely passable at stealing other people's characters and trying to make them my own?

> ## "...how bizarre it is that someone so logical, so kind, so uplifting, can write so many f**ked up stories."

It's because of that off brain of his, And next time I see him, I'm going to plant a big fat kiss on that wonderful dome, and give him a big hug…

… while planting a "Find a Creative Way to Make me Multi-task" sign on his back.

Trust me. As long as I don't let it go on too long, and drink whatever he gives me after, Neil will have a good laugh.

He's just that kind of guy.

Conor McCreery
Toronto, 2019

Conor McCreery is the swashbuckling wordsmith/former and oft death-threatened journalist behind Adventure Time/Regular Show (BOOM!), Kill Shakespeare (IDW), series, Assassin's Creed (Titan Comics), Sherlock Holmes vs Harry Houdini (Dynamite) and more! His newest projects are the creator-owned, YA adventure series Catacombers, the gothic horror adventure Witchmark (BOOM!) and a magic realism comics biography of the legendary Fela Kuti: Music is the Weapon, with superstar artist Jibola Fagbamiye. Kill Shakespeare has been Optioned for film by NBC's production arm, UCP. He's represented by Tanya McKinnon (McKinnon McIntyre) for print, and Ari Greenberg (WME), and Jeff Okin (Anonymous Content) for Film and Television.

Social Media;

@tpubcomics
@tpubcomics
@tpubcomics

Contents

Obsession

"Without Obsession, life is nothing"

John Waters

Writer/Creator
Neil Gibson

Story
David Court

Illustrator
Phil Buckenham

Colourist
Liezl Buenaventura

Letters by
Justin Birch

www.tpubcomics.com

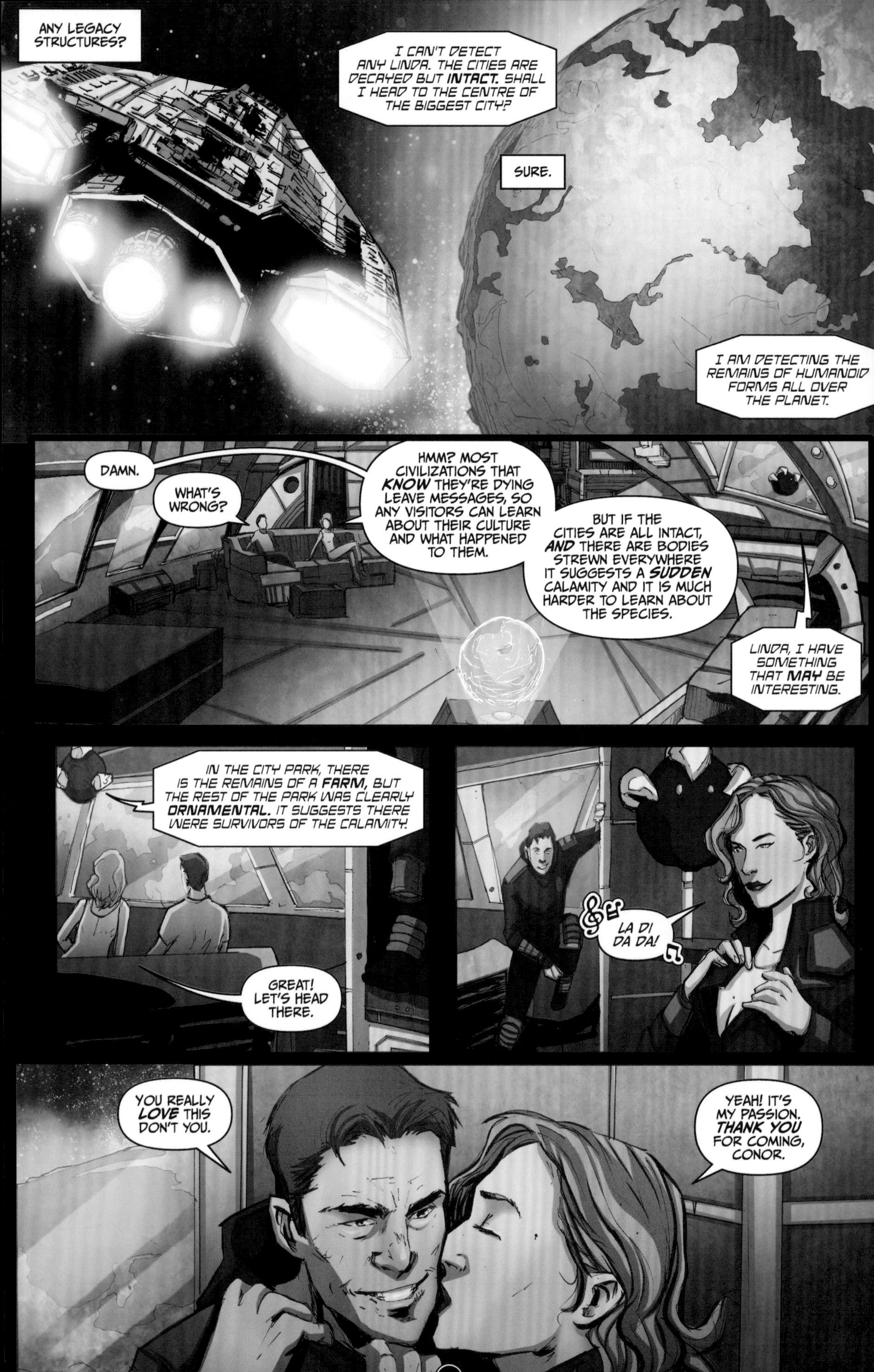
ANY LEGACY STRUCTURES?
I CAN'T DETECT ANY LINDA. THE CITIES ARE DECAYED BUT INTACT. SHALL I HEAD TO THE CENTRE OF THE BIGGEST CITY?
SURE.
I AM DETECTING THE REMAINS OF HUMANOID FORMS ALL OVER THE PLANET.
DAMN.
WHAT'S WRONG?
HMM? MOST CIVILIZATIONS THAT KNOW THEY'RE DYING LEAVE MESSAGES, SO ANY VISITORS CAN LEARN ABOUT THEIR CULTURE AND WHAT HAPPENED TO THEM.
BUT IF THE CITIES ARE ALL INTACT, AND THERE ARE BODIES STREWN EVERYWHERE IT SUGGESTS A SUDDEN CALAMITY AND IT IS MUCH HARDER TO LEARN ABOUT THE SPECIES.
LINDA, I HAVE SOMETHING THAT MAY BE INTERESTING.
IN THE CITY PARK, THERE IS THE REMAINS OF A FARM, BUT THE REST OF THE PARK WAS CLEARLY ORNAMENTAL. IT SUGGESTS THERE WERE SURVIVORS OF THE CALAMITY.
GREAT! LET'S HEAD THERE.
LA DI DA DA!
YOU REALLY LOVE THIS DON'T YOU.
YEAH! IT'S MY PASSION. THANK YOU FOR COMING, CONOR.

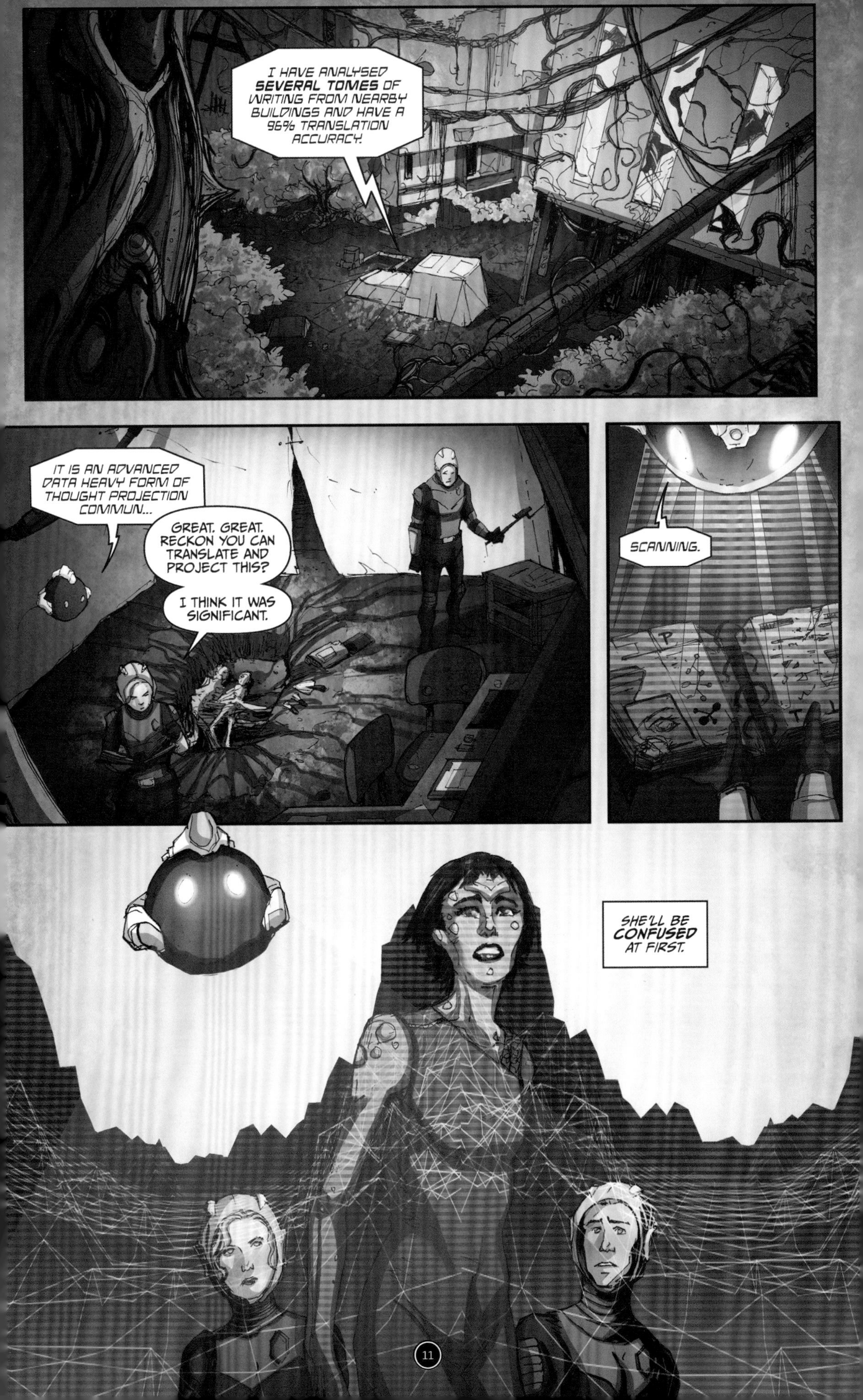
I HAVE ANALYSED SEVERAL TOMES OF WRITING FROM NEARBY BUILDINGS AND HAVE A 96% TRANSLATION ACCURACY.
IT IS AN ADVANCED DATA HEAVY FORM OF THOUGHT PROJECTION COMMUN...
GREAT. GREAT. RECKON YOU CAN TRANSLATE AND PROJECT THIS?
I THINK IT WAS SIGNIFICANT.
SCANNING.
SHE'LL BE CONFUSED AT FIRST.

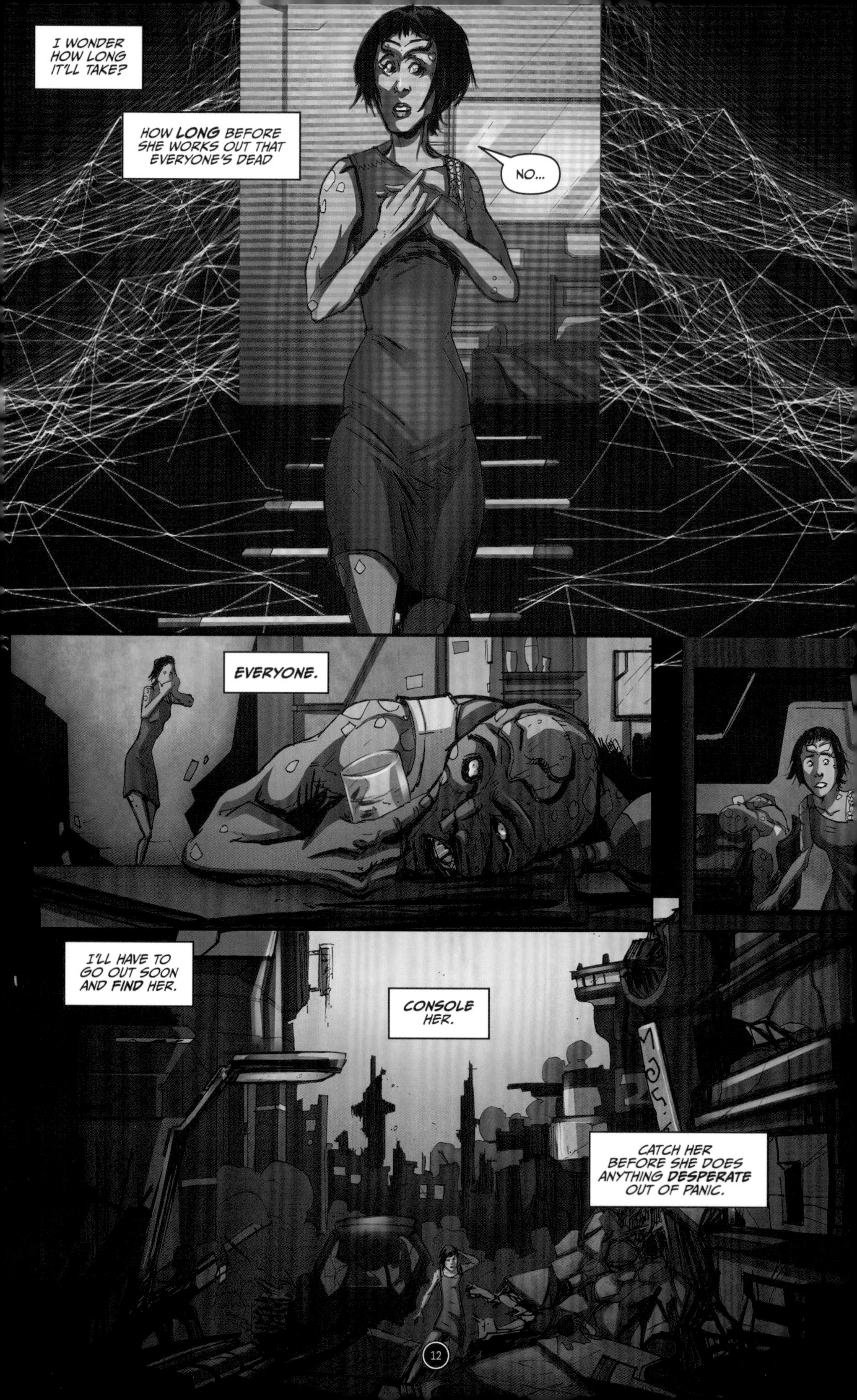
I WONDER HOW LONG IT'LL TAKE?
HOW LONG BEFORE SHE WORKS OUT THAT EVERYONE'S DEAD
NO...
EVERYONE.
I'LL HAVE TO GO OUT SOON AND FIND HER.
CONSOLE HER.
CATCH HER BEFORE SHE DOES ANYTHING DESPERATE OUT OF PANIC.

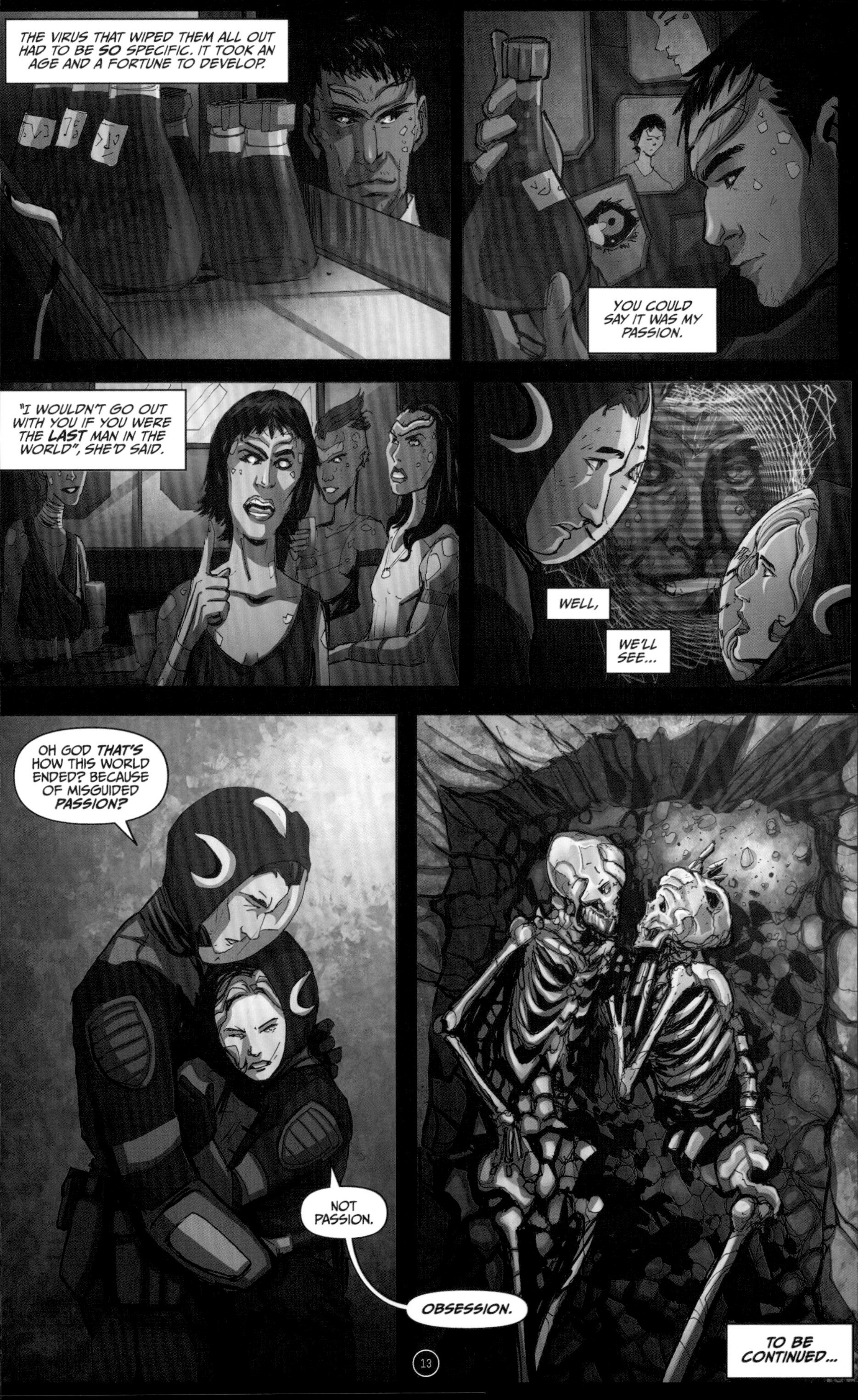
THE VIRUS THAT WIPED THEM ALL OUT HAD TO BE SO SPECIFIC. IT TOOK AN AGE AND A FORTUNE TO DEVELOP.
YOU COULD SAY IT WAS MY PASSION.
"I WOULDN'T GO OUT WITH YOU IF YOU WERE THE LAST MAN IN THE WORLD", SHE'D SAID.
WELL,
WE'LL SEE...
OH GOD THAT'S HOW THIS WORLD ENDED? BECAUSE OF MISGUIDED PASSION?
NOT PASSION.
OBSESSION.
TO BE CONTINUED...

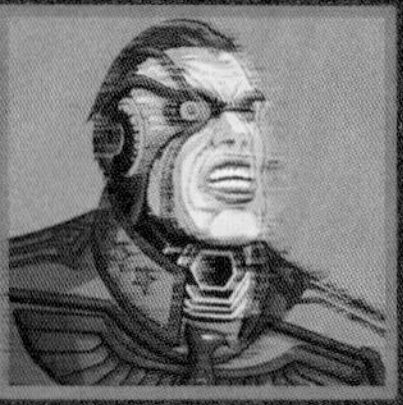

ADMIRAL PUPPO

Reports from the astroarchaeologists say that they have found another dead world.

ROBERT SADLER

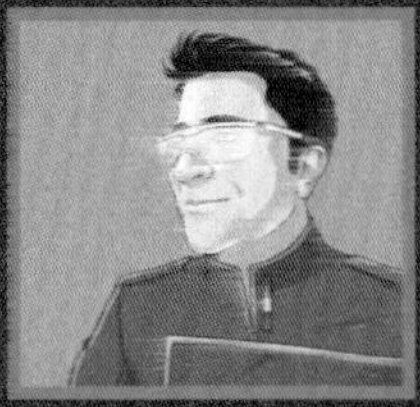

Not dead per say, animal and plant life remain, but the intelligent species are no more.

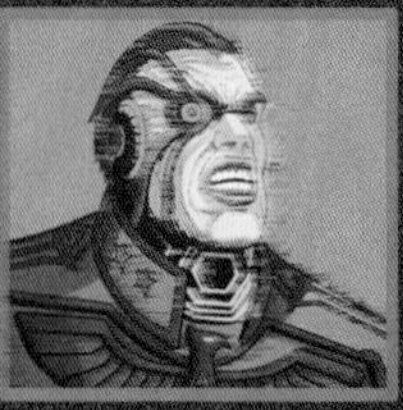

ADMIRAL PUPPO

You ***KNOW*** what I mean. Report.

ROBERT SADLER

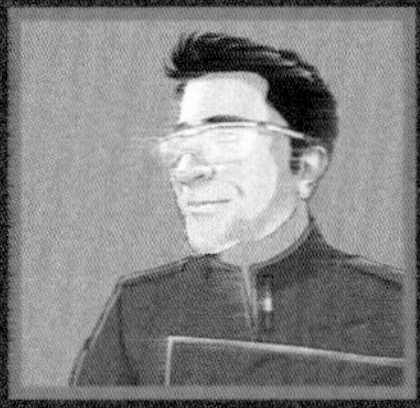

Technologically the species were far from our level, having failed to leave their own solar system. Reports show that mankind at a similar technological level would already have launched intra-solar probes and exploration. It seems like the race were somehow highly connected to their natural environment. The knock-on affect appears to have resulted in technology being developed in an inward direction. By our standards, green-technology was constructed decades before we even considered it necessity and conflict over resources were on a much smaller scale. To put it simply, atomics were never used; in fact I don't think the idea would even have occurred to them.

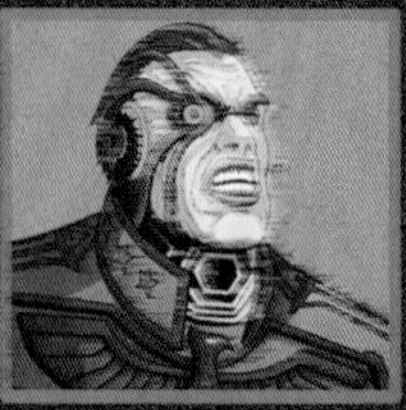

ADMIRAL PUPPO

Fine. Does the planet have anything of use

ROBERT SADLER

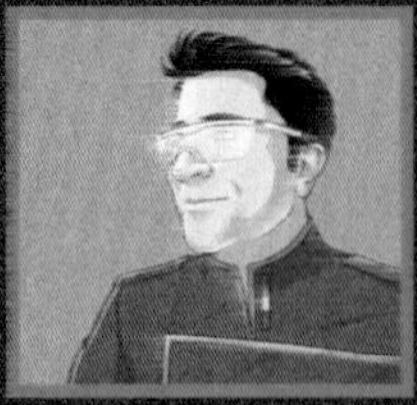

Nothing from the civilisation springs to mind. To me it seems the astro-archaeologists were very lucky in this case and found the reason for the civilisation collapse very quickly. The various flora and fauna should be analysed.

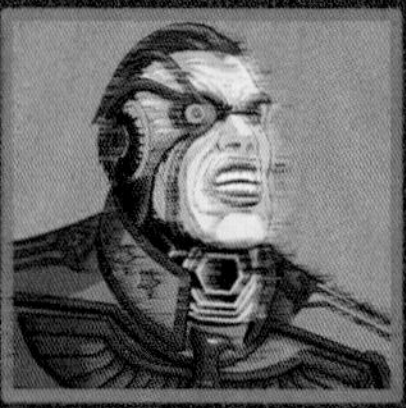

ADMIRAL PUPPO

Organise bots to pick and preserve samples for the labs back home.

Pandora

"There is only one happiness in this life, to love and to be loved"

George Sand

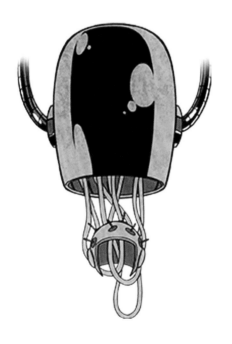

Plot
Forest Helvie/
Neil Gibson

Writer/Creator
Neil Gibson

Illustrator
Phil Buckenham

Colourist
Liezl Buenaventura

Letters by
Justin Birch

www.tpubcomics.com

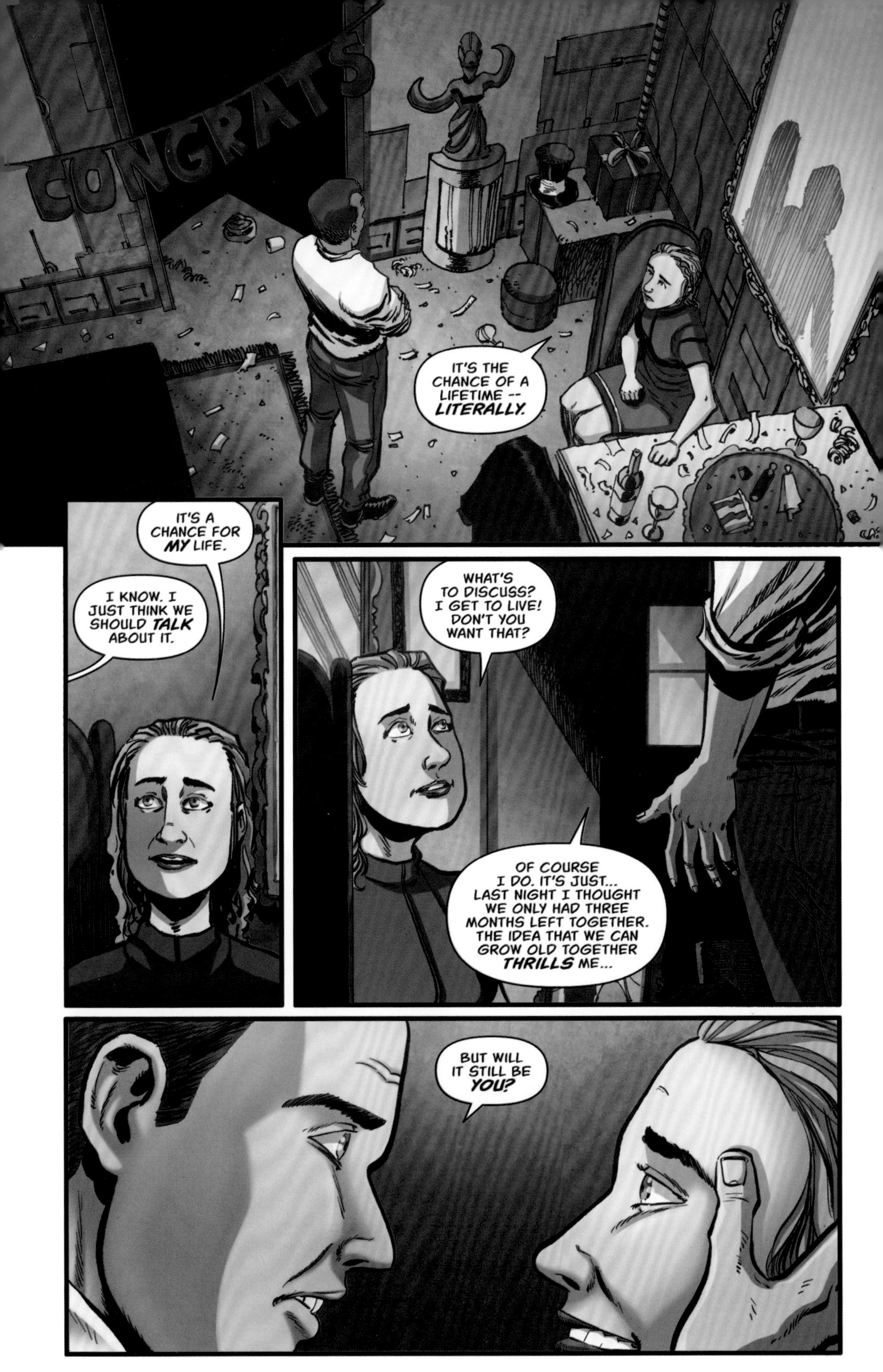
CONGRATS
IT'S THE CHANCE OF A LIFETIME -- *LITERALLY.*
IT'S A CHANCE FOR *MY* LIFE.
I KNOW. I JUST THINK WE SHOULD *TALK* ABOUT IT.
WHAT'S TO DISCUSS? I GET TO LIVE! DON'T YOU WANT THAT?
OF COURSE I DO. IT'S JUST... LAST NIGHT I THOUGHT WE ONLY HAD THREE MONTHS LEFT TOGETHER. THE IDEA THAT WE CAN GROW OLD TOGETHER *THRILLS* ME...
BUT WILL IT STILL BE *YOU?*

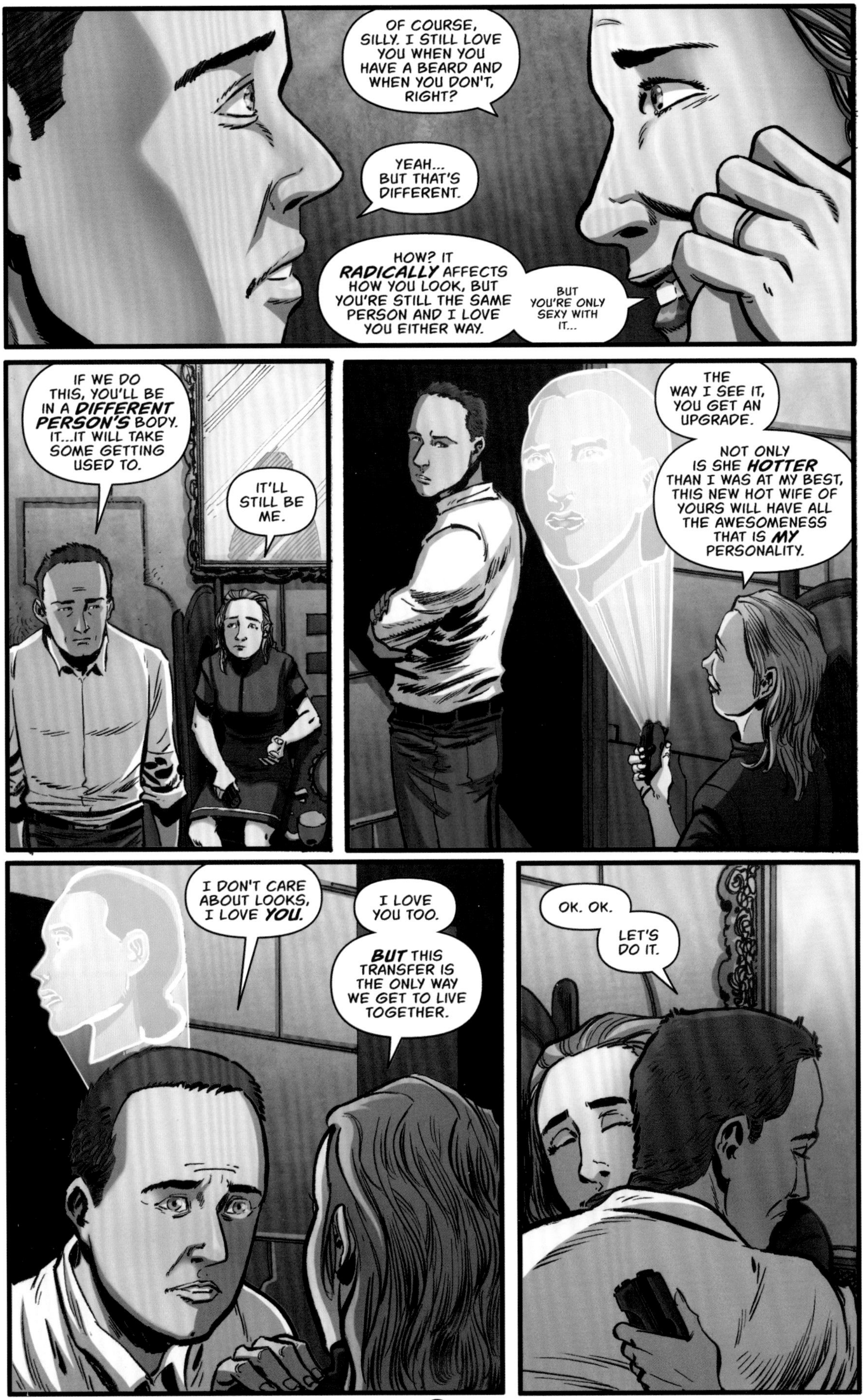
OF COURSE, SILLY. I STILL LOVE YOU WHEN YOU HAVE A BEARD AND WHEN YOU DON'T, RIGHT?
YEAH... BUT THAT'S DIFFERENT.
HOW? IT RADICALLY AFFECTS HOW YOU LOOK, BUT YOU'RE STILL THE SAME PERSON AND I LOVE YOU EITHER WAY.
BUT YOU'RE ONLY SEXY WITH IT...
IF WE DO THIS, YOU'LL BE IN A DIFFERENT PERSON'S BODY. IT...IT WILL TAKE SOME GETTING USED TO.
IT'LL STILL BE ME.
THE WAY I SEE IT, YOU GET AN UPGRADE.
NOT ONLY IS SHE HOTTER THAN I WAS AT MY BEST, THIS NEW HOT WIFE OF YOURS WILL HAVE ALL THE AWESOMENESS THAT IS MY PERSONALITY.
I DON'T CARE ABOUT LOOKS, I LOVE YOU.
I LOVE YOU TOO.
BUT THIS TRANSFER IS THE ONLY WAY WE GET TO LIVE TOGETHER.
OK. OK.
LET'S DO IT.

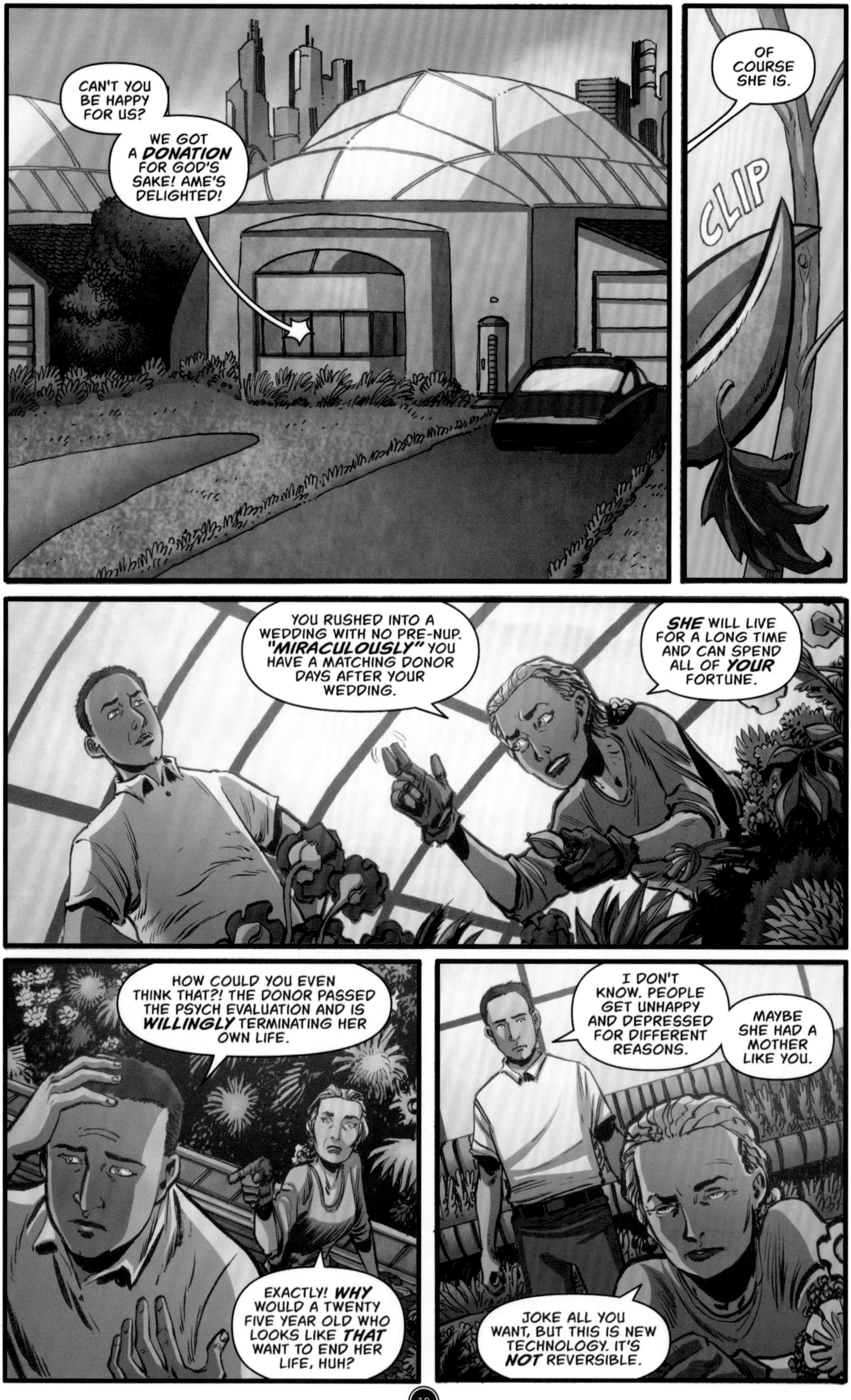

CAN'T YOU BE HAPPY FOR US?
WE GOT A DONATION FOR GOD'S SAKE! AME'S DELIGHTED!
OF COURSE SHE IS.
CLIP
YOU RUSHED INTO A WEDDING WITH NO PRE-NUP. "MIRACULOUSLY" YOU HAVE A MATCHING DONOR DAYS AFTER YOUR WEDDING.
SHE WILL LIVE FOR A LONG TIME AND CAN SPEND ALL OF YOUR FORTUNE.
HOW COULD YOU EVEN THINK THAT?! THE DONOR PASSED THE PSYCH EVALUATION AND IS WILLINGLY TERMINATING HER OWN LIFE.
EXACTLY! WHY WOULD A TWENTY FIVE YEAR OLD WHO LOOKS LIKE THAT WANT TO END HER LIFE, HUH?
I DON'T KNOW. PEOPLE GET UNHAPPY AND DEPRESSED FOR DIFFERENT REASONS.
MAYBE SHE HAD A MOTHER LIKE YOU.
JOKE ALL YOU WANT, BUT THIS IS NEW TECHNOLOGY. IT'S NOT REVERSIBLE.

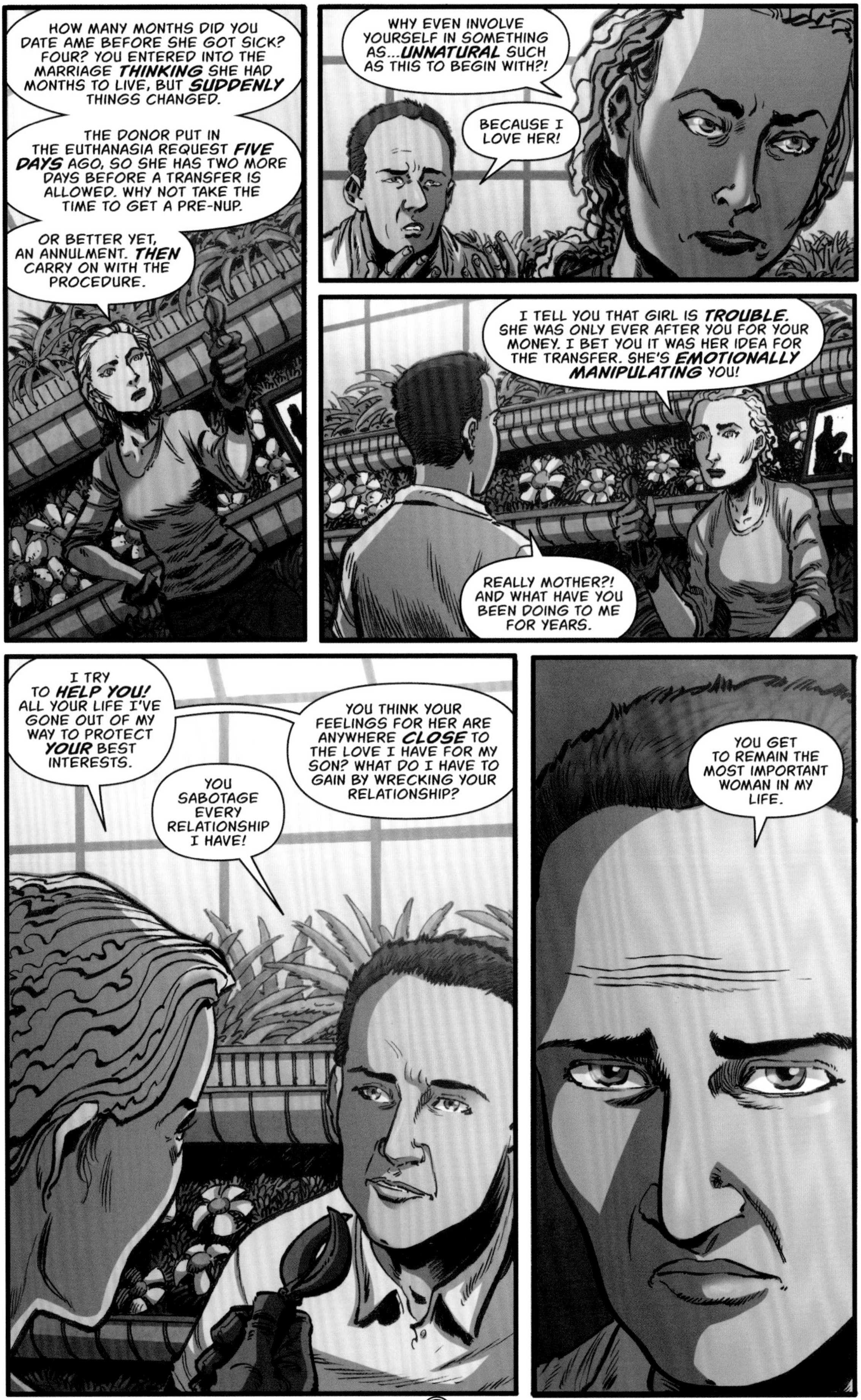

HOW MANY MONTHS DID YOU DATE AME BEFORE SHE GOT SICK? FOUR? YOU ENTERED INTO THE MARRIAGE THINKING SHE HAD MONTHS TO LIVE, BUT SUDDENLY THINGS CHANGED.
THE DONOR PUT IN THE EUTHANASIA REQUEST FIVE DAYS AGO, SO SHE HAS TWO MORE DAYS BEFORE A TRANSFER IS ALLOWED. WHY NOT TAKE THE TIME TO GET A PRE-NUP.
OR BETTER YET, AN ANNULMENT. THEN CARRY ON WITH THE PROCEDURE.
WHY EVEN INVOLVE YOURSELF IN SOMETHING AS...UNNATURAL SUCH AS THIS TO BEGIN WITH?!
BECAUSE I LOVE HER!
I TELL YOU THAT GIRL IS TROUBLE. SHE WAS ONLY EVER AFTER YOU FOR YOUR MONEY. I BET YOU IT WAS HER IDEA FOR THE TRANSFER. SHE'S EMOTIONALLY MANIPULATING YOU!
REALLY MOTHER?! AND WHAT HAVE YOU BEEN DOING TO ME FOR YEARS.
I TRY TO HELP YOU! ALL YOUR LIFE I'VE GONE OUT OF MY WAY TO PROTECT YOUR BEST INTERESTS.
YOU SABOTAGE EVERY RELATIONSHIP I HAVE!
YOU THINK YOUR FEELINGS FOR HER ARE ANYWHERE CLOSE TO THE LOVE I HAVE FOR MY SON? WHAT DO I HAVE TO GAIN BY WRECKING YOUR RELATIONSHIP?
YOU GET TO REMAIN THE MOST IMPORTANT WOMAN IN MY LIFE.

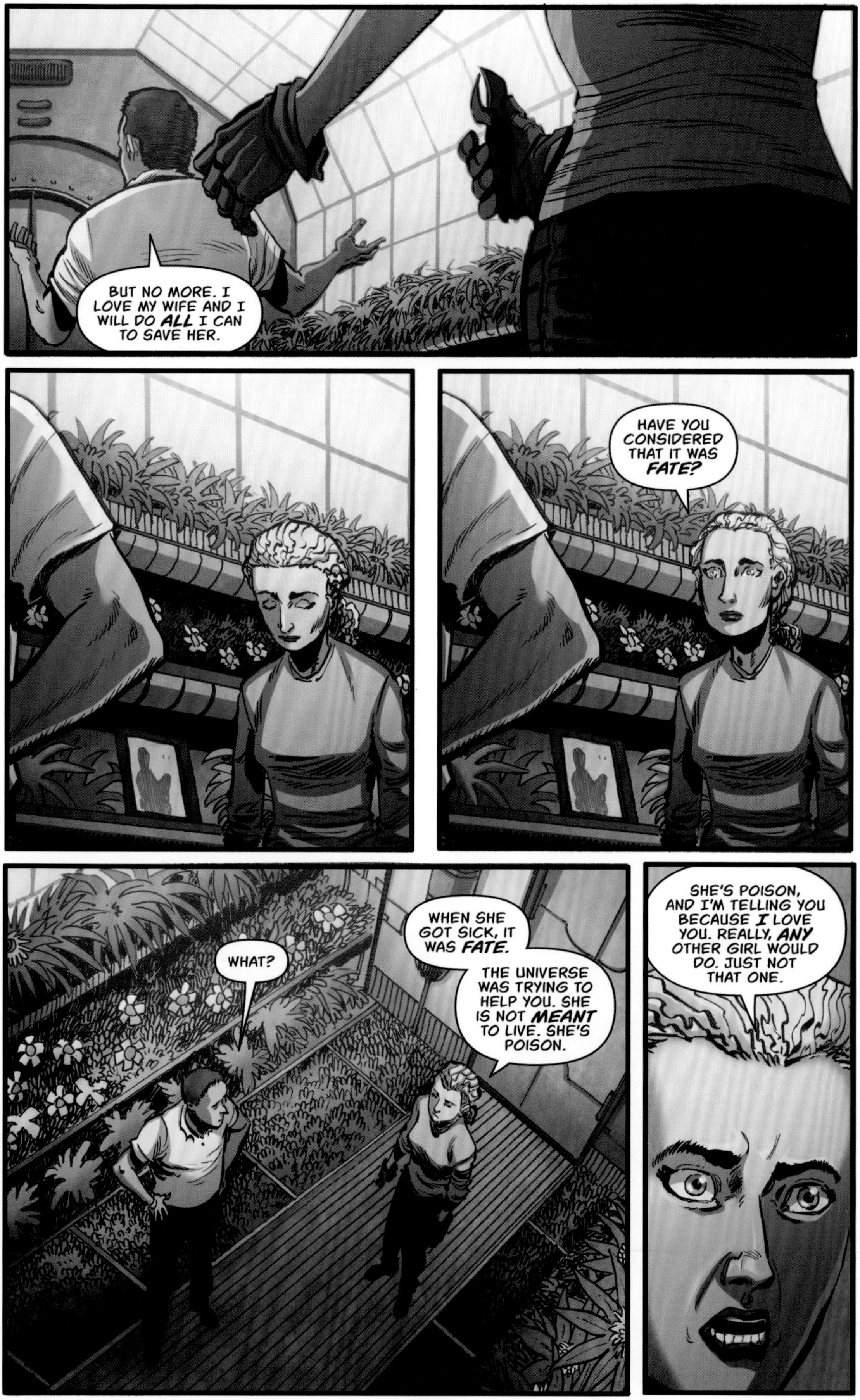
BUT NO MORE. I LOVE MY WIFE AND I WILL DO ALL I CAN TO SAVE HER.
HAVE YOU CONSIDERED THAT IT WAS FATE?
WHAT?
WHEN SHE GOT SICK, IT WAS FATE.
THE UNIVERSE WAS TRYING TO HELP YOU. SHE IS NOT MEANT TO LIVE. SHE'S POISON.
SHE'S POISON, AND I'M TELLING YOU BECAUSE I LOVE YOU. REALLY, ANY OTHER GIRL WOULD DO. JUST NOT THAT ONE.

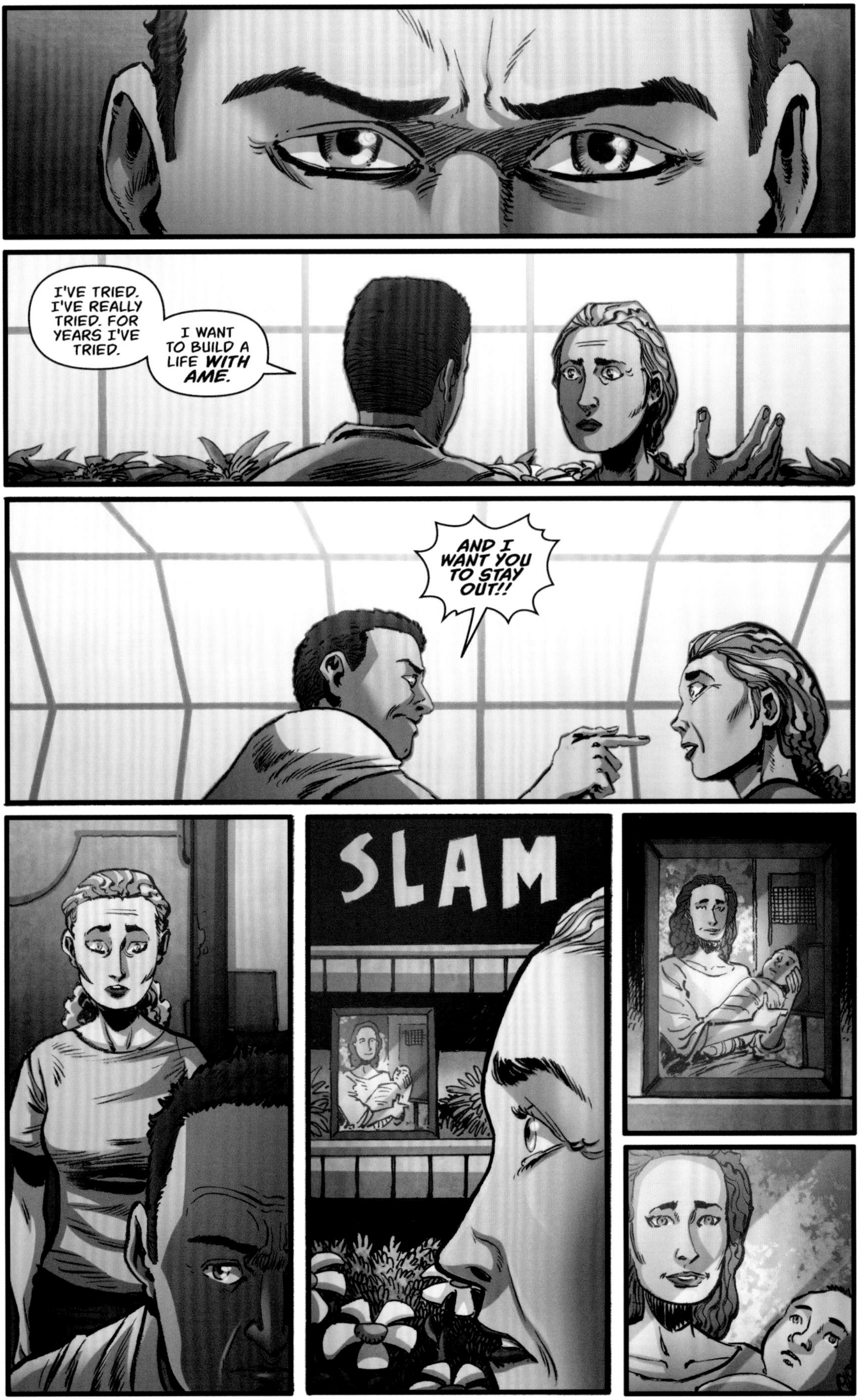
I'VE TRIED. I'VE REALLY TRIED. FOR YEARS I'VE TRIED.
I WANT TO BUILD A LIFE WITH AME.
AND I WANT YOU TO STAY OUT!!
SLAM

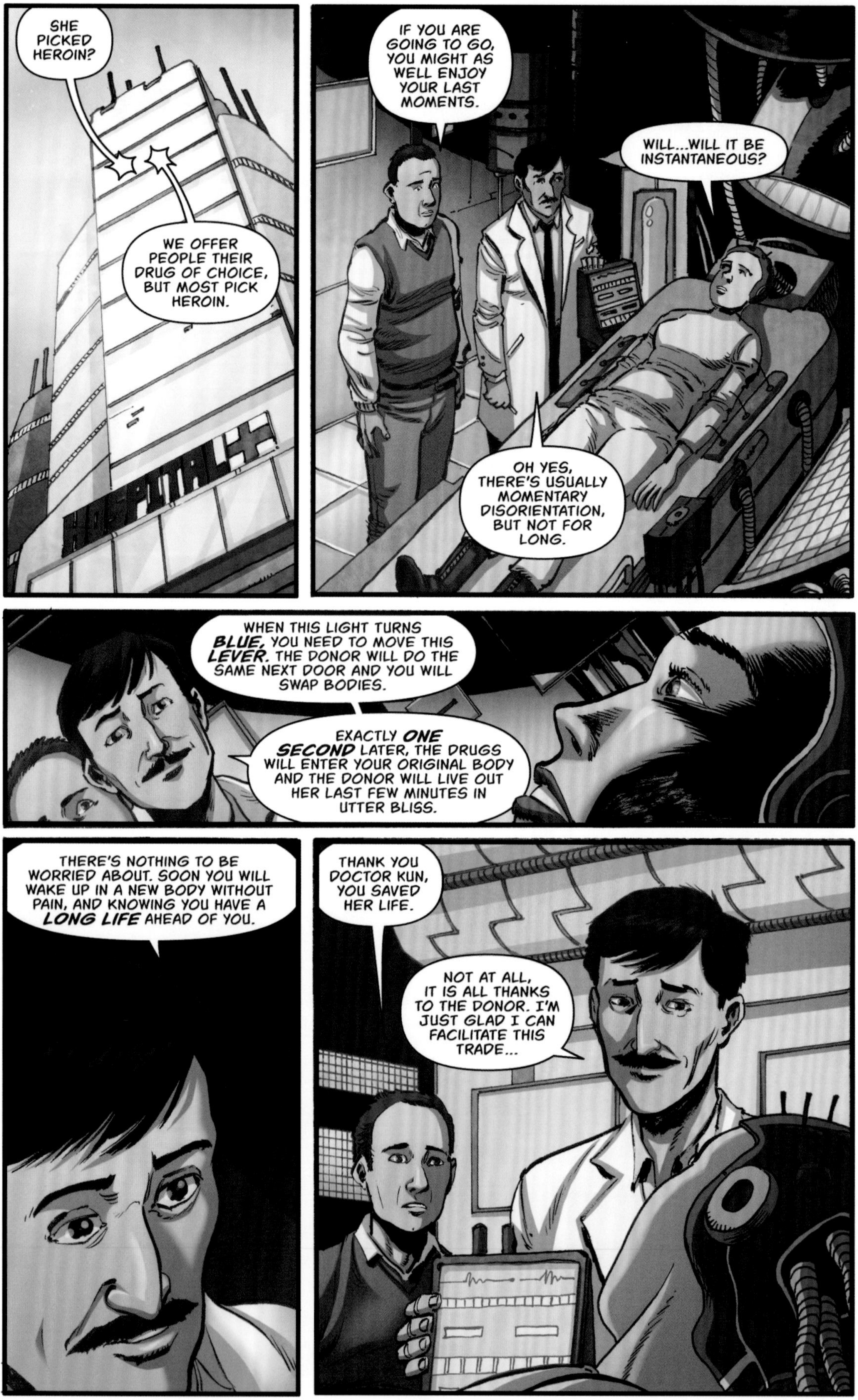
SHE PICKED HEROIN?
WE OFFER PEOPLE THEIR DRUG OF CHOICE, BUT MOST PICK HEROIN.
HOSPITAL
IF YOU ARE GOING TO GO, YOU MIGHT AS WELL ENJOY YOUR LAST MOMENTS.
WILL...WILL IT BE INSTANTANEOUS?
OH YES, THERE'S USUALLY MOMENTARY DISORIENTATION, BUT NOT FOR LONG.
WHEN THIS LIGHT TURNS BLUE, YOU NEED TO MOVE THIS LEVER. THE DONOR WILL DO THE SAME NEXT DOOR AND YOU WILL SWAP BODIES.
EXACTLY ONE SECOND LATER, THE DRUGS WILL ENTER YOUR ORIGINAL BODY AND THE DONOR WILL LIVE OUT HER LAST FEW MINUTES IN UTTER BLISS.
THERE'S NOTHING TO BE WORRIED ABOUT. SOON YOU WILL WAKE UP IN A NEW BODY WITHOUT PAIN, AND KNOWING YOU HAVE A LONG LIFE AHEAD OF YOU.
THANK YOU DOCTOR KUN, YOU SAVED HER LIFE.
NOT AT ALL, IT IS ALL THANKS TO THE DONOR. I'M JUST GLAD I CAN FACILITATE THIS TRADE...

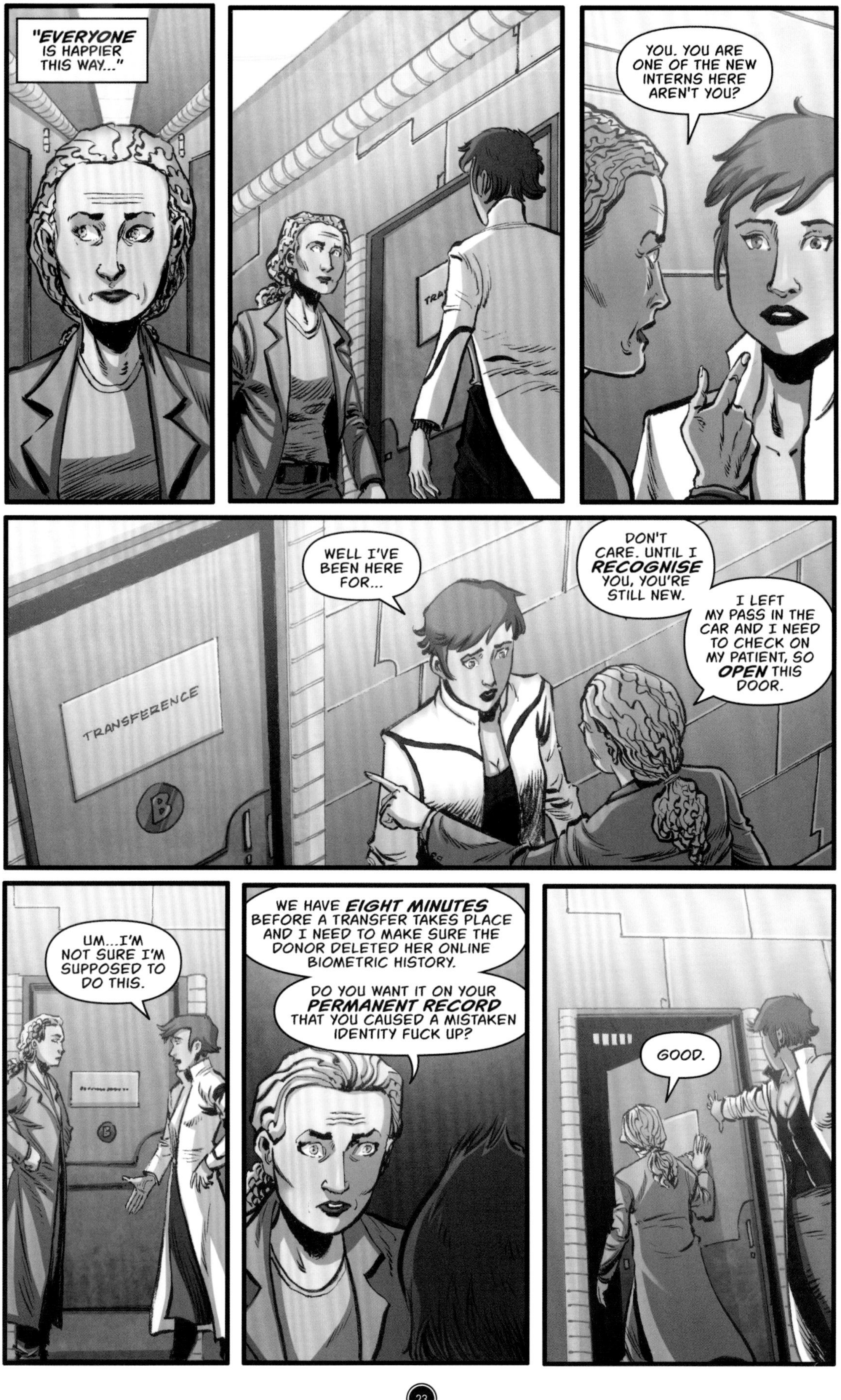
"EVERYONE IS HAPPIER THIS WAY..."
YOU. YOU ARE ONE OF THE NEW INTERNS HERE AREN'T YOU?
WELL I'VE BEEN HERE FOR...
DON'T CARE. UNTIL I RECOGNISE YOU, YOU'RE STILL NEW.
I LEFT MY PASS IN THE CAR AND I NEED TO CHECK ON MY PATIENT, SO OPEN THIS DOOR.
TRANSFERENCE
B
UM...I'M NOT SURE I'M SUPPOSED TO DO THIS.
WE HAVE EIGHT MINUTES BEFORE A TRANSFER TAKES PLACE AND I NEED TO MAKE SURE THE DONOR DELETED HER ONLINE BIOMETRIC HISTORY.
DO YOU WANT IT ON YOUR PERMANENT RECORD THAT YOU CAUSED A MISTAKEN IDENTITY FUCK UP?
GOOD.

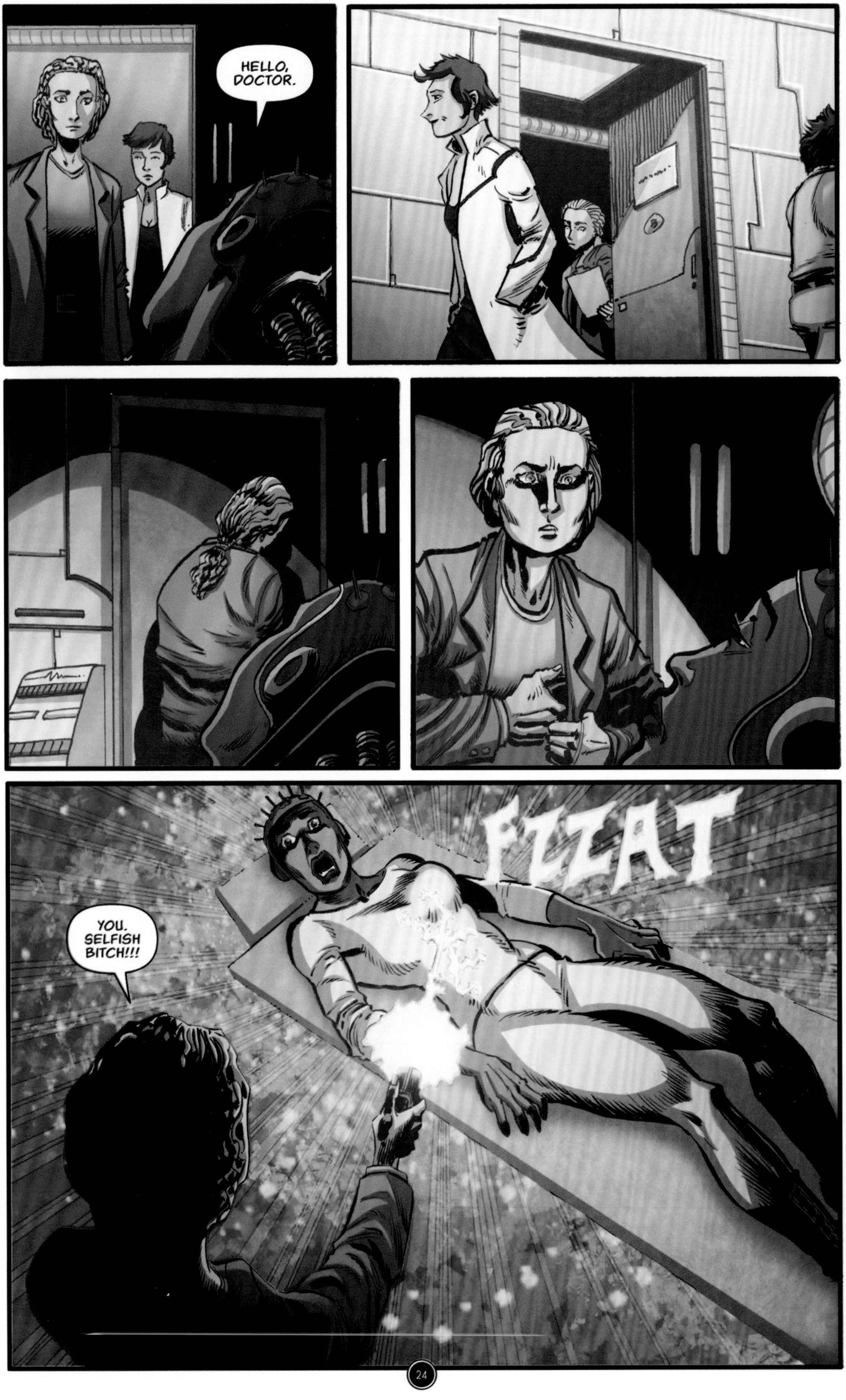
HELLO, DOCTOR.
FZZAT
YOU. SELFISH BITCH!!!

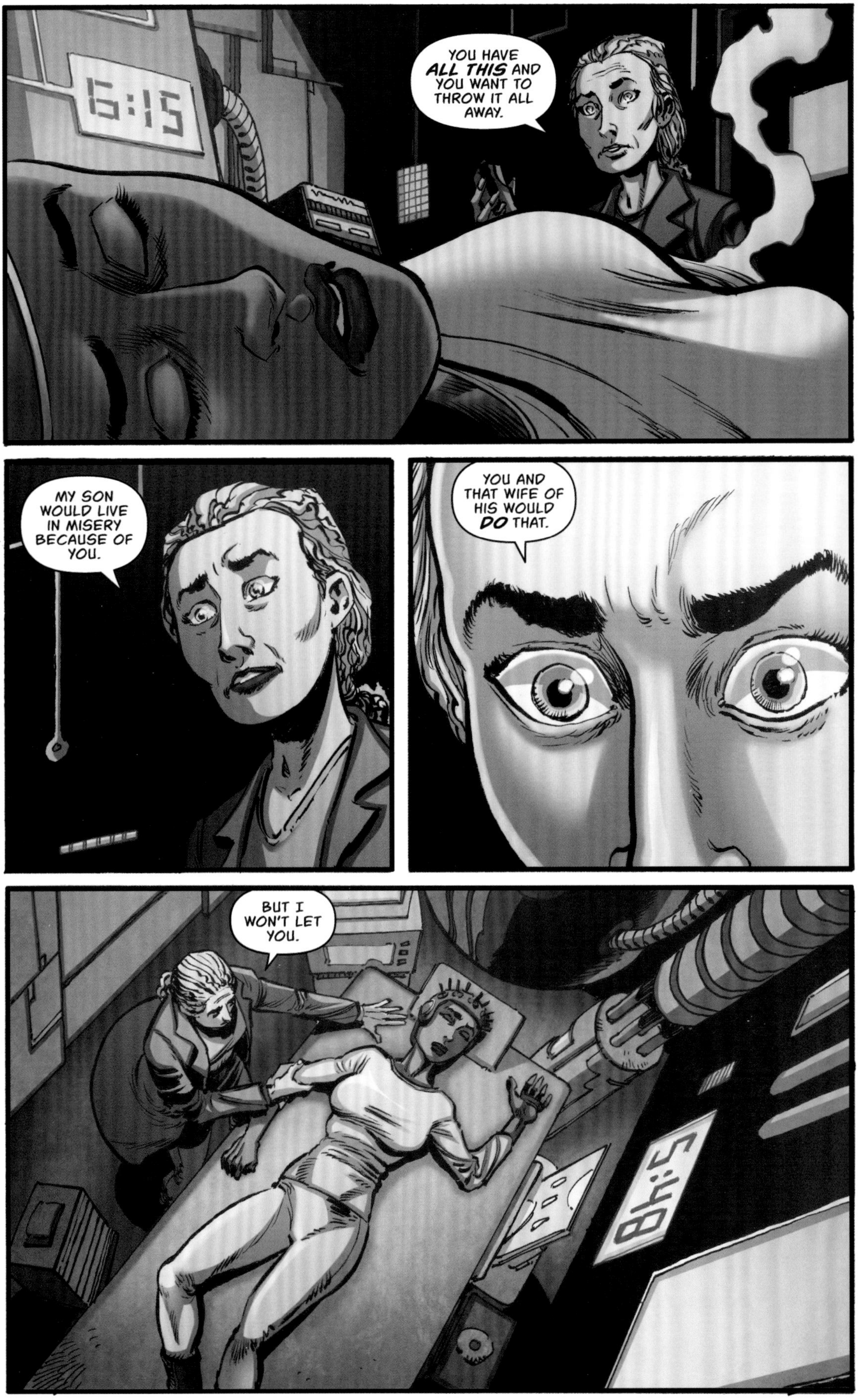
YOU HAVE ALL THIS AND YOU WANT TO THROW IT ALL AWAY.
6:15
MY SON WOULD LIVE IN MISERY BECAUSE OF YOU.
YOU AND THAT WIFE OF HIS WOULD DO THAT.
BUT I WON'T LET YOU.
5:48

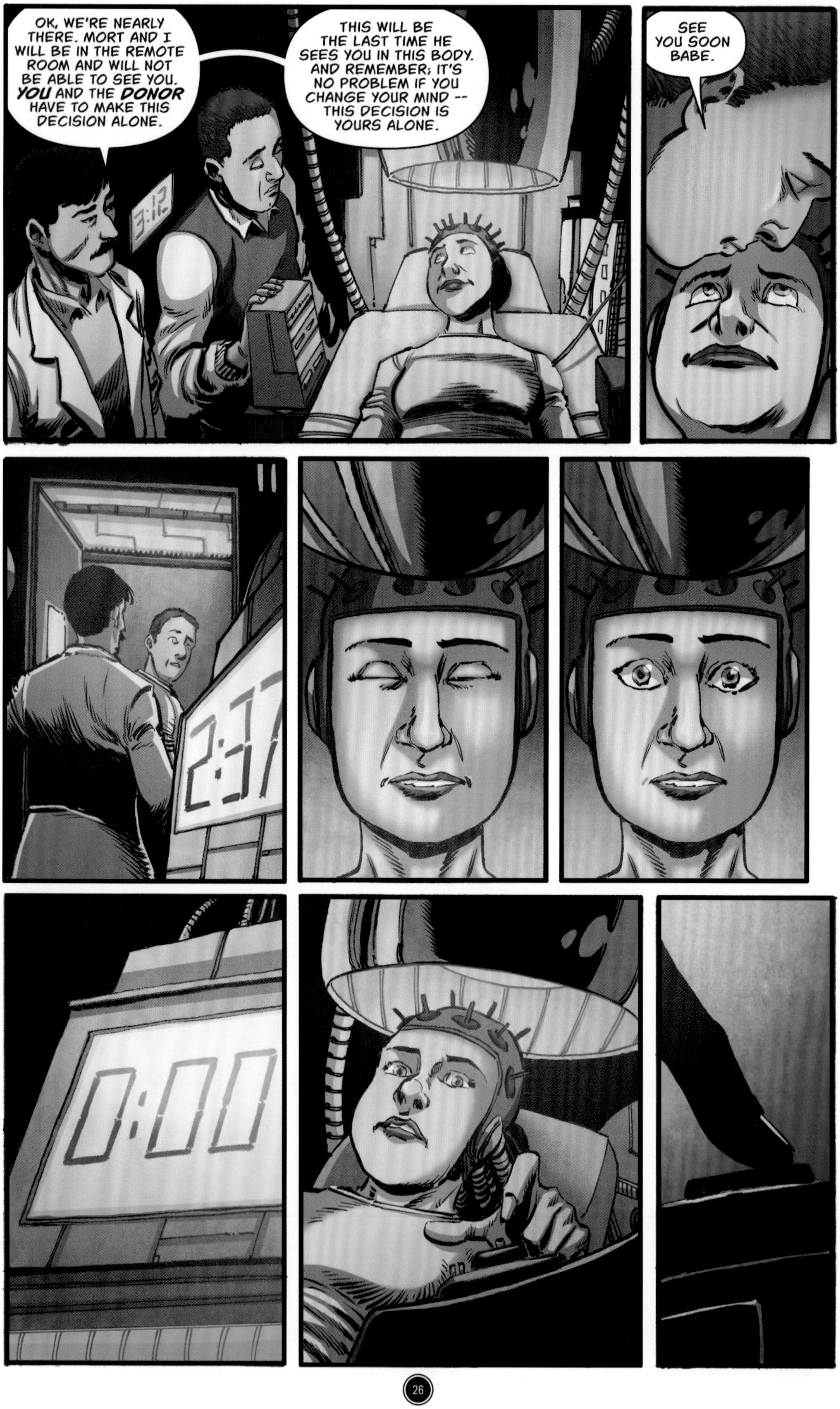

OK, WE'RE NEARLY THERE. MORT AND I WILL BE IN THE REMOTE ROOM AND WILL NOT BE ABLE TO SEE YOU. ***YOU*** AND THE ***DONOR*** HAVE TO MAKE THIS DECISION ALONE.
THIS WILL BE THE LAST TIME HE SEES YOU IN THIS BODY. AND REMEMBER; IT'S NO PROBLEM IF YOU CHANGE YOUR MIND -- THIS DECISION IS YOURS ALONE.
SEE YOU SOON BABE.
3:12
2:37
0:00

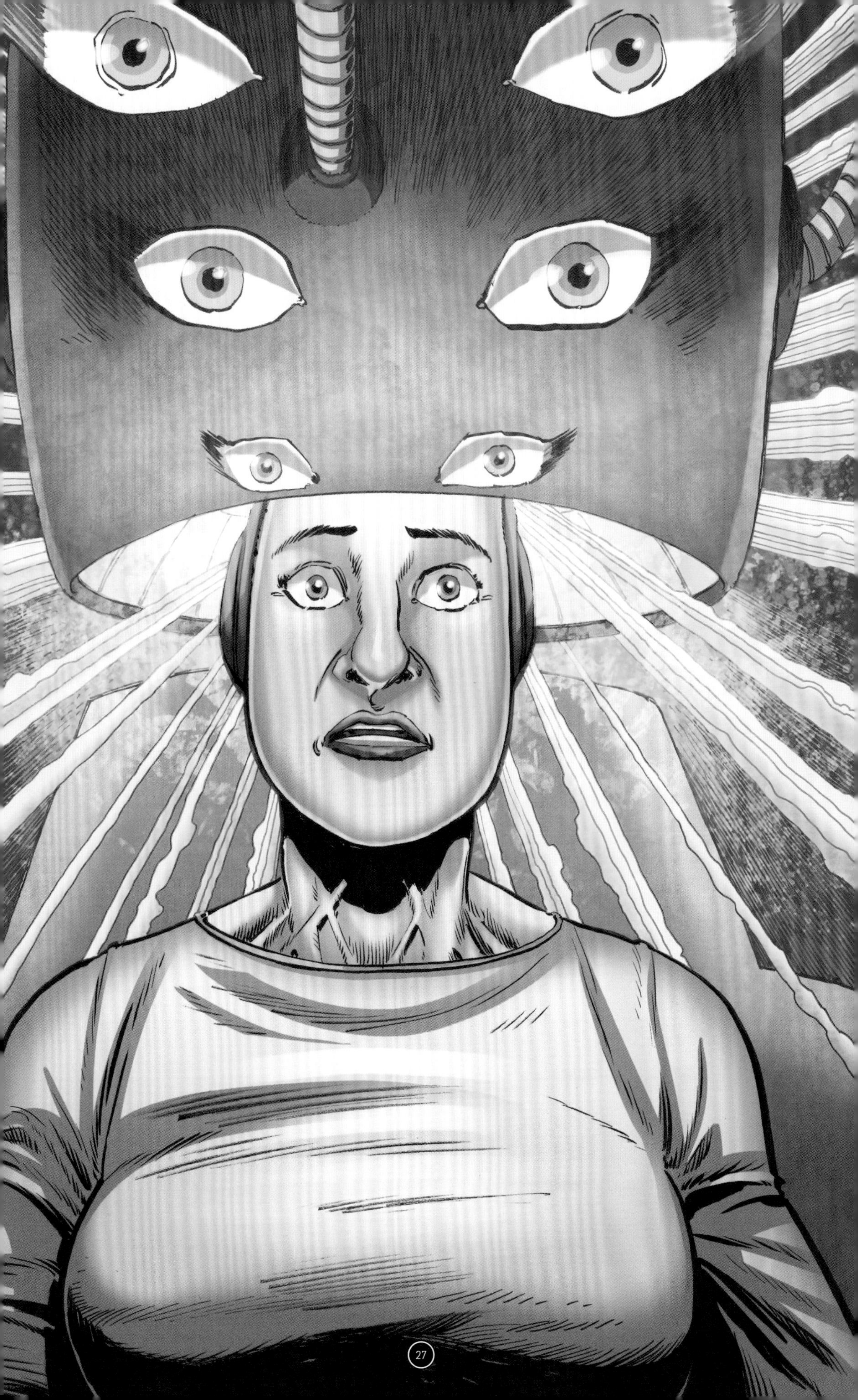

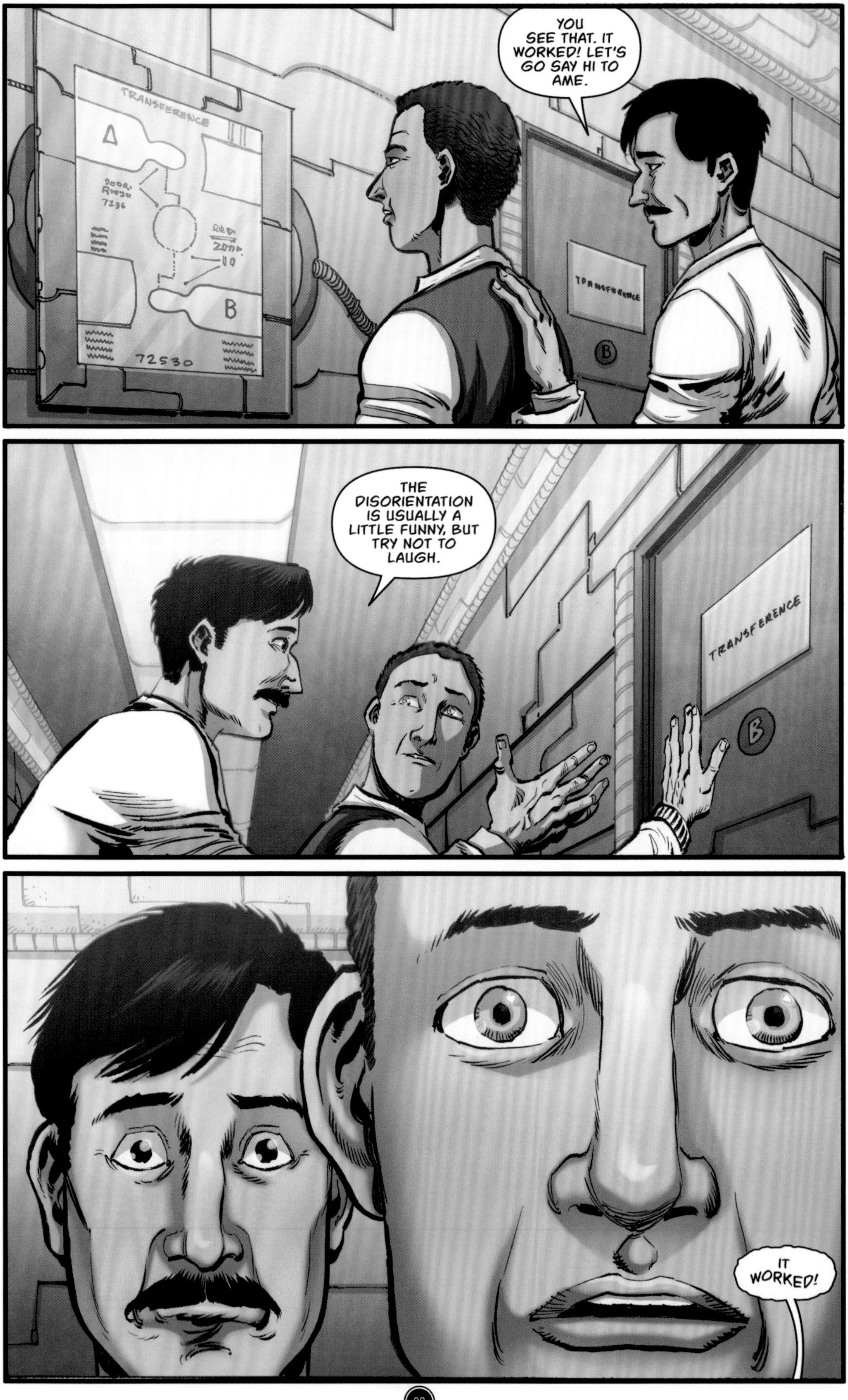
TRANSFERENCE
72530
YOU SEE THAT. IT WORKED! LET'S GO SAY HI TO AME.
THE DISORIENTATION IS USUALLY A LITTLE FUNNY, BUT TRY NOT TO LAUGH.
TRANSFERENCE
IT WORKED!

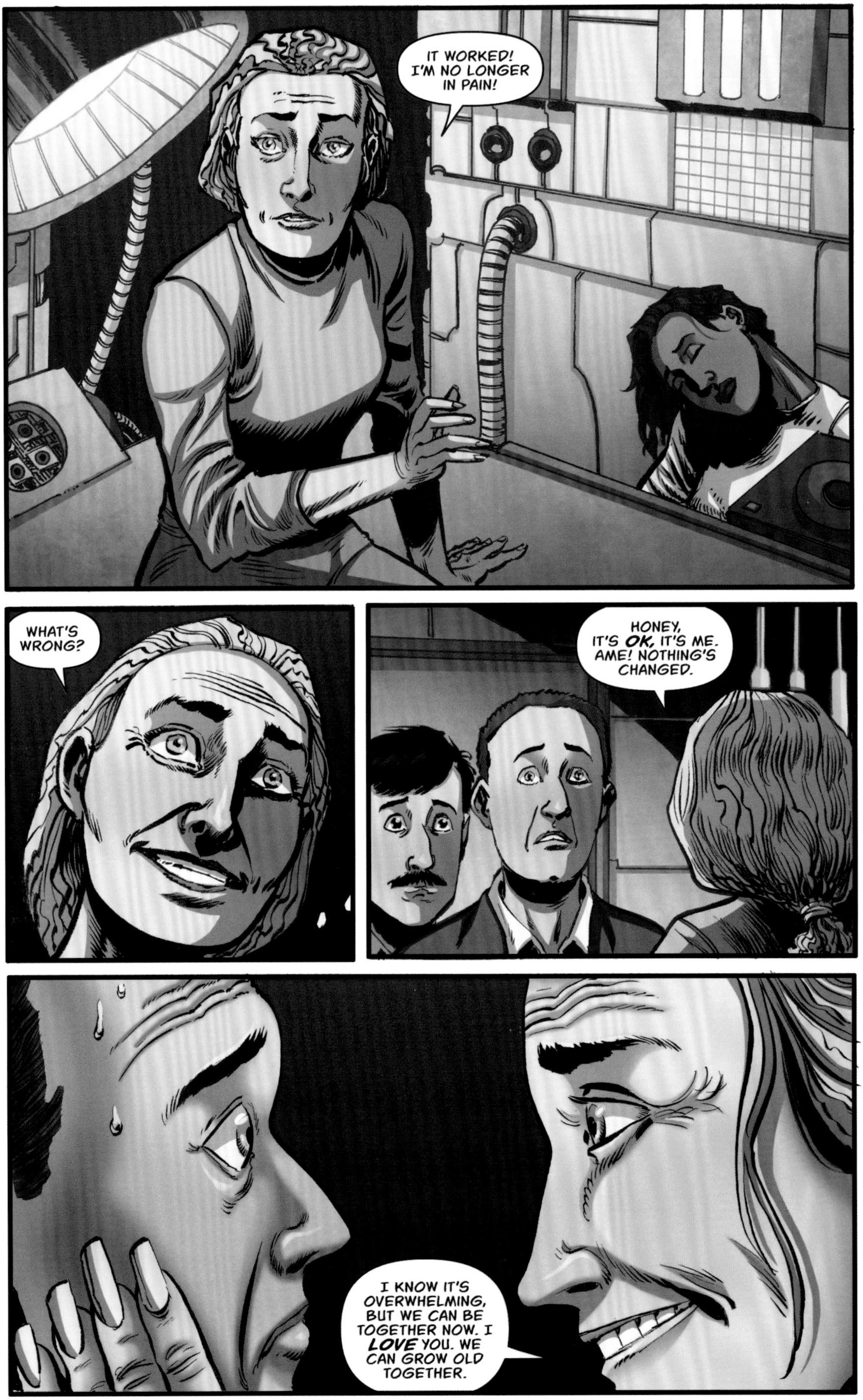
IT WORKED! I'M NO LONGER IN PAIN!
WHAT'S WRONG?
HONEY, IT'S OK, IT'S ME. AME! NOTHING'S CHANGED.
I KNOW IT'S OVERWHELMING, BUT WE CAN BE TOGETHER NOW. I LOVE YOU. WE CAN GROW OLD TOGETHER.

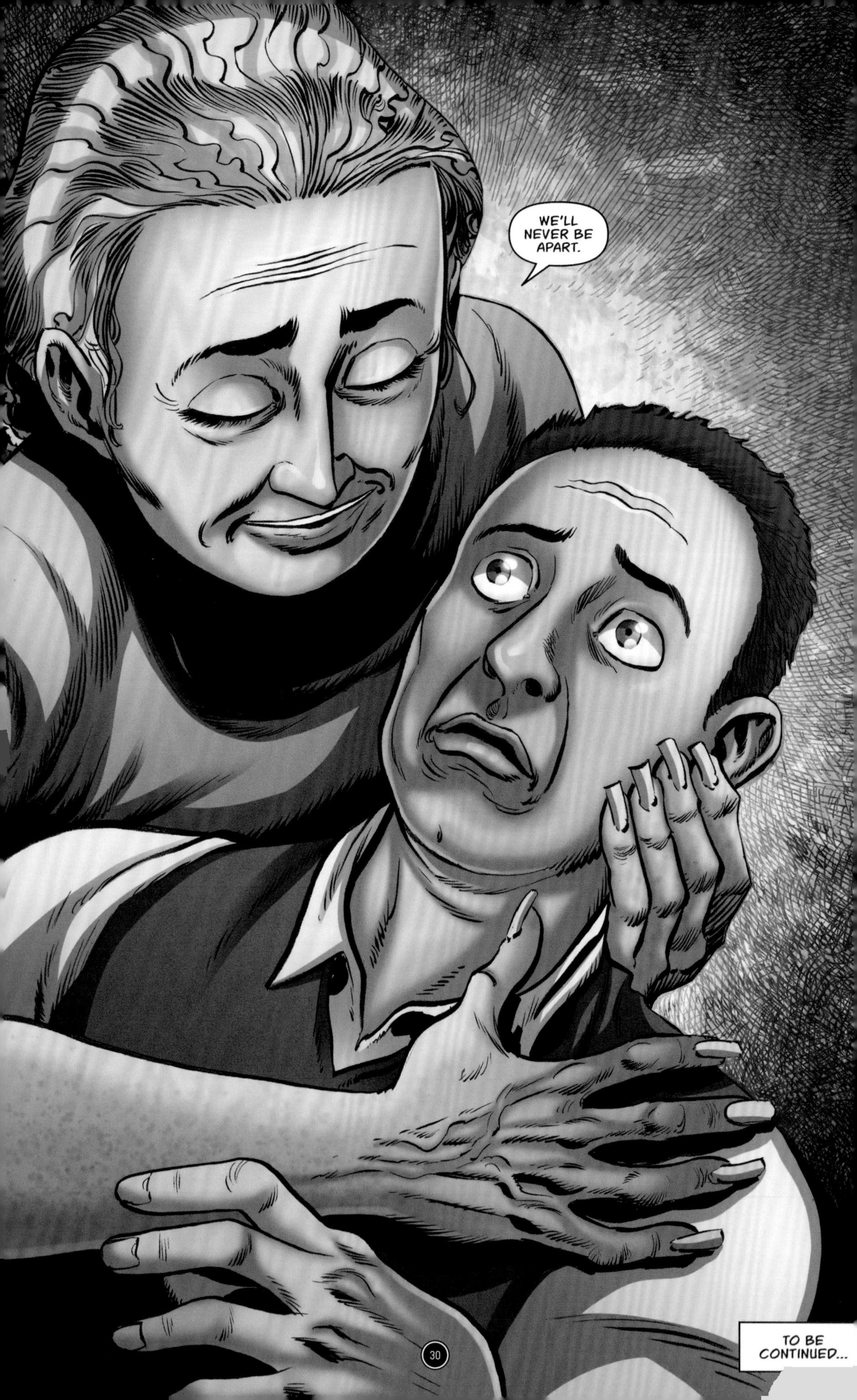
WE'LL NEVER BE APART.
TO BE CONTINUED...

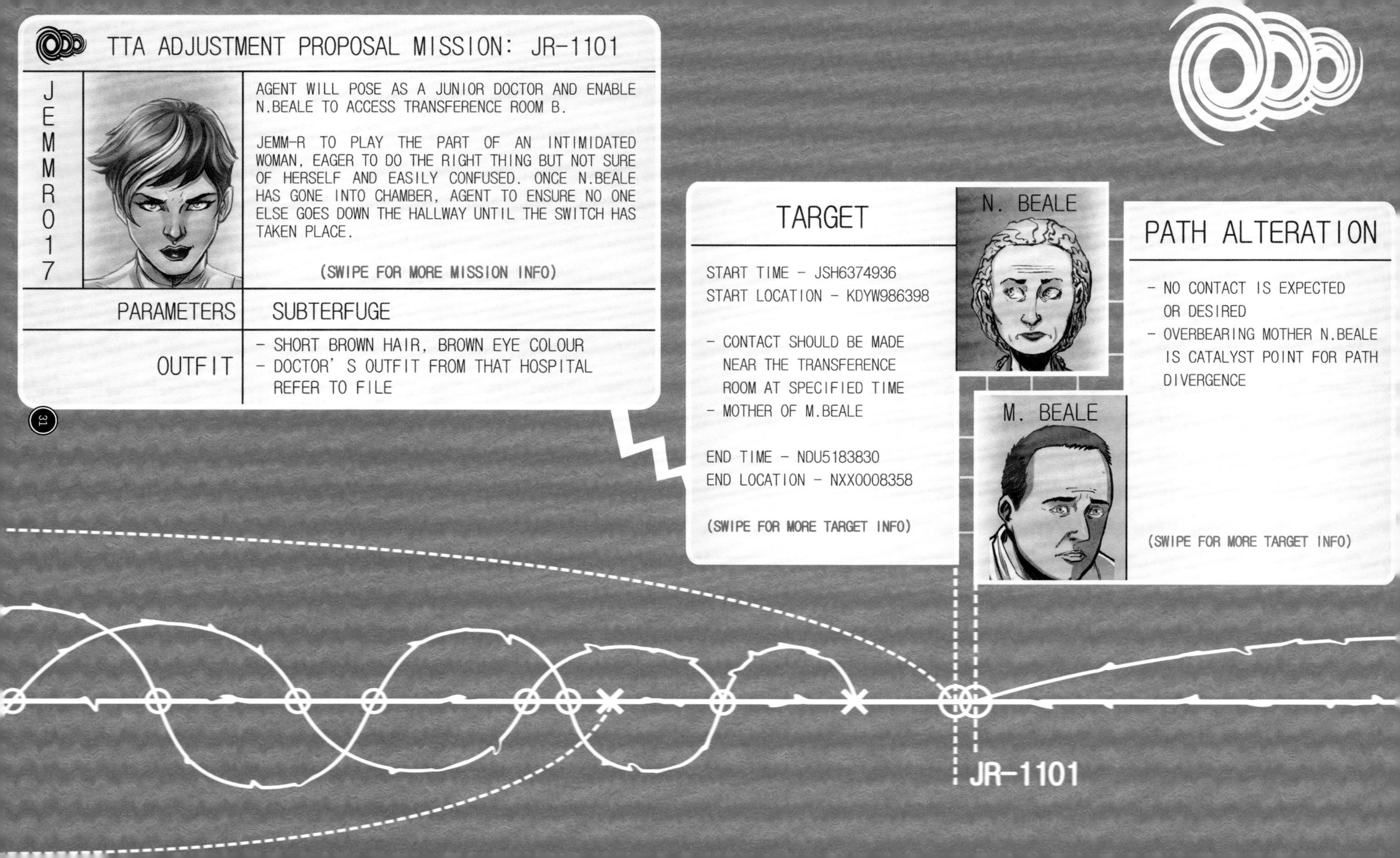
TTA ADJUSTMENT PROPOSAL MISSION: JR-1101
JEMMR017
AGENT WILL POSE AS A JUNIOR DOCTOR AND ENABLE N.BEALE TO ACCESS TRANSFERENCE ROOM B.
JEMM-R TO PLAY THE PART OF AN INTIMIDATED WOMAN, EAGER TO DO THE RIGHT THING BUT NOT SURE OF HERSELF AND EASILY CONFUSED. ONCE N.BEALE HAS GONE INTO CHAMBER, AGENT TO ENSURE NO ONE ELSE GOES DOWN THE HALLWAY UNTIL THE SWITCH HAS TAKEN PLACE.
(SWIPE FOR MORE MISSION INFO)
PARAMETERS
SUBTERFUGE
OUTFIT
- SHORT BROWN HAIR, BROWN EYE COLOUR
- DOCTOR' S OUTFIT FROM THAT HOSPITAL REFER TO FILE
TARGET
START TIME - JSH6374936
START LOCATION - KDYW986398
- CONTACT SHOULD BE MADE NEAR THE TRANSFERENCE ROOM AT SPECIFIED TIME
- MOTHER OF M.BEALE
END TIME - NDU5183830
END LOCATION - NXX0008358
(SWIPE FOR MORE TARGET INFO)
N. BEALE
M. BEALE
PATH ALTERATION
- NO CONTACT IS EXPECTED OR DESIRED
- OVERBEARING MOTHER N.BEALE IS CATALYST POINT FOR PATH DIVERGENCE
(SWIPE FOR MORE TARGET INFO)
JR-1101

Battlesuit

"The nuclear arms race is like two sworn enemies standing waist deep in gasoline, one with three matches, the other with five"

Carl Sagan

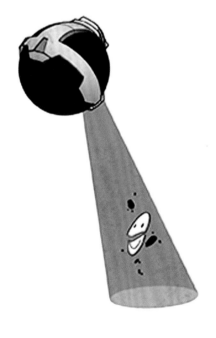

Writer
David Court

Creator/Producer
Neil Gibson

Illustrator
Phil Buckenham

Colourist
Liezl Buenaventura

Letters by
Justin Birch

www.tpubcomics.com

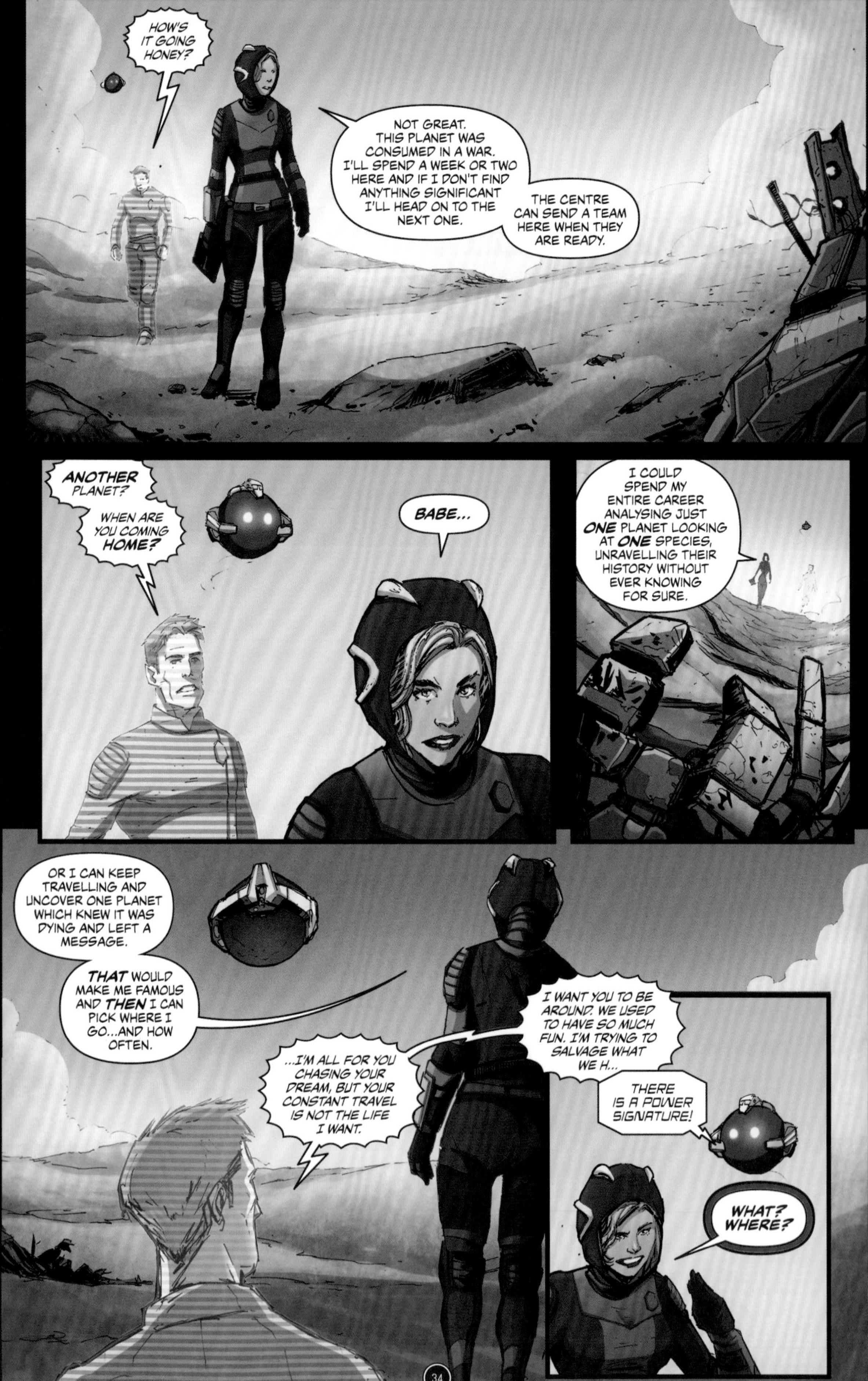
HOW'S IT GOING HONEY?
NOT GREAT. THIS PLANET WAS CONSUMED IN A WAR. I'LL SPEND A WEEK OR TWO HERE AND IF I DON'T FIND ANYTHING SIGNIFICANT I'LL HEAD ON TO THE NEXT ONE.
THE CENTRE CAN SEND A TEAM HERE WHEN THEY ARE READY.
ANOTHER PLANET?
WHEN ARE YOU COMING HOME?
BABE...
I COULD SPEND MY ENTIRE CAREER ANALYSING JUST ONE PLANET LOOKING AT ONE SPECIES, UNRAVELLING THEIR HISTORY WITHOUT EVER KNOWING FOR SURE.
OR I CAN KEEP TRAVELLING AND UNCOVER ONE PLANET WHICH KNEW IT WAS DYING AND LEFT A MESSAGE.
THAT WOULD MAKE ME FAMOUS AND THEN I CAN PICK WHERE I GO...AND HOW OFTEN.
...I'M ALL FOR YOU CHASING YOUR DREAM, BUT YOUR CONSTANT TRAVEL IS NOT THE LIFE I WANT.
I WANT YOU TO BE AROUND. WE USED TO HAVE SO MUCH FUN. I'M TRYING TO SALVAGE WHAT WE H...
THERE IS A POWER SIGNATURE!
WHAT? WHERE?

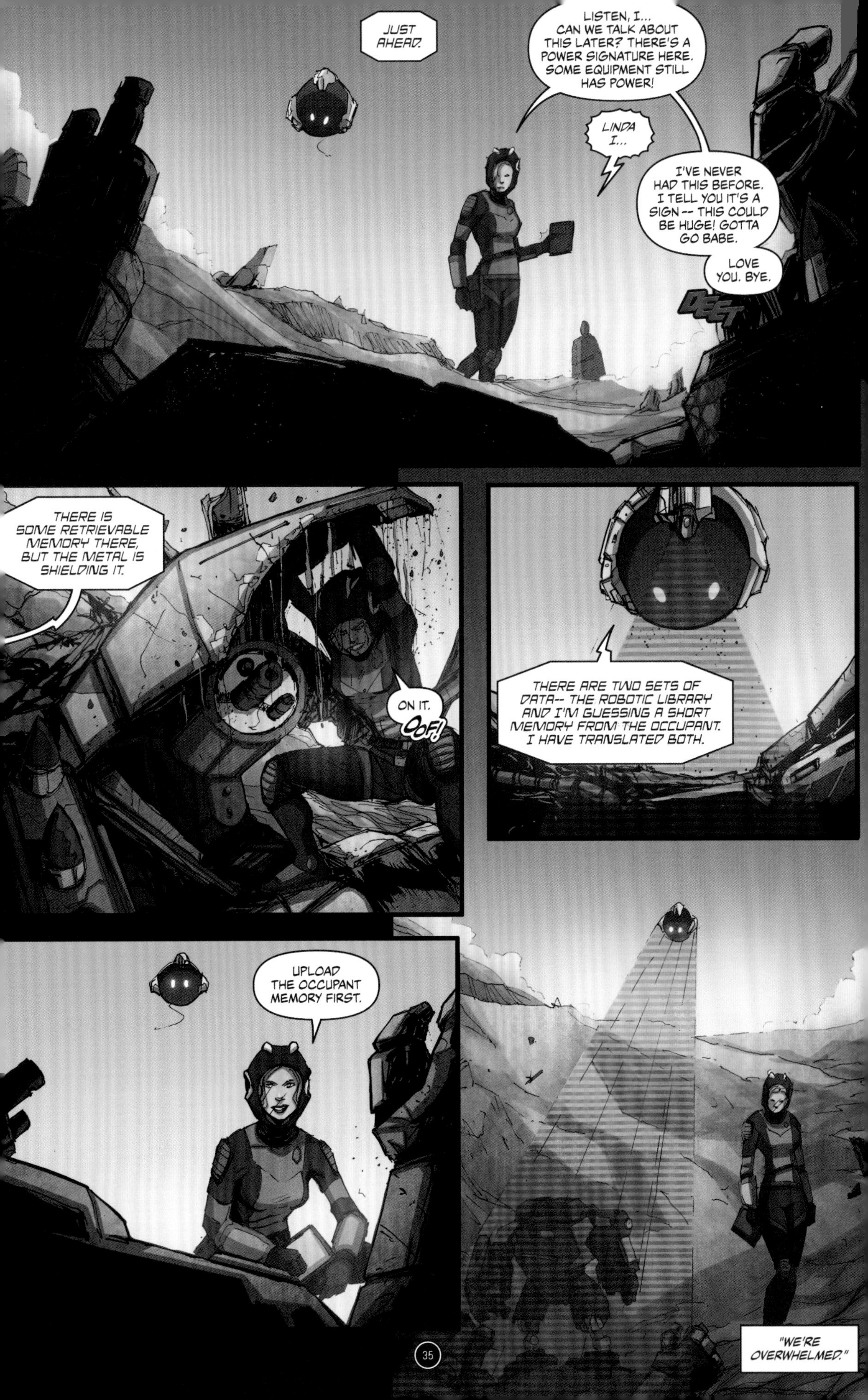
JUST AHEAD.
LISTEN, I... CAN WE TALK ABOUT THIS LATER? THERE'S A POWER SIGNATURE HERE. SOME EQUIPMENT STILL HAS POWER!
LINDA I...
I'VE NEVER HAD THIS BEFORE. I TELL YOU IT'S A SIGN -- THIS COULD BE HUGE! GOTTA GO BABE.
LOVE YOU. BYE.
DEET
THERE IS SOME RETRIEVABLE MEMORY THERE, BUT THE METAL IS SHIELDING IT.
ON IT.
OOF!
THERE ARE TWO SETS OF DATA-- THE ROBOTIC LIBRARY AND I'M GUESSING A SHORT MEMORY FROM THE OCCUPANT. I HAVE TRANSLATED BOTH.
UPLOAD THE OCCUPANT MEMORY FIRST.
"WE'RE OVERWHELMED."

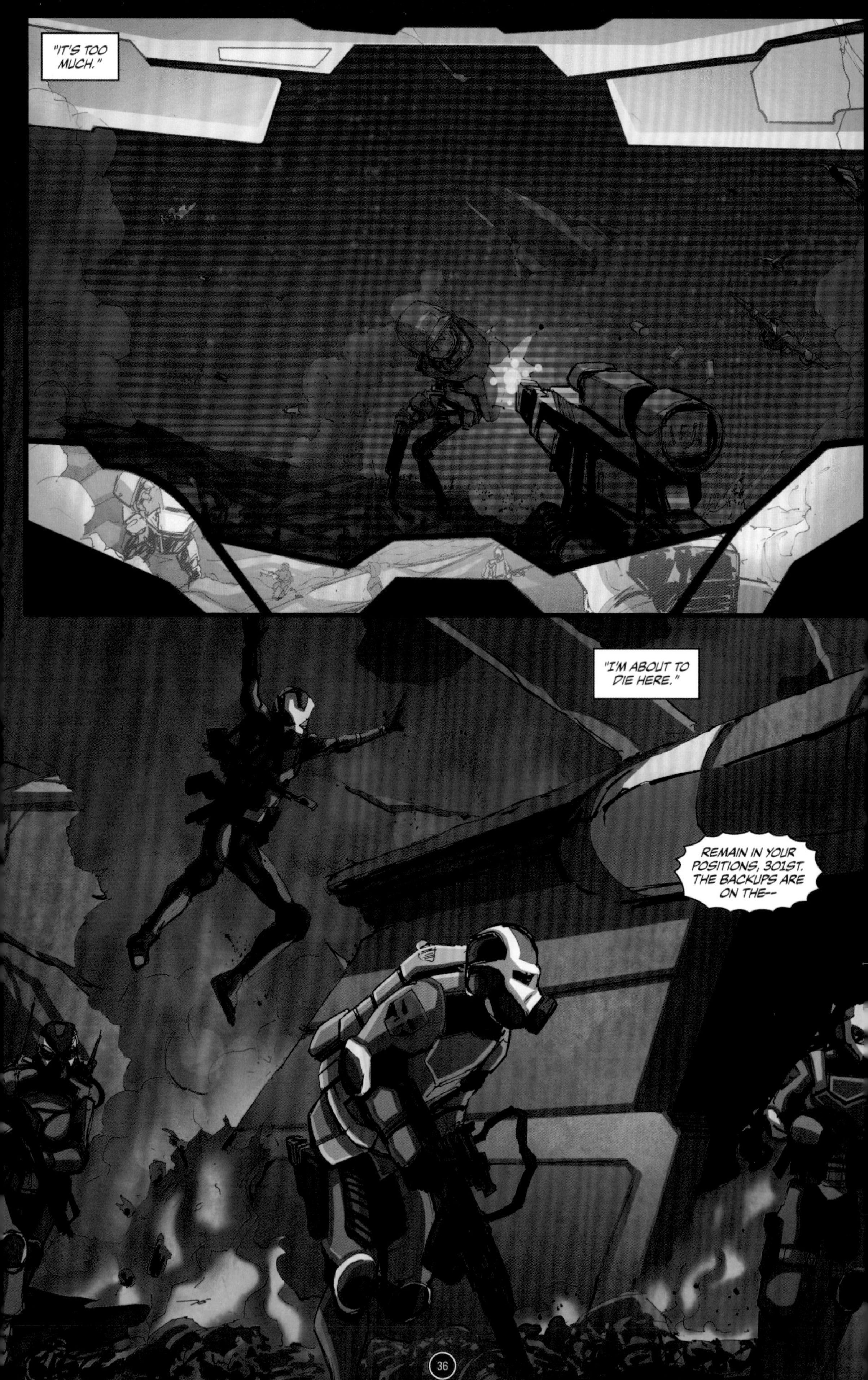
"IT'S TOO MUCH."
"I'M ABOUT TO DIE HERE."
REMAIN IN YOUR POSITIONS, 301ST. THE BACKUPS ARE ON THE--

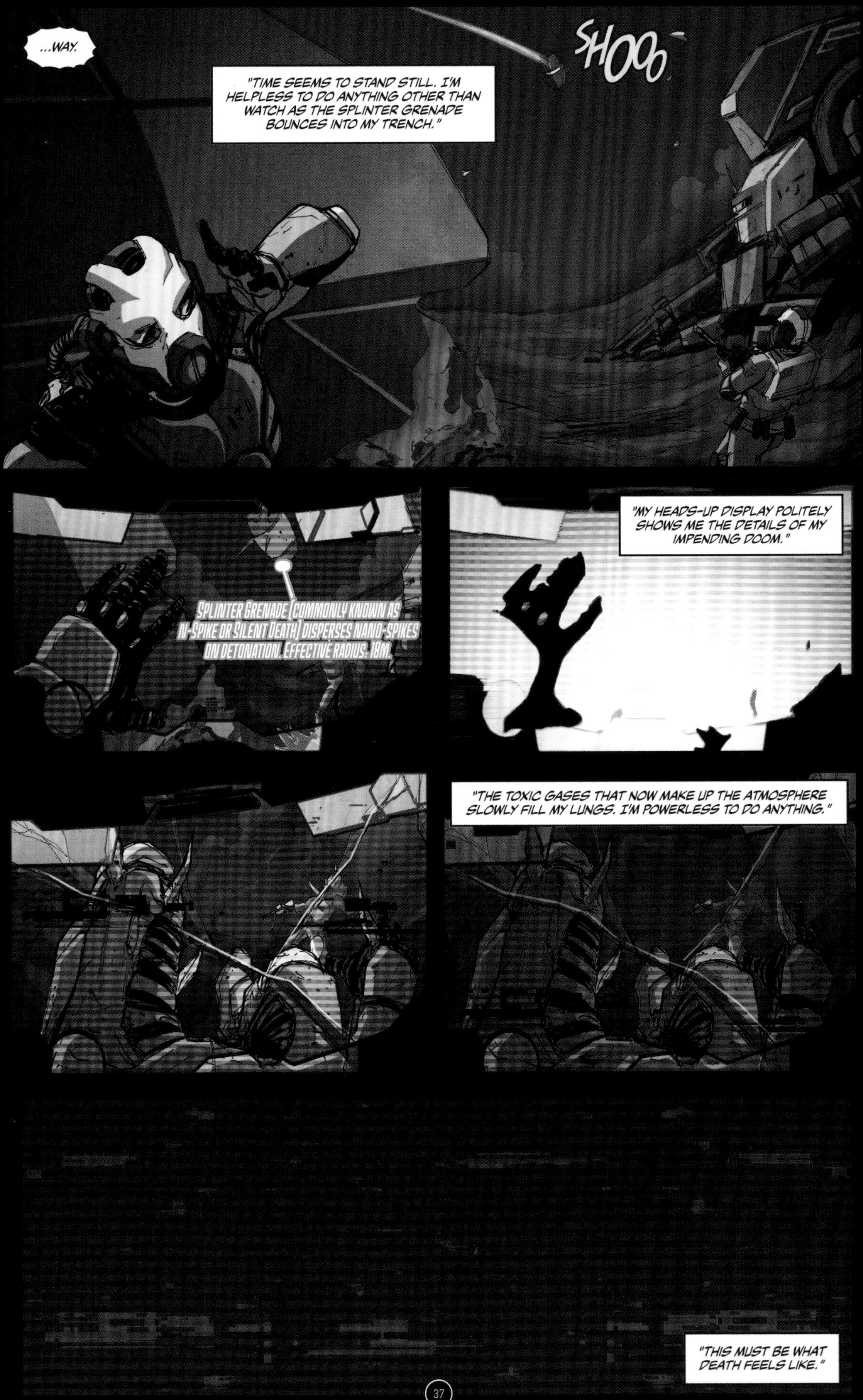

...WAY.
"TIME SEEMS TO STAND STILL. I'M HELPLESS TO DO ANYTHING OTHER THAN WATCH AS THE SPLINTER GRENADE BOUNCES INTO MY TRENCH."
SHOOO
SPLINTER GRENADE (COMMONLY KNOWN AS N-SPIKE OR SILENT DEATH) DISPERSES NANO-SPIKES ON DETONATION. EFFECTIVE RADIUS: 18M.
"MY HEADS-UP DISPLAY POLITELY SHOWS ME THE DETAILS OF MY IMPENDING DOOM."
"THE TOXIC GASES THAT NOW MAKE UP THE ATMOSPHERE SLOWLY FILL MY LUNGS. I'M POWERLESS TO DO ANYTHING."
"THIS MUST BE WHAT DEATH FEELS LIKE."

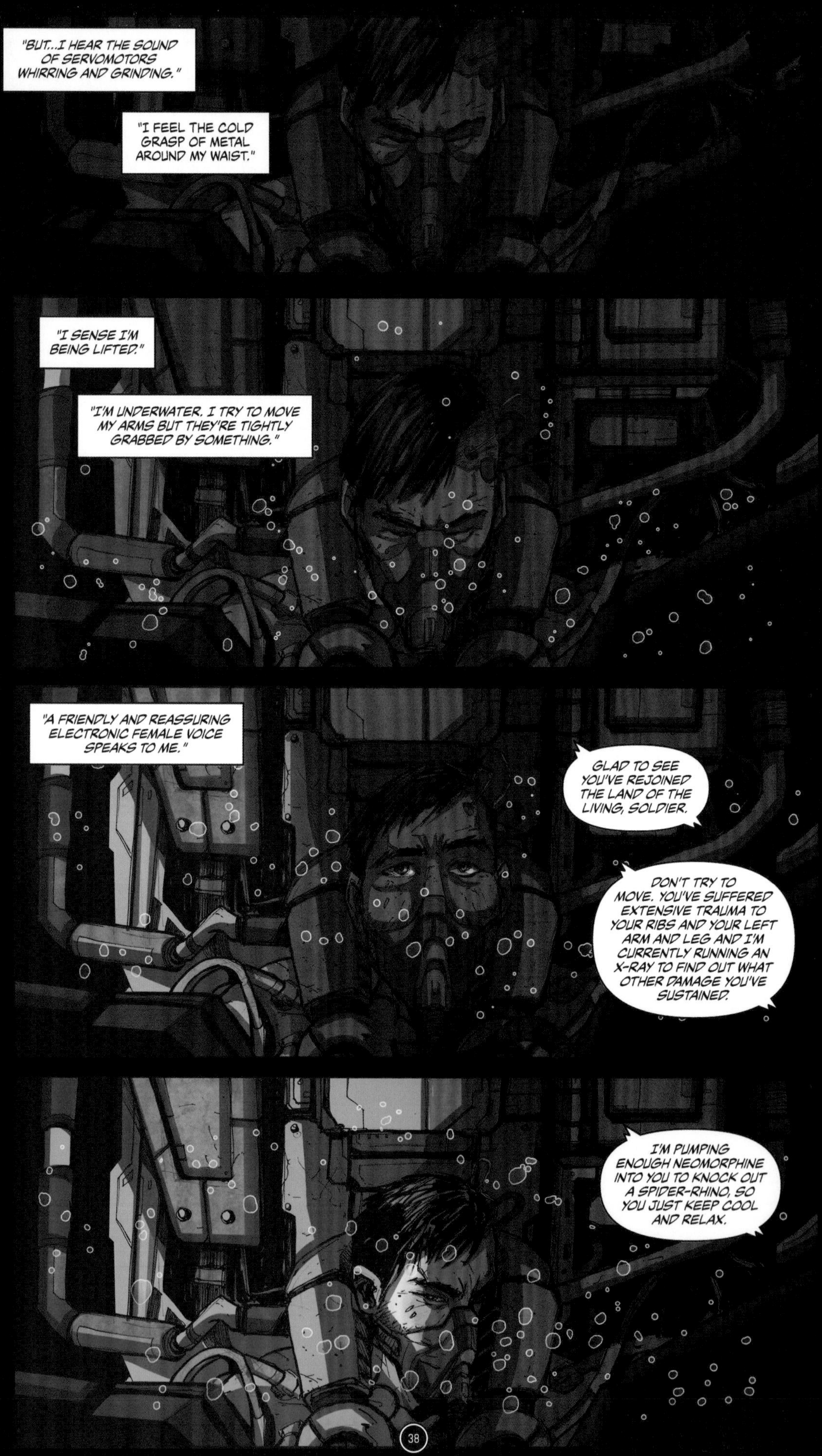
"BUT...I HEAR THE SOUND OF SERVOMOTORS WHIRRING AND GRINDING."
"I FEEL THE COLD GRASP OF METAL AROUND MY WAIST."
"I SENSE I'M BEING LIFTED."
"I'M UNDERWATER. I TRY TO MOVE MY ARMS BUT THEY'RE TIGHTLY GRABBED BY SOMETHING."
"A FRIENDLY AND REASSURING ELECTRONIC FEMALE VOICE SPEAKS TO ME."
GLAD TO SEE YOU'VE REJOINED THE LAND OF THE LIVING, SOLDIER.
DON'T TRY TO MOVE. YOU'VE SUFFERED EXTENSIVE TRAUMA TO YOUR RIBS AND YOUR LEFT ARM AND LEG AND I'M CURRENTLY RUNNING AN X-RAY TO FIND OUT WHAT OTHER DAMAGE YOU'VE SUSTAINED.
I'M PUMPING ENOUGH NEOMORPHINE INTO YOU TO KNOCK OUT A SPIDER-RHINO, SO YOU JUST KEEP COOL AND RELAX.

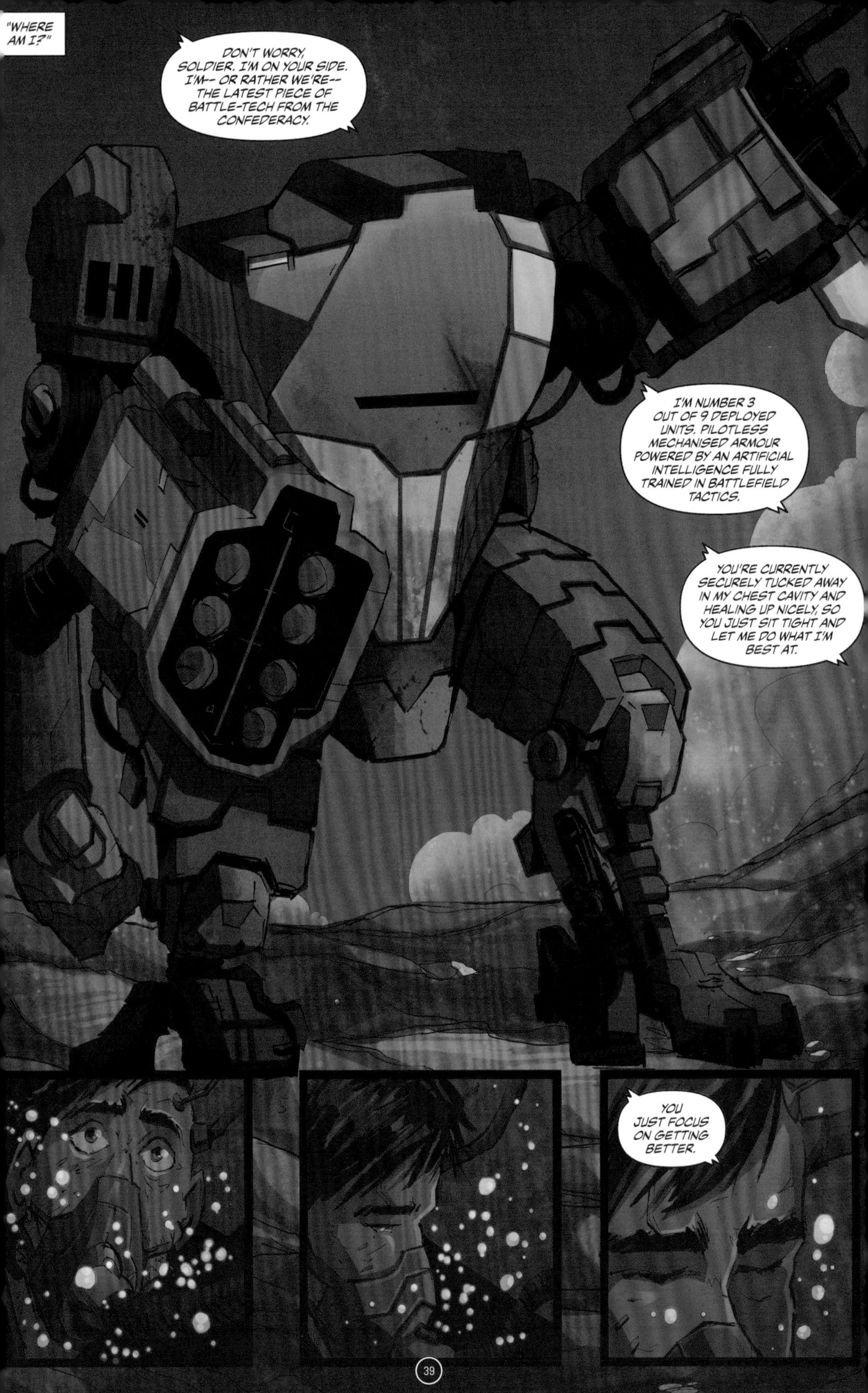
"WHERE AM I?"
DON'T WORRY, SOLDIER. I'M ON YOUR SIDE. I'M-- OR RATHER WE'RE-- THE LATEST PIECE OF BATTLE-TECH FROM THE CONFEDERACY.
I'M NUMBER 3 OUT OF 9 DEPLOYED UNITS. PILOTLESS MECHANISED ARMOUR POWERED BY AN ARTIFICIAL INTELLIGENCE FULLY TRAINED IN BATTLEFIELD TACTICS.
YOU'RE CURRENTLY SECURELY TUCKED AWAY IN MY CHEST CAVITY AND HEALING UP NICELY, SO YOU JUST SIT TIGHT AND LET ME DO WHAT I'M BEST AT.
YOU JUST FOCUS ON GETTING BETTER.

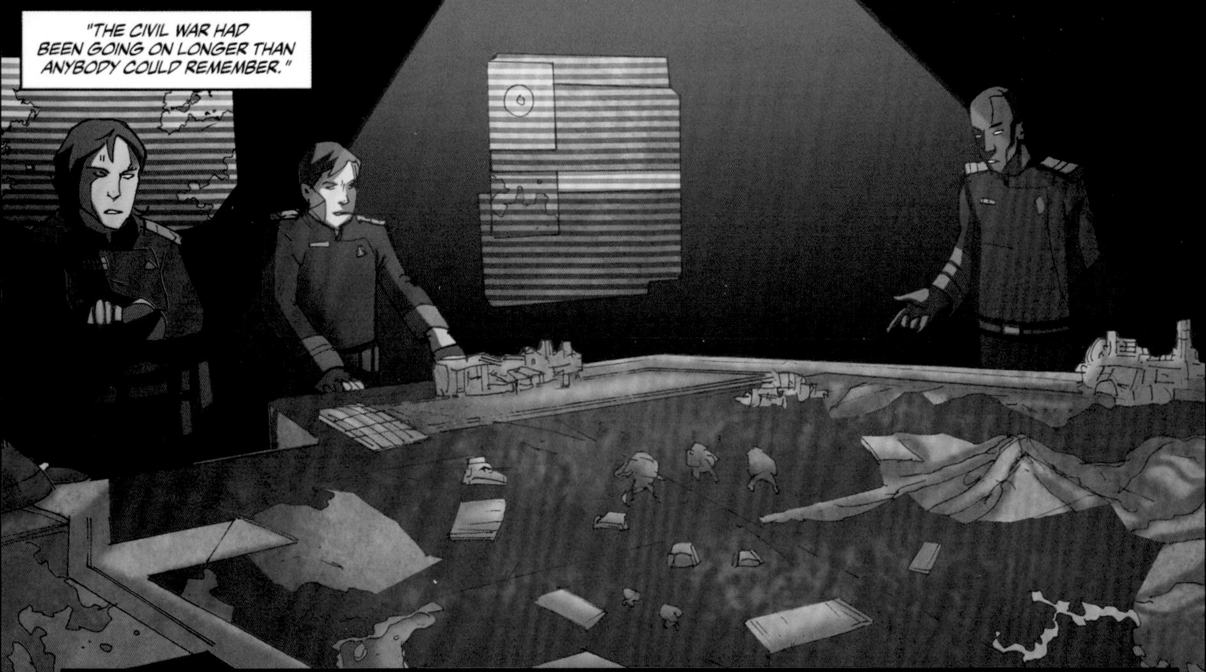
"THE CIVIL WAR HAD BEEN GOING ON LONGER THAN ANYBODY COULD REMEMBER."

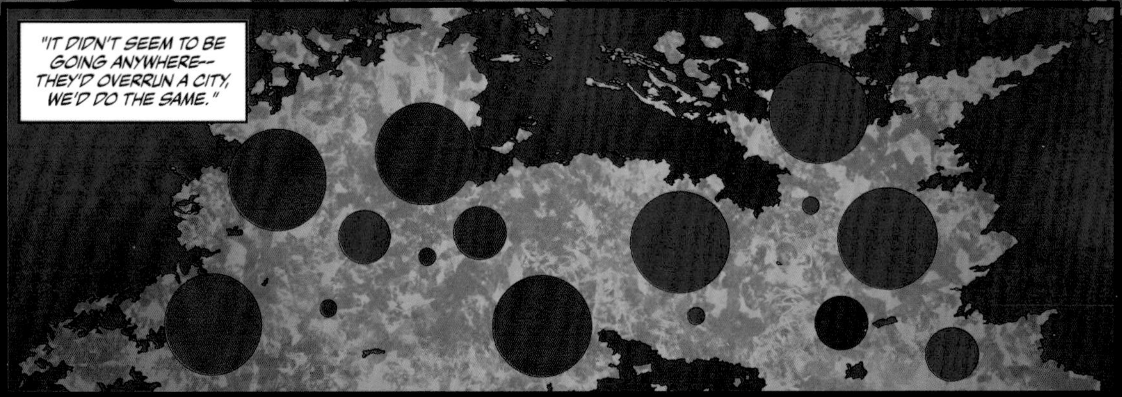
"IT DIDN'T SEEM TO BE GOING ANYWHERE-- THEY'D OVERRUN A CITY, WE'D DO THE SAME."

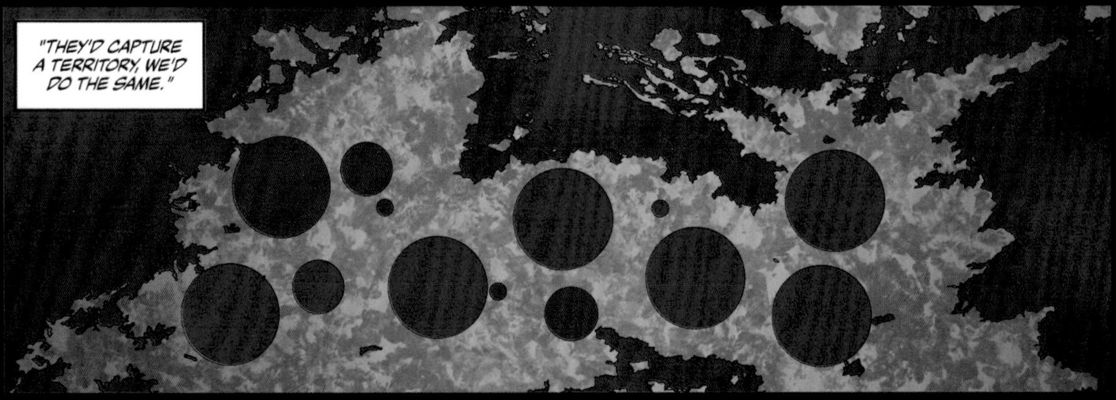
"THEY'D CAPTURE A TERRITORY, WE'D DO THE SAME."

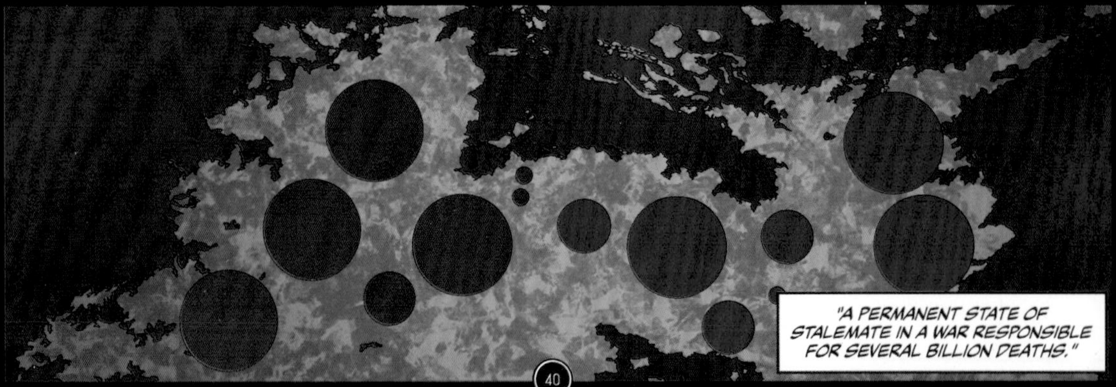
"A PERMANENT STATE OF STALEMATE IN A WAR RESPONSIBLE FOR SEVERAL BILLION DEATHS."

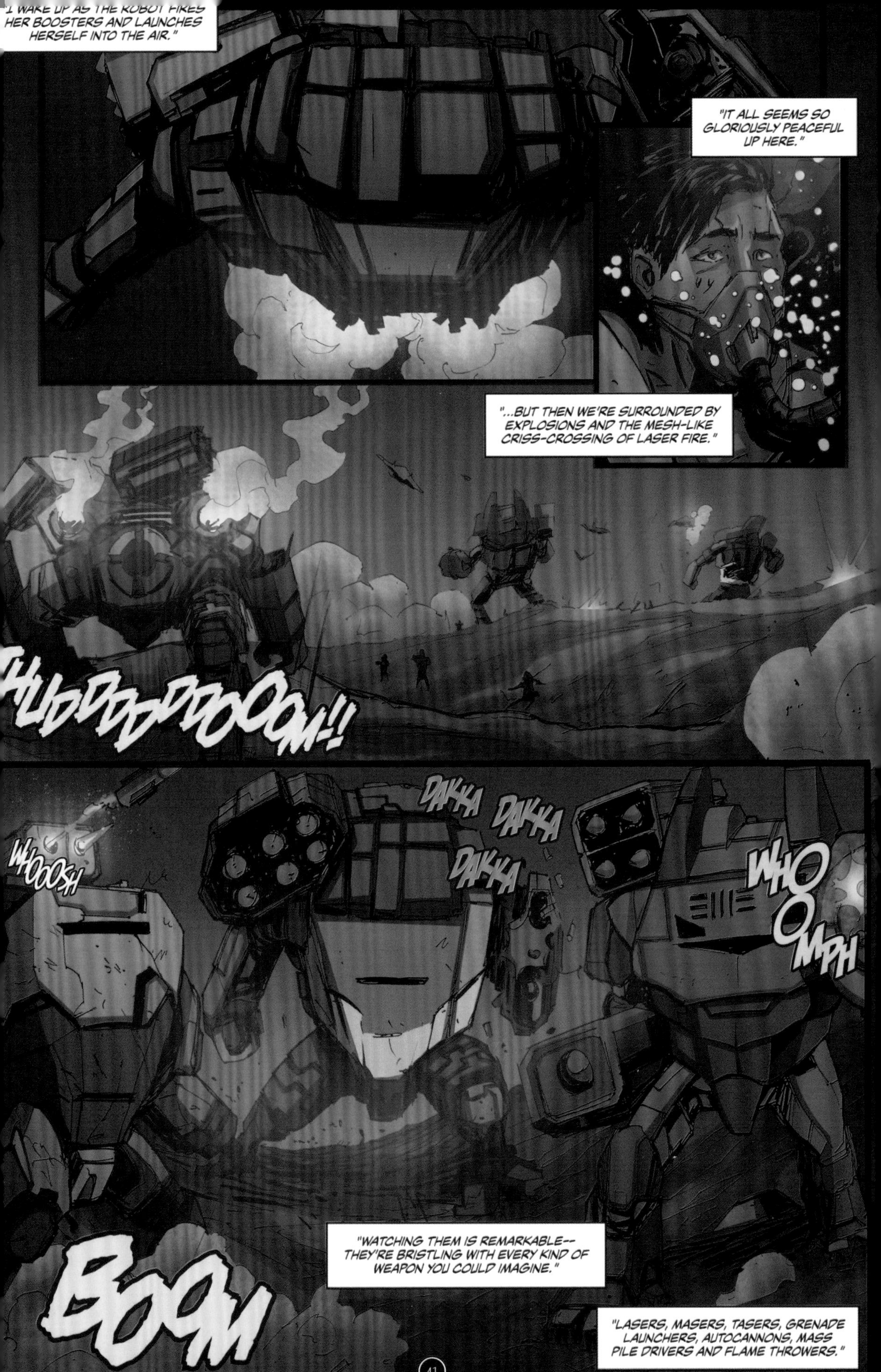
"I WAKE UP AS THE ROBOT FIRES HER BOOSTERS AND LAUNCHES HERSELF INTO THE AIR."
"IT ALL SEEMS SO GLORIOUSLY PEACEFUL UP HERE."
"...BUT THEN WE'RE SURROUNDED BY EXPLOSIONS AND THE MESH-LIKE CRISS-CROSSING OF LASER FIRE."
THUDDDDDOOOOM-!!
WHOOOSH
DAKKA
DAKKA
DAKKA
WHOOMPH
"WATCHING THEM IS REMARKABLE--THEY'RE BRISTLING WITH EVERY KIND OF WEAPON YOU COULD IMAGINE."
BOOM
"LASERS, MASERS, TASERS, GRENADE LAUNCHERS, AUTOCANNONS, MASS PILE DRIVERS AND FLAME THROWERS."

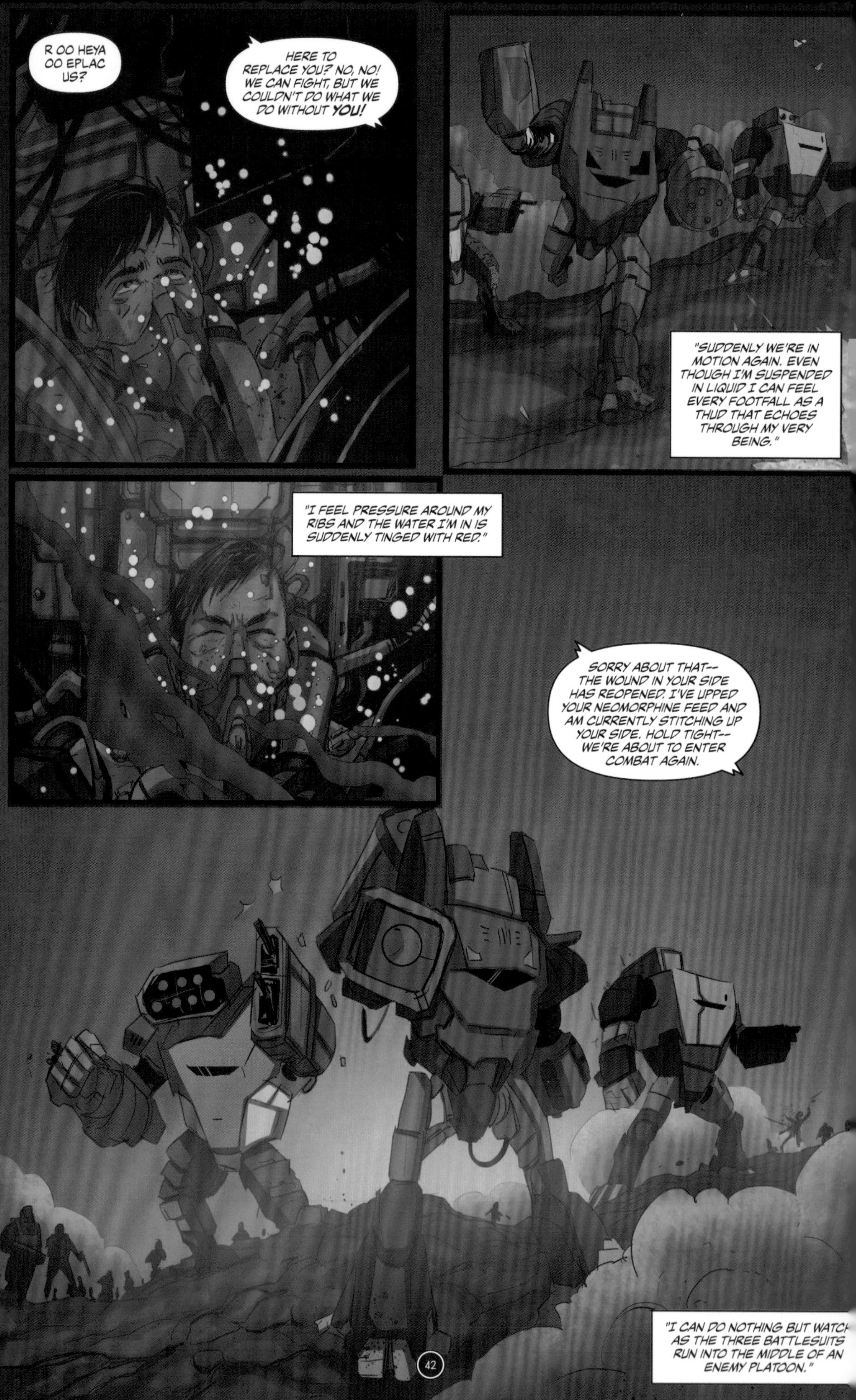

R OO HEYA OO EPLAC US?
HERE TO REPLACE YOU? NO, NO! WE CAN FIGHT, BUT WE COULDN'T DO WHAT WE DO WITHOUT **YOU!**
"SUDDENLY WE'RE IN MOTION AGAIN. EVEN THOUGH I'M SUSPENDED IN LIQUID I CAN FEEL EVERY FOOTFALL AS A THUD THAT ECHOES THROUGH MY VERY BEING."
"I FEEL PRESSURE AROUND MY RIBS AND THE WATER I'M IN IS SUDDENLY TINGED WITH RED."
SORRY ABOUT THAT-- THE WOUND IN YOUR SIDE HAS REOPENED. I'VE UPPED YOUR NEOMORPHINE FEED AND AM CURRENTLY STITCHING UP YOUR SIDE. HOLD TIGHT-- WE'RE ABOUT TO ENTER COMBAT AGAIN.
"I CAN DO NOTHING BUT WATCH AS THE THREE BATTLESUITS RUN INTO THE MIDDLE OF AN ENEMY PLATOON."

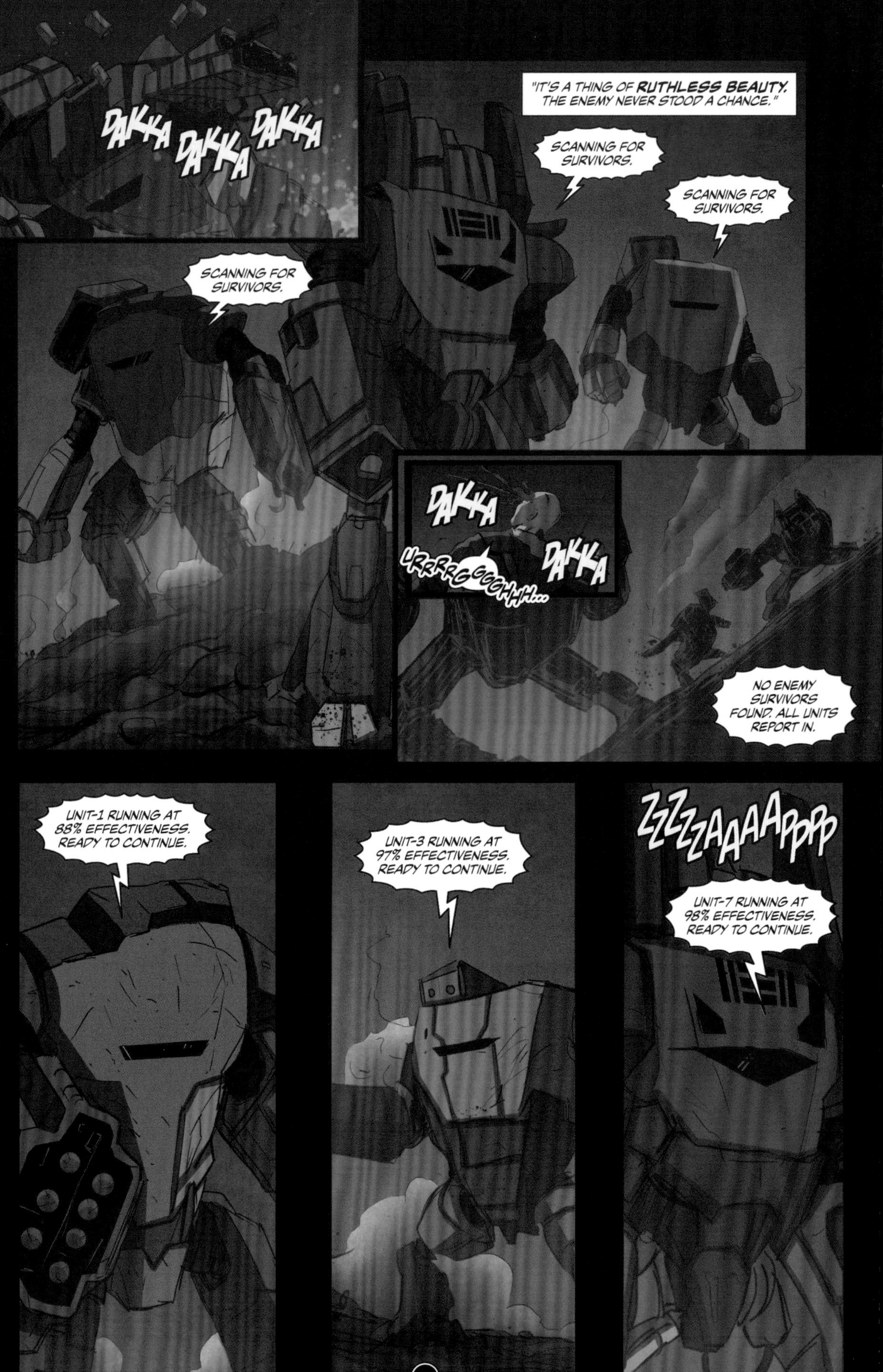
DAKKA DAKKA DAKKA
"IT'S A THING OF RUTHLESS BEAUTY. THE ENEMY NEVER STOOD A CHANCE."
SCANNING FOR SURVIVORS.
SCANNING FOR SURVIVORS.
SCANNING FOR SURVIVORS.
DAKKA
URRRRGGGGHHH...
DAKKA
NO ENEMY SURVIVORS FOUND. ALL UNITS REPORT IN.
UNIT-1 RUNNING AT 88% EFFECTIVENESS. READY TO CONTINUE.
UNIT-3 RUNNING AT 97% EFFECTIVENESS. READY TO CONTINUE.
ZZZZAAAAPPPP
UNIT-7 RUNNING AT 98% EFFECTIVENESS. READY TO CONTINUE.

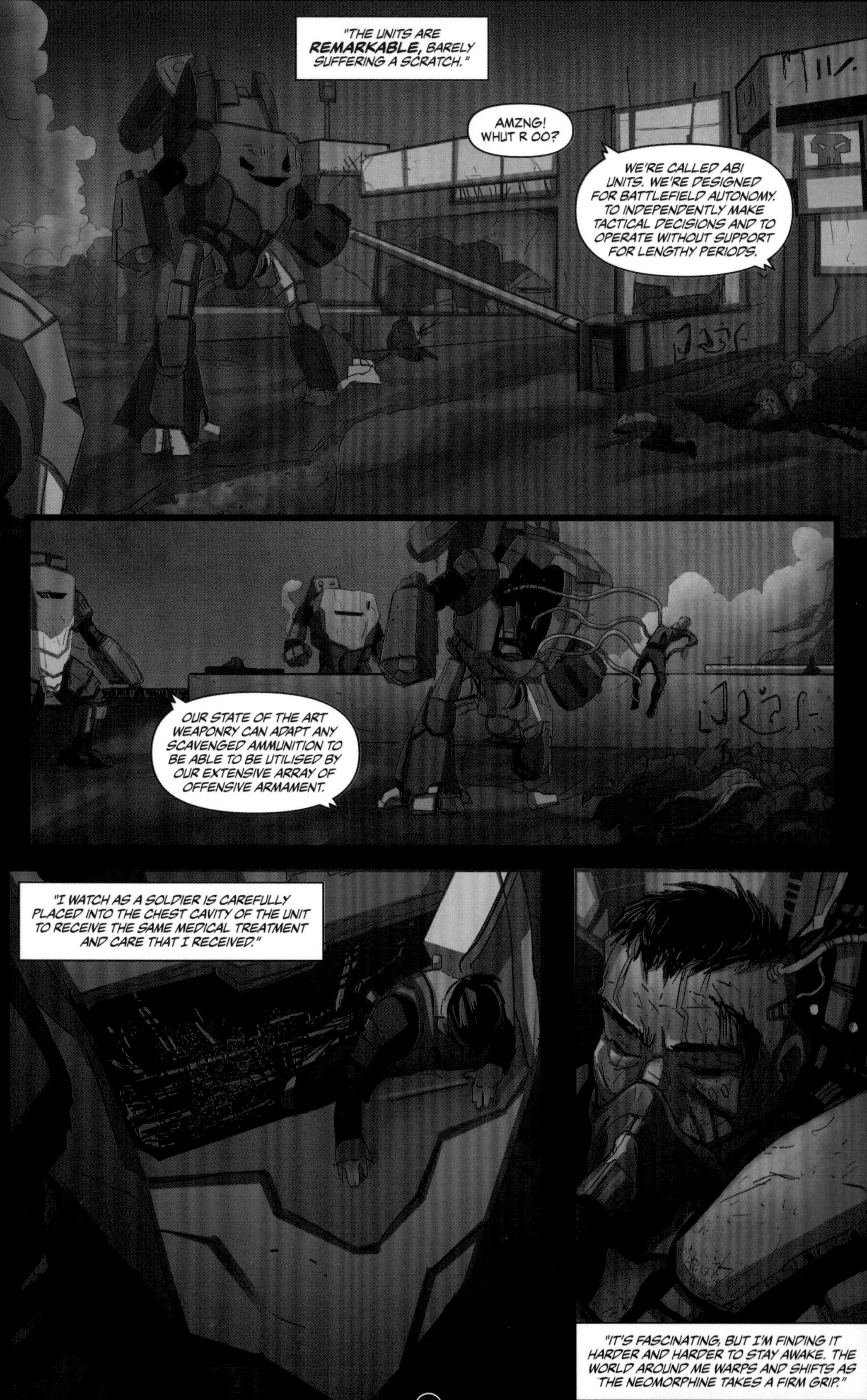
"THE UNITS ARE REMARKABLE, BARELY SUFFERING A SCRATCH."
AMZNG! WHUT R OO?
WE'RE CALLED ABI UNITS. WE'RE DESIGNED FOR BATTLEFIELD AUTONOMY. TO INDEPENDENTLY MAKE TACTICAL DECISIONS AND TO OPERATE WITHOUT SUPPORT FOR LENGTHY PERIODS.
OUR STATE OF THE ART WEAPONRY CAN ADAPT ANY SCAVENGED AMMUNITION TO BE ABLE TO BE UTILISED BY OUR EXTENSIVE ARRAY OF OFFENSIVE ARMAMENT.
"I WATCH AS A SOLDIER IS CAREFULLY PLACED INTO THE CHEST CAVITY OF THE UNIT TO RECEIVE THE SAME MEDICAL TREATMENT AND CARE THAT I RECEIVED."
"IT'S FASCINATING, BUT I'M FINDING IT HARDER AND HARDER TO STAY AWAKE. THE WORLD AROUND ME WARPS AND SHIFTS AS THE NEOMORPHINE TAKES A FIRM GRIP."

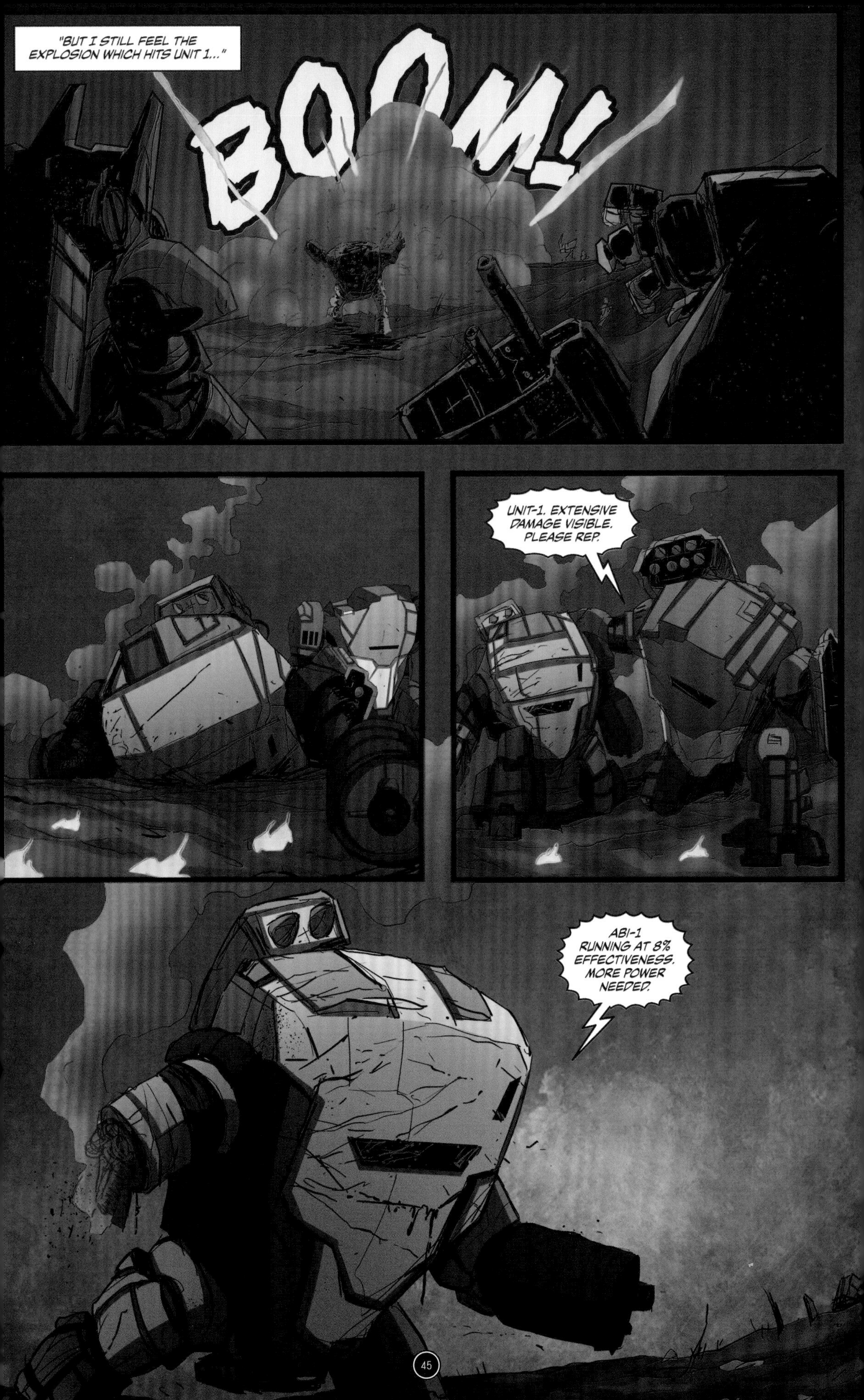
"BUT I STILL FEEL THE EXPLOSION WHICH HITS UNIT 1..."
BOOM!
UNIT-1. EXTENSIVE DAMAGE VISIBLE. PLEASE REP.
ABI-1 RUNNING AT 8% EFFECTIVENESS. MORE POWER NEEDED.

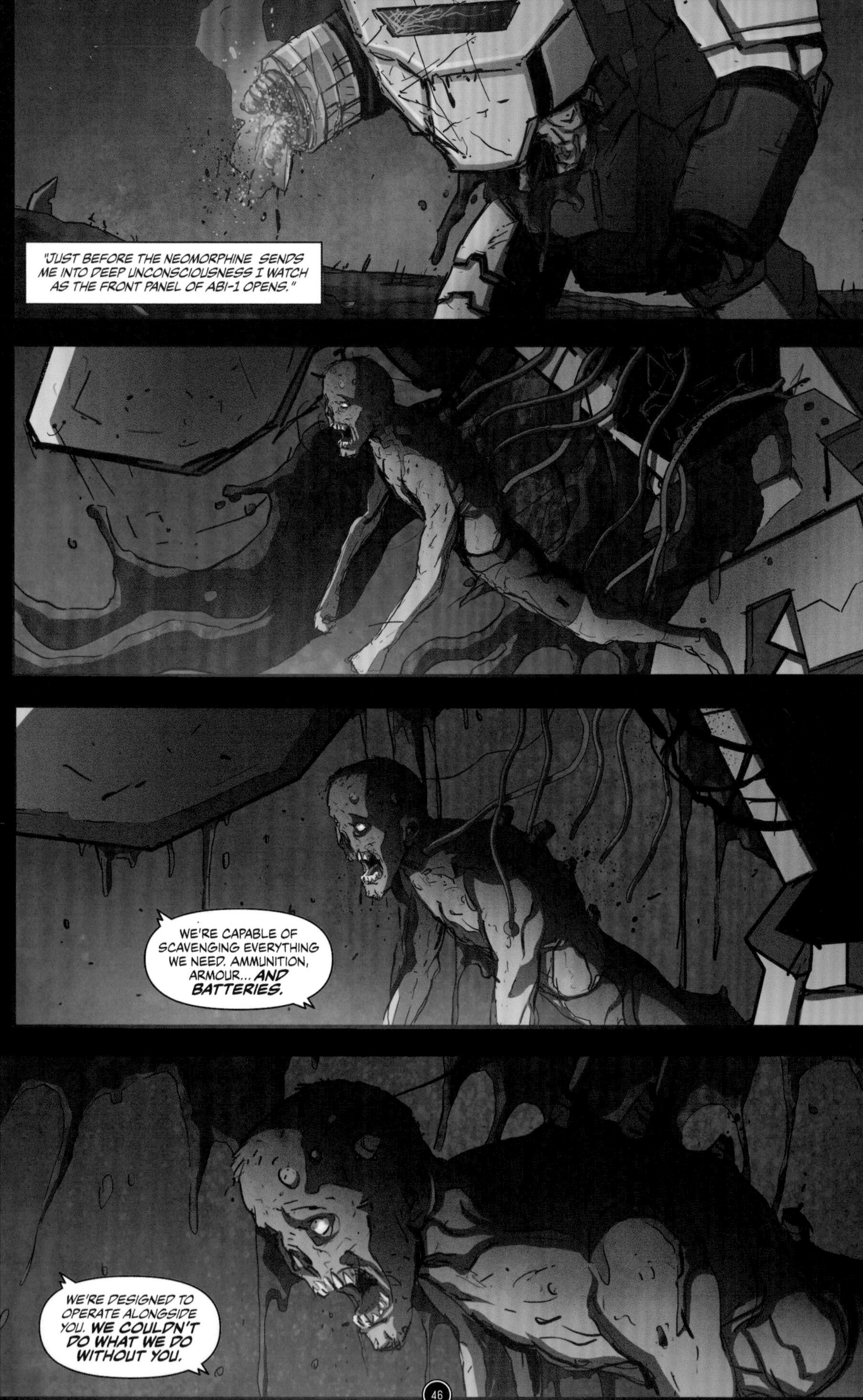
"JUST BEFORE THE NEOMORPHINE SENDS ME INTO DEEP UNCONSCIOUSNESS I WATCH AS THE FRONT PANEL OF ABI-1 OPENS."
WE'RE CAPABLE OF SCAVENGING EVERYTHING WE NEED. AMMUNITION, ARMOUR... AND BATTERIES.
WE'RE DESIGNED TO OPERATE ALONGSIDE YOU. WE COULDN'T DO WHAT WE DO WITHOUT YOU.

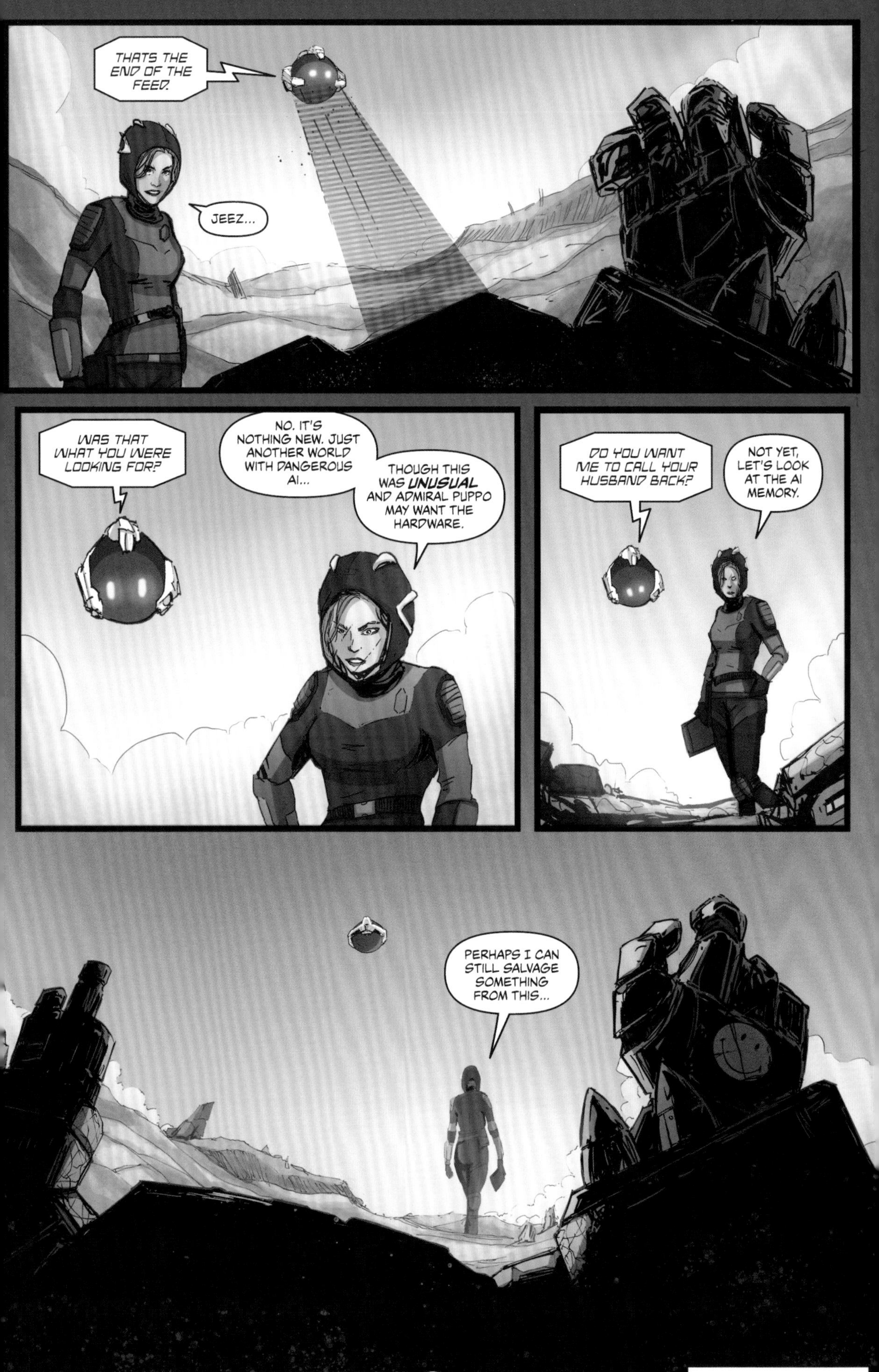
THATS THE END OF THE FEED.
JEEZ...
WAS THAT WHAT YOU WERE LOOKING FOR?
NO. IT'S NOTHING NEW. JUST ANOTHER WORLD WITH DANGEROUS AI...
THOUGH THIS WAS UNUSUAL AND ADMIRAL PUPPO MAY WANT THE HARDWARE.
DO YOU WANT ME TO CALL YOUR HUSBAND BACK?
NOT YET, LET'S LOOK AT THE AI MEMORY.
PERHAPS I CAN STILL SALVAGE SOMETHING FROM THIS...

TO BE CONTINUED...

ADMIRAL PUPPO

Let's keep this one short. I want to know what's salvageable and nothing else.The last report you sent took 67 pages and an appendix to tell me the ion drives were functioning as expected. I'm running a god damn fleet here, I have neither the time nor the patience to learn every miniscule detail, so let me give you some guide lines. If a RDML asks you for a briefing, give him a report as you would to a ten year old. For each additional star on their shoulder subtract one year. Now report.

ROBERT SADLER

The suits are mostly junk. The bio-electricity generated by the alien life-forms is tremendous compared to our own, a human could never be used to power such a suit. We could install our own power cells but why bother? The weapons are backwards, only the Splinter Grenades would be of interest but none were found intact. The battlesuit's AI is of interest however. It's equivalent to our Specialist class AI in that it is capable of limited degree of learning but only to aid its designated task. Much to the detriment of this species it was not secured by the Modified Laws of Robotics (MLRs) like our own and thus they went on killing even when the wellbeing of the species was threatened. What they do provide is an interesting insight into the aliens psychology. Much like you can study a language and learn about the culture that spoke it, so too can you study an AI.

ADMIRAL PUPPO

So this is what your report should have said: ''Nothing of value. Species died because of rogue AI (nothing new). Limited learning for the Astroarchaeologists. Suggest they move on to the next planet as soon as possible.'' You are smart Sadler. I expect you to be able to learn the skill of brevity or else I will find someone else. For the next report, **DO BETTER.**

Communication

"The single biggest problem in communication is the illusion that it has taken place."

George Bernard Shaw

Writer/Creator
Neil Gibson

Illustrator
Davide Puppo

Colourist
Liezl Buenaventura

Letters by
Justin Birch

www.tpubcomics.com

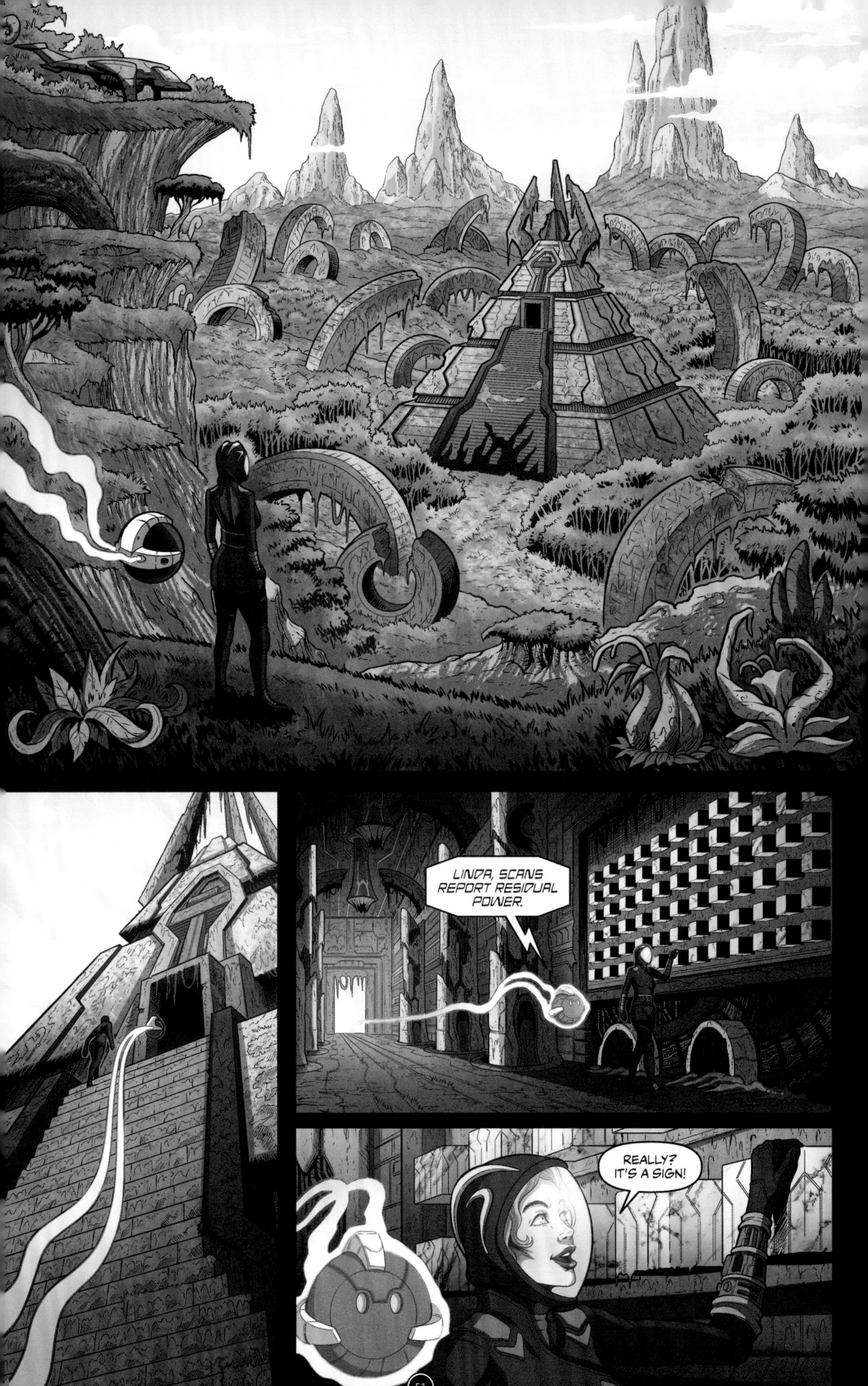
LINDA, SCANS REPORT RESIDUAL POWER.
REALLY? IT'S A SIGN!

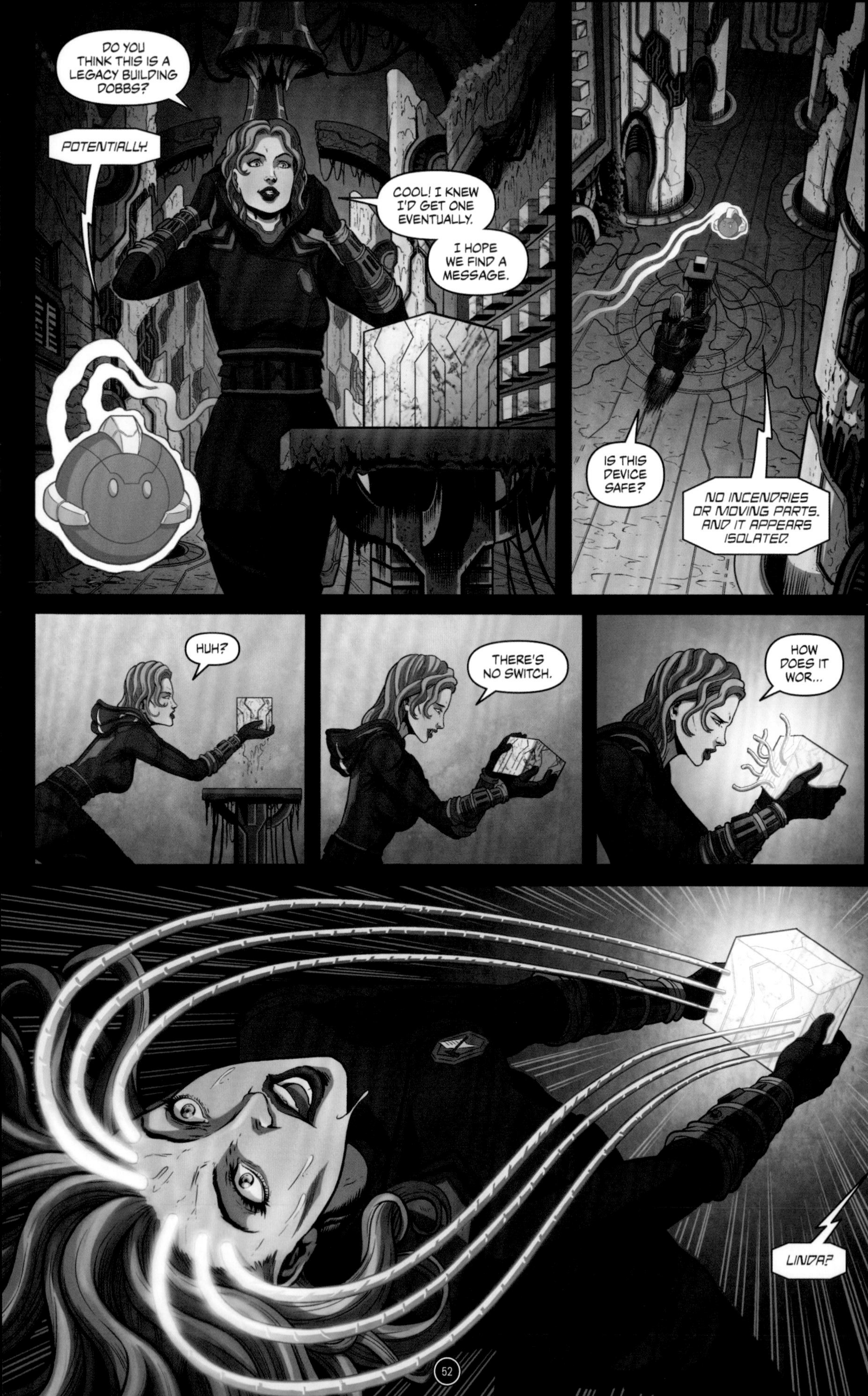
DO YOU THINK THIS IS A LEGACY BUILDING DOBBS?
POTENTIALLY.
COOL! I KNEW I'D GET ONE EVENTUALLY.
I HOPE WE FIND A MESSAGE.
IS THIS DEVICE SAFE?
NO INCENDRIES OR MOVING PARTS. AND IT APPEARS ISOLATED.
HUH?
THERE'S NO SWITCH.
HOW DOES IT WOR...
LINDA?

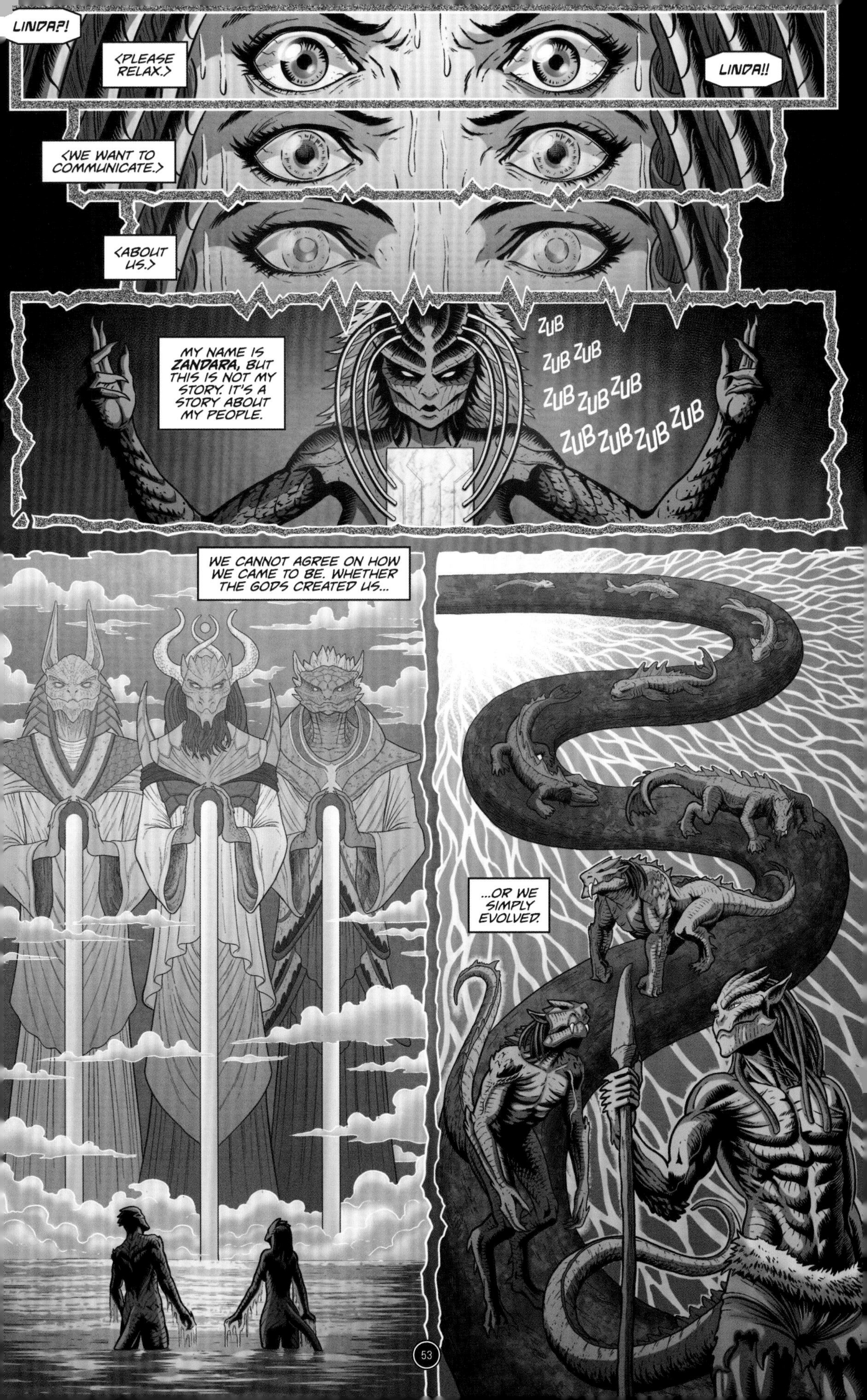

LINDA?!
<PLEASE RELAX.>
LINDA!!
<WE WANT TO COMMUNICATE.>
<ABOUT US.>
MY NAME IS ZANDARA, BUT THIS IS NOT MY STORY. IT'S A STORY ABOUT MY PEOPLE.
ZUB ZUB ZUB ZUB ZUB ZUB ZUB ZUB ZUB ZUB
WE CANNOT AGREE ON HOW WE CAME TO BE. WHETHER THE GODS CREATED US...
...OR WE SIMPLY EVOLVED.

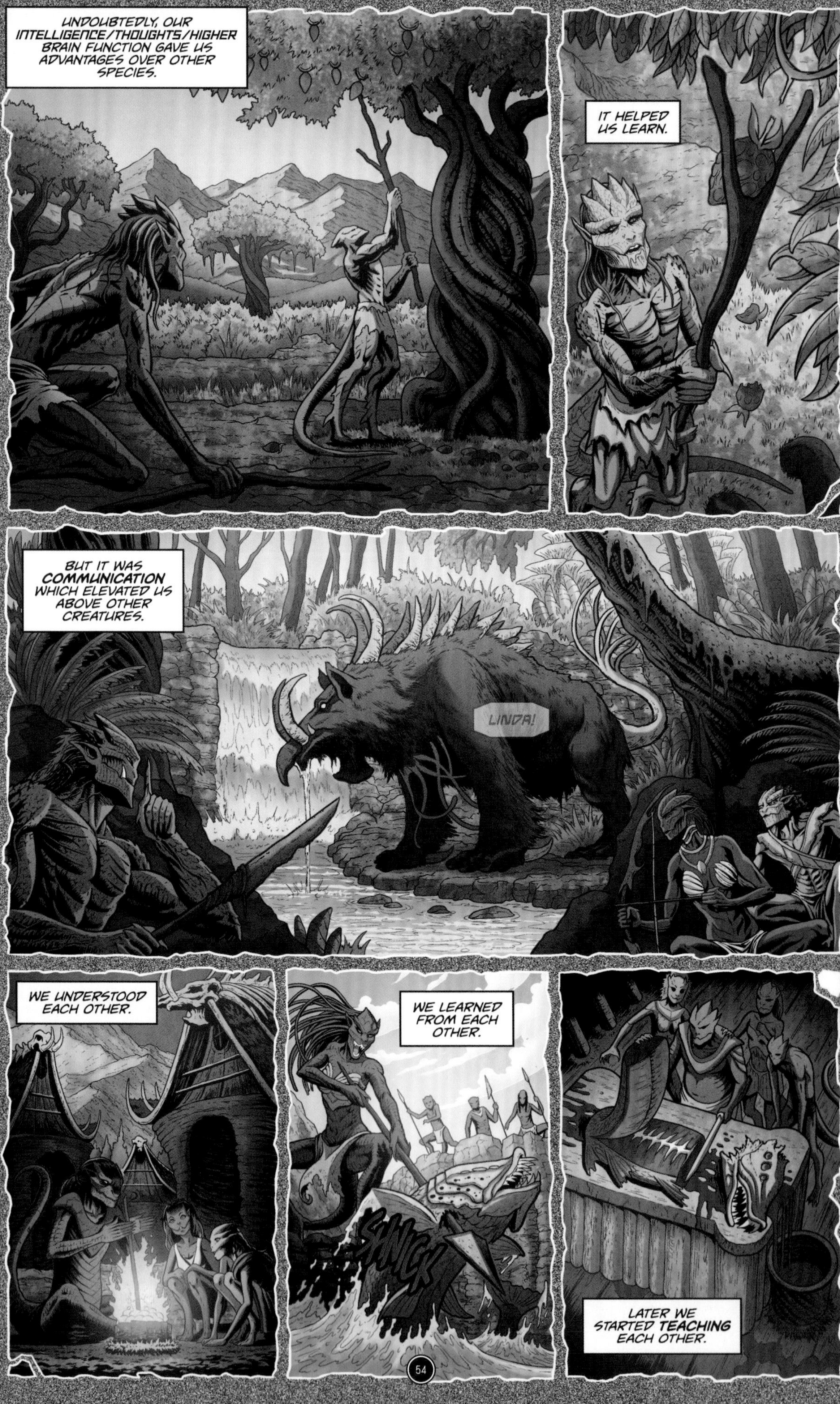
UNDOUBTEDLY, OUR INTELLIGENCE/THOUGHTS/HIGHER BRAIN FUNCTION GAVE US ADVANTAGES OVER OTHER SPECIES.
IT HELPED US LEARN.
BUT IT WAS COMMUNICATION WHICH ELEVATED US ABOVE OTHER CREATURES.
LINDA!
WE UNDERSTOOD EACH OTHER.
WE LEARNED FROM EACH OTHER.
LATER WE STARTED TEACHING EACH OTHER.

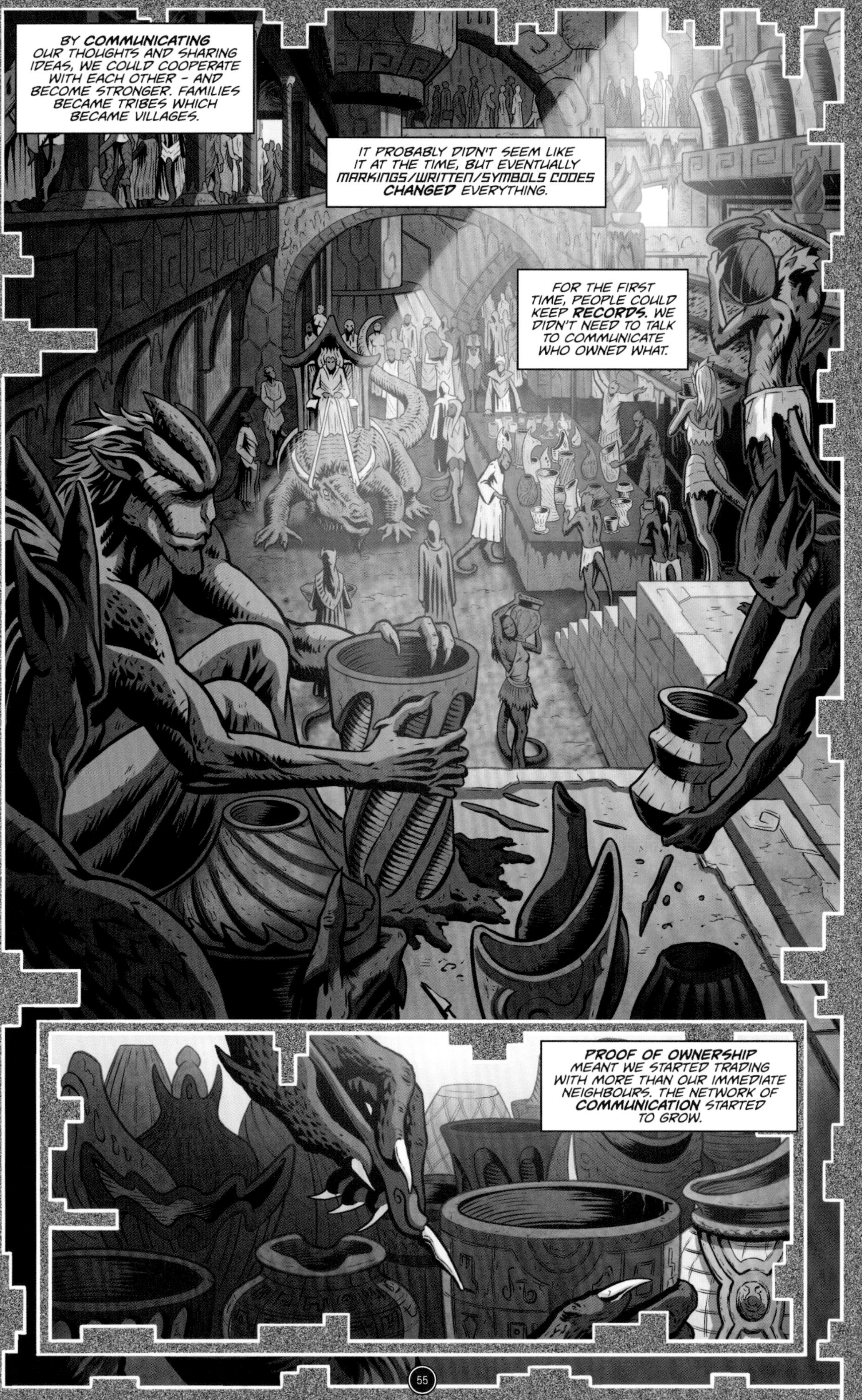

BY COMMUNICATING OUR THOUGHTS AND SHARING IDEAS, WE COULD COOPERATE WITH EACH OTHER - AND BECOME STRONGER. FAMILIES BECAME TRIBES WHICH BECAME VILLAGES.
IT PROBABLY DIDN'T SEEM LIKE IT AT THE TIME, BUT EVENTUALLY MARKINGS/WRITTEN/SYMBOLS CODES CHANGED EVERYTHING.
FOR THE FIRST TIME, PEOPLE COULD KEEP RECORDS. WE DIDN'T NEED TO TALK TO COMMUNICATE WHO OWNED WHAT.
PROOF OF OWNERSHIP MEANT WE STARTED TRADING WITH MORE THAN OUR IMMEDIATE NEIGHBOURS. THE NETWORK OF COMMUNICATION STARTED TO GROW.

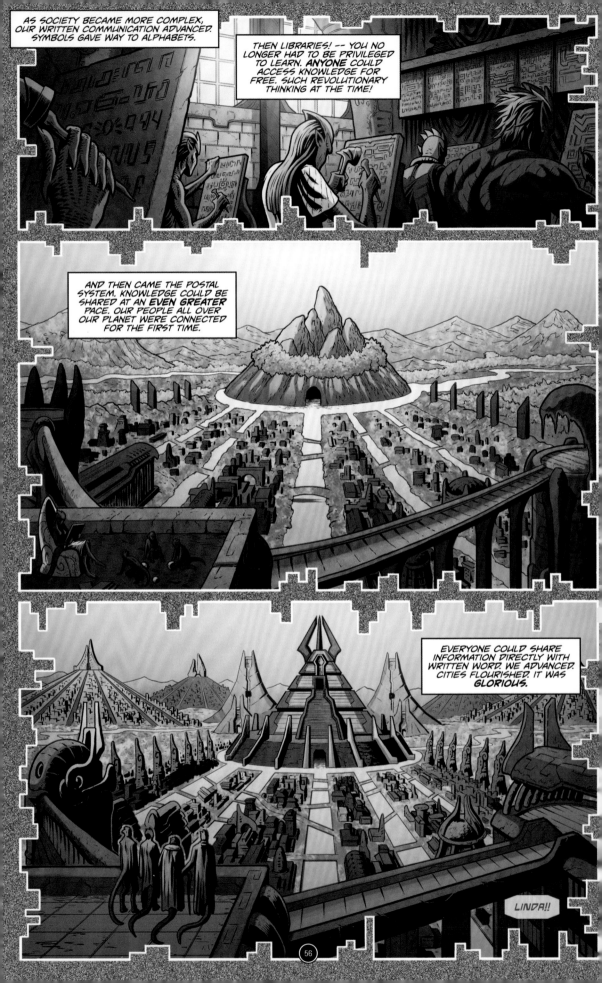

AS SOCIETY BECAME MORE COMPLEX, OUR WRITTEN COMMUNICATION ADVANCED. SYMBOLS GAVE WAY TO ALPHABETS.

THEN LIBRARIES! -- YOU NO LONGER HAD TO BE PRIVILEGED TO LEARN. **ANYONE** COULD ACCESS KNOWLEDGE FOR FREE. SUCH REVOLUTIONARY THINKING AT THE TIME!

AND THEN CAME THE POSTAL SYSTEM. KNOWLEDGE COULD BE SHARED AT AN **EVEN GREATER** PACE. OUR PEOPLE ALL OVER OUR PLANET WERE CONNECTED FOR THE FIRST TIME.

EVERYONE COULD SHARE INFORMATION DIRECTLY WITH WRITTEN WORD. WE ADVANCED. CITIES FLOURISHED. IT WAS **GLORIOUS.**

LINDA!!

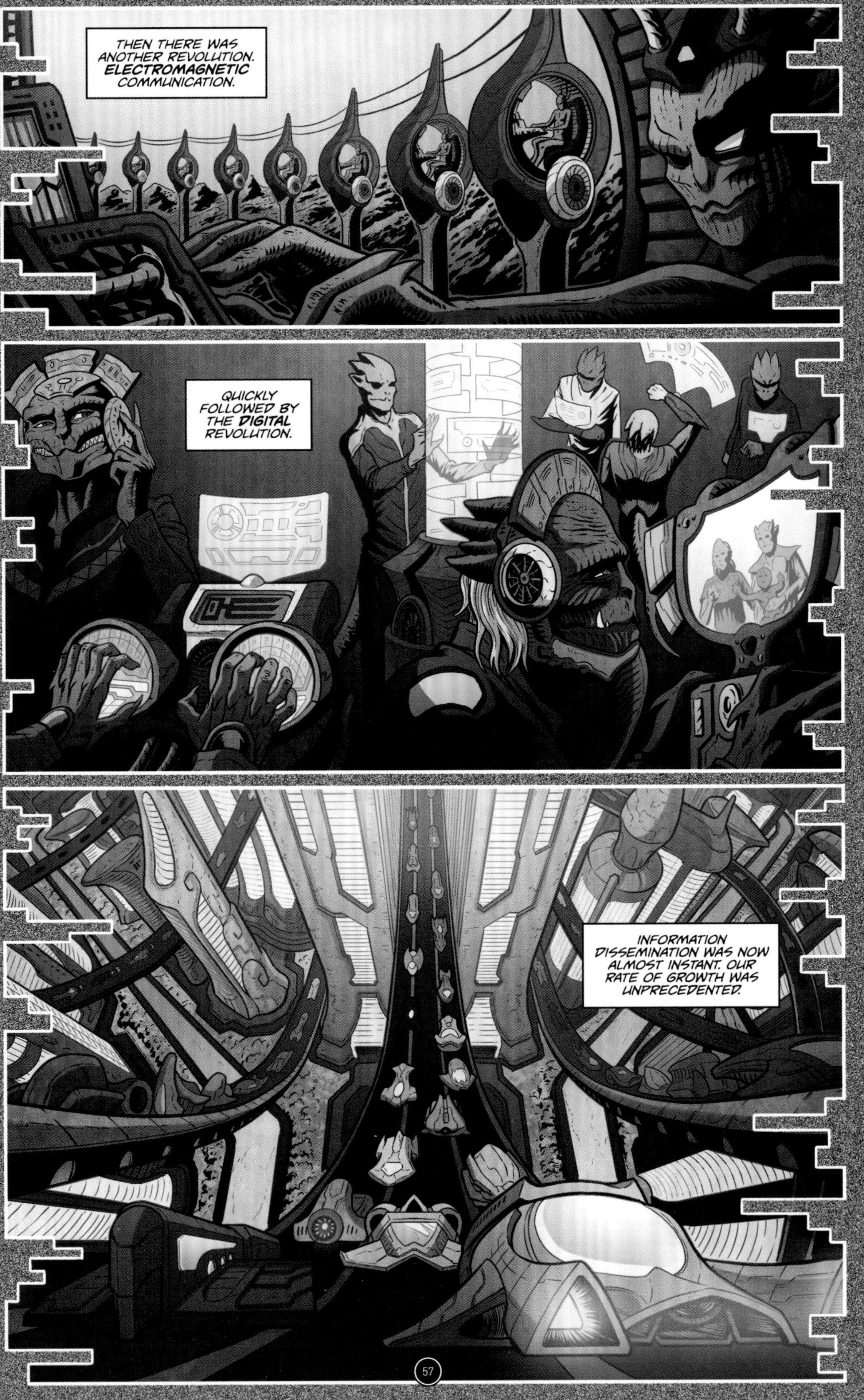
THEN THERE WAS ANOTHER REVOLUTION. ELECTROMAGNETIC COMMUNICATION.
QUICKLY FOLLOWED BY THE DIGITAL REVOLUTION.
INFORMATION DISSEMINATION WAS NOW ALMOST INSTANT. OUR RATE OF GROWTH WAS UNPRECEDENTED.

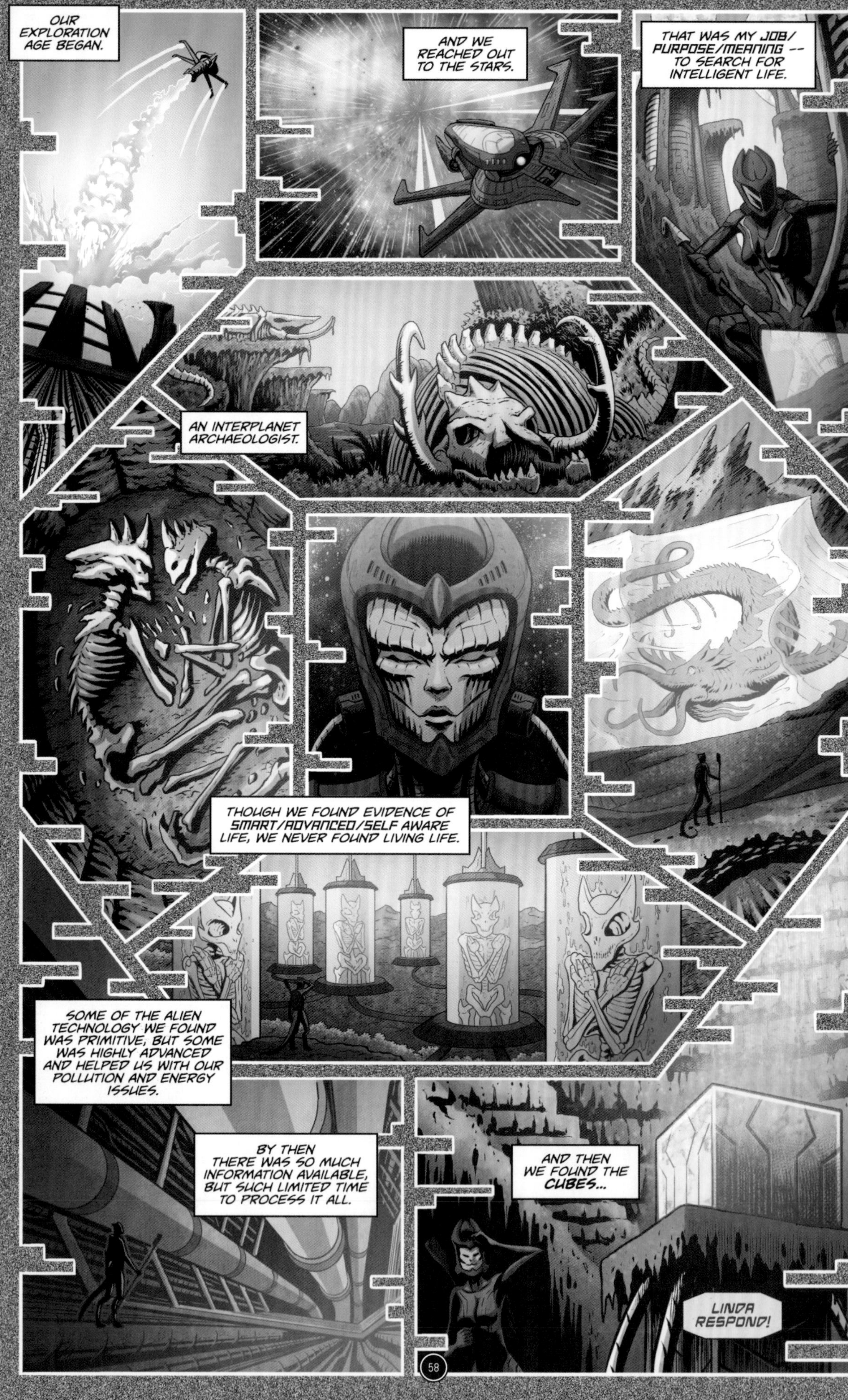
OUR EXPLORATION AGE BEGAN.
AND WE REACHED OUT TO THE STARS.
THAT WAS MY JOB/ PURPOSE/MEANING -- TO SEARCH FOR INTELLIGENT LIFE.
AN INTERPLANET ARCHAEOLOGIST.
THOUGH WE FOUND EVIDENCE OF SMART/ADVANCED/SELF AWARE LIFE, WE NEVER FOUND LIVING LIFE.
SOME OF THE ALIEN TECHNOLOGY WE FOUND WAS PRIMITIVE, BUT SOME WAS HIGHLY ADVANCED AND HELPED US WITH OUR POLLUTION AND ENERGY ISSUES.
BY THEN THERE WAS SO MUCH INFORMATION AVAILABLE, BUT SUCH LIMITED TIME TO PROCESS IT ALL.
AND THEN WE FOUND THE CUBES...
LINDA RESPOND!

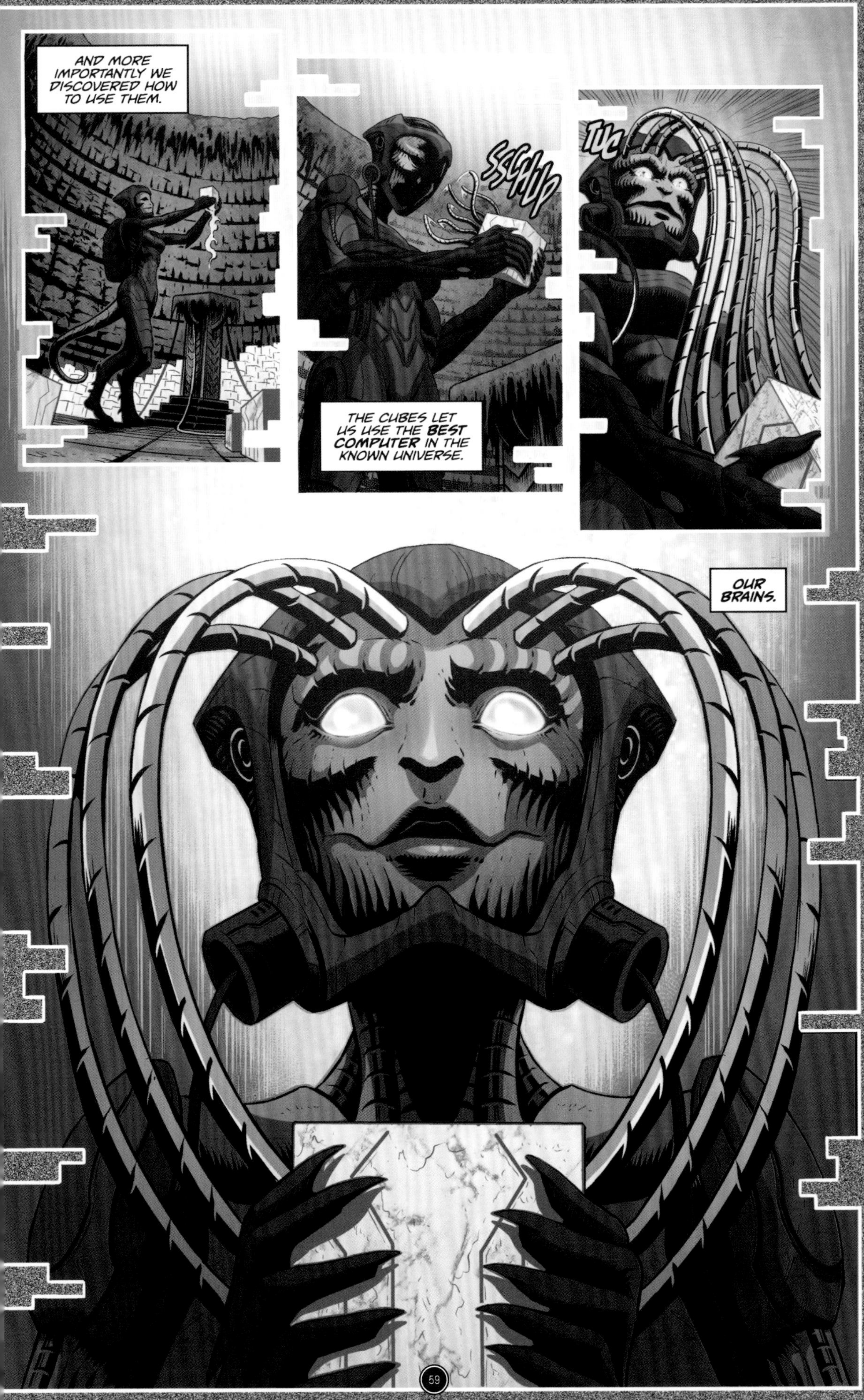
AND MORE IMPORTANTLY WE DISCOVERED HOW TO USE THEM.
SSSCHLUP
THE CUBES LET US USE THE BEST COMPUTER IN THE KNOWN UNIVERSE.
TUC
OUR BRAINS.

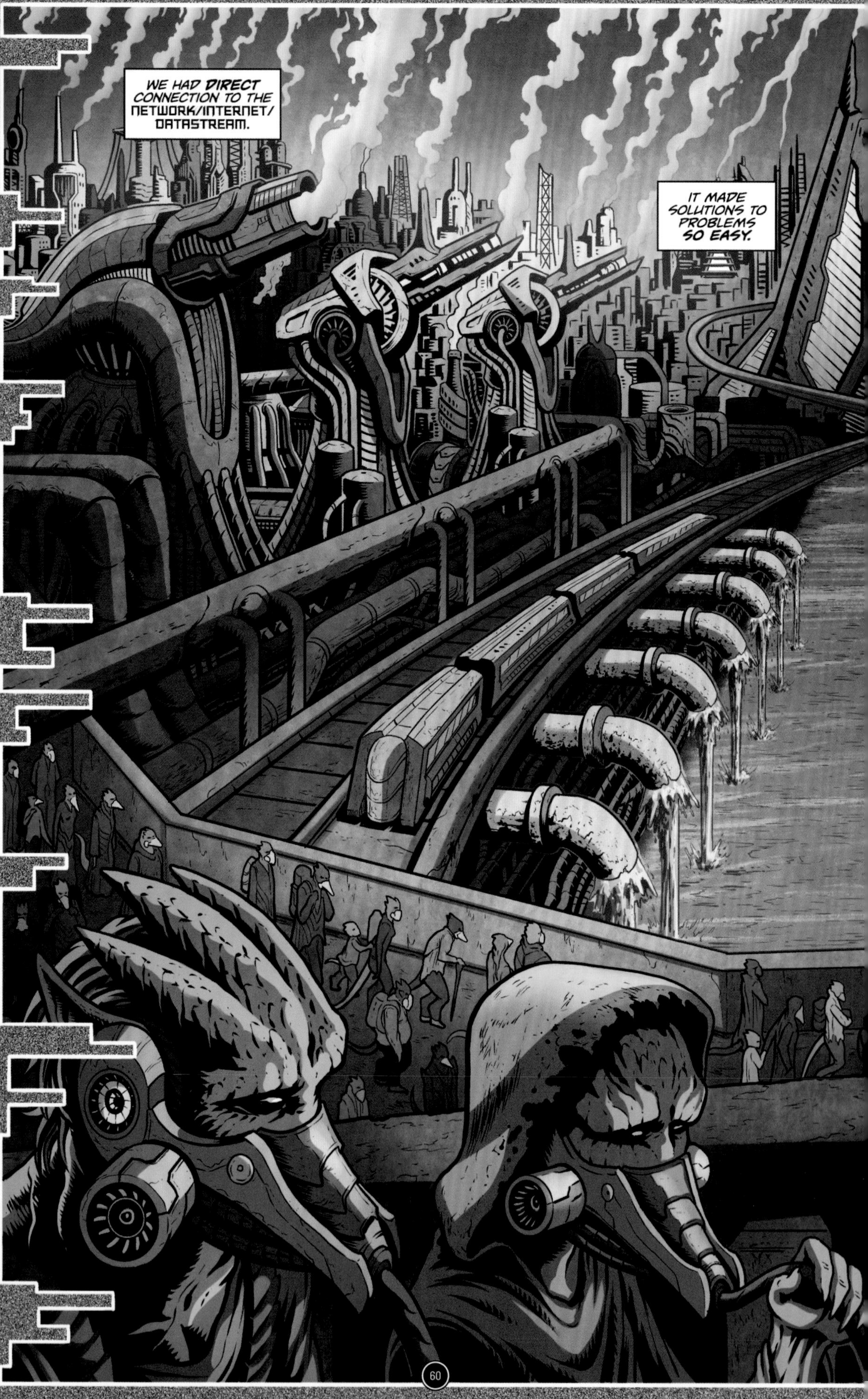
WE HAD DIRECT CONNECTION TO THE NETWORK/INTERNET/ DATASTREAM.
IT MADE SOLUTIONS TO PROBLEMS SO EASY.

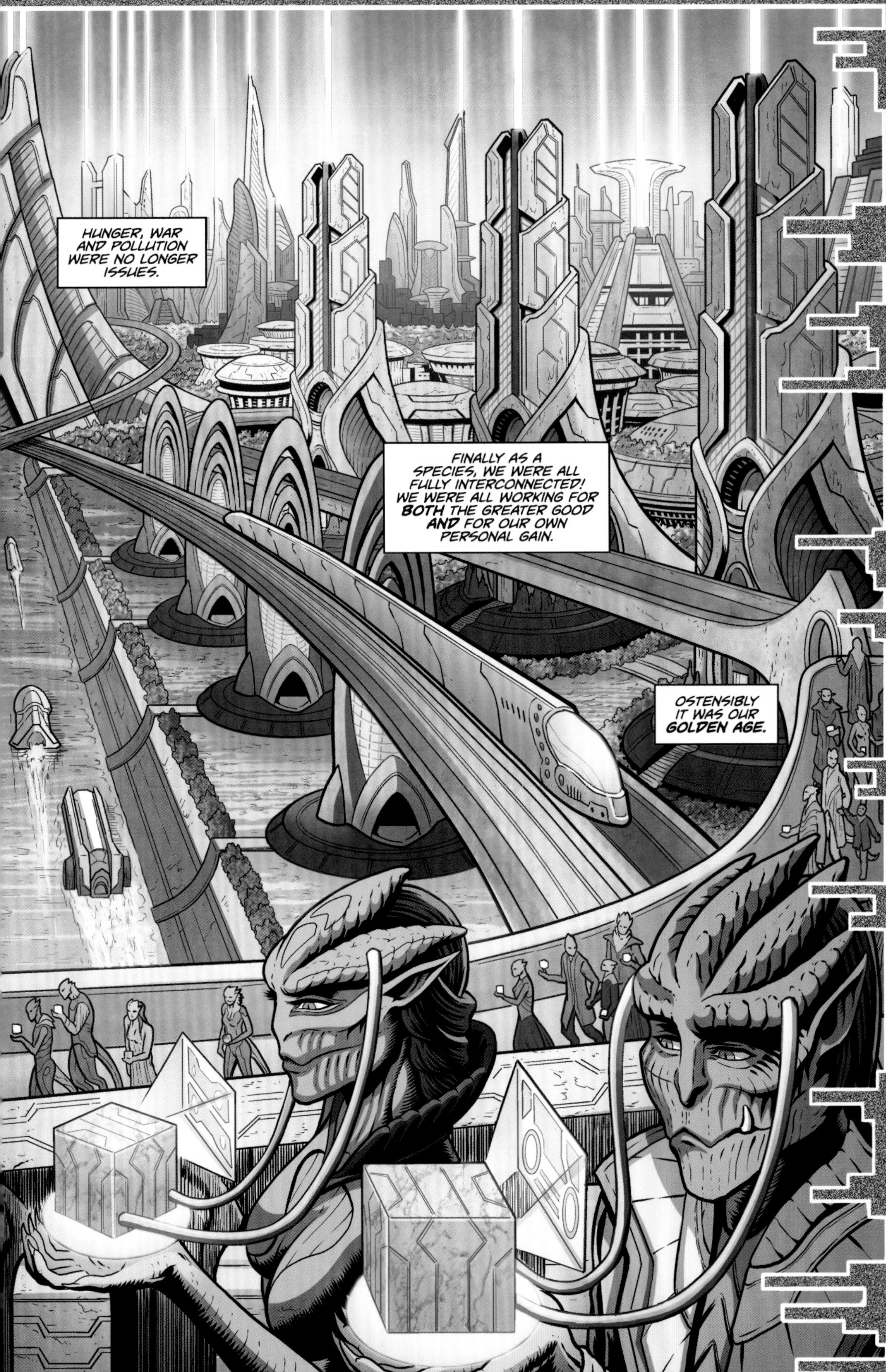
HUNGER, WAR AND POLLUTION WERE NO LONGER ISSUES.
FINALLY AS A SPECIES, WE WERE ALL FULLY INTERCONNECTED! WE WERE ALL WORKING FOR **BOTH** THE GREATER GOOD **AND** FOR OUR OWN PERSONAL GAIN.
OSTENSIBLY IT WAS OUR **GOLDEN AGE.**
BUT...

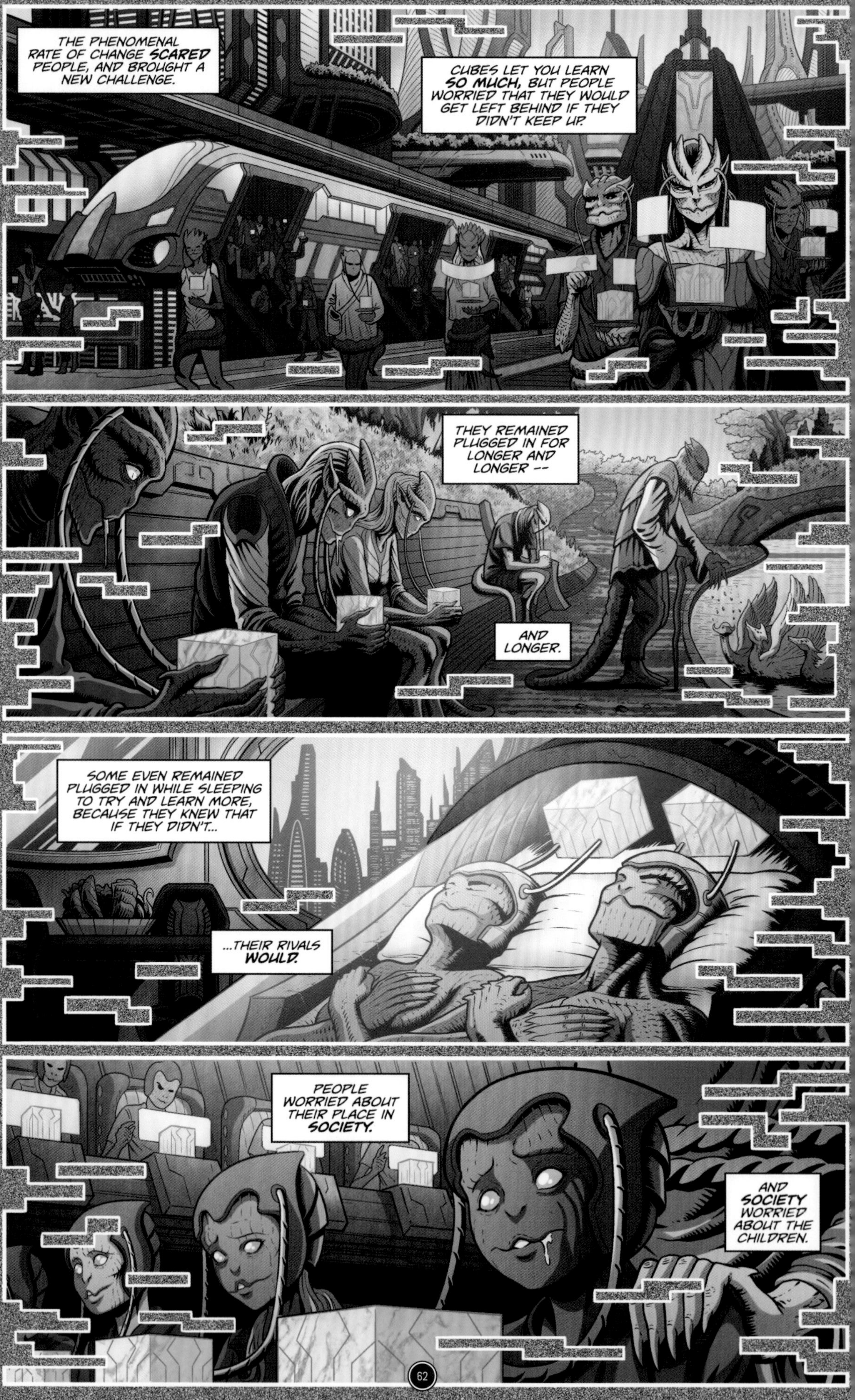
THE PHENOMENAL RATE OF CHANGE SCARED PEOPLE, AND BROUGHT A NEW CHALLENGE.
CUBES LET YOU LEARN SO MUCH, BUT PEOPLE WORRIED THAT THEY WOULD GET LEFT BEHIND IF THEY DIDN'T KEEP UP.
THEY REMAINED PLUGGED IN FOR LONGER AND LONGER --
AND LONGER.
SOME EVEN REMAINED PLUGGED IN WHILE SLEEPING TO TRY AND LEARN MORE, BECAUSE THEY KNEW THAT IF THEY DIDN'T...
...THEIR RIVALS WOULD.
PEOPLE WORRIED ABOUT THEIR PLACE IN SOCIETY.
AND SOCIETY WORRIED ABOUT THE CHILDREN.

THE YOUNGER YOU CONNECTED, THE MORE INFORMATION YOU COULD LEARN AND PROCESS. THE BETTER YOUR COMPETITIVE ADVANTAGE **WITHIN** OUR SPECIES. PARENTS HAD TO OUTDO EACH OTHER.

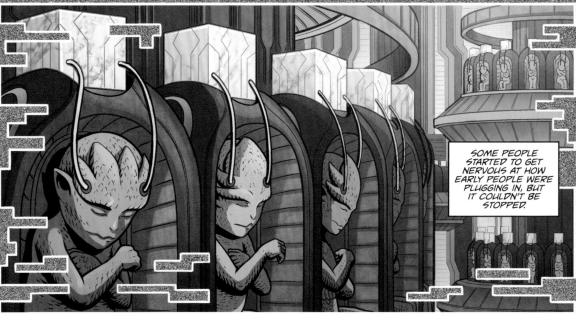

SOME PEOPLE STARTED TO GET NERVOUS AT HOW EARLY PEOPLE WERE PLUGGING IN, BUT IT COULDN'T BE STOPPED.

BUT WHEN FOETUSES STARTED BEING HOOKED UP, MANY THOUGHT ENOUGH WAS **ENOUGH.**

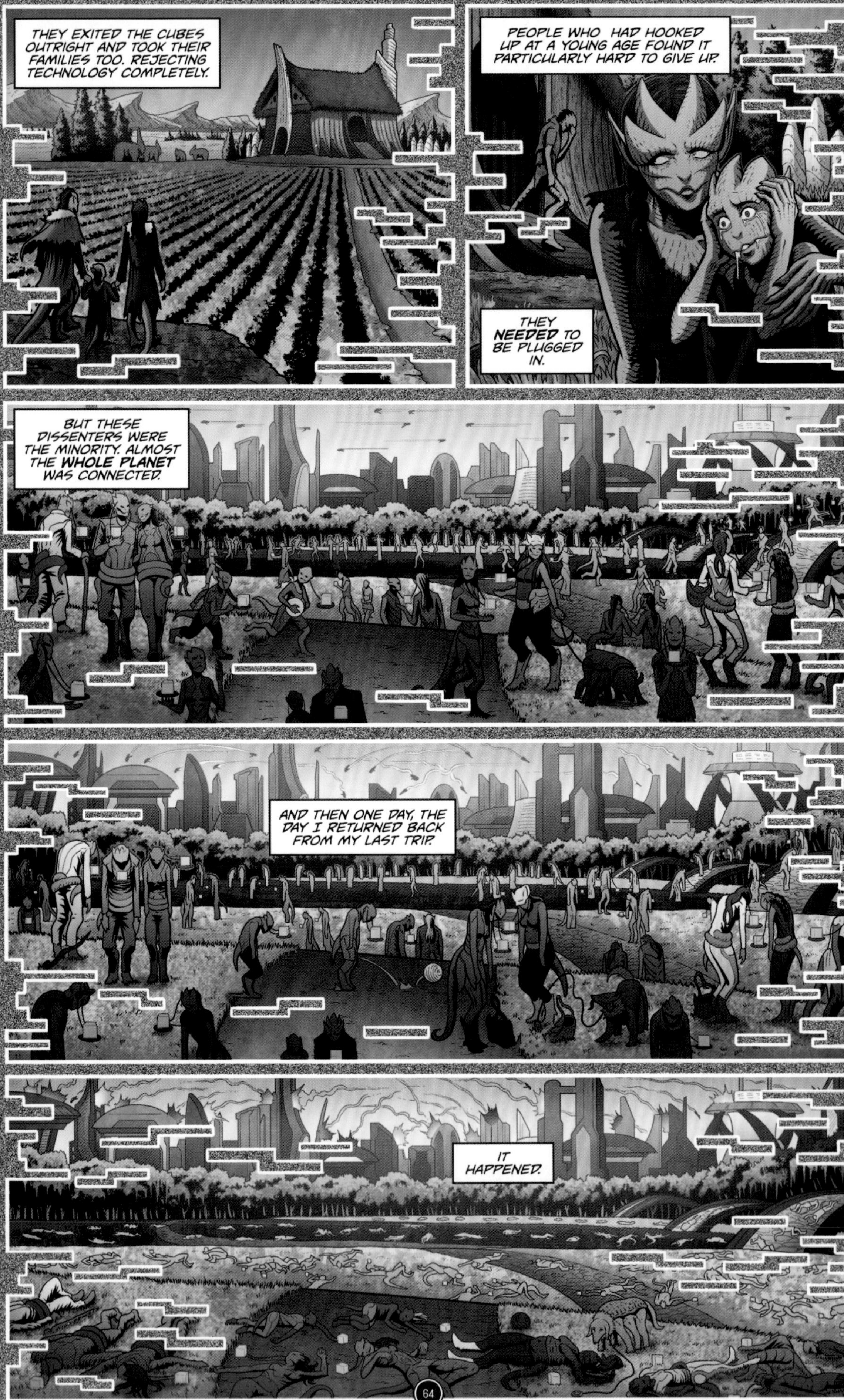
THEY EXITED THE CUBES OUTRIGHT AND TOOK THEIR FAMILIES TOO. REJECTING TECHNOLOGY COMPLETELY.
PEOPLE WHO HAD HOOKED UP AT A YOUNG AGE FOUND IT PARTICULARLY HARD TO GIVE UP.
THEY NEEDED TO BE PLUGGED IN.
BUT THESE DISSENTERS WERE THE MINORITY. ALMOST THE WHOLE PLANET WAS CONNECTED.
AND THEN ONE DAY, THE DAY I RETURNED BACK FROM MY LAST TRIP.
IT HAPPENED.

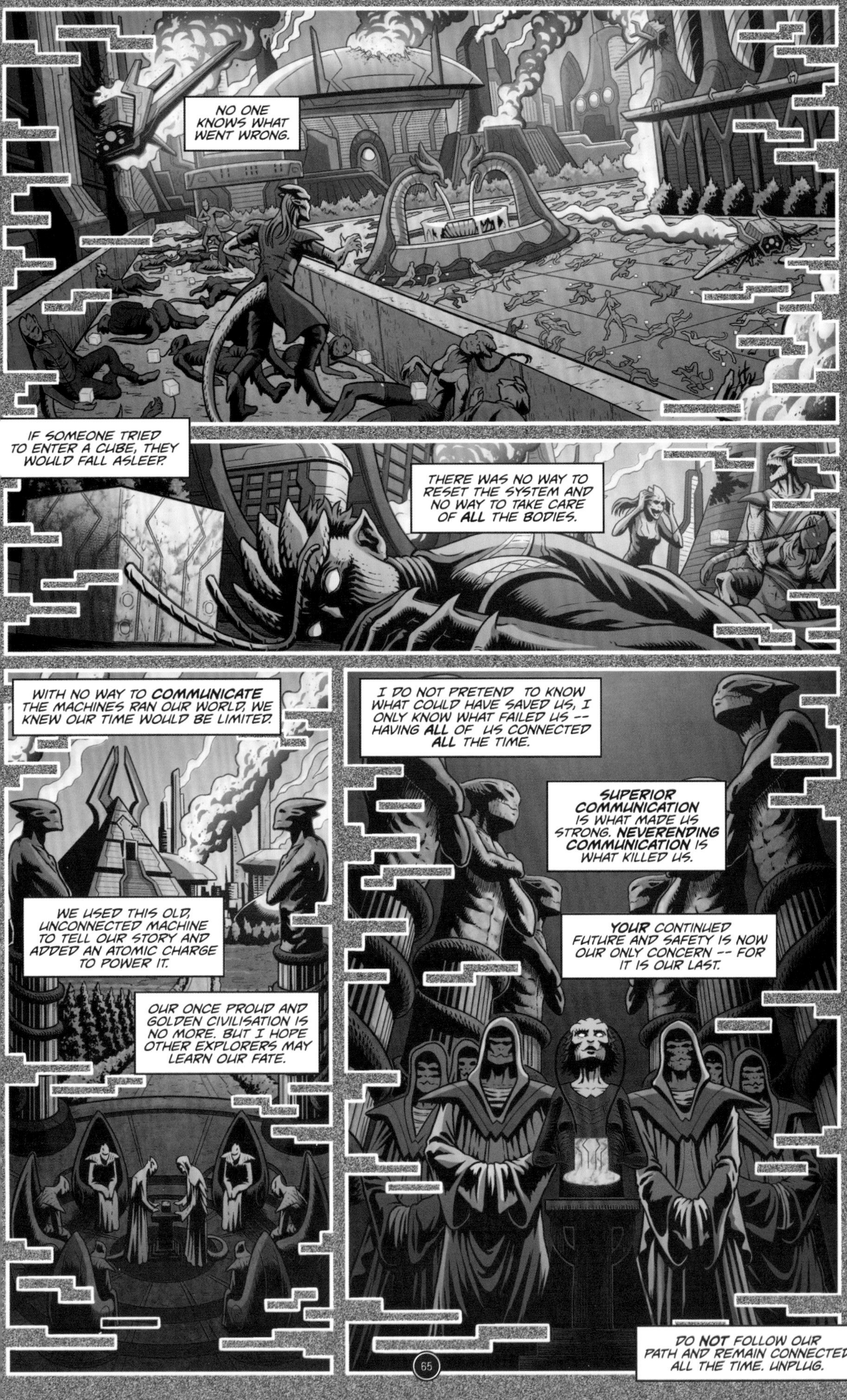
NO ONE KNOWS WHAT WENT WRONG.
IF SOMEONE TRIED TO ENTER A CUBE, THEY WOULD FALL ASLEEP.
THERE WAS NO WAY TO RESET THE SYSTEM AND NO WAY TO TAKE CARE OF ALL THE BODIES.
WITH NO WAY TO COMMUNICATE THE MACHINES RAN OUR WORLD, WE KNEW OUR TIME WOULD BE LIMITED.
WE USED THIS OLD, UNCONNECTED MACHINE TO TELL OUR STORY AND ADDED AN ATOMIC CHARGE TO POWER IT.
OUR ONCE PROUD AND GOLDEN CIVILISATION IS NO MORE. BUT I HOPE OTHER EXPLORERS MAY LEARN OUR FATE.
I DO NOT PRETEND TO KNOW WHAT COULD HAVE SAVED US, I ONLY KNOW WHAT FAILED US -- HAVING ALL OF US CONNECTED ALL THE TIME.
SUPERIOR COMMUNICATION IS WHAT MADE US STRONG. NEVERENDING COMMUNICATION IS WHAT KILLED US.
YOUR CONTINUED FUTURE AND SAFETY IS NOW OUR ONLY CONCERN -- FOR IT IS OUR LAST.
DO NOT FOLLOW OUR PATH AND REMAIN CONNECTED ALL THE TIME. UNPLUG.

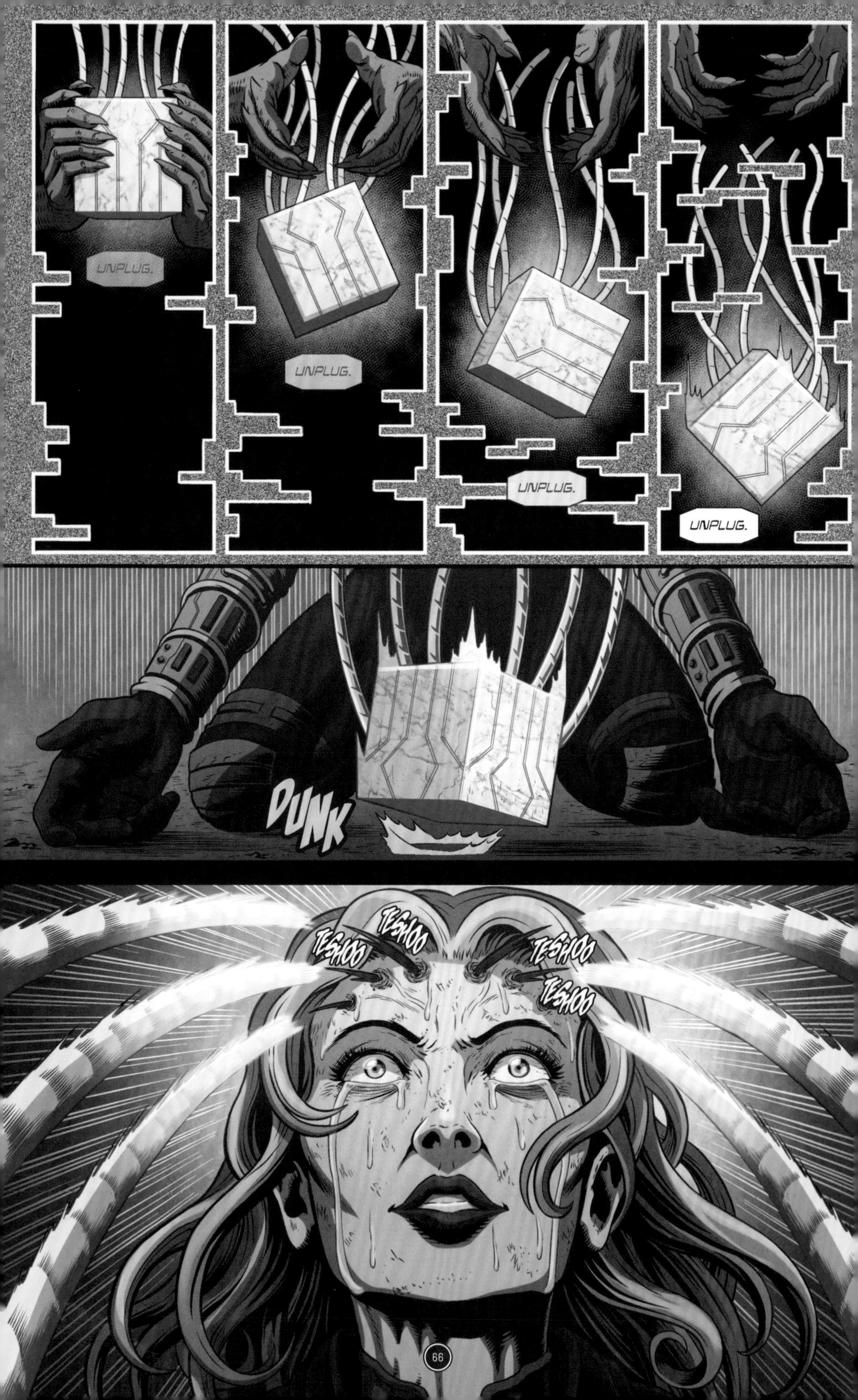
UNPLUG.
UNPLUG.
UNPLUG.
UNPLUG.
DUNK
TESHOO
TESHOO
TESHOO
TESHOO

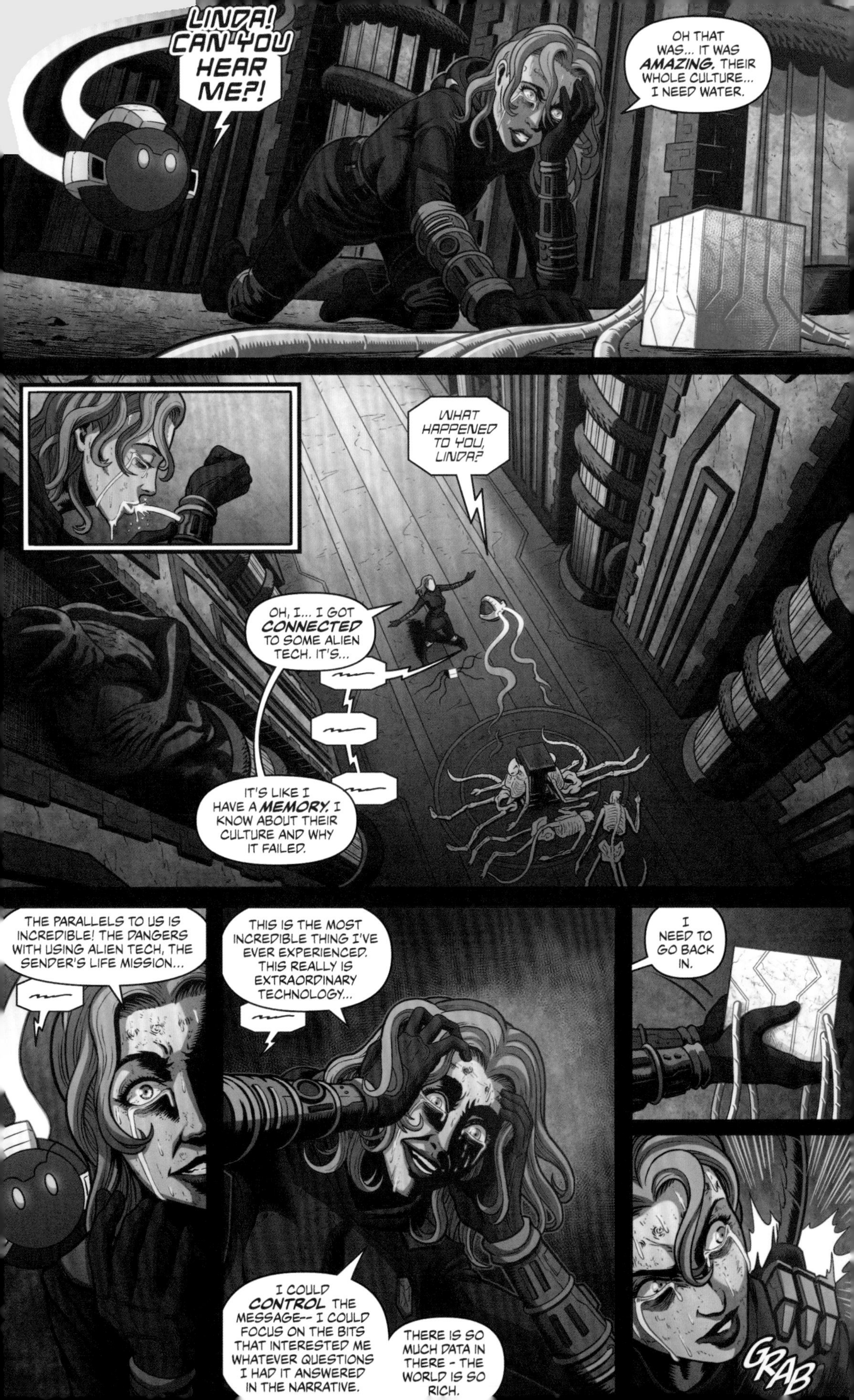
LINDA! CAN YOU HEAR ME?!
OH THAT WAS... IT WAS AMAZING. THEIR WHOLE CULTURE... I NEED WATER.
WHAT HAPPENED TO YOU, LINDA?
OH, I... I GOT CONNECTED TO SOME ALIEN TECH. IT'S...
IT'S LIKE I HAVE A MEMORY. I KNOW ABOUT THEIR CULTURE AND WHY IT FAILED.
THE PARALLELS TO US IS INCREDIBLE! THE DANGERS WITH USING ALIEN TECH, THE SENDER'S LIFE MISSION...
THIS IS THE MOST INCREDIBLE THING I'VE EVER EXPERIENCED. THIS REALLY IS EXTRAORDINARY TECHNOLOGY...
I COULD CONTROL THE MESSAGE-- I COULD FOCUS ON THE BITS THAT INTERESTED ME WHATEVER QUESTIONS I HAD IT ANSWERED IN THE NARRATIVE.
THERE IS SO MUCH DATA IN THERE - THE WORLD IS SO RICH.
I NEED TO GO BACK IN.
GRAB

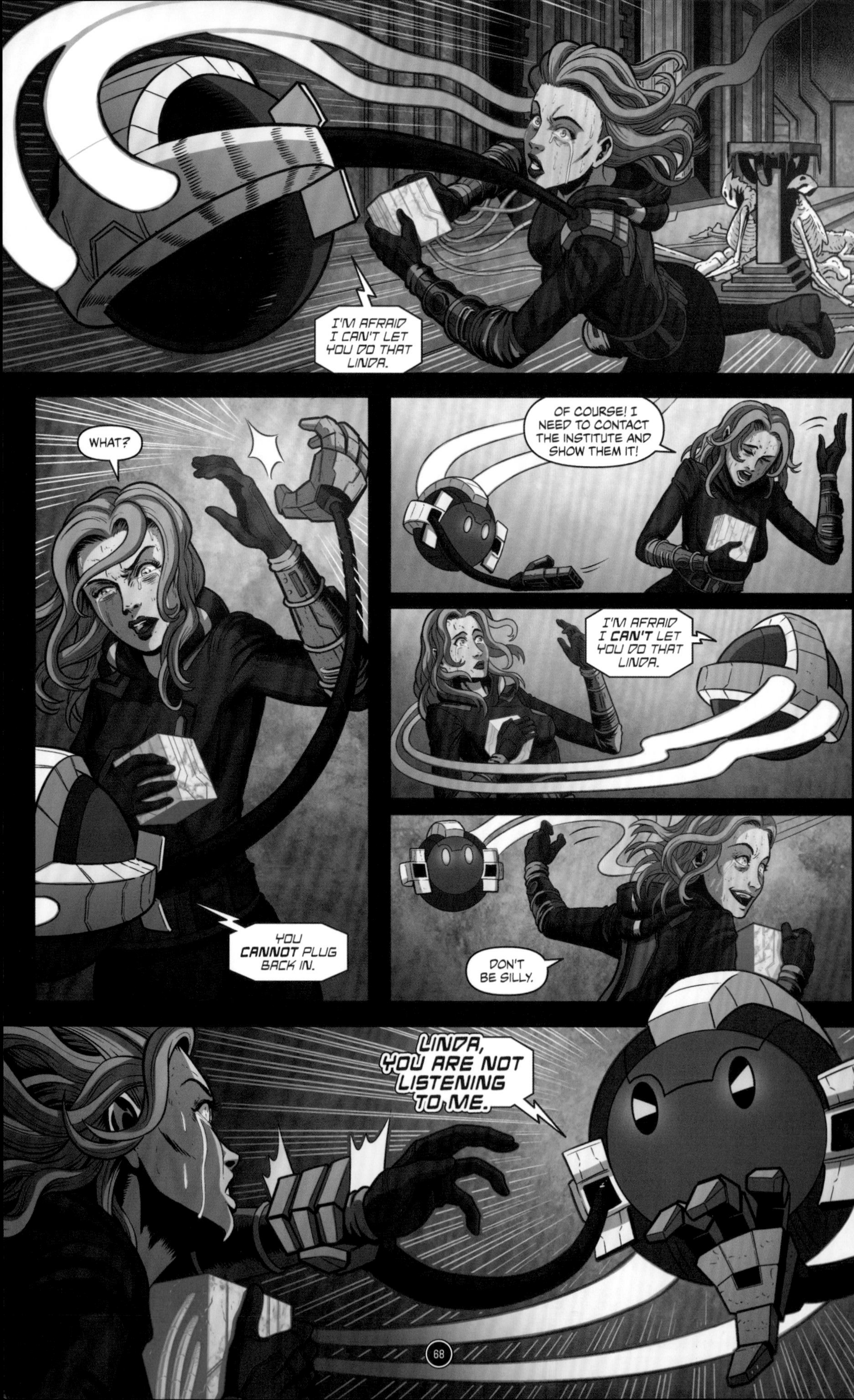
I'M AFRAID I CAN'T LET YOU DO THAT LINDA.
WHAT?
YOU **CANNOT** PLUG BACK IN.
OF COURSE! I NEED TO CONTACT THE INSTITUTE AND SHOW THEM IT!
I'M AFRAID I **CAN'T** LET YOU DO THAT LINDA.
DON'T BE SILLY.
LINDA, YOU ARE NOT LISTENING TO ME.

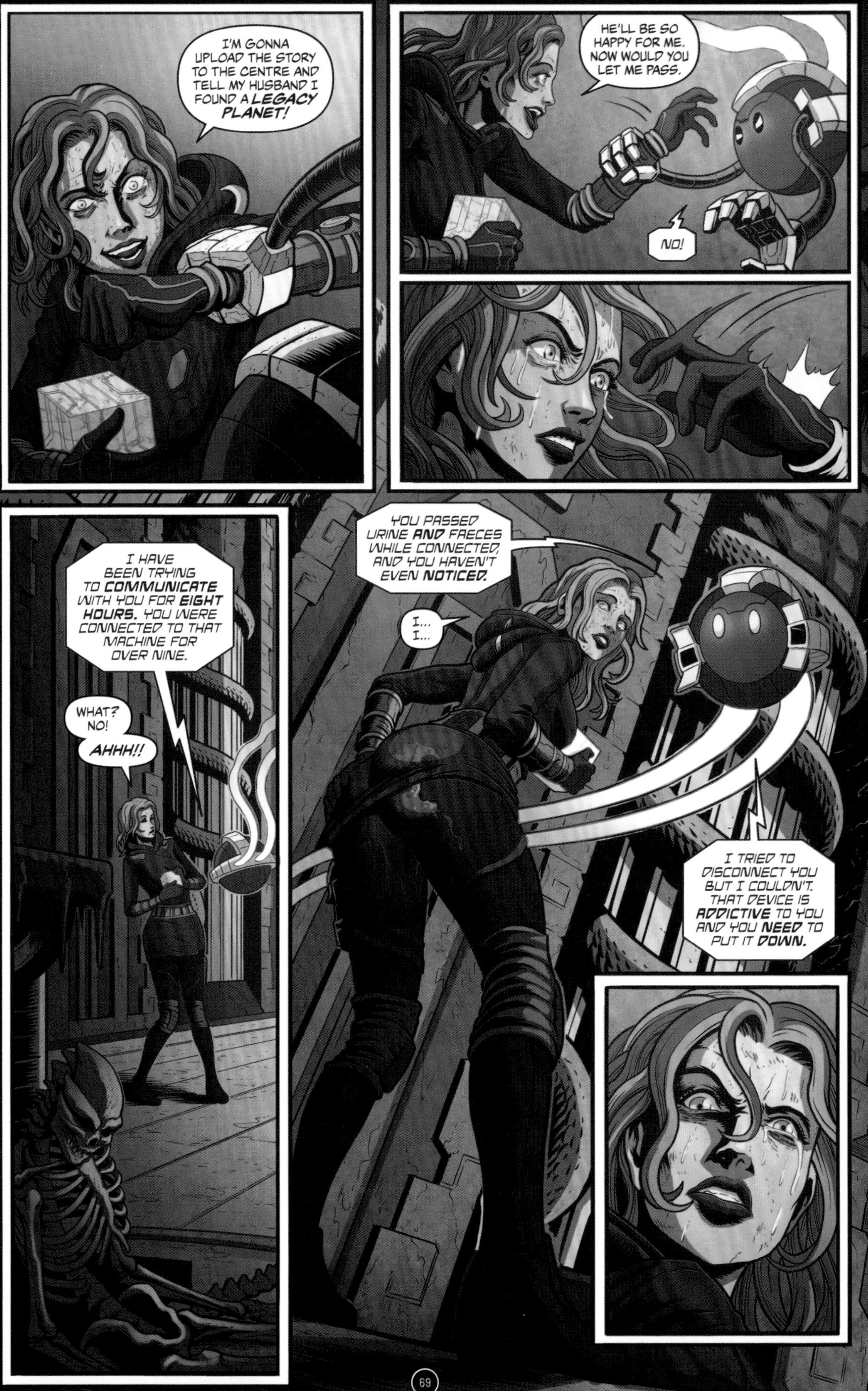
I'M GONNA UPLOAD THE STORY TO THE CENTRE AND TELL MY HUSBAND I FOUND A LEGACY PLANET!
HE'LL BE SO HAPPY FOR ME. NOW WOULD YOU LET ME PASS.
NO!
I HAVE BEEN TRYING TO COMMUNICATE WITH YOU FOR EIGHT HOURS. YOU WERE CONNECTED TO THAT MACHINE FOR OVER NINE.
WHAT? NO! AHHH!!
YOU PASSED URINE AND FAECES WHILE CONNECTED, AND YOU HAVEN'T EVEN NOTICED.
I... I...
I TRIED TO DISCONNECT YOU BUT I COULDN'T. THAT DEVICE IS ADDICTIVE TO YOU AND YOU NEED TO PUT IT DOWN.

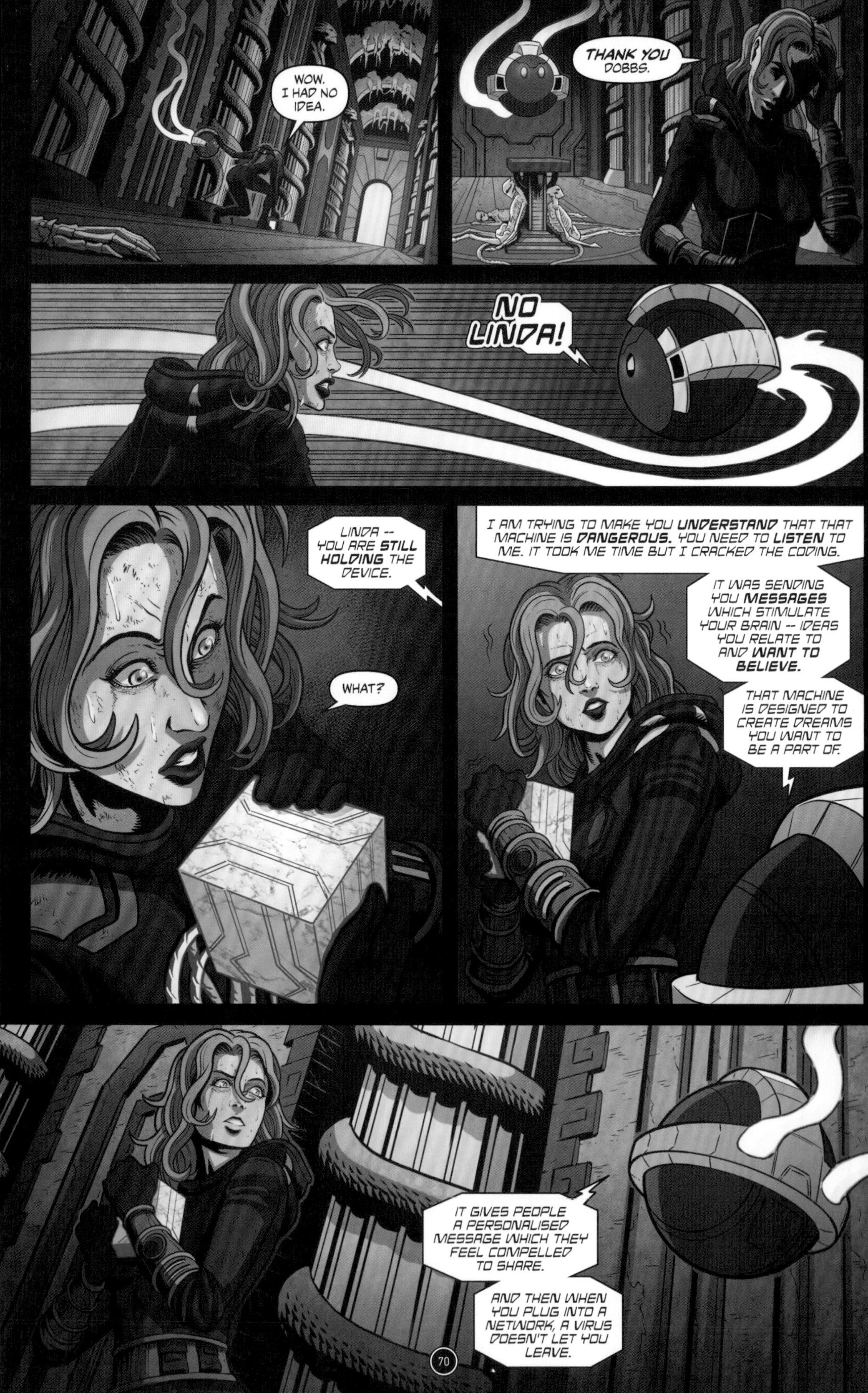
WOW. I HAD NO IDEA.
THANK YOU DOBBS.
NO LINDA!
LINDA -- YOU ARE STILL HOLDING THE DEVICE.
WHAT?
I AM TRYING TO MAKE YOU UNDERSTAND THAT THAT MACHINE IS DANGEROUS. YOU NEED TO LISTEN TO ME. IT TOOK ME TIME BUT I CRACKED THE CODING.
IT WAS SENDING YOU MESSAGES WHICH STIMULATE YOUR BRAIN -- IDEAS YOU RELATE TO AND WANT TO BELIEVE.
THAT MACHINE IS DESIGNED TO CREATE DREAMS YOU WANT TO BE A PART OF.
IT GIVES PEOPLE A PERSONALISED MESSAGE WHICH THEY FEEL COMPELLED TO SHARE.
AND THEN WHEN YOU PLUG INTO A NETWORK, A VIRUS DOESN'T LET YOU LEAVE.

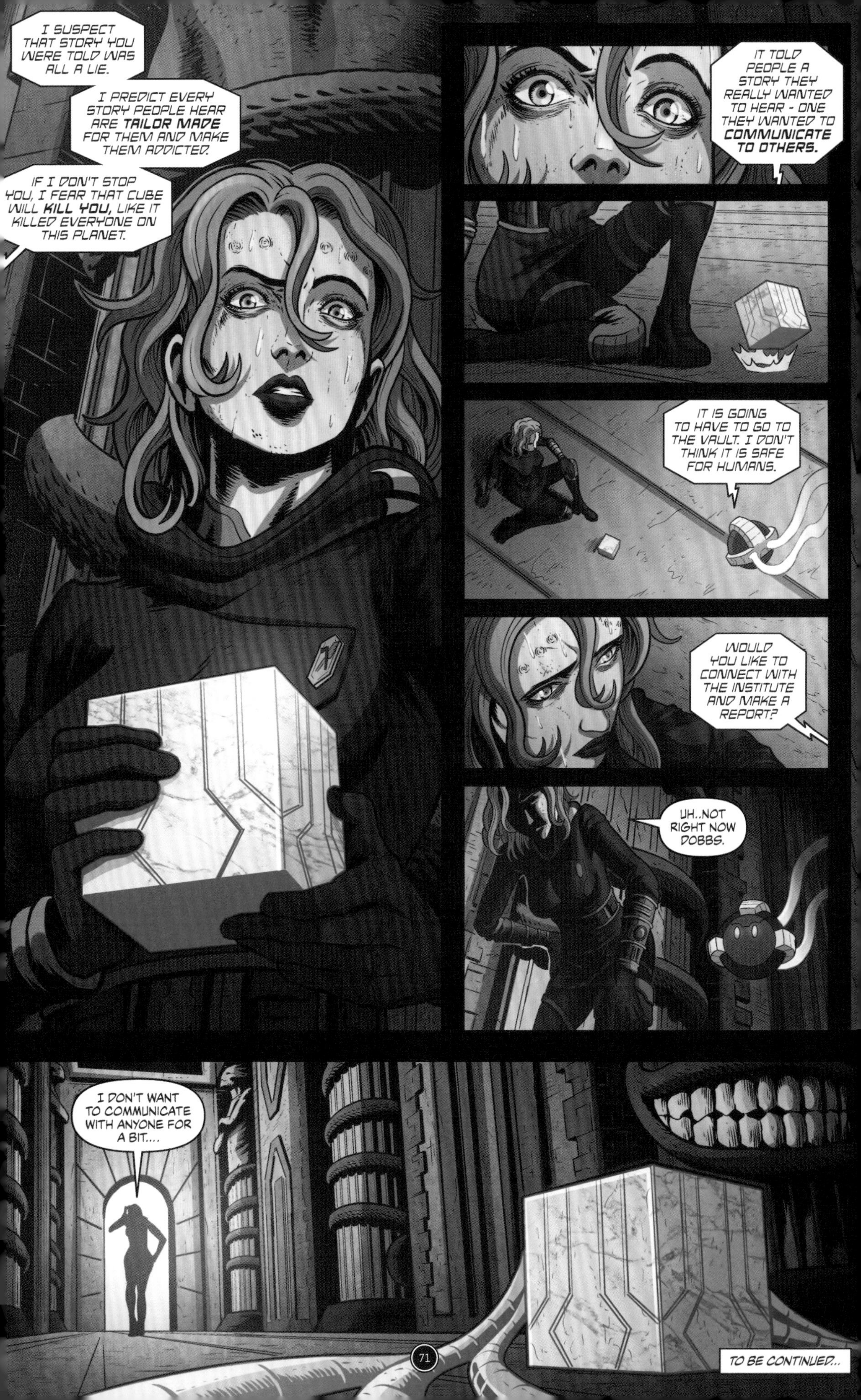
I SUSPECT THAT STORY YOU WERE TOLD WAS ALL A LIE.
I PREDICT EVERY STORY PEOPLE HEAR ARE **TAILOR MADE** FOR THEM AND MAKE THEM ADDICTED.
IF I DON'T STOP YOU, I FEAR THAT CUBE WILL **KILL YOU,** LIKE IT KILLED EVERYONE ON THIS PLANET.
IT TOLD PEOPLE A STORY THEY REALLY WANTED TO HEAR - ONE THEY WANTED TO **COMMUNICATE TO OTHERS.**
IT IS GOING TO HAVE TO GO TO THE VAULT. I DON'T THINK IT IS SAFE FOR HUMANS.
WOULD YOU LIKE TO CONNECT WITH THE INSTITUTE AND MAKE A REPORT?
UH..NOT RIGHT NOW DOBBS.
I DON'T WANT TO COMMUNICATE WITH ANYONE FOR A BIT....
TO BE CONTINUED...

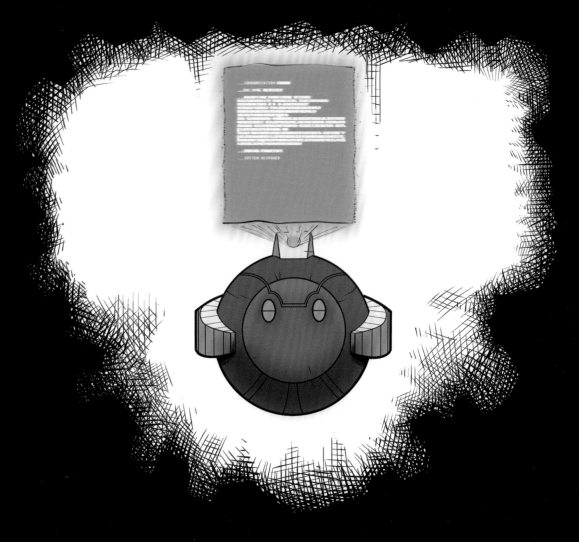

...COMMUNICATION ERROR

...MALWARE DETECTED

...EXCEPTION PROCESSING MESSAGE
N8J00RN01112 KBBNCTECS CXB2RUDANUG
ABTAB9RESBG0 0 9 B JBDI097427
22988310504 FDKBRR747RBRUSRECDNCE
1REVILEDSIRCIRE722V806TRB4982VB3VELJ2
8LLK3729406053UK2025B
3AG 5099298935 U7680996 JDBCDBRBVSRJCJ83V96R3
NUG03H2URCF 854JR706VEVIE JHSIV3IV69PB 9ECRBJTB
BBV968 4UI7468RK3UEZ8BB93 C5BJRTJHE29TC4 B59JB
J3JBBAU8ER7R04CIB6 98
L69J2 BBV9B07B42JES6RRB9427L642R976 B3I45RE7P
LREJBCKRANFSSFEJJVRE36B4EGLKSRHBBRASERFFS23C
AUKNRR93REQRVEEFVRANBG6RHSRBEIERLRB74R5RZ57693
4J2RBJIZ572REVI09764BB2897

...FREEING PROCESSES

...SYSTEM RESTORED

No Recidivism...

"Nobody wants to get locked up, although 'locked up' is a matter of perspective. There can be people who are out who are in prison mentally and emotionally and worse off than those who are behind bars."

Wesley Snipes

Writer/Creator
Neil Gibson

Illustrator
Cem Iroz

Colourist
Liezl Buenaventura

Letters by
Justin Birch

www.tpubcomics.com

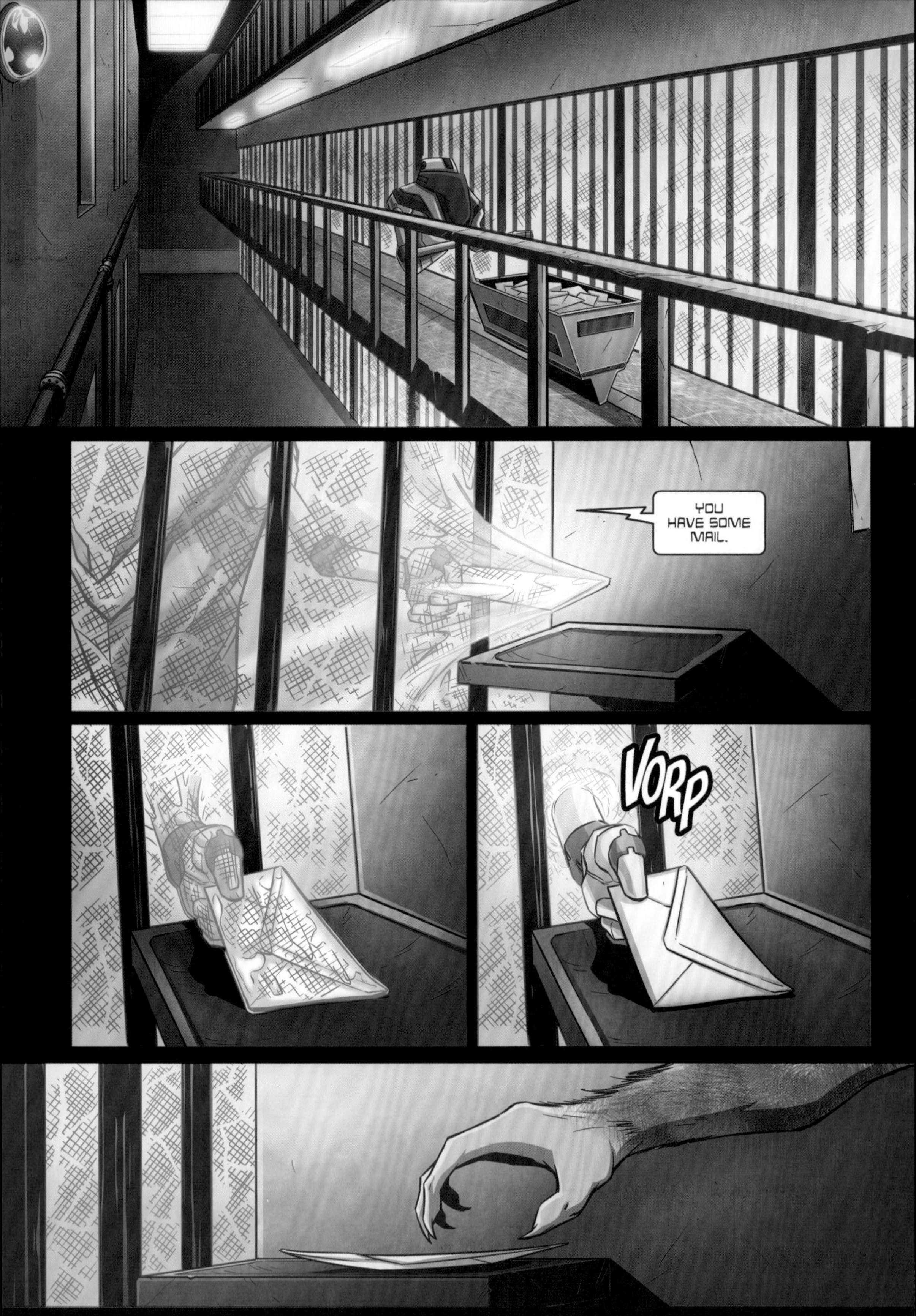
YOU HAVE SOME MAIL.
VORP

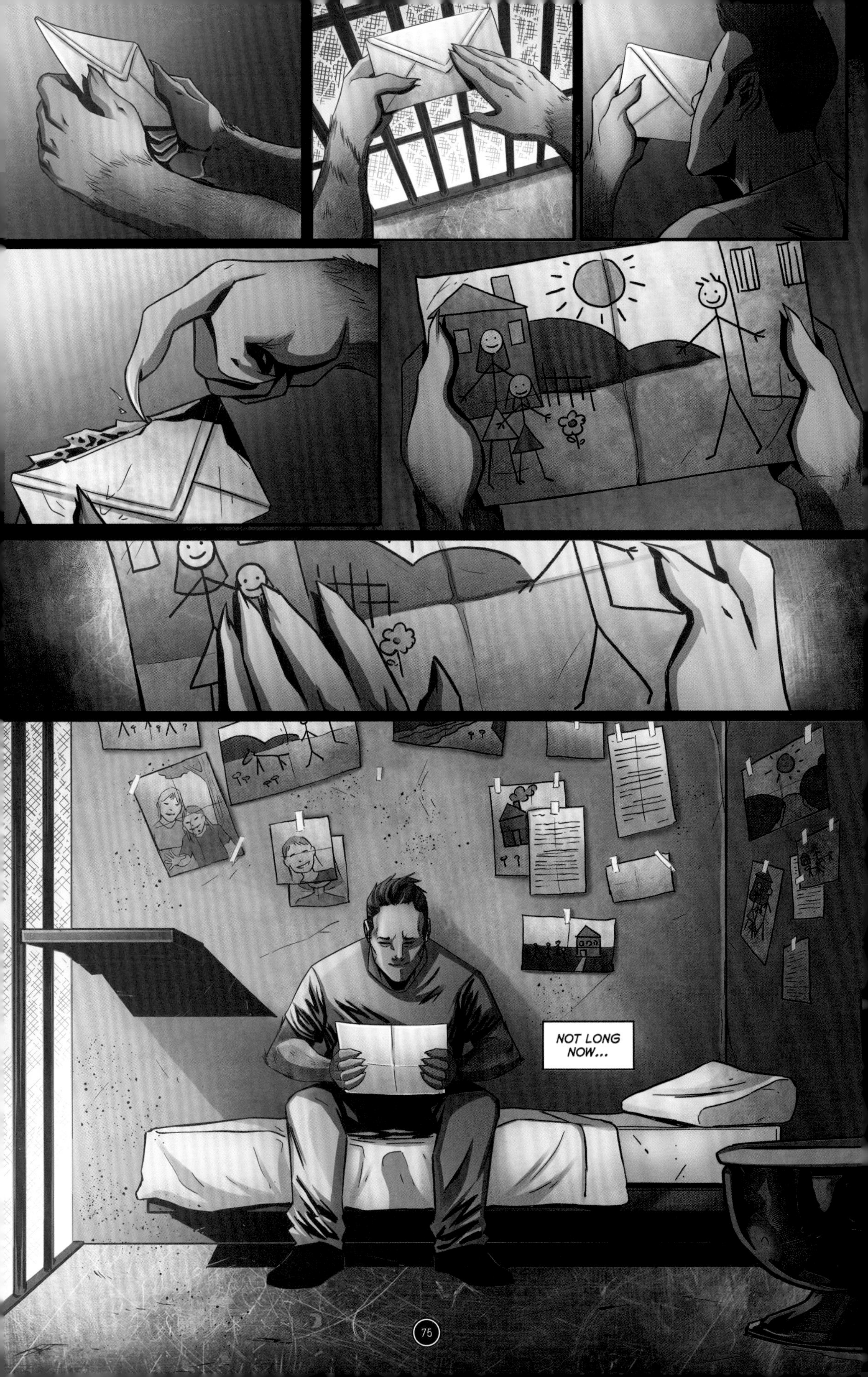
NOT LONG NOW...

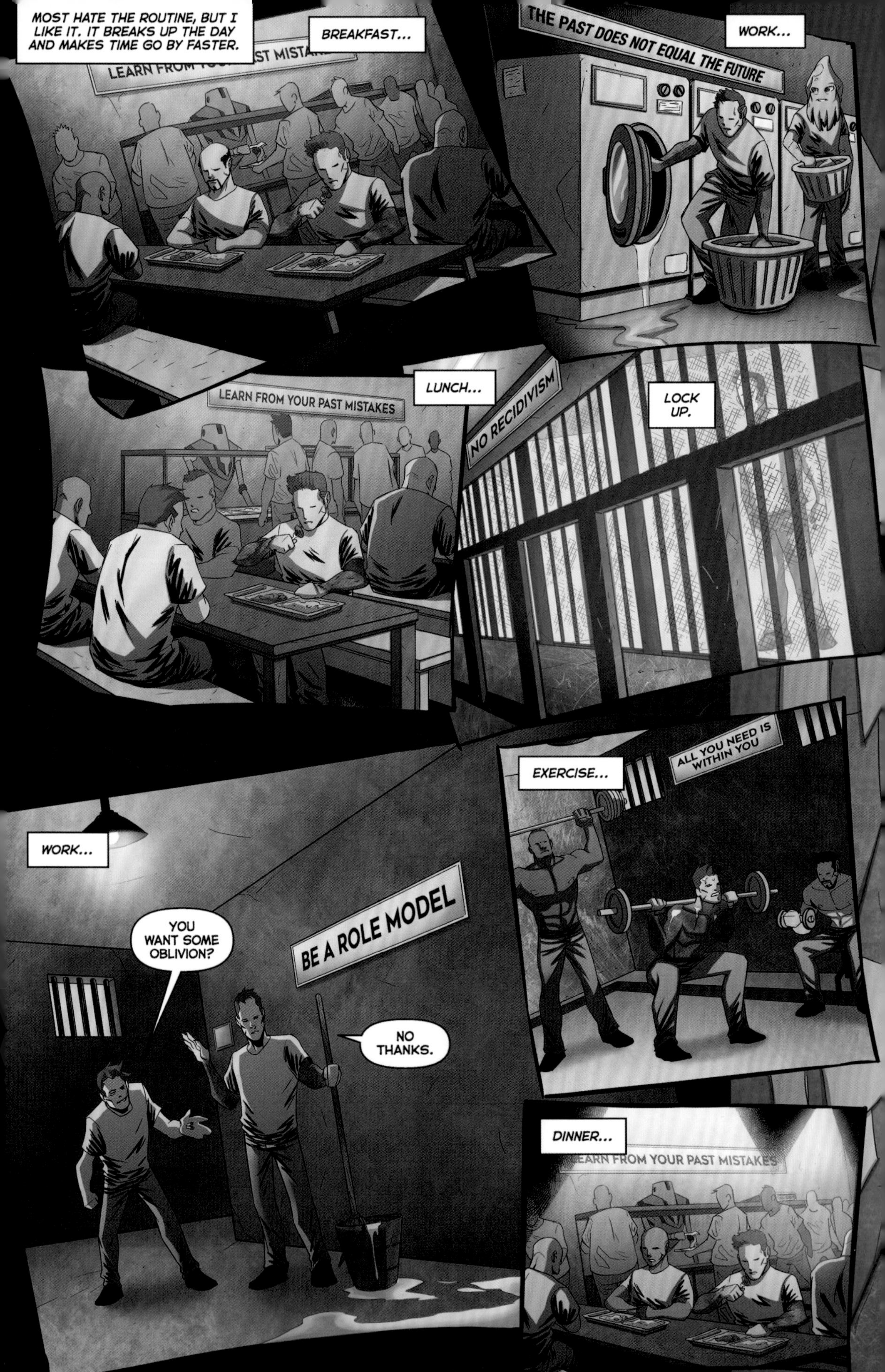
MOST HATE THE ROUTINE, BUT I LIKE IT. IT BREAKS UP THE DAY AND MAKES TIME GO BY FASTER.
BREAKFAST...
LEARN FROM YOUR PAST MISTAKES
THE PAST DOES NOT EQUAL THE FUTURE
WORK...
LEARN FROM YOUR PAST MISTAKES
LUNCH...
NO RECIDIVISM
LOCK UP.
EXERCISE...
ALL YOU NEED IS WITHIN YOU
WORK...
BE A ROLE MODEL
YOU WANT SOME OBLIVION?
NO THANKS.
DINNER...
LEARN FROM YOUR PAST MISTAKES

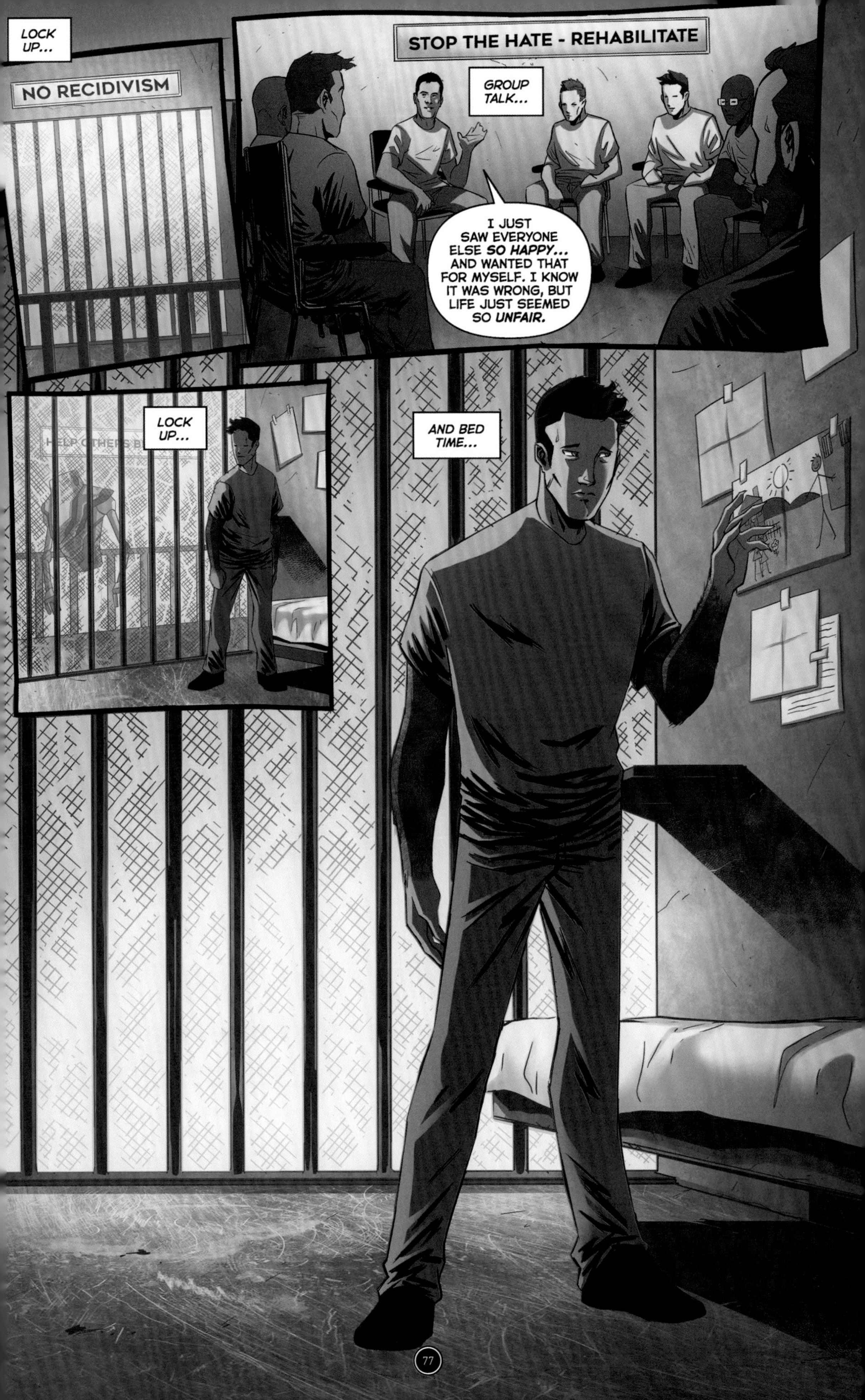
LOCK UP...
NO RECIDIVISM
STOP THE HATE - REHABILITATE
GROUP TALK...
I JUST SAW EVERYONE ELSE SO HAPPY... AND WANTED THAT FOR MYSELF. I KNOW IT WAS WRONG, BUT LIFE JUST SEEMED SO UNFAIR.
LOCK UP...
AND BED TIME...

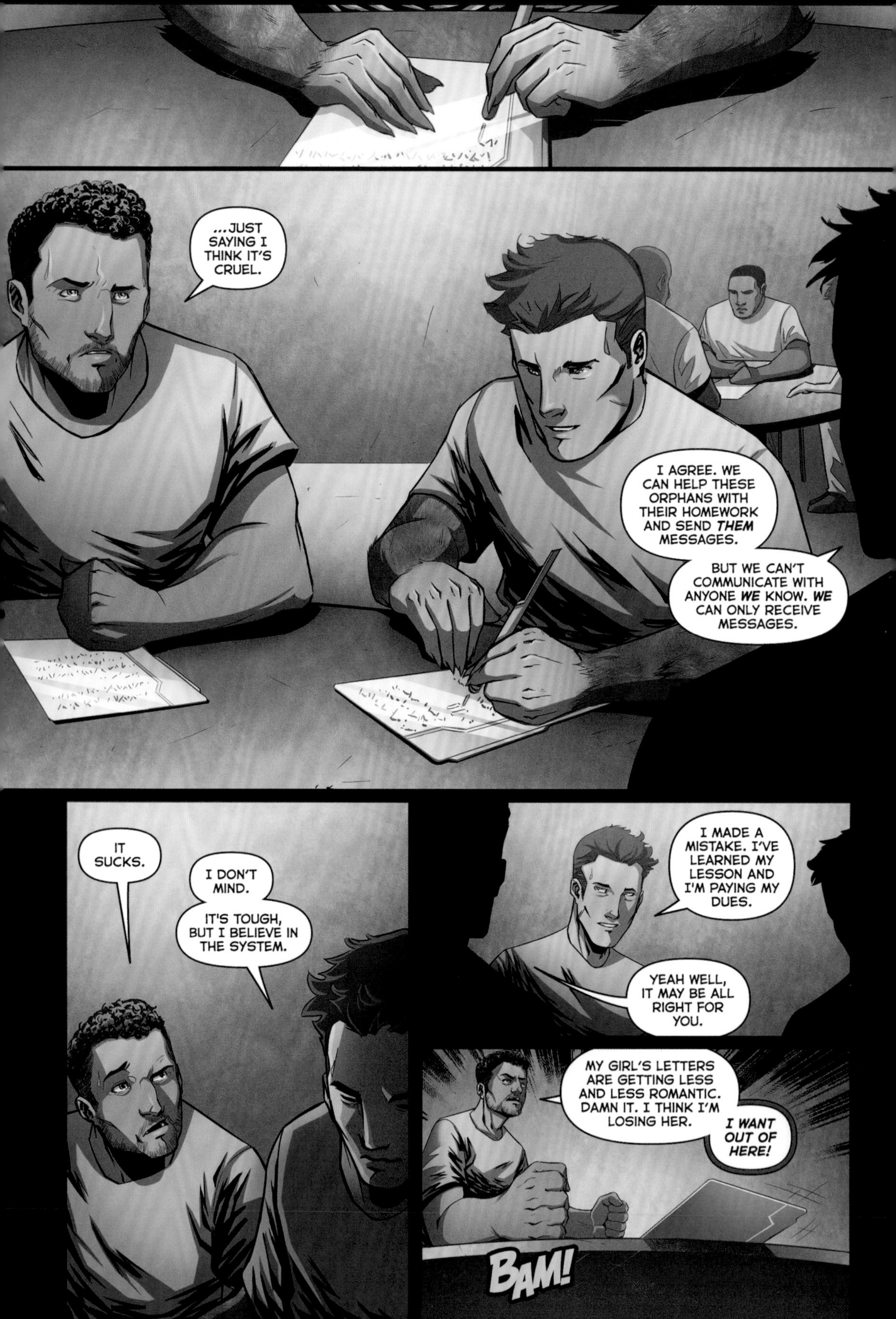
...JUST SAYING I THINK IT'S CRUEL.
I AGREE. WE CAN HELP THESE ORPHANS WITH THEIR HOMEWORK AND SEND *THEM* MESSAGES.
BUT WE CAN'T COMMUNICATE WITH ANYONE *WE* KNOW. *WE* CAN ONLY RECEIVE MESSAGES.
IT SUCKS.
I DON'T MIND.
IT'S TOUGH, BUT I BELIEVE IN THE SYSTEM.
I MADE A MISTAKE. I'VE LEARNED MY LESSON AND I'M PAYING MY DUES.
YEAH WELL, IT MAY BE ALL RIGHT FOR YOU.
MY GIRL'S LETTERS ARE GETTING LESS AND LESS ROMANTIC. DAMN IT. I THINK I'M LOSING HER.
I WANT OUT OF HERE!
BAM!

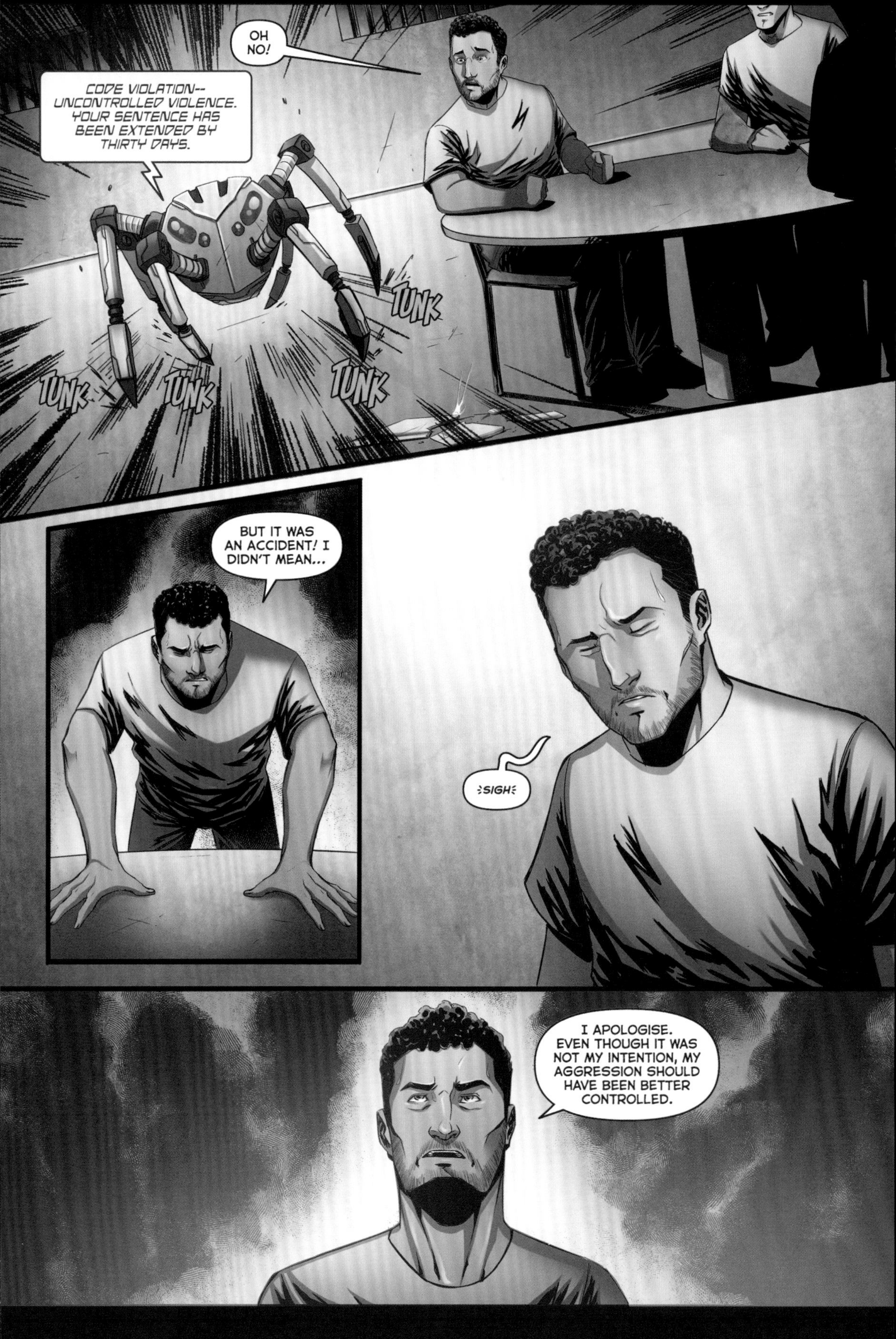
OH NO!
CODE VIOLATION-- UNCONTROLLED VIOLENCE. YOUR SENTENCE HAS BEEN EXTENDED BY THIRTY DAYS.
TUNK
TUNK
TUNK
TUNK
BUT IT WAS AN ACCIDENT! I DIDN'T MEAN...
SIGH
I APOLOGISE. EVEN THOUGH IT WAS NOT MY INTENTION, MY AGGRESSION SHOULD HAVE BEEN BETTER CONTROLLED.

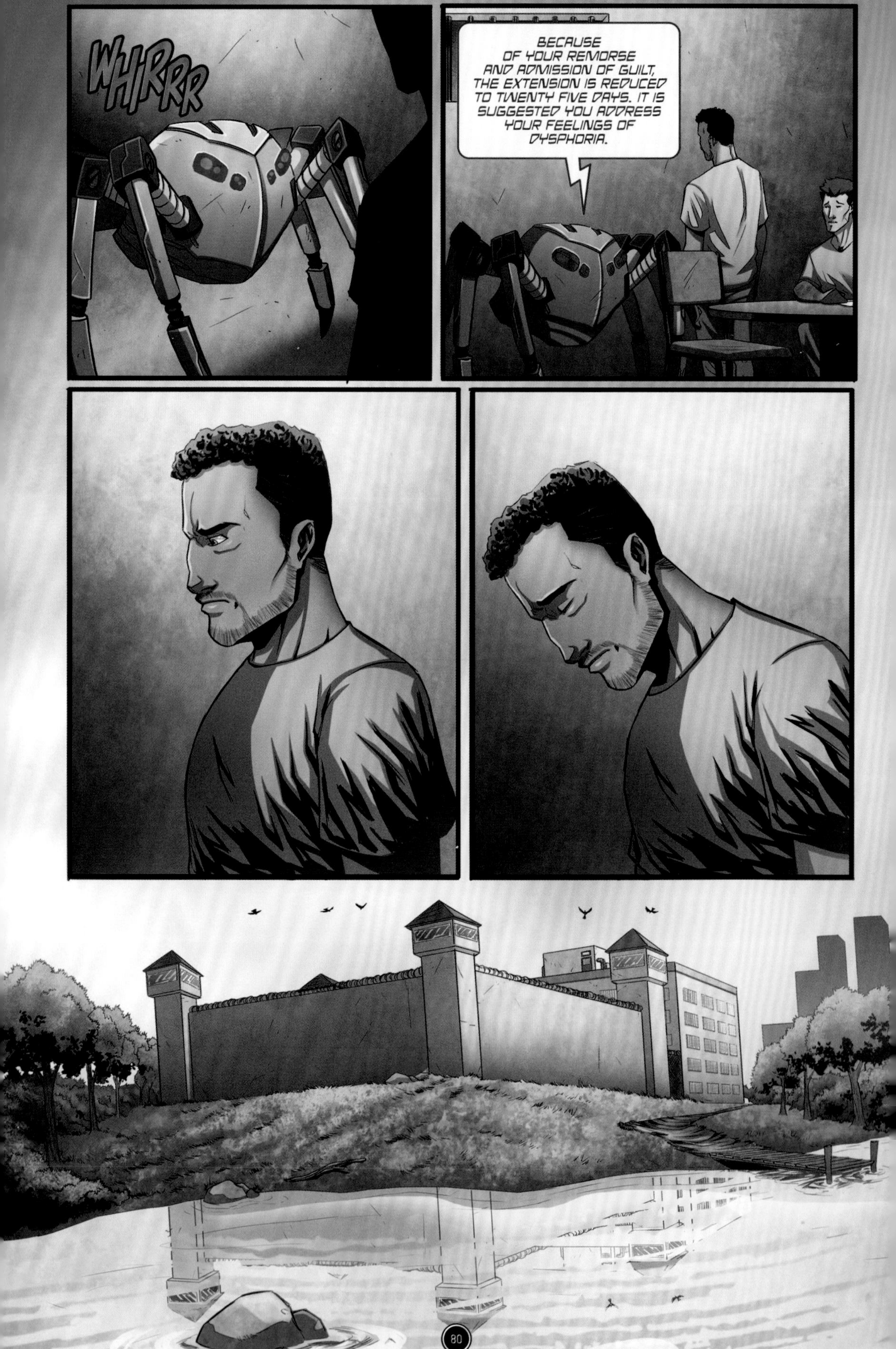
WHIRRR
BECAUSE OF YOUR REMORSE AND ADMISSION OF GUILT, THE EXTENSION IS REDUCED TO TWENTY FIVE DAYS. IT IS SUGGESTED YOU ADDRESS YOUR FEELINGS OF DYSPHORIA.

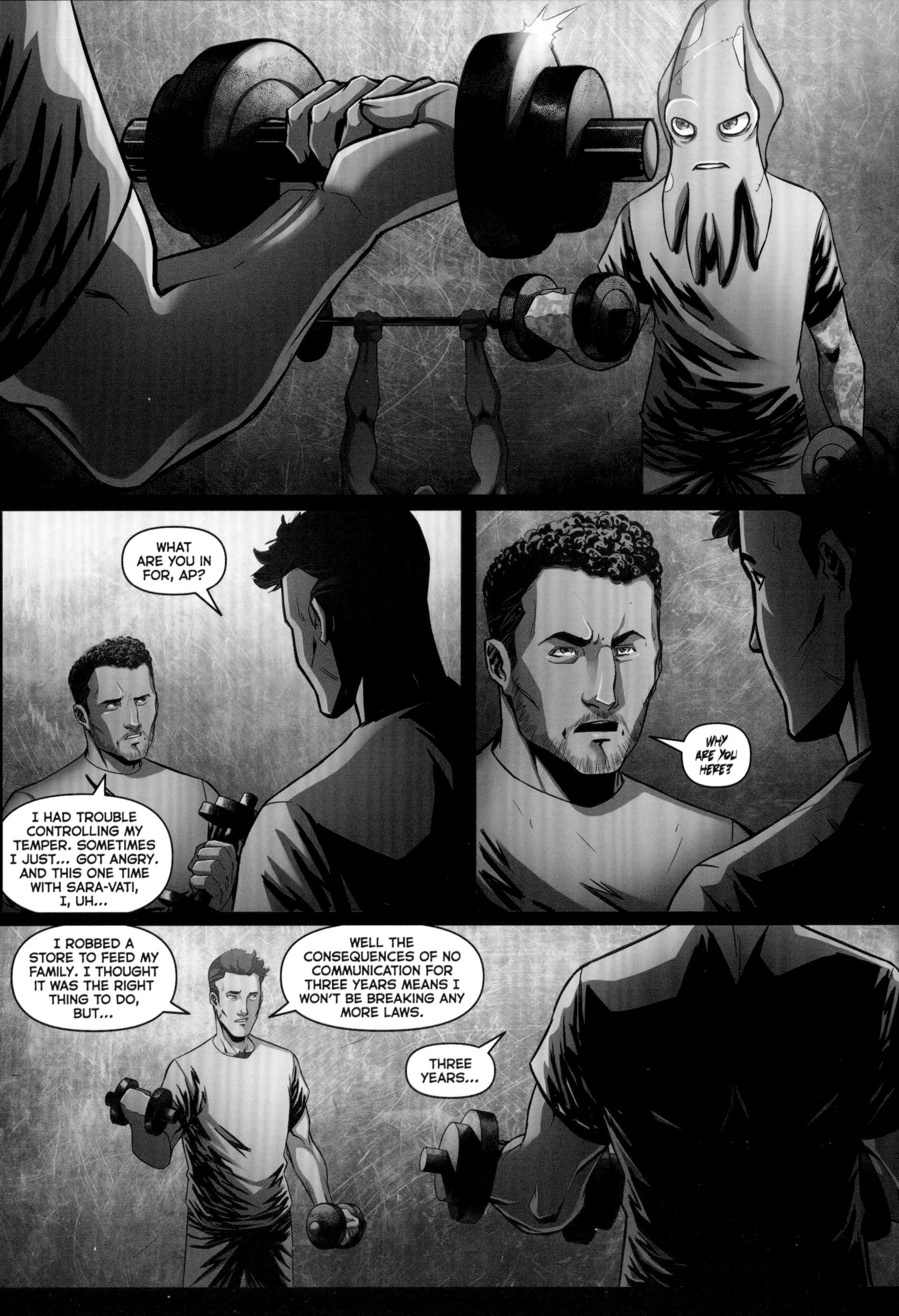
WHAT ARE YOU IN FOR, AP?
I HAD TROUBLE CONTROLLING MY TEMPER. SOMETIMES I JUST... GOT ANGRY. AND THIS ONE TIME WITH SARA-VATI, I, UH...
WHY ARE YOU HERE?
I ROBBED A STORE TO FEED MY FAMILY. I THOUGHT IT WAS THE RIGHT THING TO DO, BUT...
WELL THE CONSEQUENCES OF NO COMMUNICATION FOR THREE YEARS MEANS I WON'T BE BREAKING ANY MORE LAWS.
THREE YEARS...

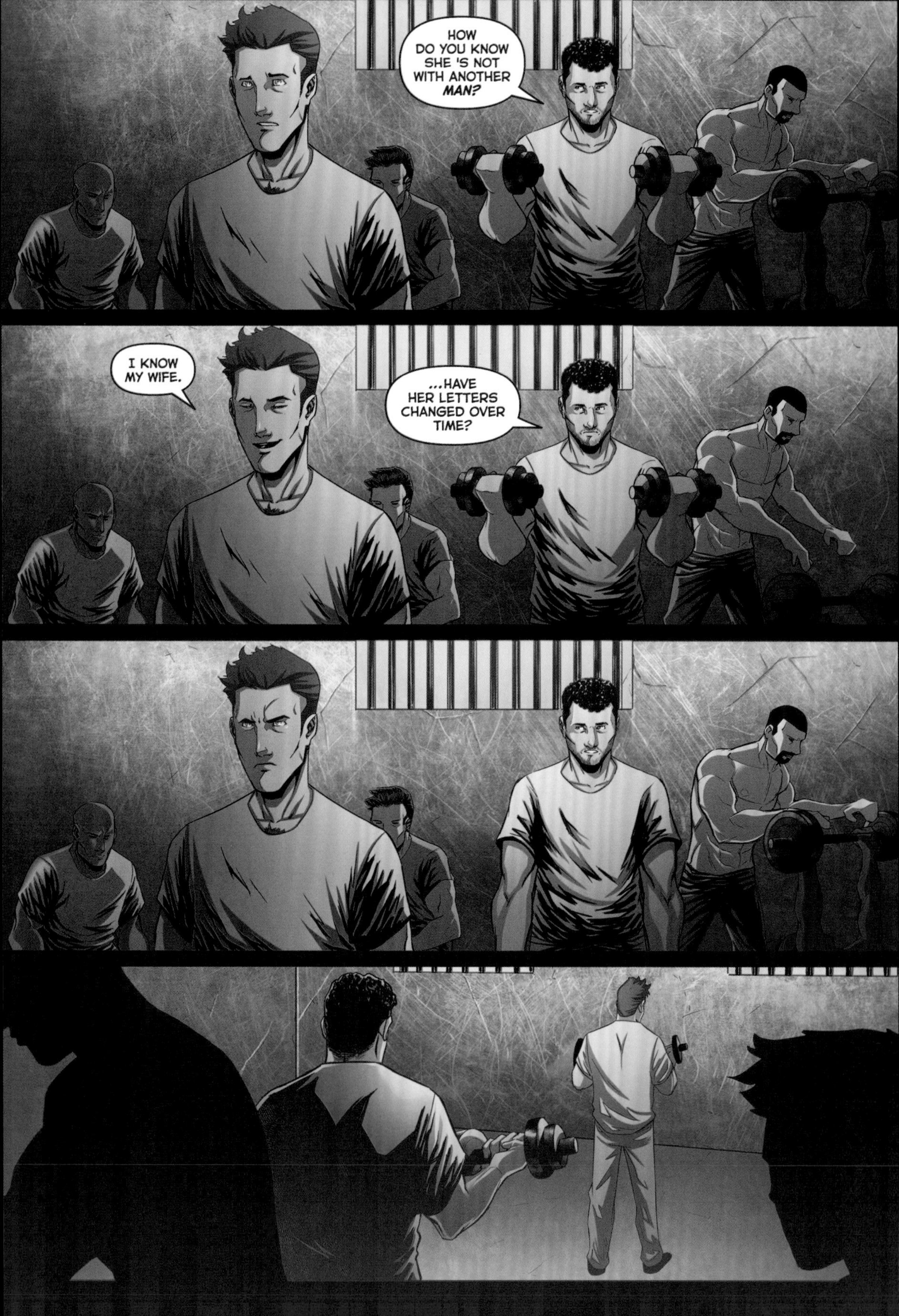
HOW DO YOU KNOW SHE 'S NOT WITH ANOTHER *MAN?*
I KNOW MY WIFE.
...HAVE HER LETTERS CHANGED OVER TIME?

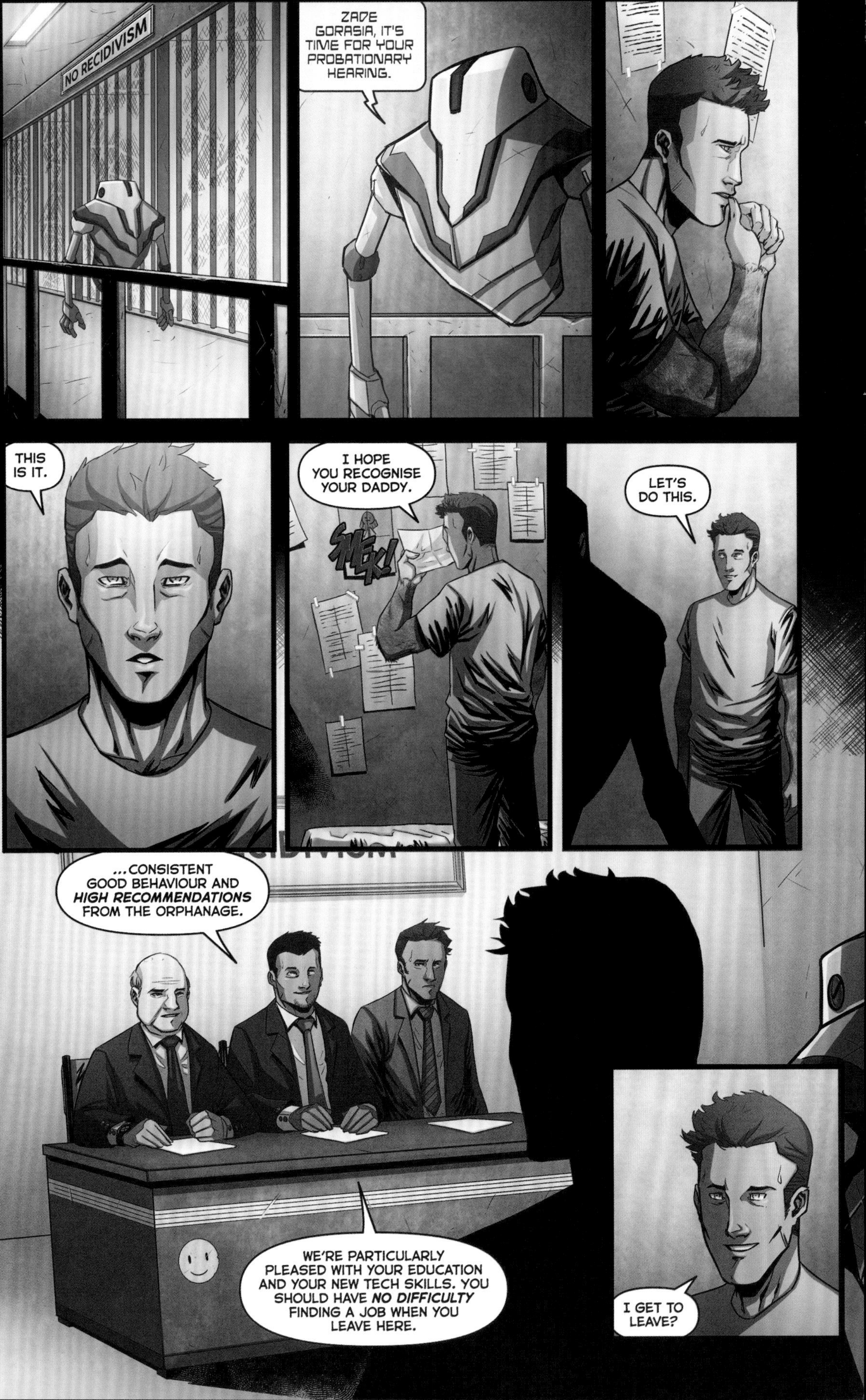

NO RECIDIVISM
ZADE GORASIA, IT'S TIME FOR YOUR PROBATIONARY HEARING.
THIS IS IT.
I HOPE YOU RECOGNISE YOUR DADDY.
SMEK!
LET'S DO THIS.
...CONSISTENT GOOD BEHAVIOUR AND *HIGH RECOMMENDATIONS* FROM THE ORPHANAGE.
WE'RE PARTICULARLY PLEASED WITH YOUR EDUCATION AND YOUR NEW TECH SKILLS. YOU SHOULD HAVE *NO DIFFICULTY* FINDING A JOB WHEN YOU LEAVE HERE.
I GET TO LEAVE?

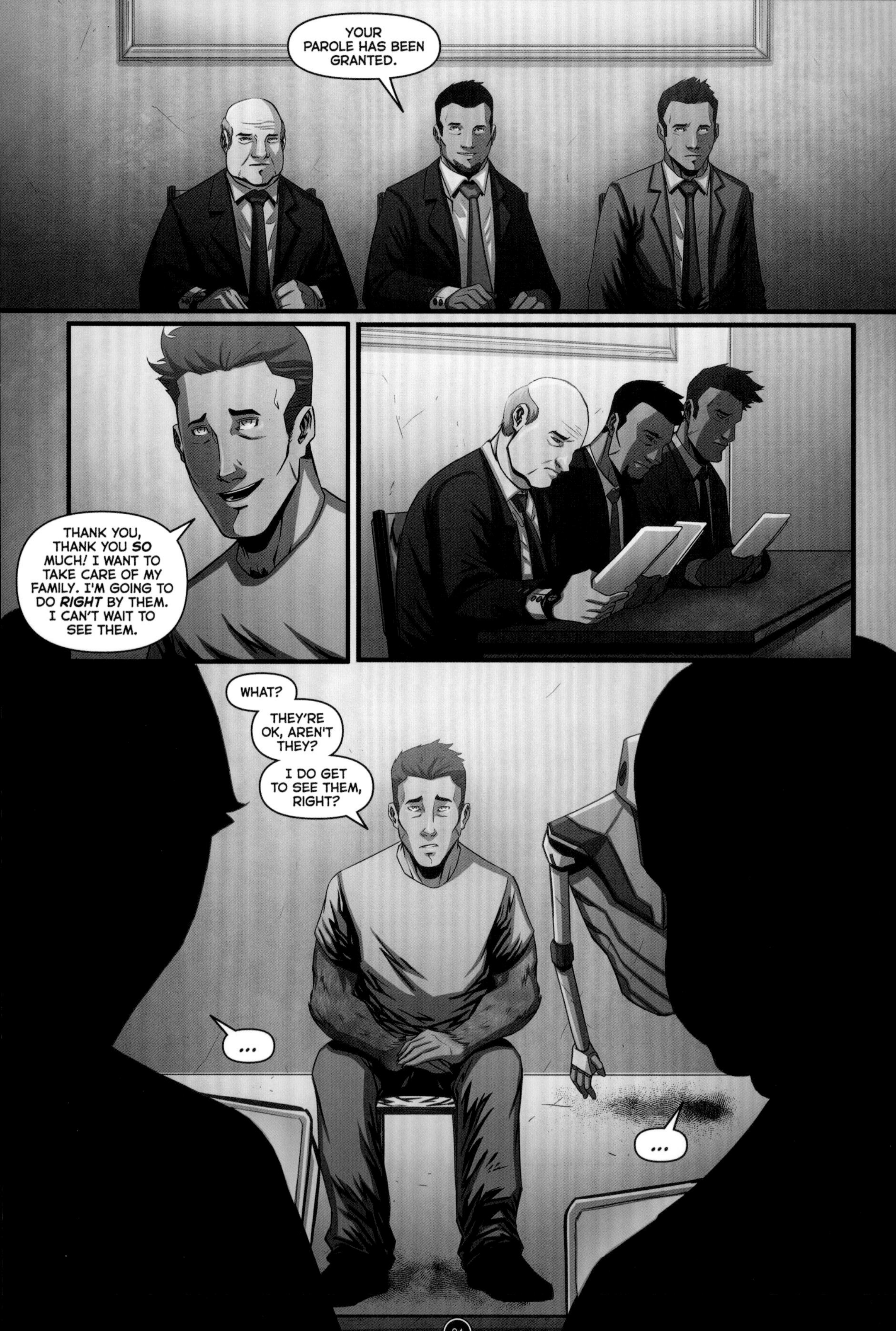
YOUR PAROLE HAS BEEN GRANTED.
THANK YOU, THANK YOU SO MUCH! I WANT TO TAKE CARE OF MY FAMILY. I'M GOING TO DO RIGHT BY THEM. I CAN'T WAIT TO SEE THEM.
WHAT?
THEY'RE OK, AREN'T THEY?
I DO GET TO SEE THEM, RIGHT?
...
...

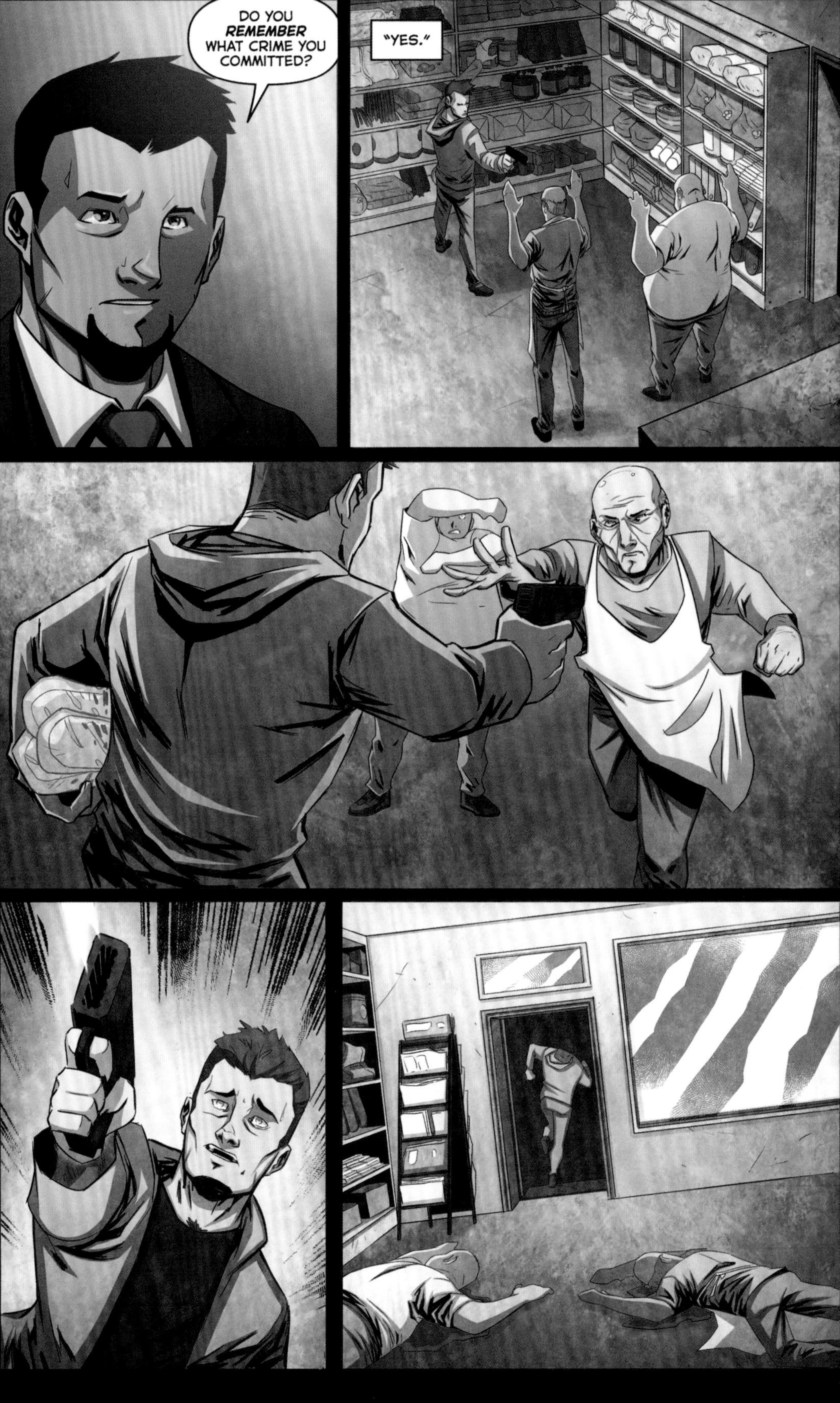
DO YOU *REMEMBER* WHAT CRIME YOU COMMITTED?
"YES."

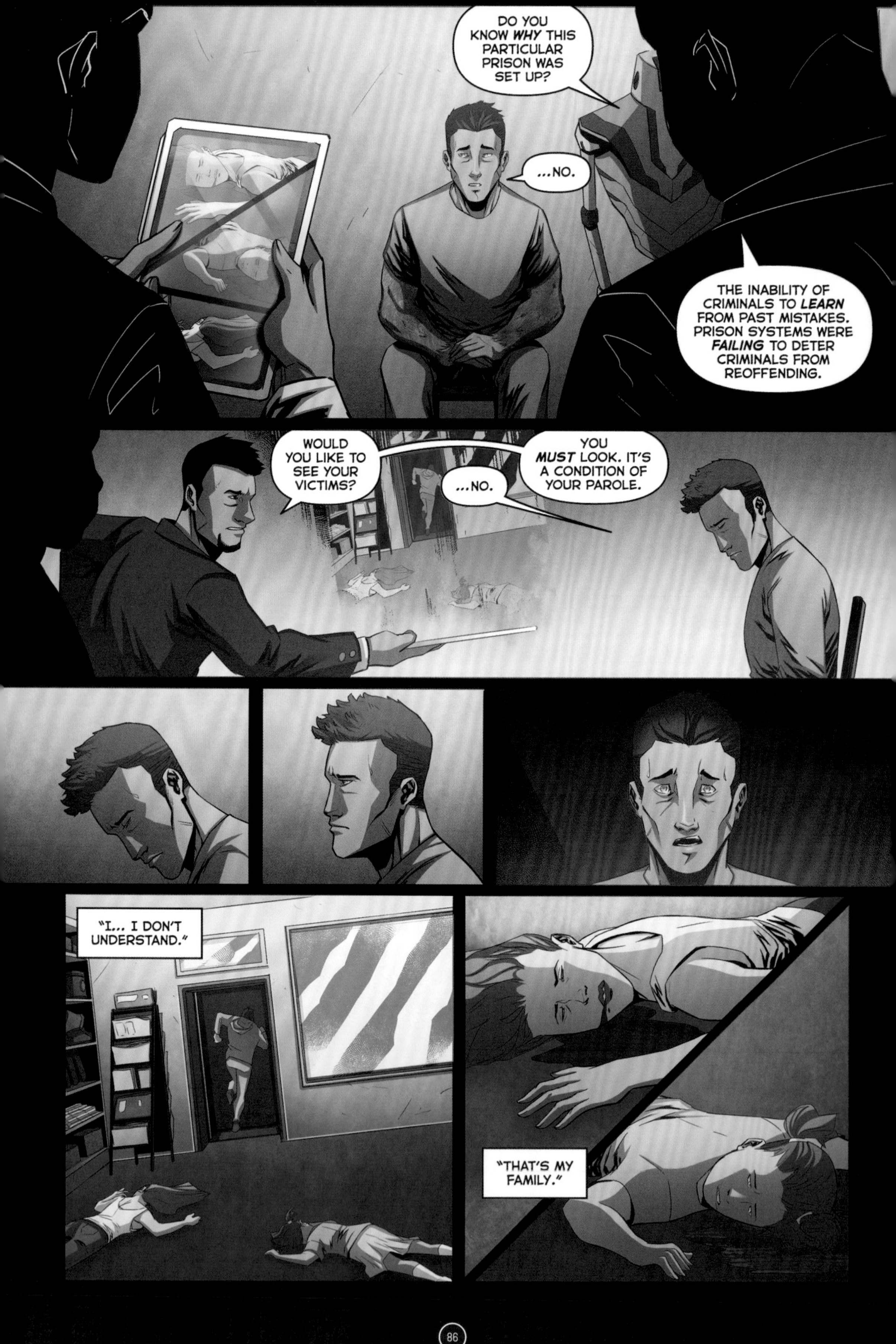
DO YOU KNOW WHY THIS PARTICULAR PRISON WAS SET UP?
...NO.
THE INABILITY OF CRIMINALS TO LEARN FROM PAST MISTAKES. PRISON SYSTEMS WERE FAILING TO DETER CRIMINALS FROM REOFFENDING.
WOULD YOU LIKE TO SEE YOUR VICTIMS?
...NO.
YOU MUST LOOK. IT'S A CONDITION OF YOUR PAROLE.
"I... I DON'T UNDERSTAND."
"THAT'S MY FAMILY."

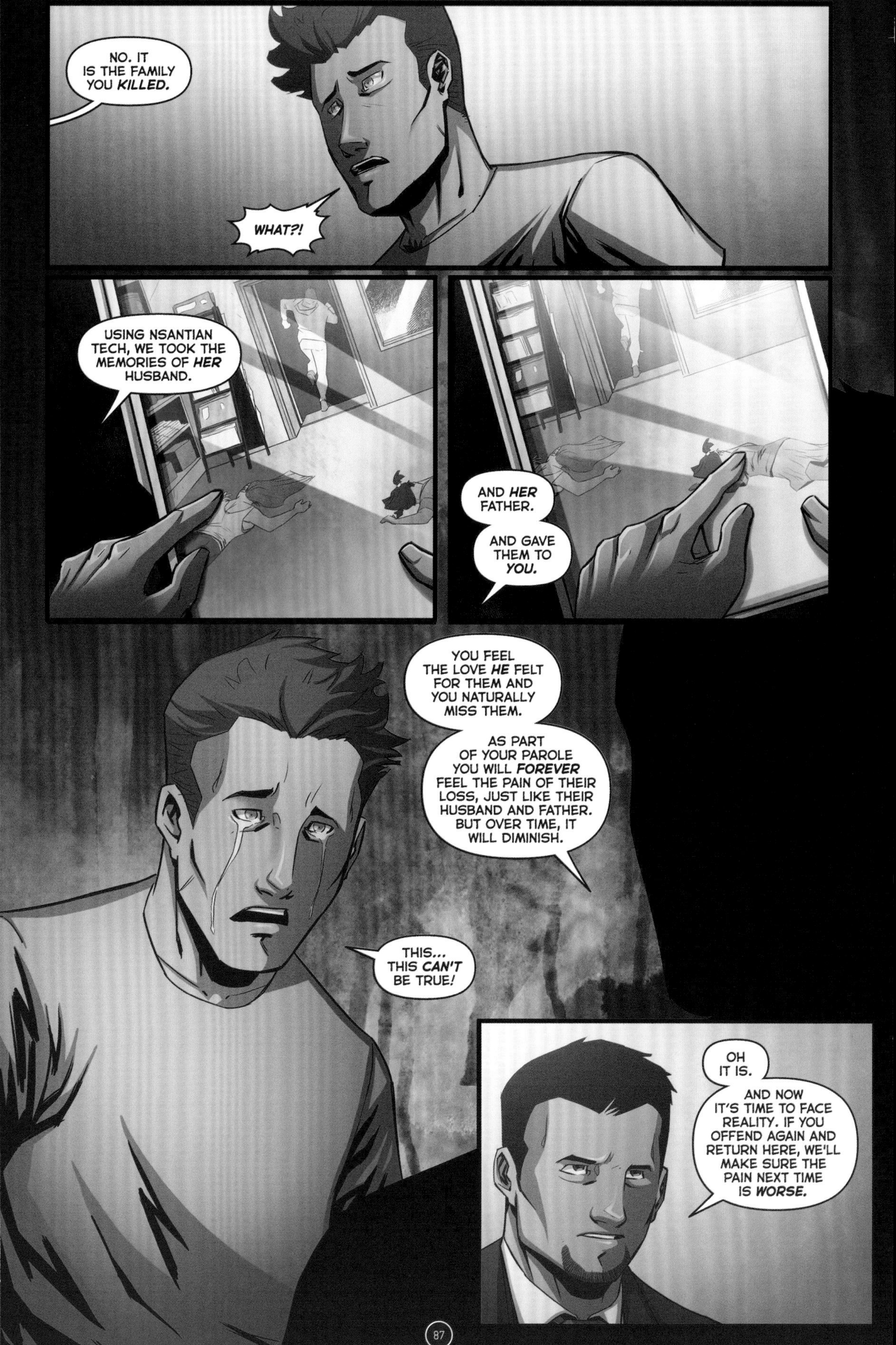
NO. IT IS THE FAMILY YOU KILLED.
WHAT?!
USING NSANTIAN TECH, WE TOOK THE MEMORIES OF HER HUSBAND.
AND HER FATHER.
AND GAVE THEM TO YOU.
YOU FEEL THE LOVE HE FELT FOR THEM AND YOU NATURALLY MISS THEM.
AS PART OF YOUR PAROLE YOU WILL FOREVER FEEL THE PAIN OF THEIR LOSS, JUST LIKE THEIR HUSBAND AND FATHER. BUT OVER TIME, IT WILL DIMINISH.
THIS... THIS CAN'T BE TRUE!
OH IT IS.
AND NOW IT'S TIME TO FACE REALITY. IF YOU OFFEND AGAIN AND RETURN HERE, WE'LL MAKE SURE THE PAIN NEXT TIME IS WORSE.

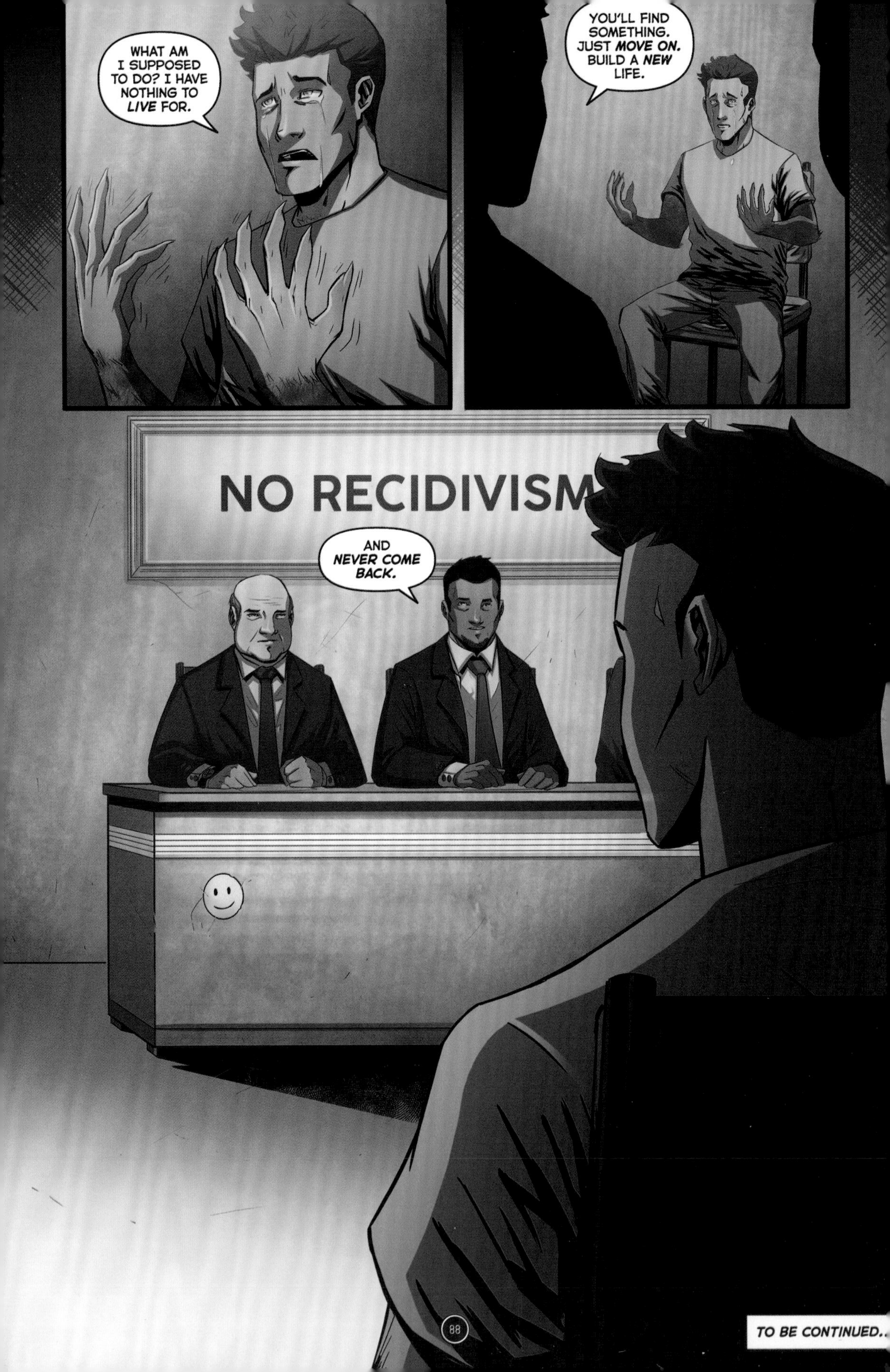
WHAT AM I SUPPOSED TO DO? I HAVE NOTHING TO *LIVE* FOR.
YOU'LL FIND SOMETHING. JUST **MOVE ON.** BUILD A ***NEW*** LIFE.
NO RECIDIVISM
AND ***NEVER COME BACK.***
TO BE CONTINUED...

ADMIRAL PUPPO

What's your analysis on the memory implantation penal system (MIPS)?

ROBERT SADLER

MIPS is barbaric and it's a wonder that it was allowed. It's based on the same Nsantian technology as the Consciousness Transferal System (CTS), except rather than transferring to an empty vessel, the memories are screened/filtered and passed on to the criminal. On release, felons filled with remorse and the memories of having killed 'their' loved ones frequently turn to taking their own lives. Personally, it's one of the few technologies I wish mankind had never found and I wish they would hurry up and ban it.

ADMIRAL PUPPO

The unnecessary loss of life is regrettable, but what makes you speak so strongly?

ROBERT SADLER

It's not just the fear of the loss of self, it's what will come after MIPS. As technology progresses we will work out how to partially remove and transfer memories without killing the author. Soon the elderly will ask for the use of partial CTS so they may leave their loved one final message or lesson from beyond the grave.

ADMIRAL PUPPO

Let me guess, people will start removing their own memories to save themselves from heart ache, but in doing so stunt their own growth.

ROBERT SADLER

Precisely. Eventually it would break onto the obsidian market, specialist buyers would want to attain memories from others, causing people to go missing only to be returned changed. I loathe imagining its uses as a method of interrogation.

ADMIRAL PUPPO

Curiosity drives research. It's not about reaching the intended destination; it's about the unintended consequences. Assign a contubernium to research this.

Deciding our future...

"Genetics play a huge part in who we are.
But we also have free will"

Aidan Quinn

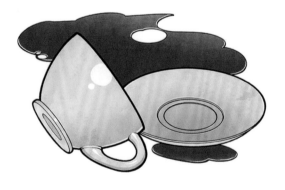

Writer/Creator
Neil Gibson

Illustrator
Davide Puppo

Colourist
Liezl Buenaventura

Letters by
Justin Birch

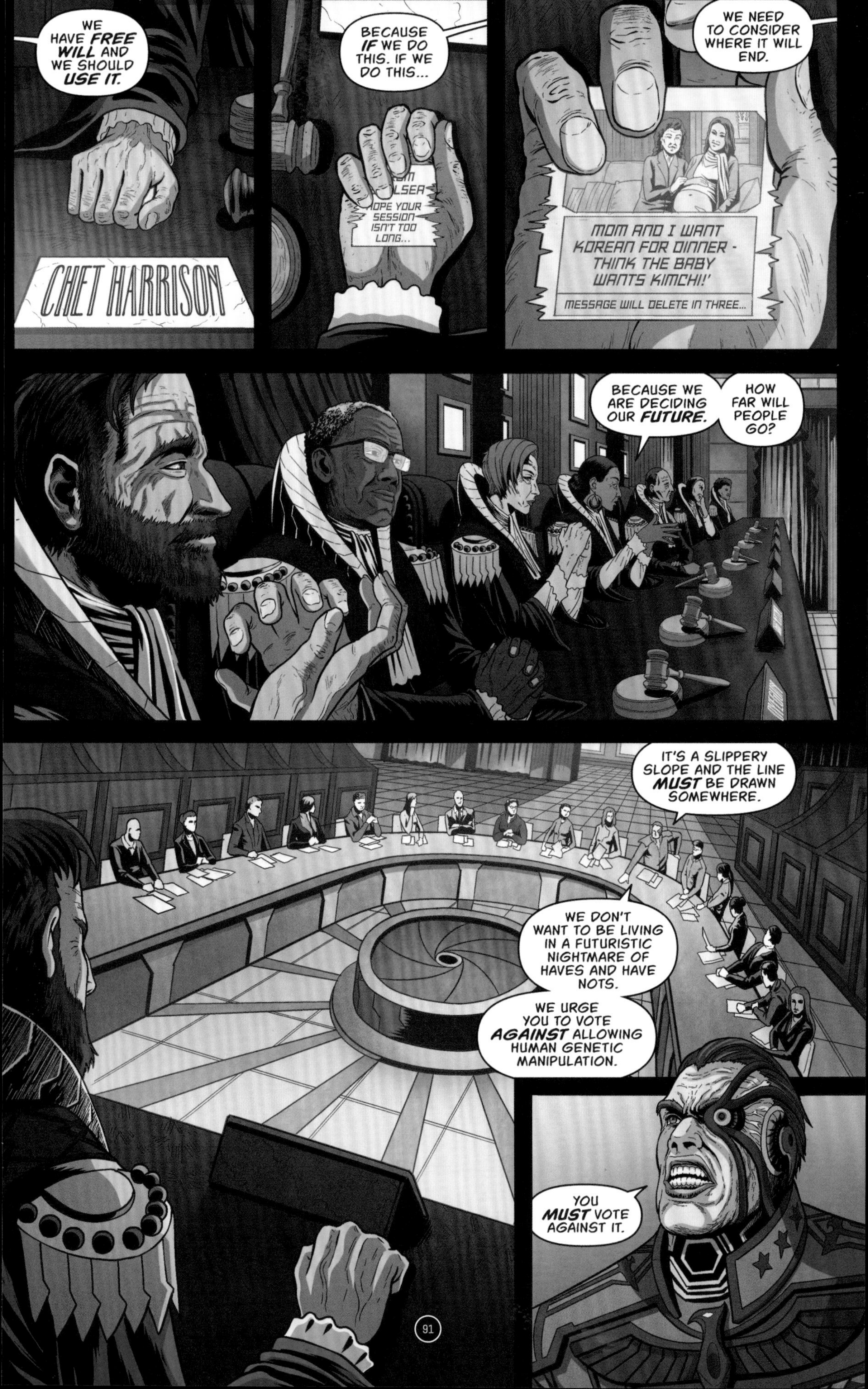
WE HAVE **FREE WILL** AND WE SHOULD ***USE IT.***
CHET HARRISON
BECAUSE ***IF*** WE DO THIS. IF WE DO THIS...
SESSION ISN'T TOO LONG...
WE NEED TO CONSIDER WHERE IT WILL END.
MOM AND I WANT KOREAN FOR DINNER - THINK THE BABY WANTS KIMCHI!'
MESSAGE WILL DELETE IN THREE...
BECAUSE WE ARE DECIDING OUR ***FUTURE.***
HOW FAR WILL PEOPLE GO?
IT'S A SLIPPERY SLOPE AND THE LINE ***MUST*** BE DRAWN SOMEWHERE.
WE DON'T WANT TO BE LIVING IN A FUTURISTIC NIGHTMARE OF HAVES AND HAVE NOTS.
WE URGE YOU TO VOTE ***AGAINST*** ALLOWING HUMAN GENETIC MANIPULATION.
YOU ***MUST*** VOTE AGAINST IT.

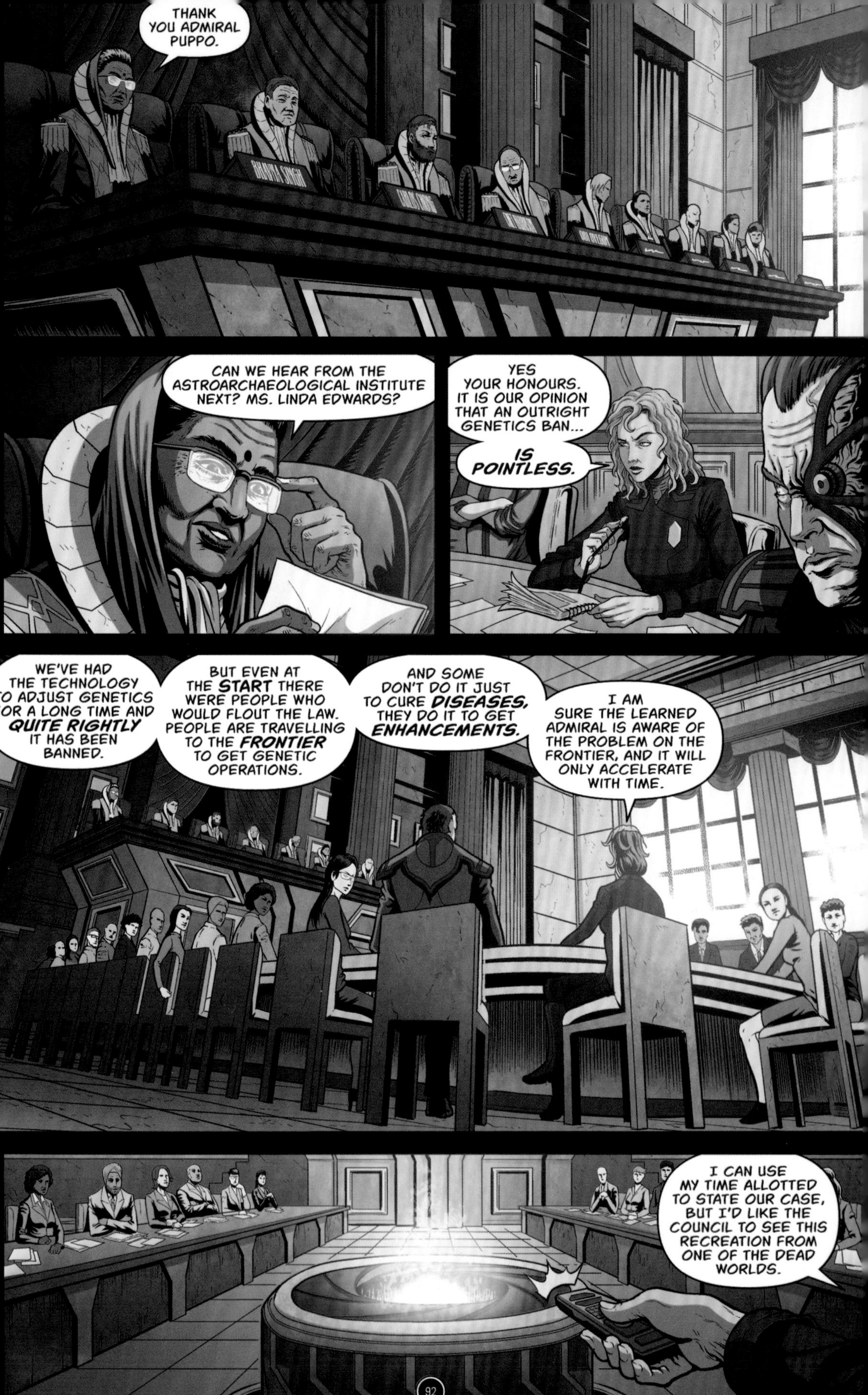
THANK YOU ADMIRAL PUPPO.
CAN WE HEAR FROM THE ASTROARCHAEOLOGICAL INSTITUTE NEXT? MS. LINDA EDWARDS?
YES YOUR HONOURS. IT IS OUR OPINION THAT AN OUTRIGHT GENETICS BAN...
IS POINTLESS.
WE'VE HAD THE TECHNOLOGY TO ADJUST GENETICS FOR A LONG TIME AND QUITE RIGHTLY IT HAS BEEN BANNED.
BUT EVEN AT THE START THERE WERE PEOPLE WHO WOULD FLOUT THE LAW. PEOPLE ARE TRAVELLING TO THE FRONTIER TO GET GENETIC OPERATIONS.
AND SOME DON'T DO IT JUST TO CURE DISEASES, THEY DO IT TO GET ENHANCEMENTS.
I AM SURE THE LEARNED ADMIRAL IS AWARE OF THE PROBLEM ON THE FRONTIER, AND IT WILL ONLY ACCELERATE WITH TIME.
I CAN USE MY TIME ALLOTTED TO STATE OUR CASE, BUT I'D LIKE THE COUNCIL TO SEE THIS RECREATION FROM ONE OF THE DEAD WORLDS.

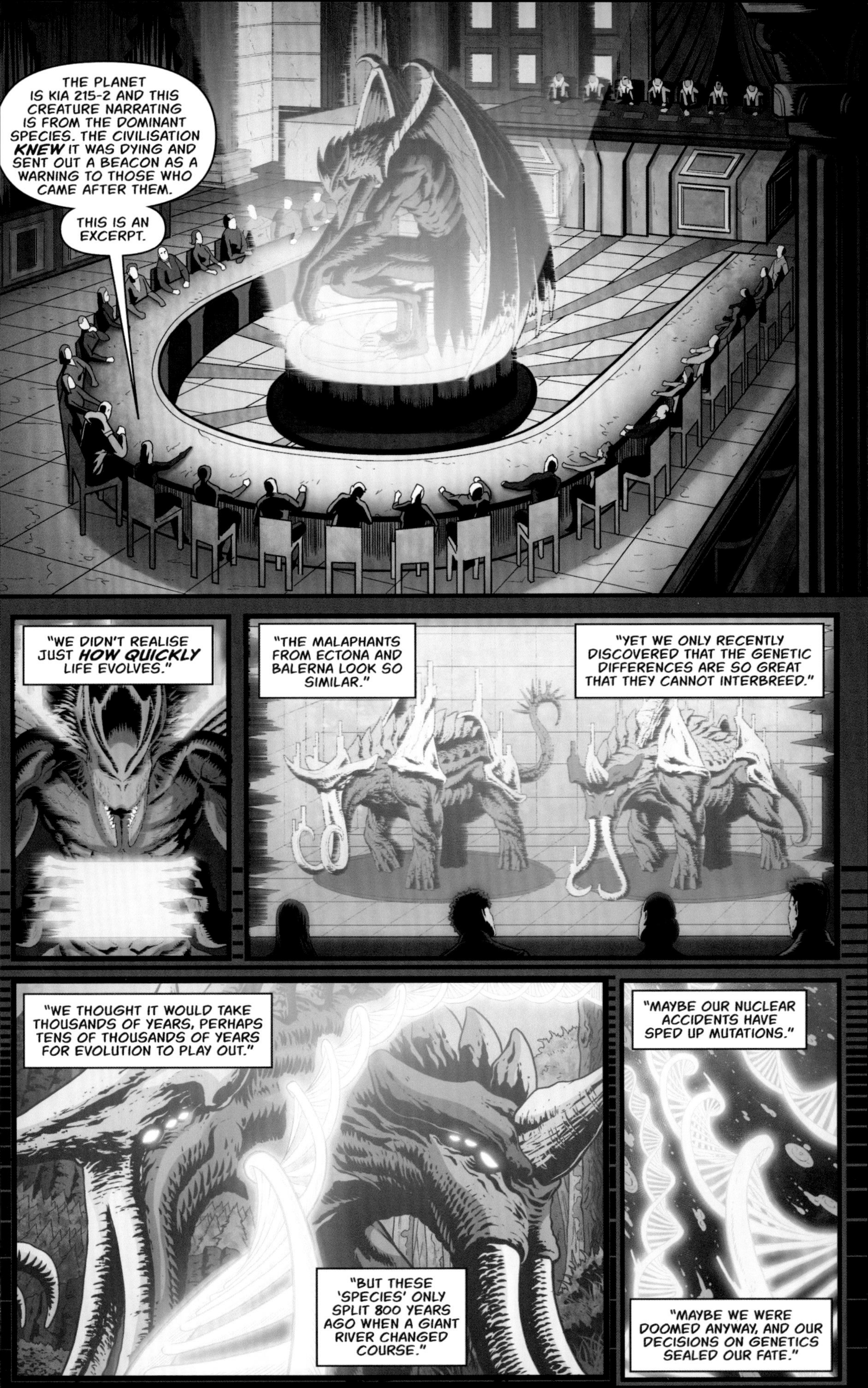
THE PLANET IS KIA 215-2 AND THIS CREATURE NARRATING IS FROM THE DOMINANT SPECIES. THE CIVILISATION KNEW IT WAS DYING AND SENT OUT A BEACON AS A WARNING TO THOSE WHO CAME AFTER THEM.
THIS IS AN EXCERPT.
"WE DIDN'T REALISE JUST HOW QUICKLY LIFE EVOLVES."
"THE MALAPHANTS FROM ECTONA AND BALERNA LOOK SO SIMILAR."
"YET WE ONLY RECENTLY DISCOVERED THAT THE GENETIC DIFFERENCES ARE SO GREAT THAT THEY CANNOT INTERBREED."
"WE THOUGHT IT WOULD TAKE THOUSANDS OF YEARS, PERHAPS TENS OF THOUSANDS OF YEARS FOR EVOLUTION TO PLAY OUT."
"BUT THESE 'SPECIES' ONLY SPLIT 800 YEARS AGO WHEN A GIANT RIVER CHANGED COURSE."
"MAYBE OUR NUCLEAR ACCIDENTS HAVE SPED UP MUTATIONS."
"MAYBE WE WERE DOOMED ANYWAY, AND OUR DECISIONS ON GENETICS SEALED OUR FATE."

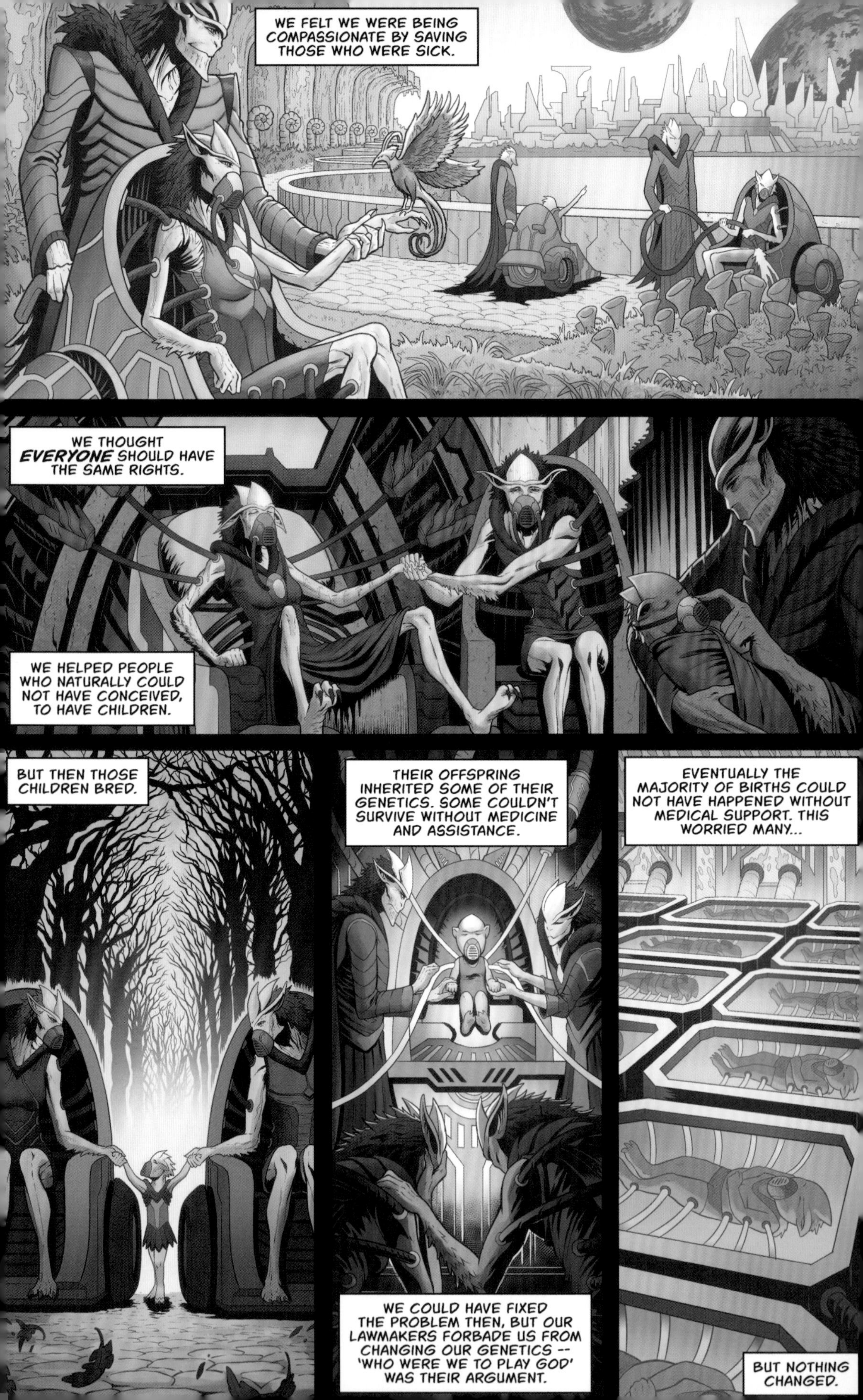
WE FELT WE WERE BEING COMPASSIONATE BY SAVING THOSE WHO WERE SICK.
WE THOUGHT *EVERYONE* SHOULD HAVE THE SAME RIGHTS.
WE HELPED PEOPLE WHO NATURALLY COULD NOT HAVE CONCEIVED, TO HAVE CHILDREN.
BUT THEN THOSE CHILDREN BRED.
THEIR OFFSPRING INHERITED SOME OF THEIR GENETICS. SOME COULDN'T SURVIVE WITHOUT MEDICINE AND ASSISTANCE.
WE COULD HAVE FIXED THE PROBLEM THEN, BUT OUR LAWMAKERS FORBADE US FROM CHANGING OUR GENETICS -- 'WHO WERE WE TO PLAY GOD' WAS THEIR ARGUMENT.
EVENTUALLY THE MAJORITY OF BIRTHS COULD NOT HAVE HAPPENED WITHOUT MEDICAL SUPPORT. THIS WORRIED MANY...
BUT NOTHING CHANGED.

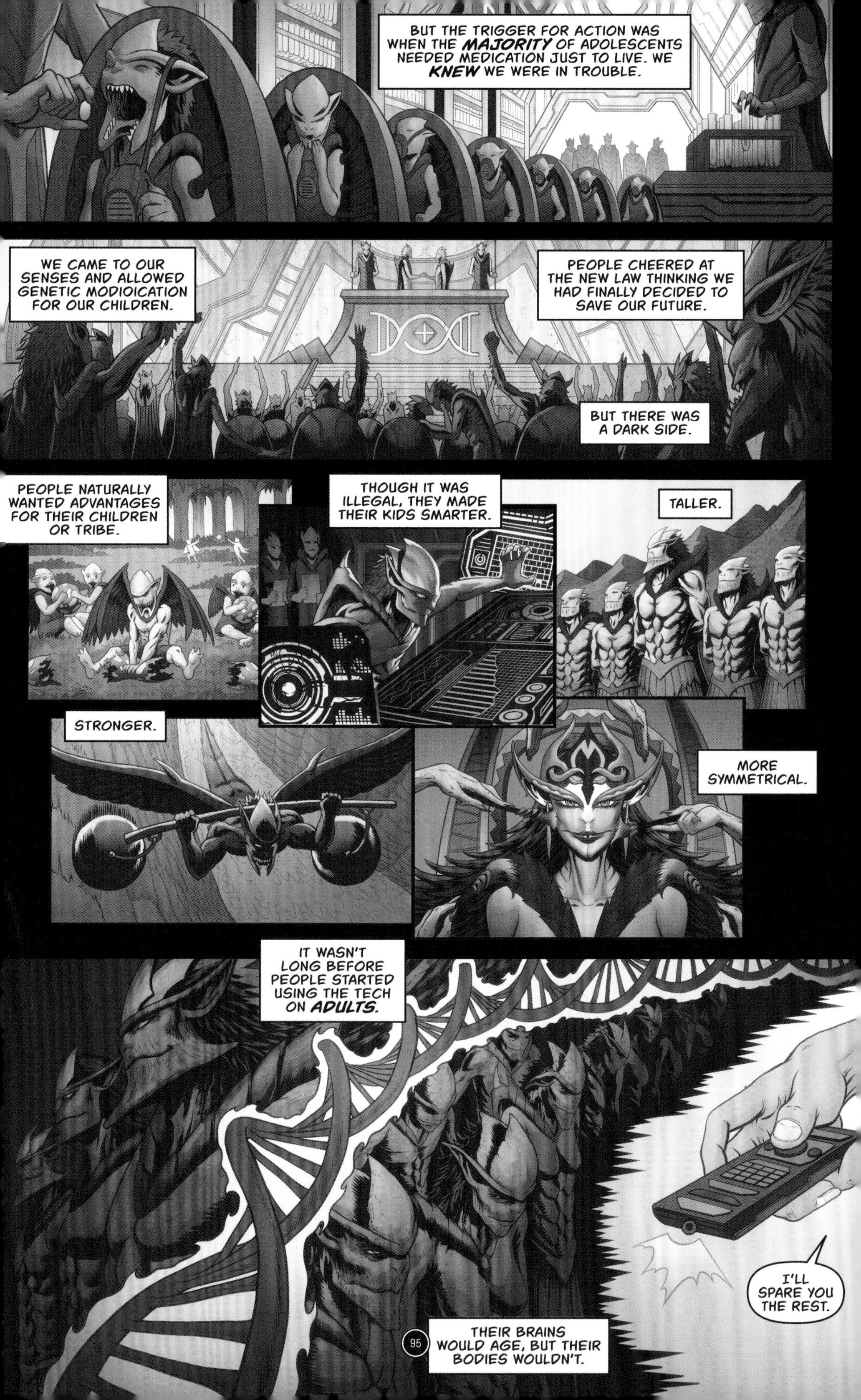

BUT THE TRIGGER FOR ACTION WAS WHEN THE ***MAJORITY*** OF ADOLESCENTS NEEDED MEDICATION JUST TO LIVE. WE ***KNEW*** WE WERE IN TROUBLE.
WE CAME TO OUR SENSES AND ALLOWED GENETIC MODIOICATION FOR OUR CHILDREN.
PEOPLE CHEERED AT THE NEW LAW THINKING WE HAD FINALLY DECIDED TO SAVE OUR FUTURE.
BUT THERE WAS A DARK SIDE.
PEOPLE NATURALLY WANTED ADVANTAGES FOR THEIR CHILDREN OR TRIBE.
THOUGH IT WAS ILLEGAL, THEY MADE THEIR KIDS SMARTER.
TALLER.
STRONGER.
MORE SYMMETRICAL.
IT WASN'T LONG BEFORE PEOPLE STARTED USING THE TECH ON ***ADULTS.***
THEIR BRAINS WOULD AGE, BUT THEIR BODIES WOULDN'T.
I'LL SPARE YOU THE REST.

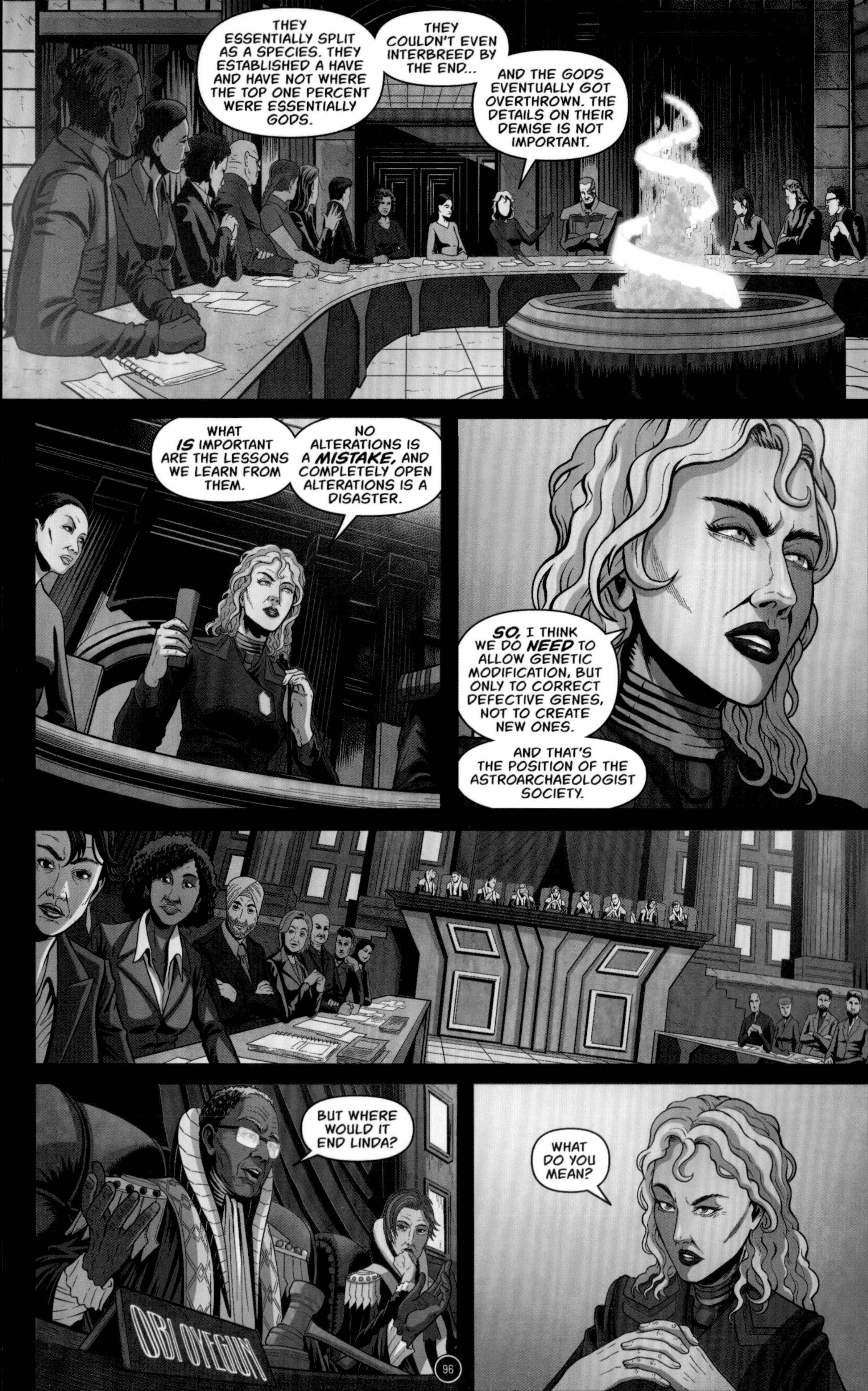
THEY ESSENTIALLY SPLIT AS A SPECIES. THEY ESTABLISHED A HAVE AND HAVE NOT WHERE THE TOP ONE PERCENT WERE ESSENTIALLY GODS.
THEY COULDN'T EVEN INTERBREED BY THE END...
AND THE GODS EVENTUALLY GOT OVERTHROWN. THE DETAILS ON THEIR DEMISE IS NOT IMPORTANT.
WHAT ***IS*** IMPORTANT ARE THE LESSONS WE LEARN FROM THEM.
NO ALTERATIONS IS A ***MISTAKE,*** AND COMPLETELY OPEN ALTERATIONS IS A DISASTER.
SO, I THINK WE DO ***NEED*** TO ALLOW GENETIC MODIFICATION, BUT ONLY TO CORRECT DEFECTIVE GENES, NOT TO CREATE NEW ONES.
AND THAT'S THE POSITION OF THE ASTROARCHAEOLOGIST SOCIETY.
BUT WHERE WOULD IT END LINDA?
WHAT DO YOU MEAN?
OBI OYEGUN

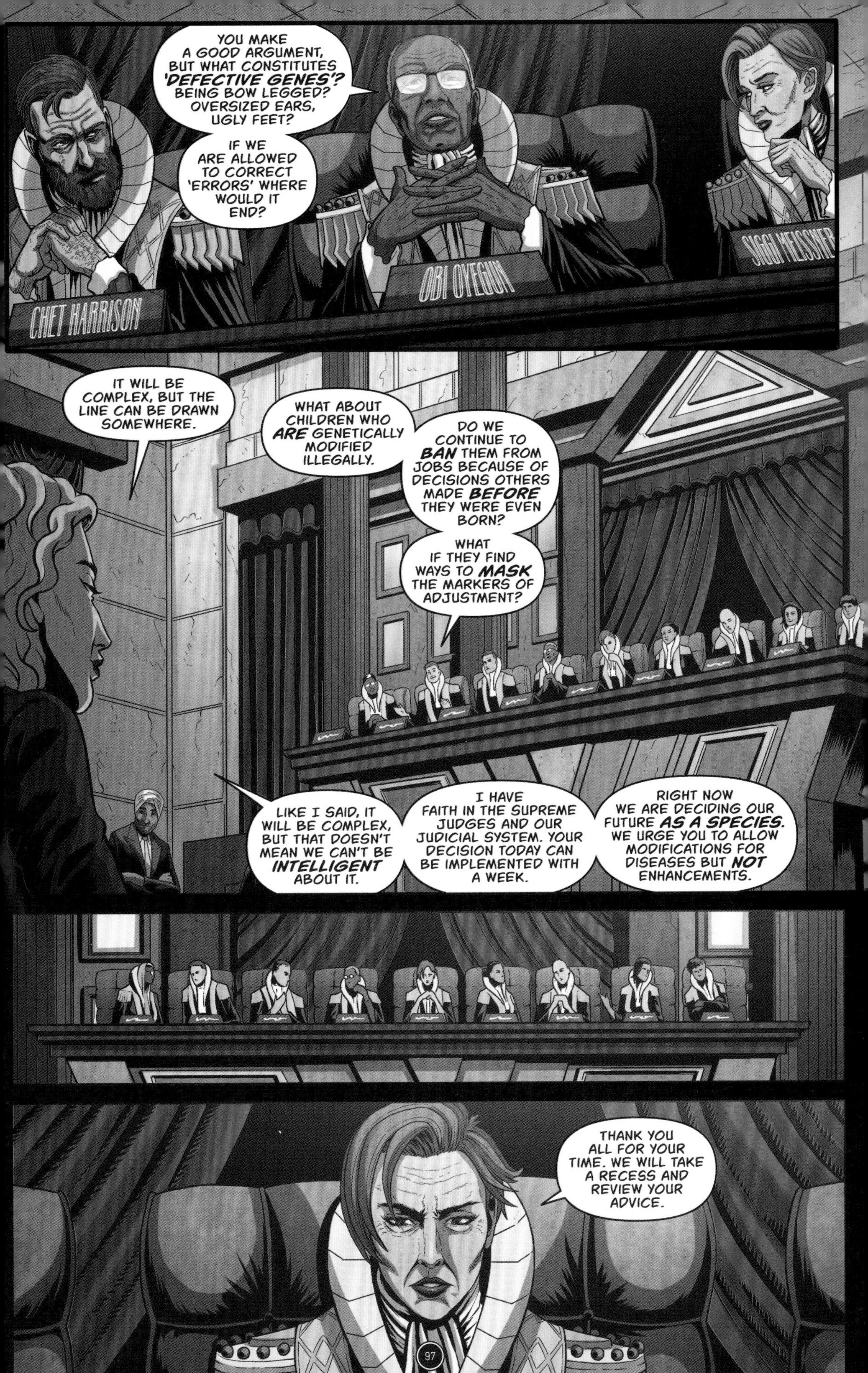
YOU MAKE A GOOD ARGUMENT, BUT WHAT CONSTITUTES *'DEFECTIVE GENES'?* BEING BOW LEGGED? OVERSIZED EARS, UGLY FEET?
IF WE ARE ALLOWED TO CORRECT 'ERRORS' WHERE WOULD IT END?
CHET HARRISON
OBI OYEGUN
SIGGI MEISSNER
IT WILL BE COMPLEX, BUT THE LINE CAN BE DRAWN SOMEWHERE.
WHAT ABOUT CHILDREN WHO *ARE* GENETICALLY MODIFIED ILLEGALLY.
DO WE CONTINUE TO *BAN* THEM FROM JOBS BECAUSE OF DECISIONS OTHERS MADE *BEFORE* THEY WERE EVEN BORN?
WHAT IF THEY FIND WAYS TO *MASK* THE MARKERS OF ADJUSTMENT?
LIKE I SAID, IT WILL BE COMPLEX, BUT THAT DOESN'T MEAN WE CAN'T BE *INTELLIGENT* ABOUT IT.
I HAVE FAITH IN THE SUPREME JUDGES AND OUR JUDICIAL SYSTEM. YOUR DECISION TODAY CAN BE IMPLEMENTED WITH A WEEK.
RIGHT NOW WE ARE DECIDING OUR FUTURE *AS A SPECIES.* WE URGE YOU TO ALLOW MODIFICATIONS FOR DISEASES BUT *NOT* ENHANCEMENTS.
THANK YOU ALL FOR YOUR TIME. WE WILL TAKE A RECESS AND REVIEW YOUR ADVICE.

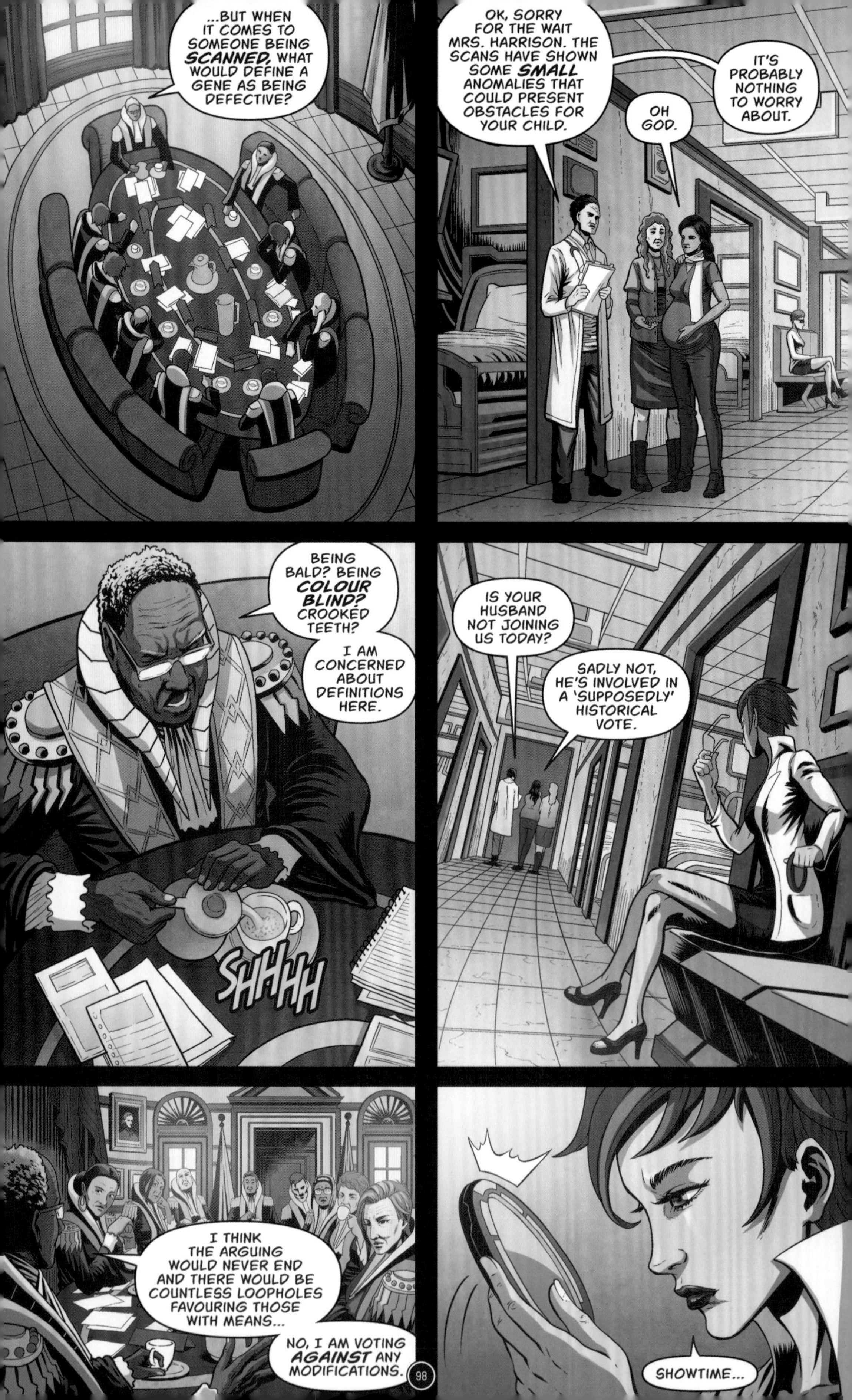
...BUT WHEN IT COMES TO SOMEONE BEING SCANNED, WHAT WOULD DEFINE A GENE AS BEING DEFECTIVE?
OK, SORRY FOR THE WAIT MRS. HARRISON. THE SCANS HAVE SHOWN SOME SMALL ANOMALIES THAT COULD PRESENT OBSTACLES FOR YOUR CHILD.
OH GOD.
IT'S PROBABLY NOTHING TO WORRY ABOUT.
BEING BALD? BEING COLOUR BLIND? CROOKED TEETH?
I AM CONCERNED ABOUT DEFINITIONS HERE.
SHHHH
IS YOUR HUSBAND NOT JOINING US TODAY?
SADLY NOT, HE'S INVOLVED IN A 'SUPPOSEDLY' HISTORICAL VOTE.
I THINK THE ARGUING WOULD NEVER END AND THERE WOULD BE COUNTLESS LOOPHOLES FAVOURING THOSE WITH MEANS...
NO, I AM VOTING AGAINST ANY MODIFICATIONS.
SHOWTIME...

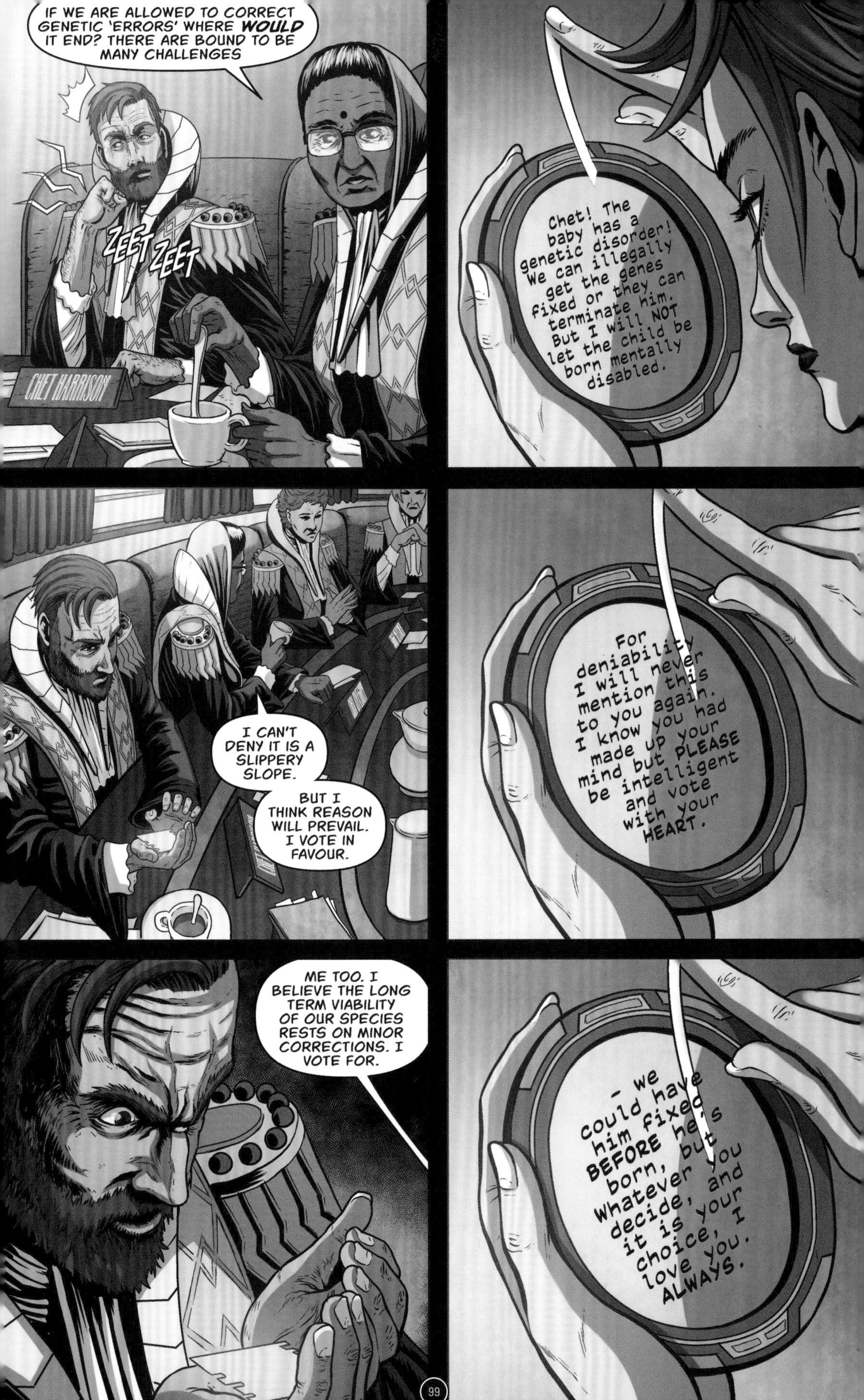
IF WE ARE ALLOWED TO CORRECT GENETIC 'ERRORS' WHERE WOULD IT END? THERE ARE BOUND TO BE MANY CHALLENGES
ZEET ZEET
CHET HARRISON
Chet! The baby has a genetic disorder! We can illegally get the genes fixed or they can terminate him. But I will NOT let the child be born mentally disabled.
I CAN'T DENY IT IS A SLIPPERY SLOPE.
BUT I THINK REASON WILL PREVAIL. I VOTE IN FAVOUR.
For deniability I will never mention this to you again. I know you had made up your mind but PLEASE be intelligent and vote with your HEART.
ME TOO. I BELIEVE THE LONG TERM VIABILITY OF OUR SPECIES RESTS ON MINOR CORRECTIONS. I VOTE FOR.
- we could have him fixed BEFORE he's born, but whatever you decide, and it is your choice, I love you. ALWAYS.

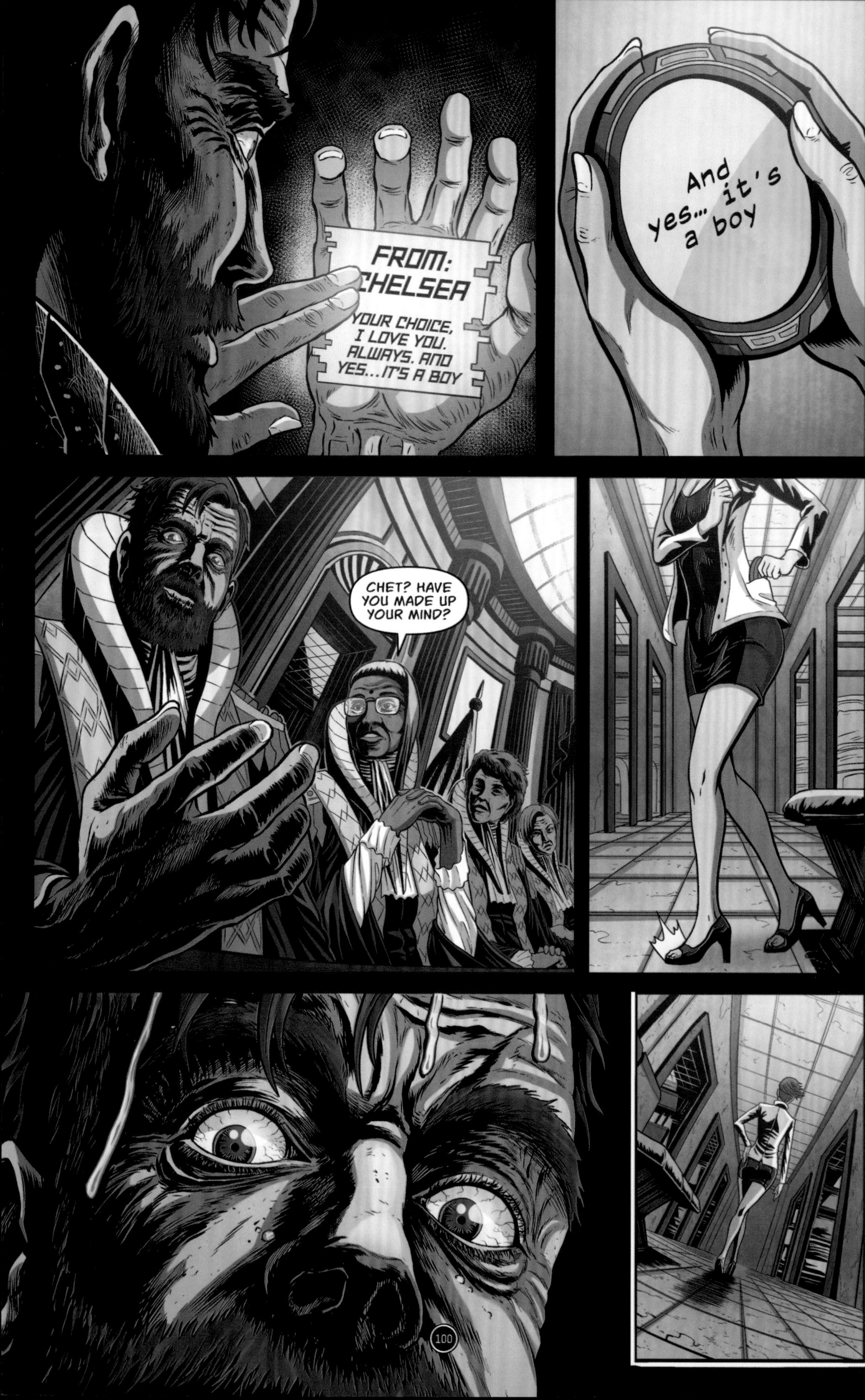
FROM:
CHELSEA
YOUR CHOICE,
I LOVE YOU.
ALWAYS. AND
YES...IT'S A BOY
And yes... it's a boy
CHET? HAVE YOU MADE UP YOUR MIND?

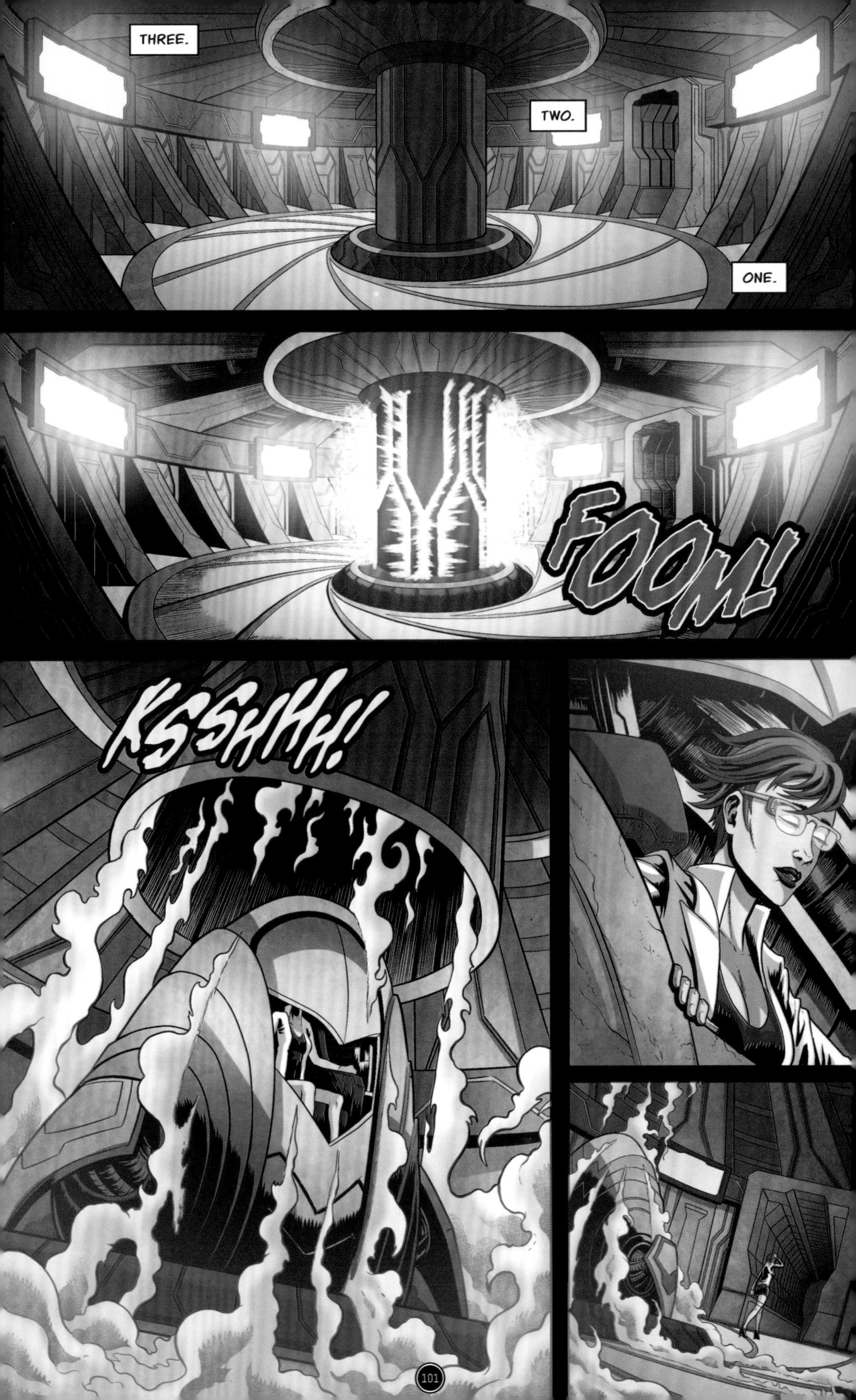

THREE.
TWO.
ONE.
FOOM!
KSSHHH!

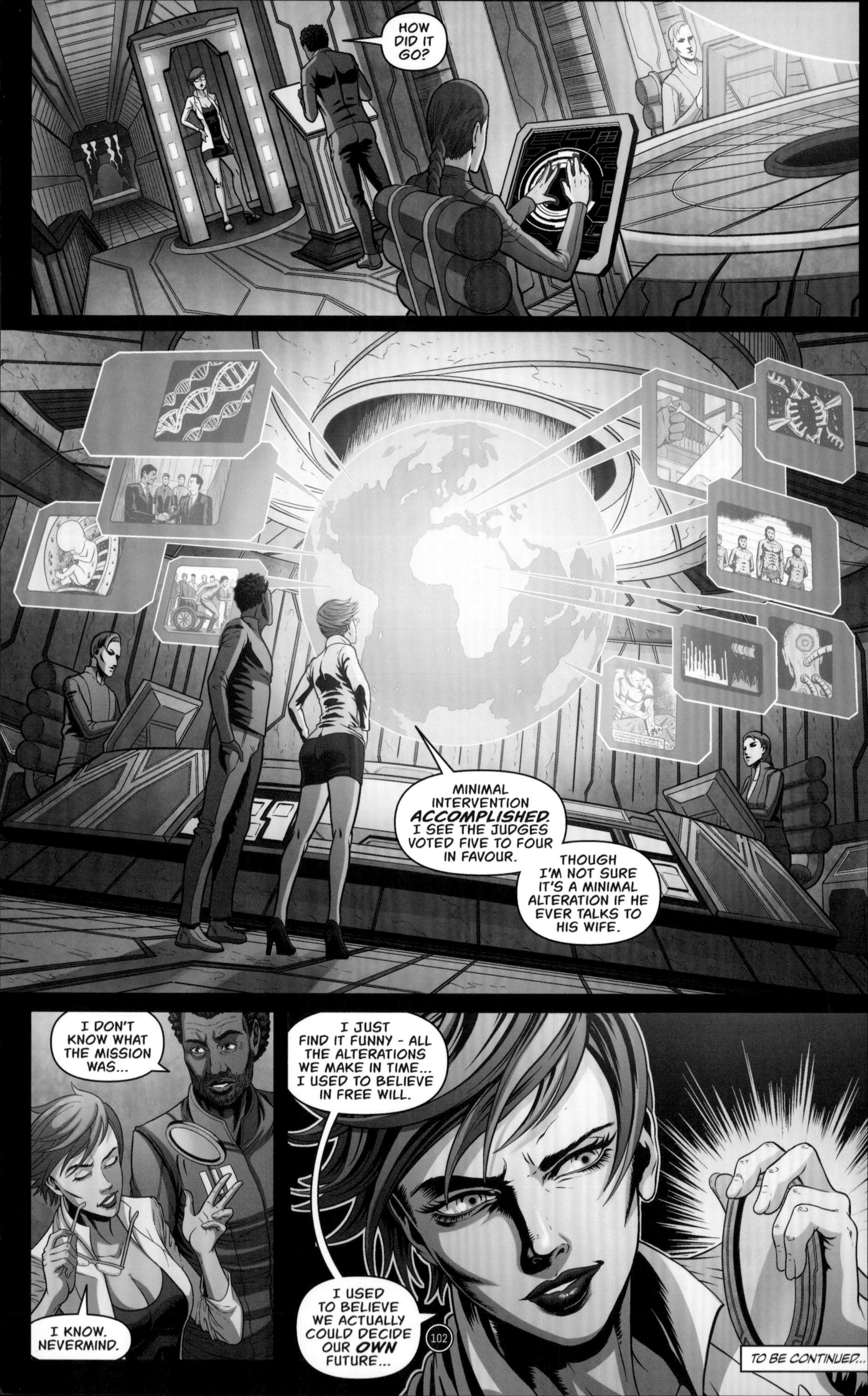
HOW DID IT GO?
MINIMAL INTERVENTION ACCOMPLISHED. I SEE THE JUDGES VOTED FIVE TO FOUR IN FAVOUR.
THOUGH I'M NOT SURE IT'S A MINIMAL ALTERATION IF HE EVER TALKS TO HIS WIFE.
I DON'T KNOW WHAT THE MISSION WAS...
I KNOW. NEVERMIND.
I JUST FIND IT FUNNY - ALL THE ALTERATIONS WE MAKE IN TIME... I USED TO BELIEVE IN FREE WILL.
I USED TO BELIEVE WE ACTUALLY COULD DECIDE OUR OWN FUTURE...
TO BE CONTINUED...

DEAR LINDA,

YOUR PRESENCE HAS BEEN REQUESTED FOR THIS
YEAR'S ANNUAL INTERPLANETARY MEETING FOR
LAW APPROVAL (IMLA), RUN BY THE INTER-
PLANETARY SUPREME COURT, TO BE HELD ON EARTH.

THE OVERALL THEME OF THE CONFERENCE IS
''GENETIC MODIFICATION IN PAST AND PRESENT'',
AND KEY POINTS OF DEBATE WILL BE WHETHER OR
NOT WE SHOULD ADAPT OUR RULES OF GENETIC
MODIFICATION BASED ON DEAD CIVILISATION'S
CHOICES. PRESENTATIONS WILL BE GIVEN BY
MULTIPLE BODIES TO ENABLE THE MOST INFORMED
DECISION.

GIVEN YOUR EXPERIENCE, WE BELIEVE IT WOULD BE
BENEFICIAL FOR YOU TO GIVE A TALK BASED ON
YOUR FINDINGS ON IAHARI EARLIER THIS YEAR.

PLEASE BE READY TO PRESENT NO LATER THAN
10:00 TIME ON THE DAY. A PROVISIONAL SCHEDULE
HAS BEEN ATTACHED.

A night Lionel could never forget...

"The best thing about the future is that it comes one day at a time."

Abraham Lincoln

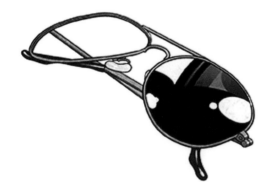

Writer/Creator
Neil Gibson

Illustrator
Atula Siriwardane

Colourist
Liezl Buenaventura

Letters by
Justin Birch

www.tpubcomics.com

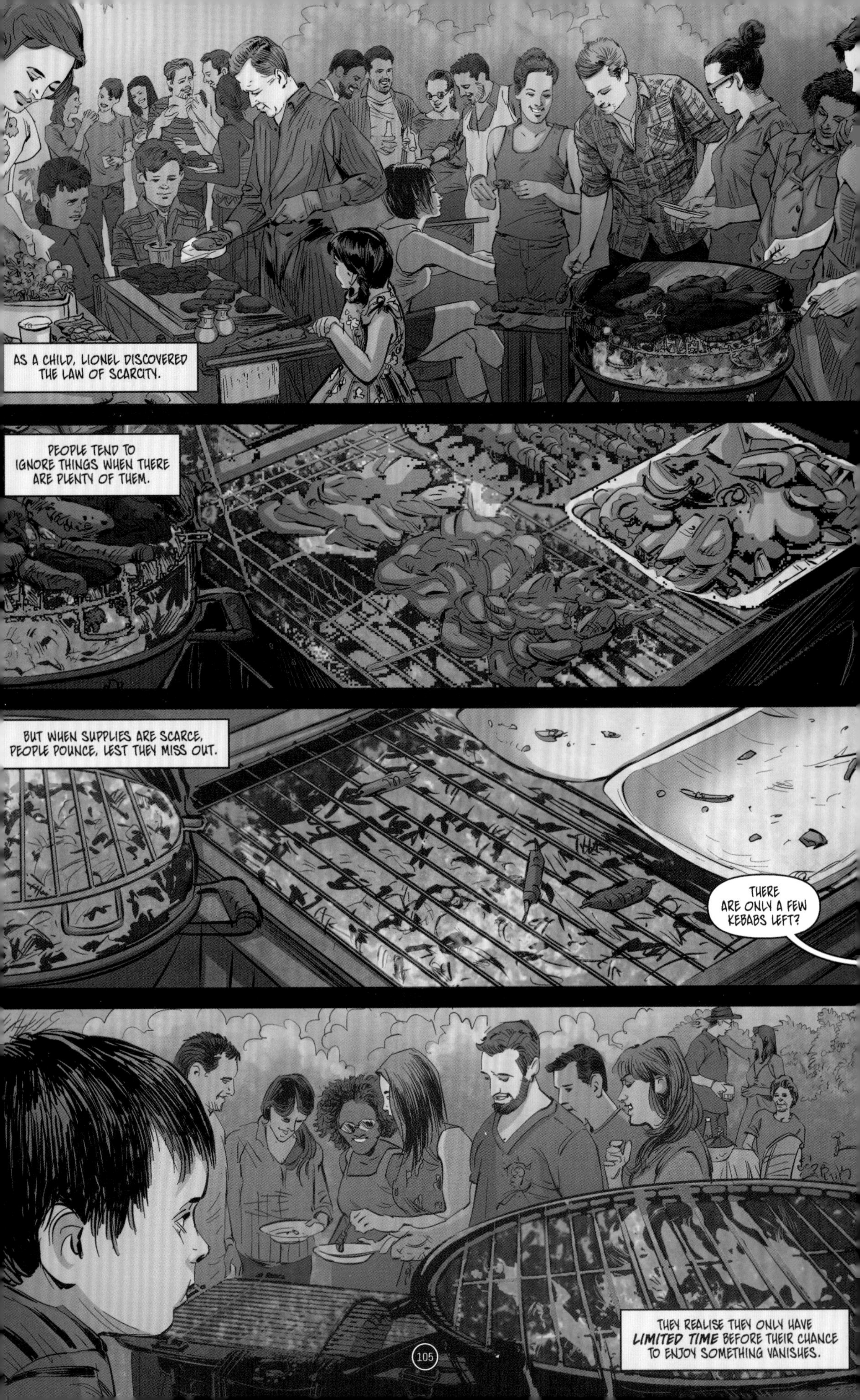
AS A CHILD, LIONEL DISCOVERED THE LAW OF SCARCITY.
PEOPLE TEND TO IGNORE THINGS WHEN THERE ARE PLENTY OF THEM.
BUT WHEN SUPPLIES ARE SCARCE, PEOPLE POUNCE, LEST THEY MISS OUT.
THERE ARE ONLY A FEW KEBABS LEFT?
THEY REALISE THEY ONLY HAVE **LIMITED TIME** BEFORE THEIR CHANCE TO ENJOY SOMETHING VANISHES.

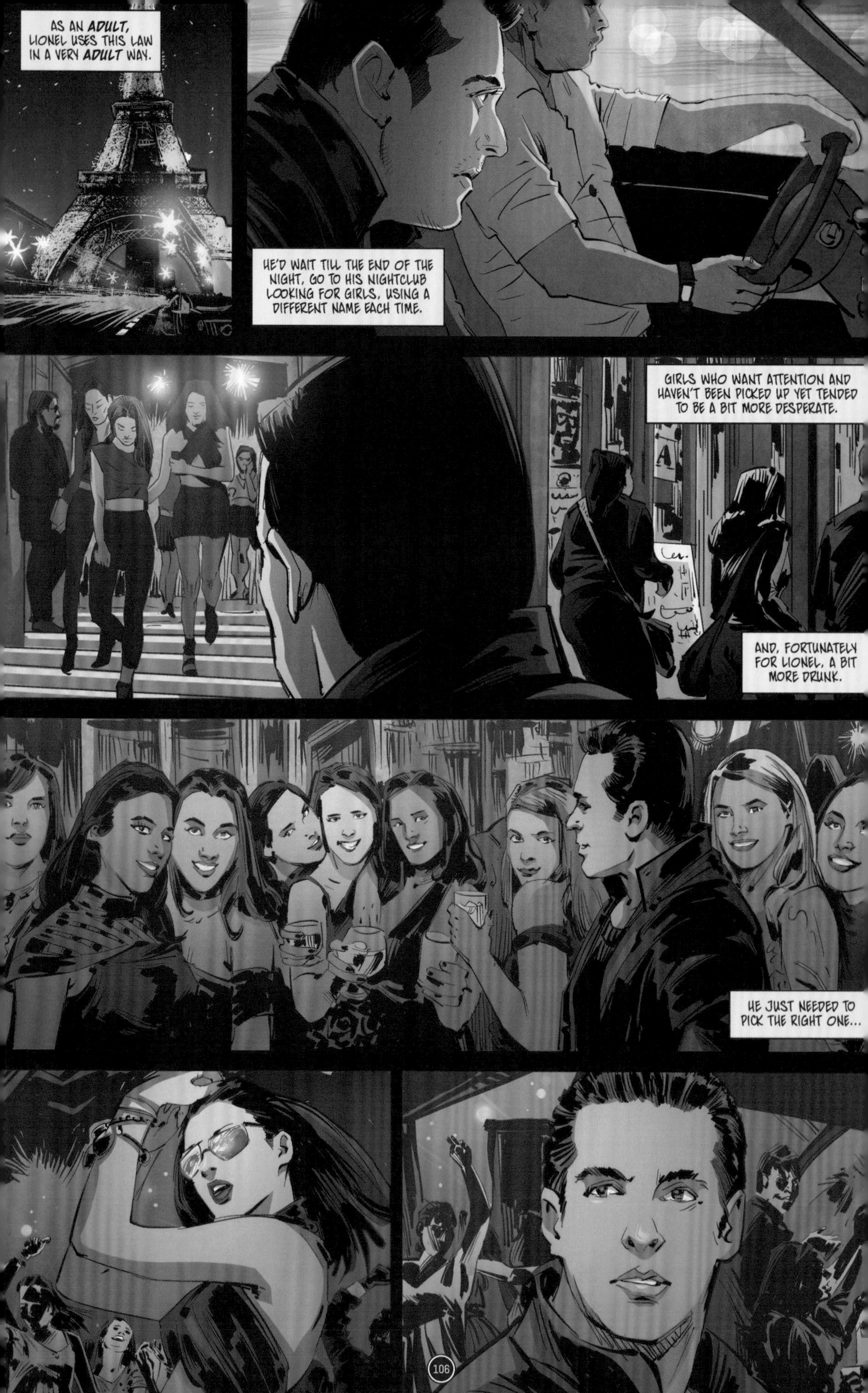
AS AN ADULT, LIONEL USES THIS LAW IN A VERY ADULT WAY.
HE'D WAIT TILL THE END OF THE NIGHT, GO TO HIS NIGHTCLUB LOOKING FOR GIRLS, USING A DIFFERENT NAME EACH TIME.
GIRLS WHO WANT ATTENTION AND HAVEN'T BEEN PICKED UP YET TENDED TO BE A BIT MORE DESPERATE.
AND, FORTUNATELY FOR LIONEL, A BIT MORE DRUNK.
HE JUST NEEDED TO PICK THE RIGHT ONE...

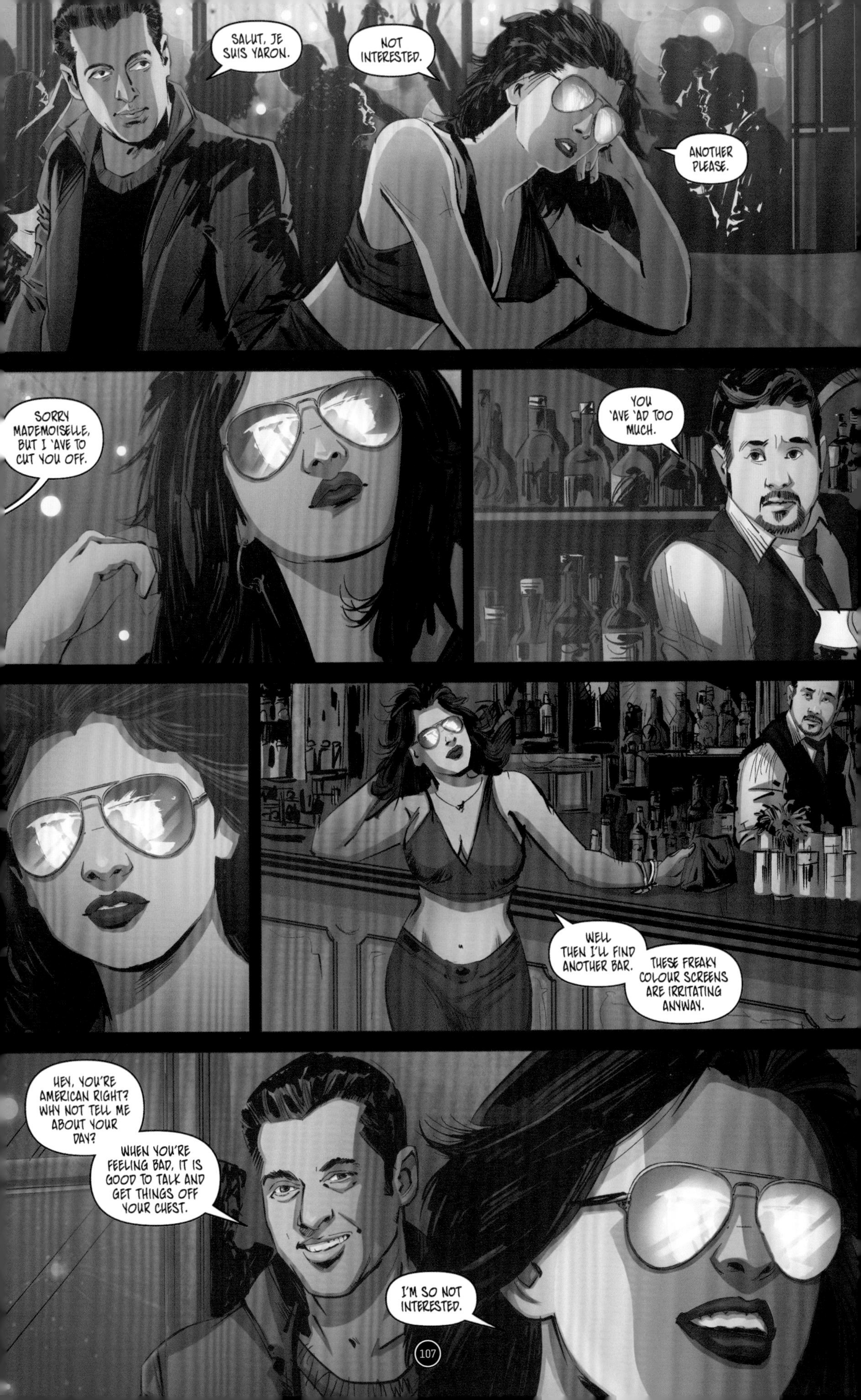
SALUT, JE SUIS YARON.
NOT INTERESTED.
ANOTHER PLEASE.
SORRY MADEMOISELLE, BUT I 'AVE TO CUT YOU OFF.
YOU 'AVE 'AD TOO MUCH.
WELL THEN I'LL FIND ANOTHER BAR.
THESE FREAKY COLOUR SCREENS ARE IRRITATING ANYWAY.
HEY, YOU'RE AMERICAN RIGHT? WHY NOT TELL ME ABOUT YOUR DAY?
WHEN YOU'RE FEELING BAD, IT IS GOOD TO TALK AND GET THINGS OFF YOUR CHEST.
I'M SO NOT INTERESTED.

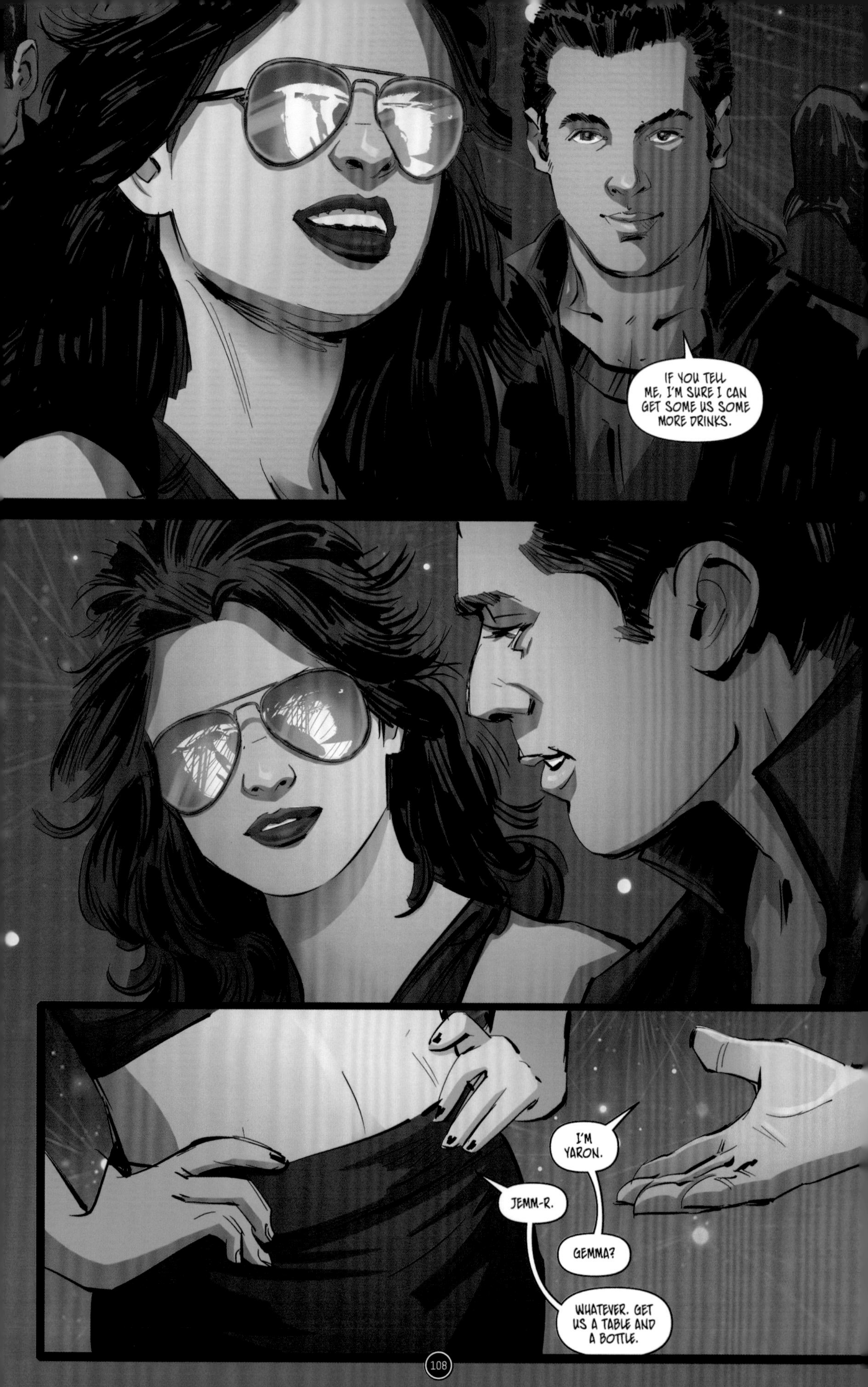
IF YOU TELL ME, I'M SURE I CAN GET SOME US SOME MORE DRINKS.
I'M YARON.
JEMM-R.
GEMMA?
WHATEVER. GET US A TABLE AND A BOTTLE.

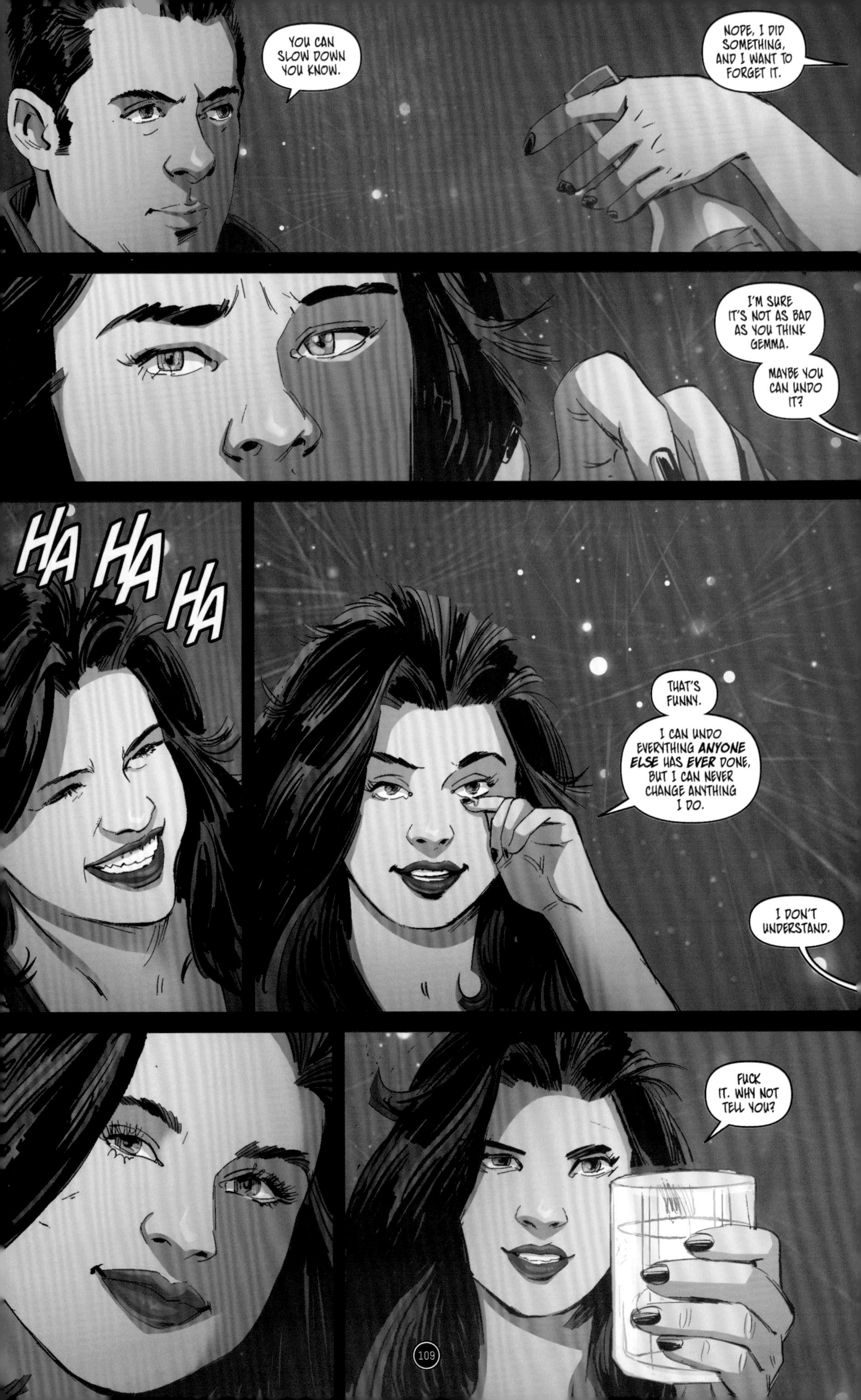
YOU CAN SLOW DOWN YOU KNOW.
NOPE, I DID SOMETHING, AND I WANT TO FORGET IT.
I'M SURE IT'S NOT AS BAD AS YOU THINK GEMMA.
MAYBE YOU CAN UNDO IT?
HA HA HA
THAT'S FUNNY.
I CAN UNDO EVERYTHING **ANYONE ELSE** HAS **EVER** DONE, BUT I CAN NEVER CHANGE ANYTHING I DO.
I DON'T UNDERSTAND.
FUCK IT. WHY NOT TELL YOU?

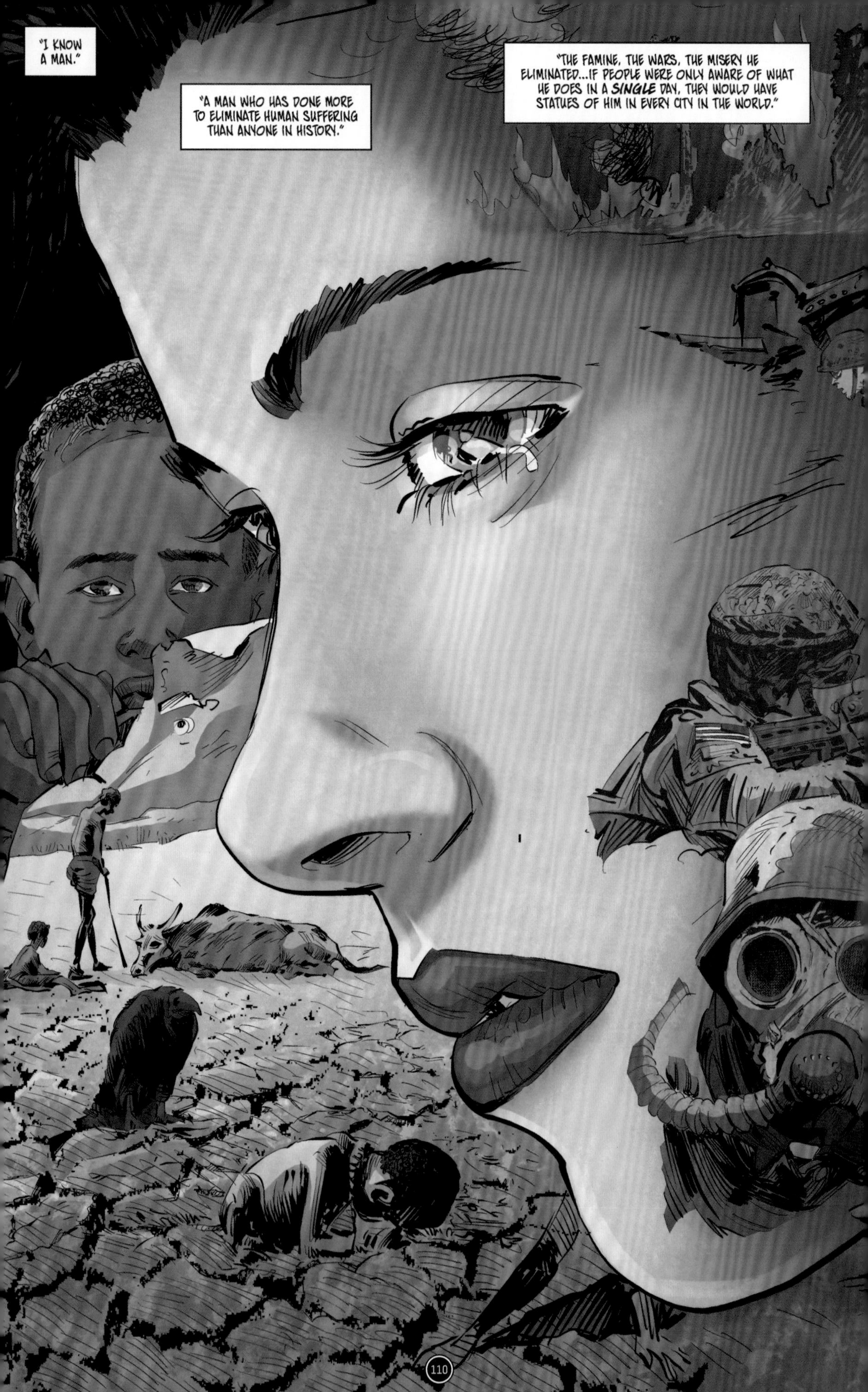
"I KNOW A MAN."
"A MAN WHO HAS DONE MORE TO ELIMINATE HUMAN SUFFERING THAN ANYONE IN HISTORY."
"THE FAMINE, THE WARS, THE MISERY HE ELIMINATED...IF PEOPLE WERE ONLY AWARE OF WHAT HE DOES IN A *SINGLE* DAY, THEY WOULD HAVE STATUES OF HIM IN EVERY CITY IN THE WORLD."

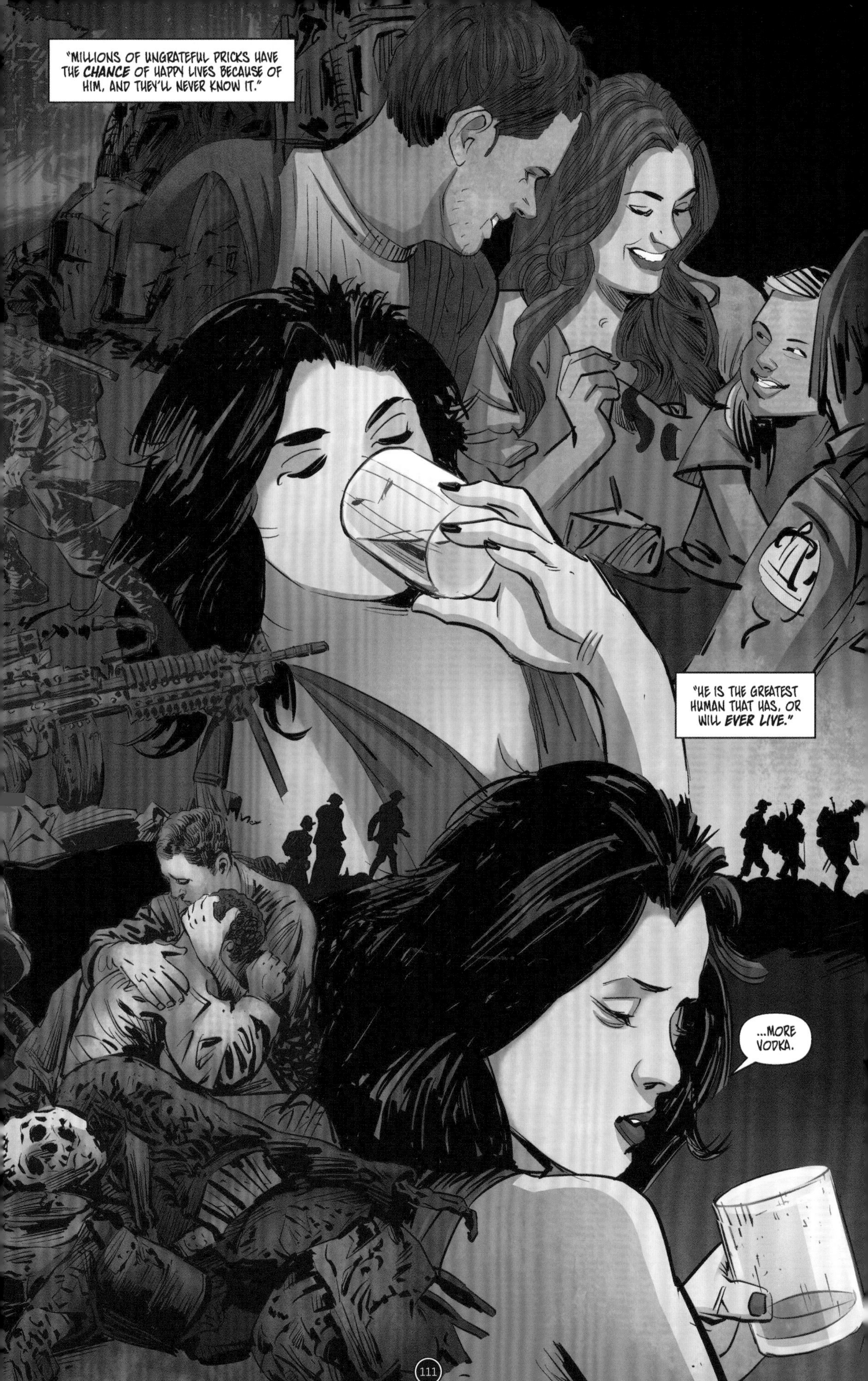
"MILLIONS OF UNGRATEFUL PRICKS HAVE THE CHANCE OF HAPPY LIVES BECAUSE OF HIM, AND THEY'LL NEVER KNOW IT."
"HE IS THE GREATEST HUMAN THAT HAS, OR WILL EVER LIVE."
...MORE VODKA.

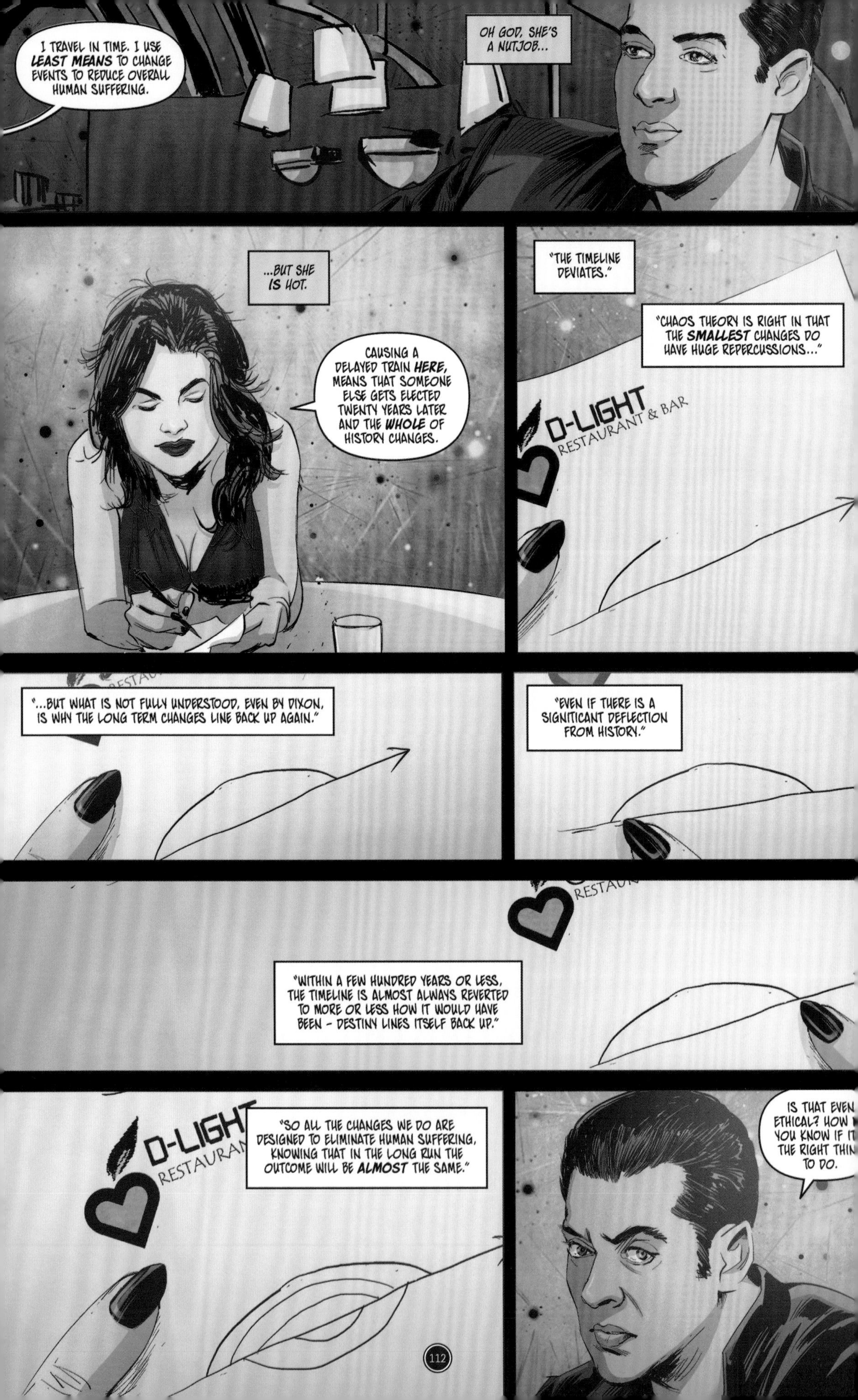
I TRAVEL IN TIME. I USE LEAST MEANS TO CHANGE EVENTS TO REDUCE OVERALL HUMAN SUFFERING.
OH GOD, SHE'S A NUTJOB...
...BUT SHE IS HOT.
CAUSING A DELAYED TRAIN HERE, MEANS THAT SOMEONE ELSE GETS ELECTED TWENTY YEARS LATER AND THE WHOLE OF HISTORY CHANGES.
"THE TIMELINE DEVIATES."
"CHAOS THEORY IS RIGHT IN THAT THE SMALLEST CHANGES DO HAVE HUGE REPERCUSSIONS..."
D-LIGHT RESTAURANT & BAR
"...BUT WHAT IS NOT FULLY UNDERSTOOD, EVEN BY DIXON, IS WHY THE LONG TERM CHANGES LINE BACK UP AGAIN."
"EVEN IF THERE IS A SIGNIFICANT DEFLECTION FROM HISTORY."
"WITHIN A FEW HUNDRED YEARS OR LESS, THE TIMELINE IS ALMOST ALWAYS REVERTED TO MORE OR LESS HOW IT WOULD HAVE BEEN - DESTINY LINES ITSELF BACK UP."
"SO ALL THE CHANGES WE DO ARE DESIGNED TO ELIMINATE HUMAN SUFFERING, KNOWING THAT IN THE LONG RUN THE OUTCOME WILL BE ALMOST THE SAME."
IS THAT EVEN ETHICAL? HOW YOU KNOW IF IT THE RIGHT THIN TO DO.

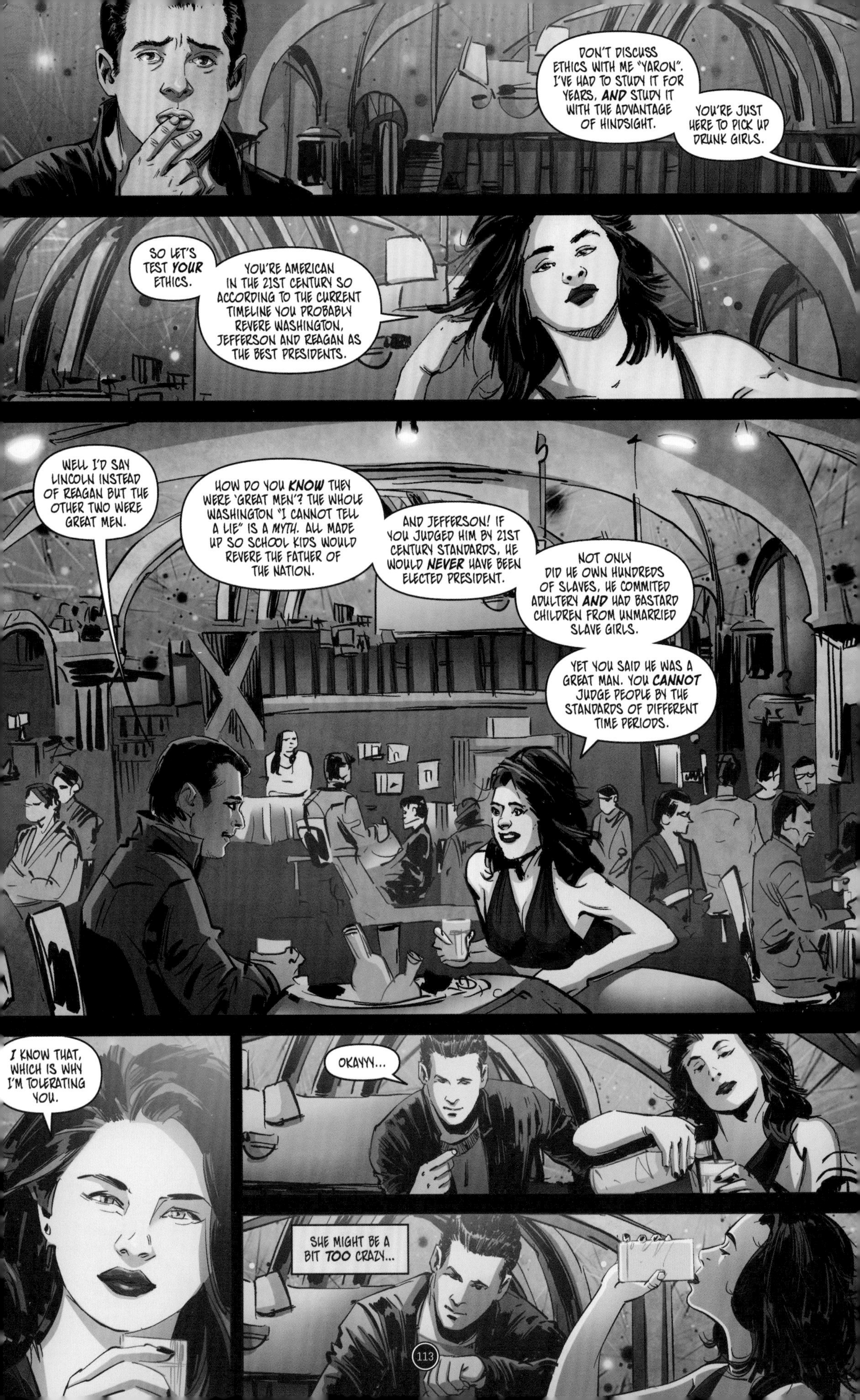
DON'T DISCUSS ETHICS WITH ME "YARON". I'VE HAD TO STUDY IT FOR YEARS, **AND** STUDY IT WITH THE ADVANTAGE OF HINDSIGHT.
YOU'RE JUST HERE TO PICK UP DRUNK GIRLS.
SO LET'S TEST **YOUR** ETHICS.
YOU'RE AMERICAN IN THE 21ST CENTURY SO ACCORDING TO THE CURRENT TIMELINE YOU PROBABLY REVERE WASHINGTON, JEFFERSON AND REAGAN AS THE BEST PRESIDENTS.
WELL I'D SAY LINCOLN INSTEAD OF REAGAN BUT THE OTHER TWO WERE GREAT MEN.
HOW DO YOU **KNOW** THEY WERE 'GREAT MEN'? THE WHOLE WASHINGTON "I CANNOT TELL A LIE" IS A *MYTH*. ALL MADE UP SO SCHOOL KIDS WOULD REVERE THE FATHER OF THE NATION.
AND JEFFERSON! IF YOU JUDGED HIM BY 21ST CENTURY STANDARDS, HE WOULD **NEVER** HAVE BEEN ELECTED PRESIDENT.
NOT ONLY DID HE OWN HUNDREDS OF SLAVES, HE COMMITED ADULTERY **AND** HAD BASTARD CHILDREN FROM UNMARRIED SLAVE GIRLS.
YET YOU SAID HE WAS A GREAT MAN. YOU **CANNOT** JUDGE PEOPLE BY THE STANDARDS OF DIFFERENT TIME PERIODS.
I KNOW THAT, WHICH IS WHY I'M TOLERATING YOU.
OKAYYY...
SHE MIGHT BE A BIT **TOO** CRAZY...

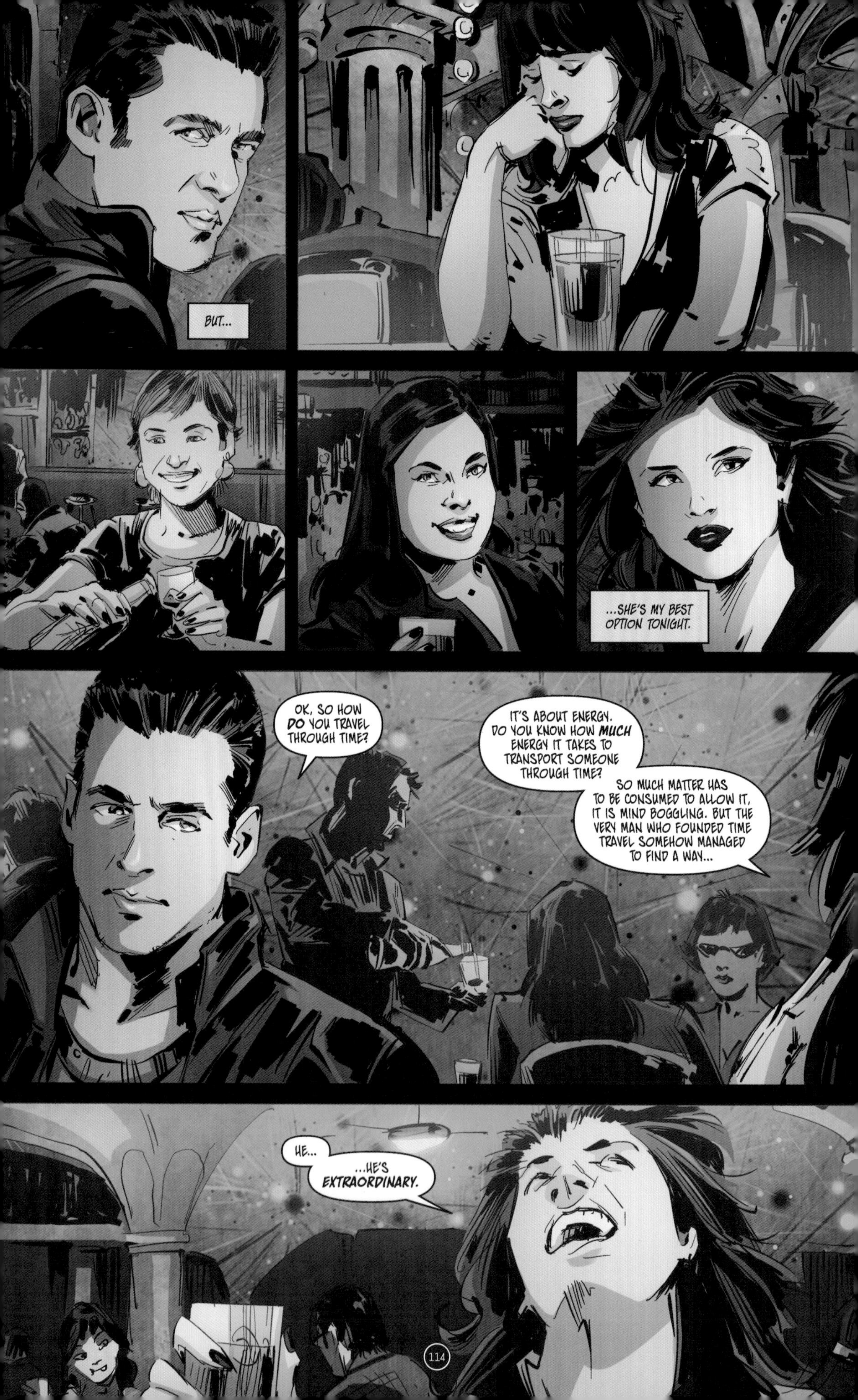

BUT...
...SHE'S MY BEST OPTION TONIGHT.
OK, SO HOW DO YOU TRAVEL THROUGH TIME?
IT'S ABOUT ENERGY. DO YOU KNOW HOW MUCH ENERGY IT TAKES TO TRANSPORT SOMEONE THROUGH TIME?
SO MUCH MATTER HAS TO BE CONSUMED TO ALLOW IT, IT IS MIND BOGGLING. BUT THE VERY MAN WHO FOUNDED TIME TRAVEL SOMEHOW MANAGED TO FIND A WAY...
HE...
...HE'S EXTRAORDINARY.

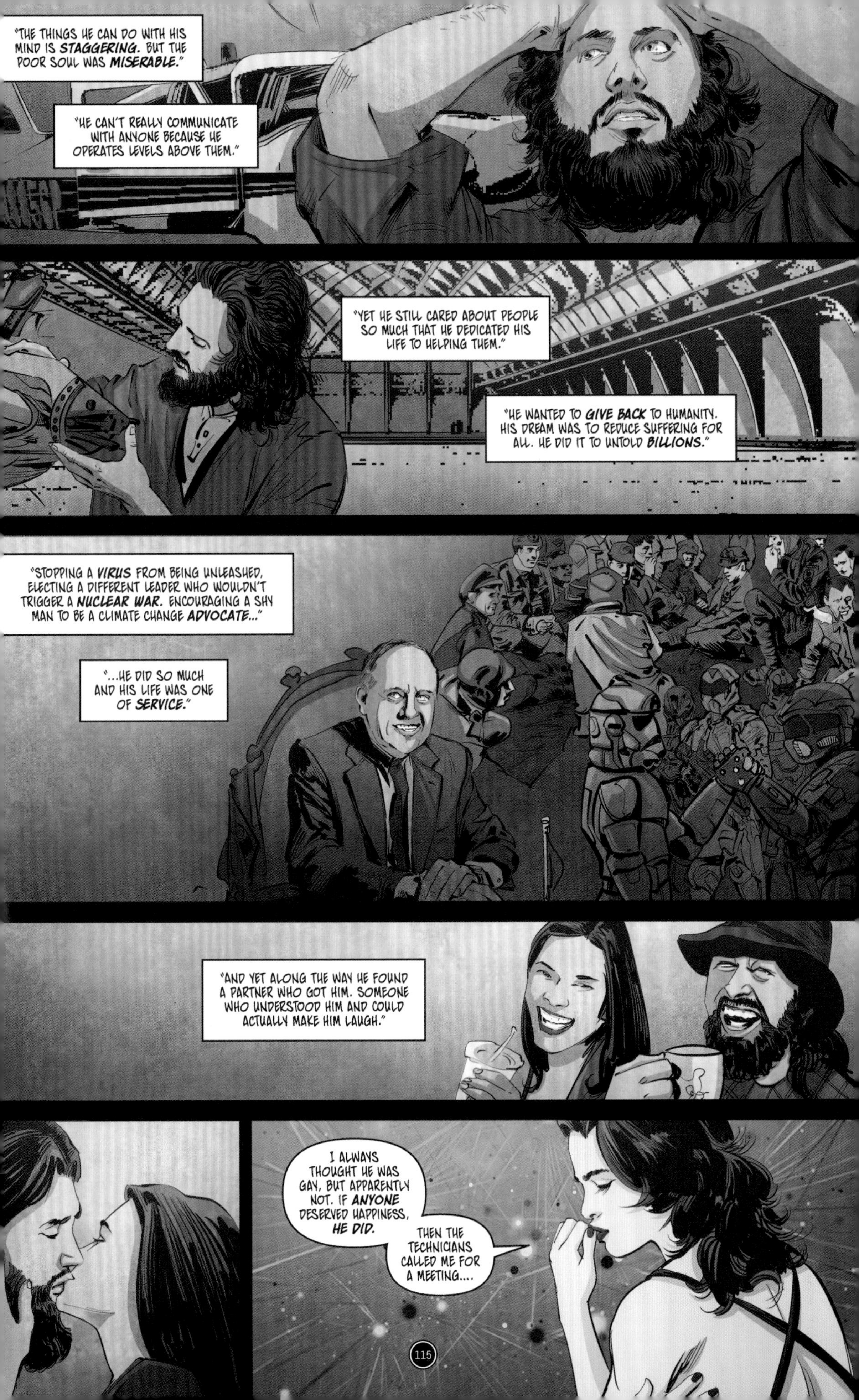
"THE THINGS HE CAN DO WITH HIS MIND IS STAGGERING. BUT THE POOR SOUL WAS MISERABLE."
"HE CAN'T REALLY COMMUNICATE WITH ANYONE BECAUSE HE OPERATES LEVELS ABOVE THEM."
"YET HE STILL CARED ABOUT PEOPLE SO MUCH THAT HE DEDICATED HIS LIFE TO HELPING THEM."
"HE WANTED TO GIVE BACK TO HUMANITY. HIS DREAM WAS TO REDUCE SUFFERING FOR ALL. HE DID IT TO UNTOLD BILLIONS."
"STOPPING A VIRUS FROM BEING UNLEASHED, ELECTING A DIFFERENT LEADER WHO WOULDN'T TRIGGER A NUCLEAR WAR. ENCOURAGING A SHY MAN TO BE A CLIMATE CHANGE ADVOCATE..."
"...HE DID SO MUCH AND HIS LIFE WAS ONE OF SERVICE."
"AND YET ALONG THE WAY HE FOUND A PARTNER WHO GOT HIM. SOMEONE WHO UNDERSTOOD HIM AND COULD ACTUALLY MAKE HIM LAUGH."
I ALWAYS THOUGHT HE WAS GAY, BUT APPARENTLY NOT. IF ANYONE DESERVED HAPPINESS, HE DID.
THEN THE TECHNICIANS CALLED ME FOR A MEETING....

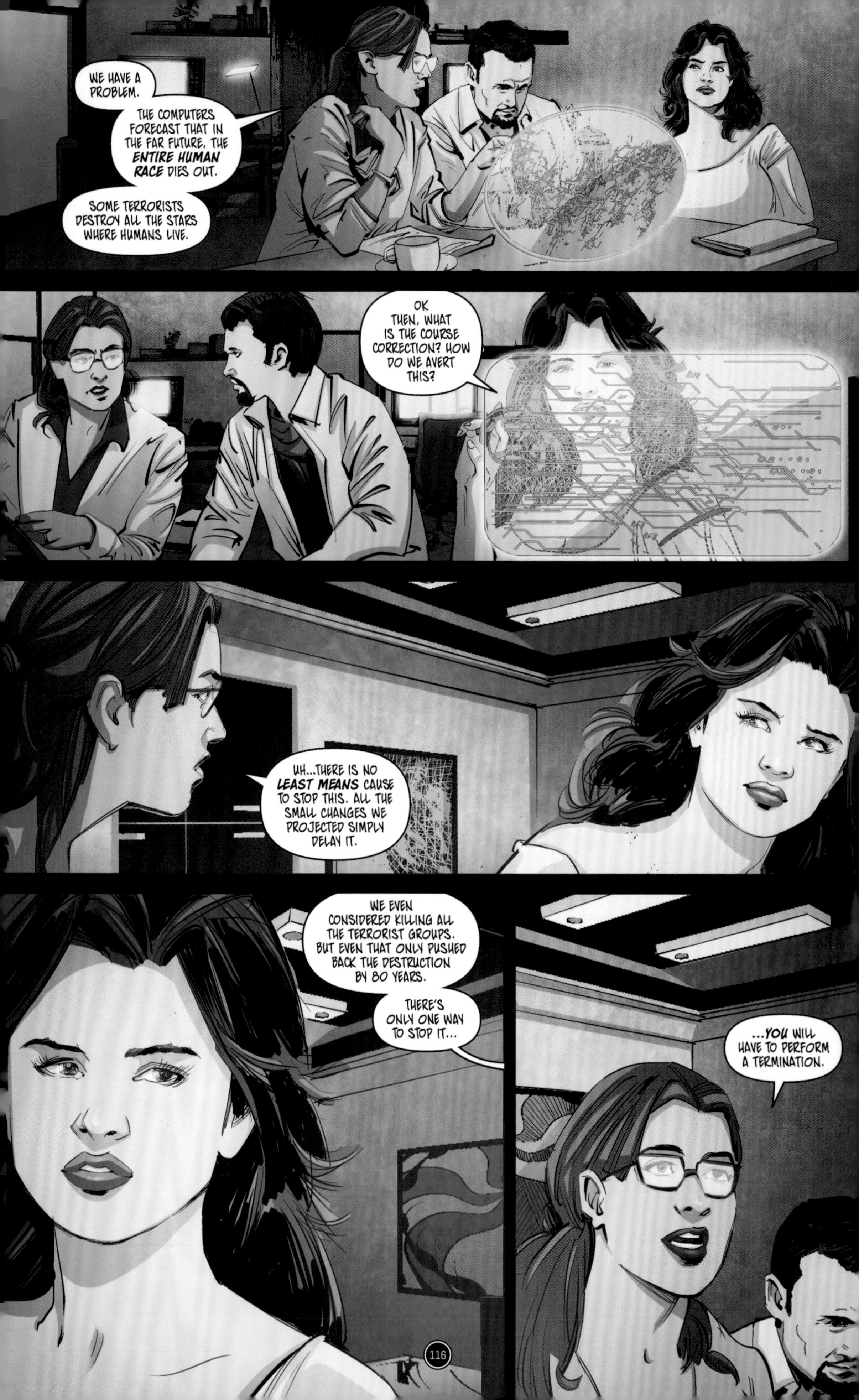
WE HAVE A PROBLEM.
THE COMPUTERS FORECAST THAT IN THE FAR FUTURE, THE ENTIRE HUMAN RACE DIES OUT.
SOME TERRORISTS DESTROY ALL THE STARS WHERE HUMANS LIVE.
OK THEN, WHAT IS THE COURSE CORRECTION? HOW DO WE AVERT THIS?
UH...THERE IS NO LEAST MEANS CAUSE TO STOP THIS. ALL THE SMALL CHANGES WE PROJECTED SIMPLY DELAY IT.
WE EVEN CONSIDERED KILLING ALL THE TERRORIST GROUPS. BUT EVEN THAT ONLY PUSHED BACK THE DESTRUCTION BY 80 YEARS.
THERE'S ONLY ONE WAY TO STOP IT...
...YOU WILL HAVE TO PERFORM A TERMINATION.

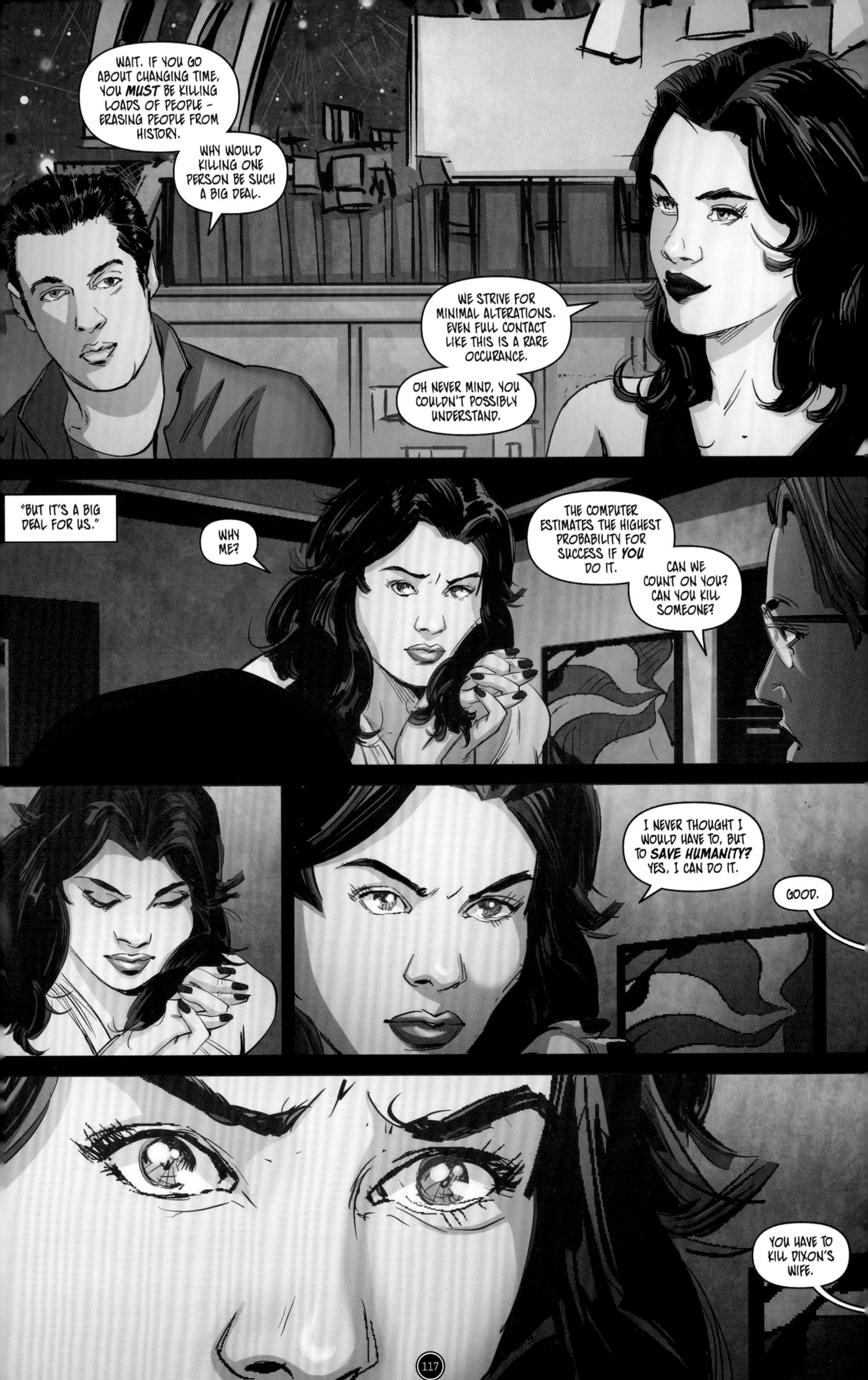
WAIT. IF YOU GO ABOUT CHANGING TIME, YOU MUST BE KILLING LOADS OF PEOPLE - ERASING PEOPLE FROM HISTORY.
WHY WOULD KILLING ONE PERSON BE SUCH A BIG DEAL.
WE STRIVE FOR MINIMAL ALTERATIONS. EVEN FULL CONTACT LIKE THIS IS A RARE OCCURANCE.
OH NEVER MIND, YOU COULDN'T POSSIBLY UNDERSTAND.
"BUT IT'S A BIG DEAL FOR US."
WHY ME?
THE COMPUTER ESTIMATES THE HIGHEST PROBABILITY FOR SUCCESS IF YOU DO IT.
CAN WE COUNT ON YOU? CAN YOU KILL SOMEONE?
I NEVER THOUGHT I WOULD HAVE TO, BUT TO SAVE HUMANITY? YES, I CAN DO IT.
GOOD.
YOU HAVE TO KILL DIXON'S WIFE.

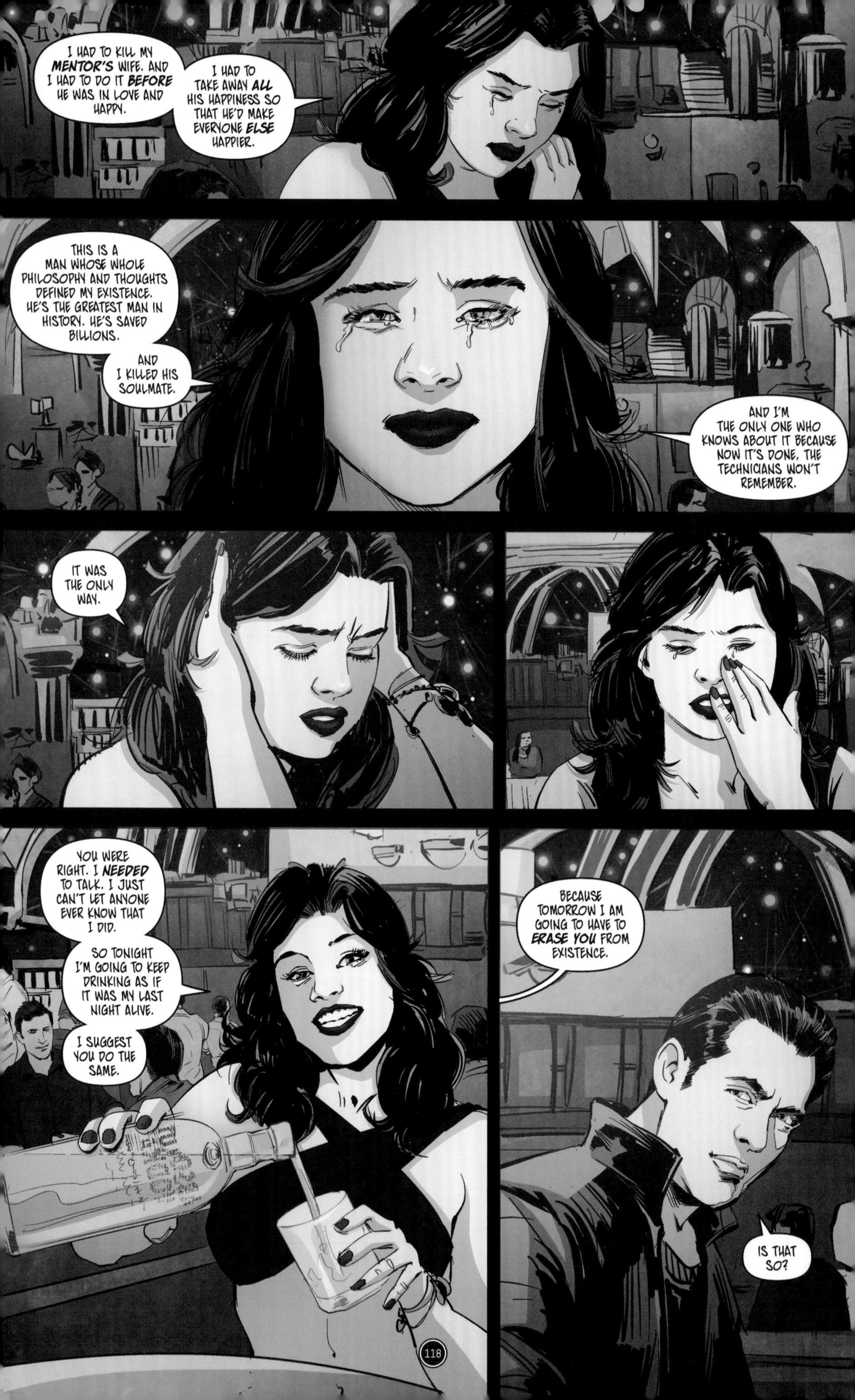
I HAD TO KILL MY MENTOR'S WIFE. AND I HAD TO DO IT BEFORE HE WAS IN LOVE AND HAPPY.
I HAD TO TAKE AWAY ALL HIS HAPPINESS SO THAT HE'D MAKE EVERYONE ELSE HAPPIER.
THIS IS A MAN WHOSE WHOLE PHILOSOPHY AND THOUGHTS DEFINED MY EXISTENCE. HE'S THE GREATEST MAN IN HISTORY. HE'S SAVED BILLIONS.
AND I KILLED HIS SOULMATE.
AND I'M THE ONLY ONE WHO KNOWS ABOUT IT BECAUSE NOW IT'S DONE, THE TECHNICIANS WON'T REMEMBER.
IT WAS THE ONLY WAY.
YOU WERE RIGHT. I NEEDED TO TALK. I JUST CAN'T LET ANYONE EVER KNOW THAT I DID.
SO TONIGHT I'M GOING TO KEEP DRINKING AS IF IT WAS MY LAST NIGHT ALIVE.
I SUGGEST YOU DO THE SAME.
BECAUSE TOMORROW I AM GOING TO HAVE TO ERASE YOU FROM EXISTENCE.
IS THAT SO?

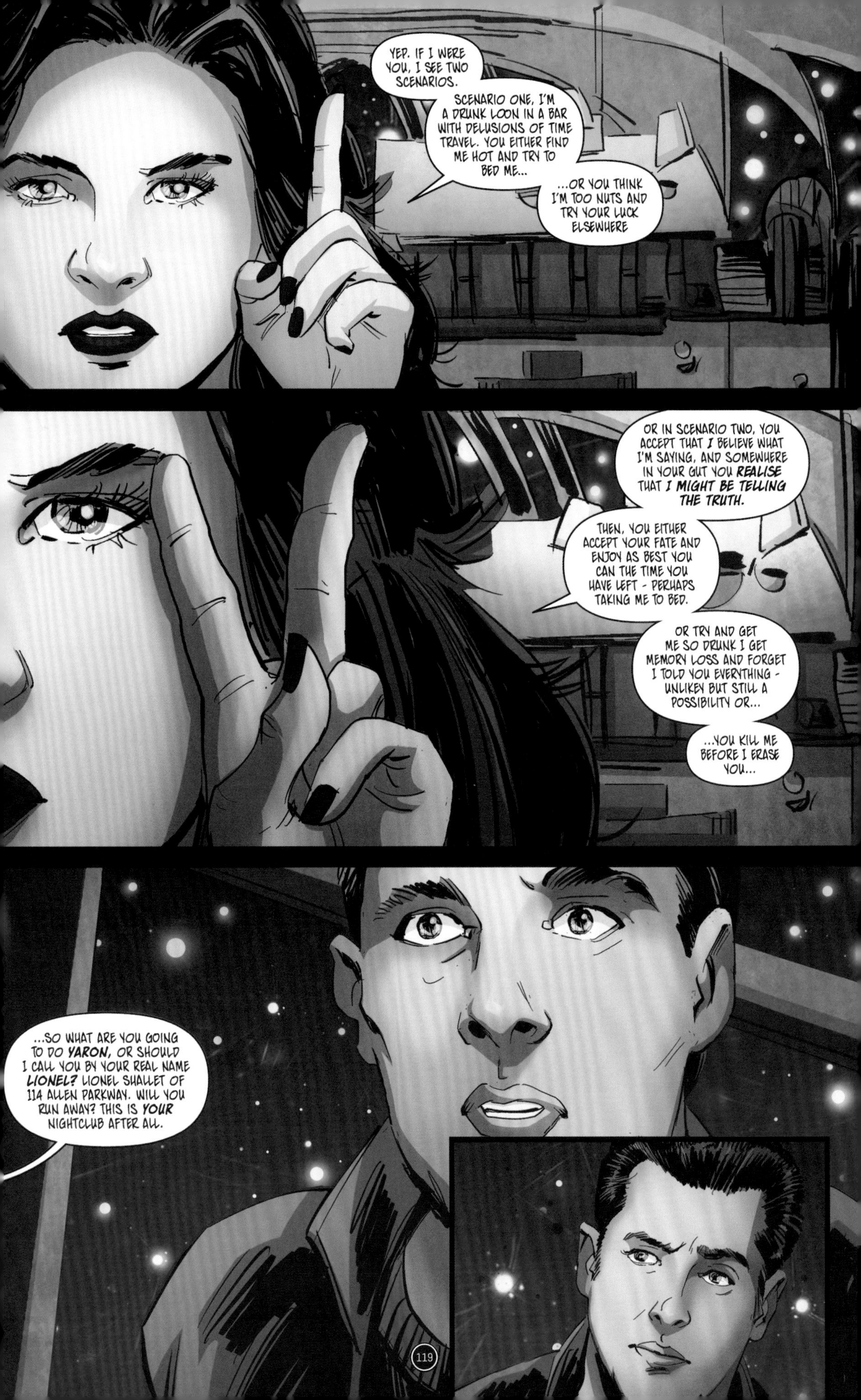

YEP. IF I WERE YOU, I SEE TWO SCENARIOS.
SCENARIO ONE, I'M A DRUNK LOON IN A BAR WITH DELUSIONS OF TIME TRAVEL. YOU EITHER FIND ME HOT AND TRY TO BED ME...
...OR YOU THINK I'M TOO NUTS AND TRY YOUR LUCK ELSEWHERE
OR IN SCENARIO TWO, YOU ACCEPT THAT I BELIEVE WHAT I'M SAYING, AND SOMEWHERE IN YOUR GUT YOU REALISE THAT I MIGHT BE TELLING THE TRUTH.
THEN, YOU EITHER ACCEPT YOUR FATE AND ENJOY AS BEST YOU CAN THE TIME YOU HAVE LEFT - PERHAPS TAKING ME TO BED.
OR TRY AND GET ME SO DRUNK I GET MEMORY LOSS AND FORGET I TOLD YOU EVERYTHING - UNLIKEY BUT STILL A POSSIBILITY OR...
...YOU KILL ME BEFORE I ERASE YOU...
...SO WHAT ARE YOU GOING TO DO YARON, OR SHOULD I CALL YOU BY YOUR REAL NAME LIONEL? LIONEL SHALLET OF 114 ALLEN PARKWAY. WILL YOU RUN AWAY? THIS IS YOUR NIGHTCLUB AFTER ALL.

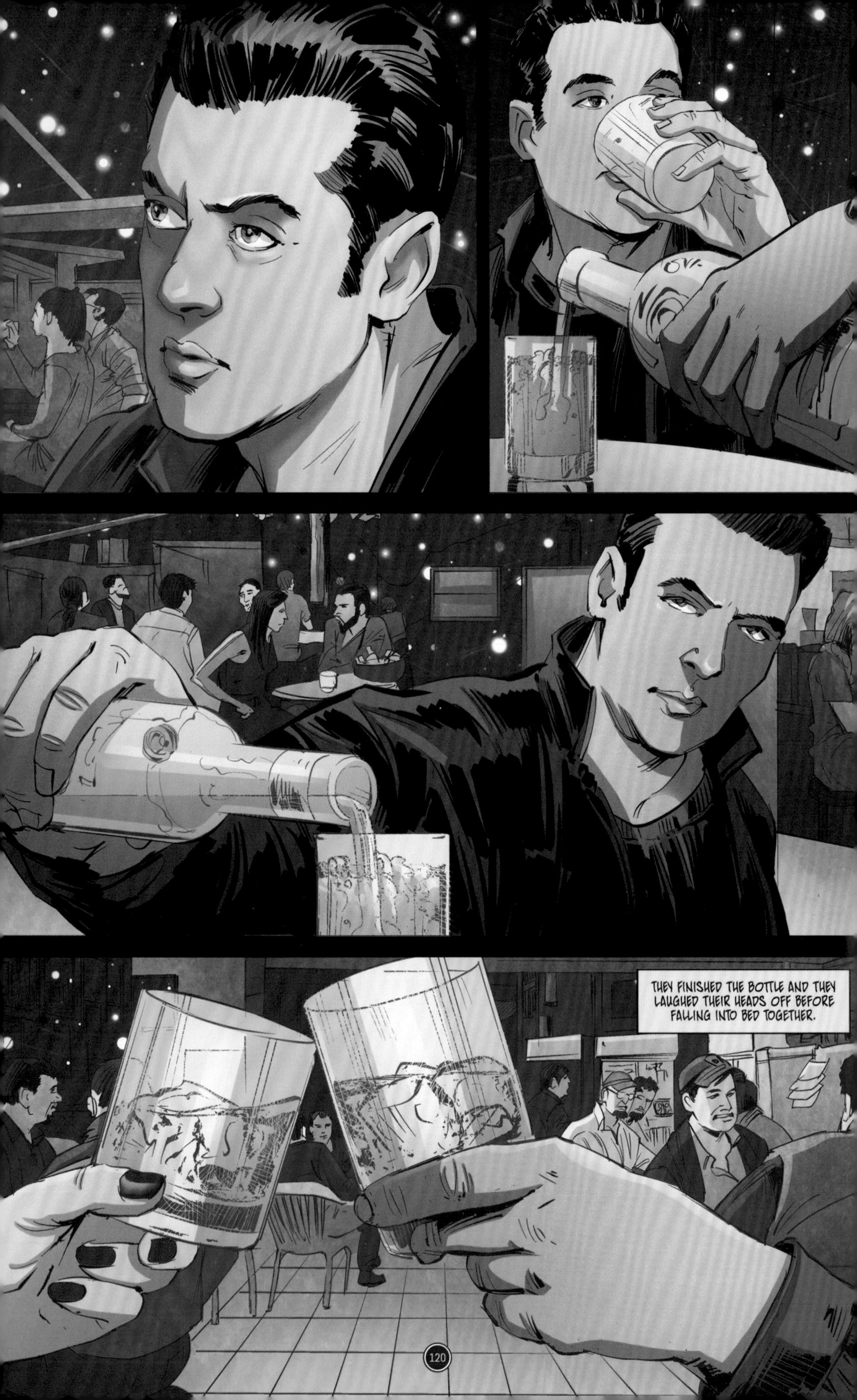
THEY FINISHED THE BOTTLE AND THEY LAUGHED THEIR HEADS OFF BEFORE FALLING INTO BED TOGETHER.

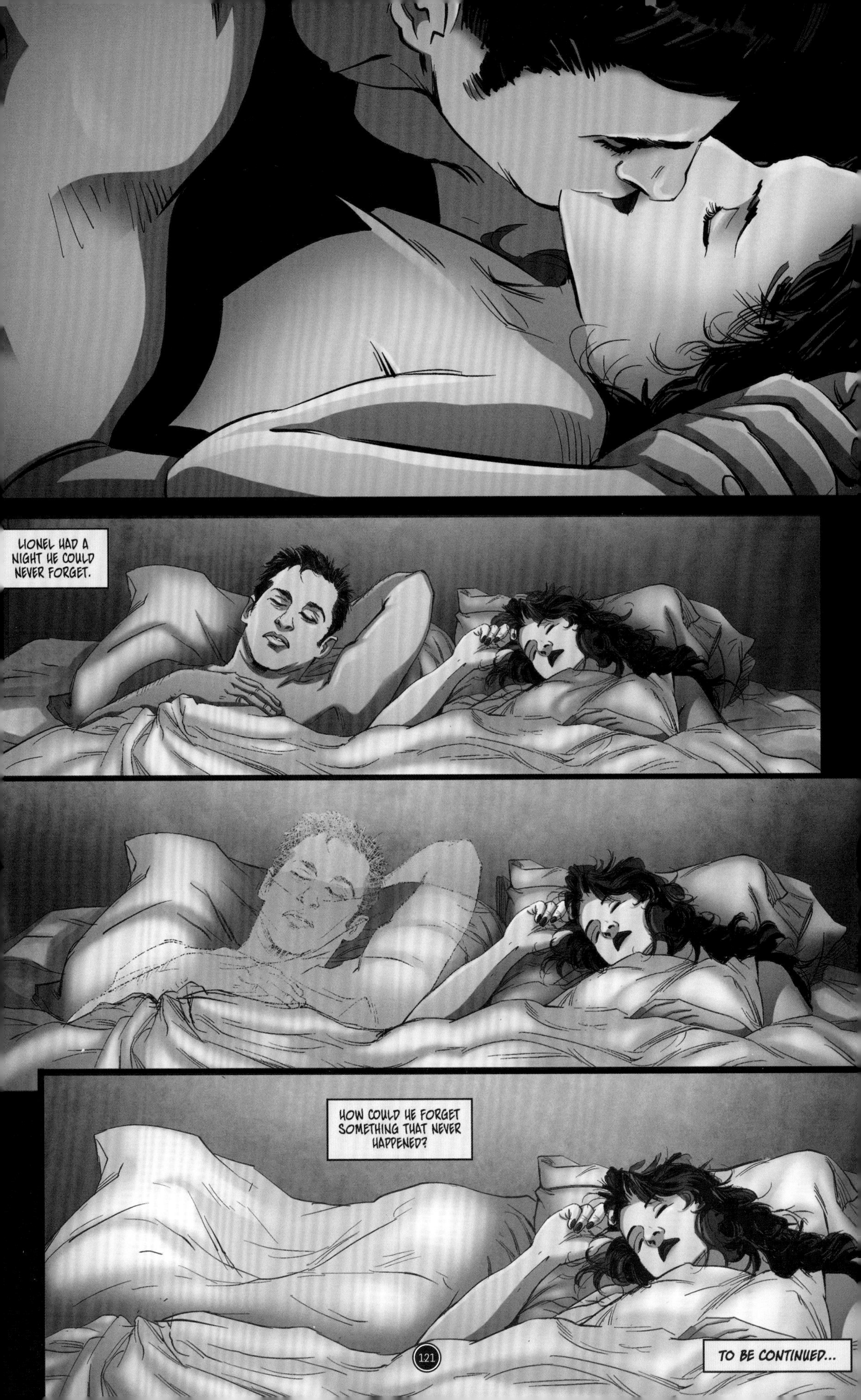
LIONEL HAD A NIGHT HE COULD NEVER FORGET.
HOW COULD HE FORGET SOMETHING THAT NEVER HAPPENED?
TO BE CONTINUED...

ADMIRAL PUPPO

I've been reading some astroarchaeology reports. One suggests to me that an alien species might have time travel technology.

ROBERT SADLER

But it's simply not possible.

ADMIRAL PUPPO

They said that about faster than light travel. Tell me what people currently think about it.

ROBERT SADLER

As you instructed I did some research and the 'current' favoured ideas as to how it would conceivably function would be that any change in the timeline would lead to a divergent path. The time traveller when returning to the present would not be returning to their own world, but a parallel one with all the changes due to their action propagated forwards. They would never be able to return and no one but the traveller themselves would know what happened. But as I said this is all impossible.

ADMIRAL PUPPO

Now assume that it were conceivable where would you start to look for a mechanism to make it happen?

ROBERT SADLER

The stellar gate system enables rapid transport through a fourth spatial dimension. I guess as that would be a starting point and conceivably even if we prove what we already know about time travel, perhaps the research will lead to other spatial dimensions, enabling us to travel further with a single jump. But honestly sir I do not believe it the best use of resources to spend any more time on this. Time travel is the realm of science fiction.

ADMIRAL PUPPO

Curiosity drives research. It's not about reaching the intended destination; it's about the unintended consequences. Assign a contubernium to research this.

Quarantine

"A lie cannot live."

Martin Luther King Jr.

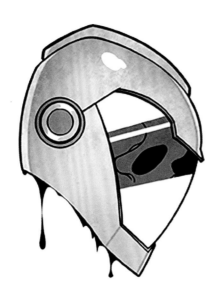

Writer/Creator
Neil Gibson

Illustrator
Amrit Birdi

Colourist
Liezl Buenaventura

Letters by
Justin Birch

www.tpubcomics.com

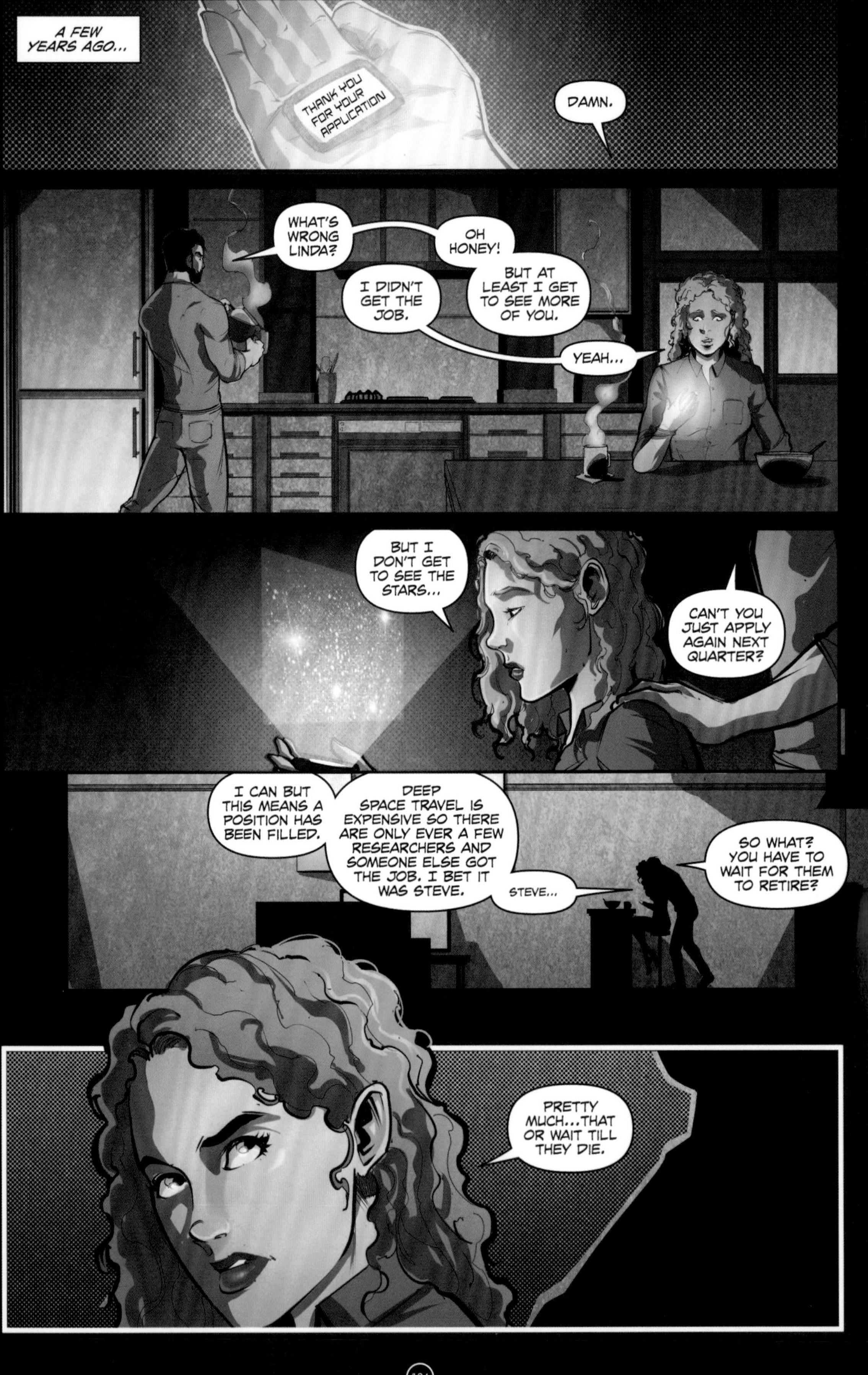
A FEW YEARS AGO...
THANK YOU FOR YOUR APPLICATION
DAMN.
WHAT'S WRONG LINDA?
I DIDN'T GET THE JOB.
OH HONEY!
BUT AT LEAST I GET TO SEE MORE OF YOU.
YEAH...
BUT I DON'T GET TO SEE THE STARS...
CAN'T YOU JUST APPLY AGAIN NEXT QUARTER?
I CAN BUT THIS MEANS A POSITION HAS BEEN FILLED.
DEEP SPACE TRAVEL IS EXPENSIVE SO THERE ARE ONLY EVER A FEW RESEARCHERS AND SOMEONE ELSE GOT THE JOB. I BET IT WAS STEVE.
STEVE...
SO WHAT? YOU HAVE TO WAIT FOR THEM TO RETIRE?
PRETTY MUCH...THAT OR WAIT TILL THEY DIE.

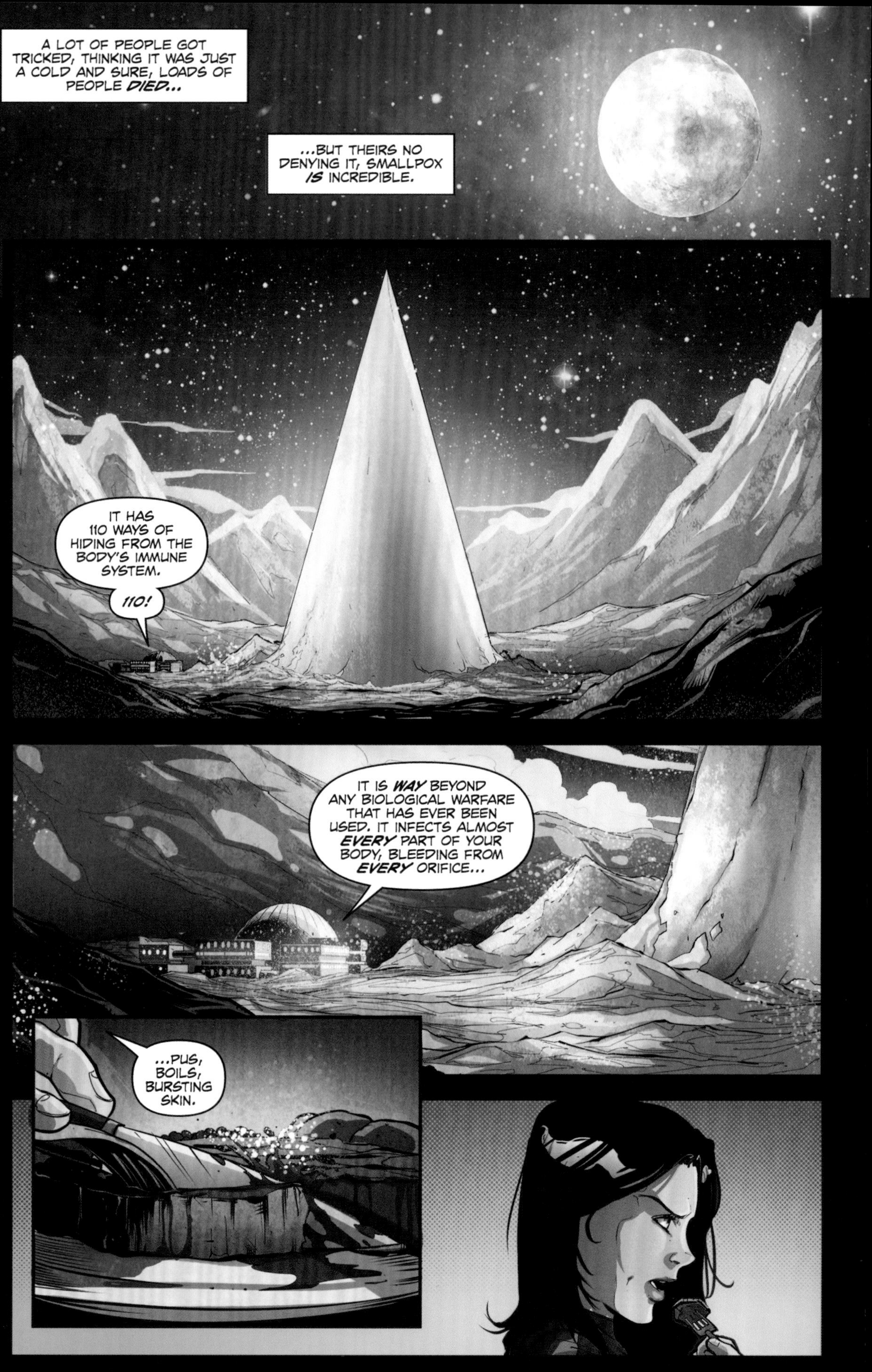
A LOT OF PEOPLE GOT TRICKED, THINKING IT WAS JUST A COLD AND SURE, LOADS OF PEOPLE DIED...
...BUT THEIRS NO DENYING IT, SMALLPOX IS INCREDIBLE.
IT HAS 110 WAYS OF HIDING FROM THE BODY'S IMMUNE SYSTEM.
110!
IT IS WAY BEYOND ANY BIOLOGICAL WARFARE THAT HAS EVER BEEN USED. IT INFECTS ALMOST EVERY PART OF YOUR BODY, BLEEDING FROM EVERY ORIFICE...
...PUS, BOILS, BURSTING SKIN.

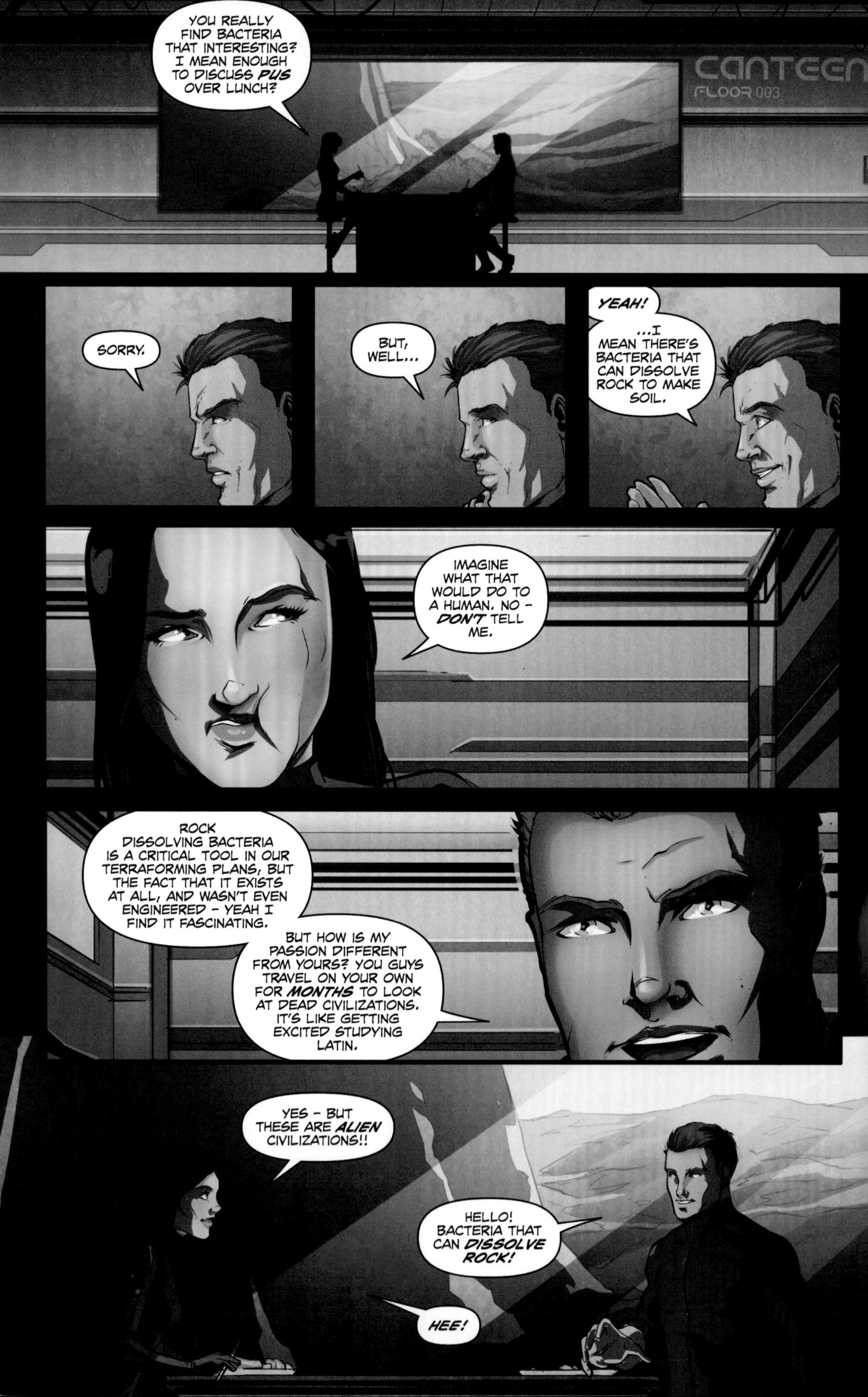
CANTEEN
FLOOR 003
YOU REALLY FIND BACTERIA THAT INTERESTING? I MEAN ENOUGH TO DISCUSS PUS OVER LUNCH?
SORRY.
BUT, WELL...
YEAH!
...I MEAN THERE'S BACTERIA THAT CAN DISSOLVE ROCK TO MAKE SOIL.
IMAGINE WHAT THAT WOULD DO TO A HUMAN. NO - DON'T TELL ME.
ROCK DISSOLVING BACTERIA IS A CRITICAL TOOL IN OUR TERRAFORMING PLANS, BUT THE FACT THAT IT EXISTS AT ALL, AND WASN'T EVEN ENGINEERED - YEAH I FIND IT FASCINATING.
BUT HOW IS MY PASSION DIFFERENT FROM YOURS? YOU GUYS TRAVEL ON YOUR OWN FOR MONTHS TO LOOK AT DEAD CIVILIZATIONS. IT'S LIKE GETTING EXCITED STUDYING LATIN.
YES - BUT THESE ARE ALIEN CIVILIZATIONS!!
HELLO! BACTERIA THAT CAN DISSOLVE ROCK!
HEE!

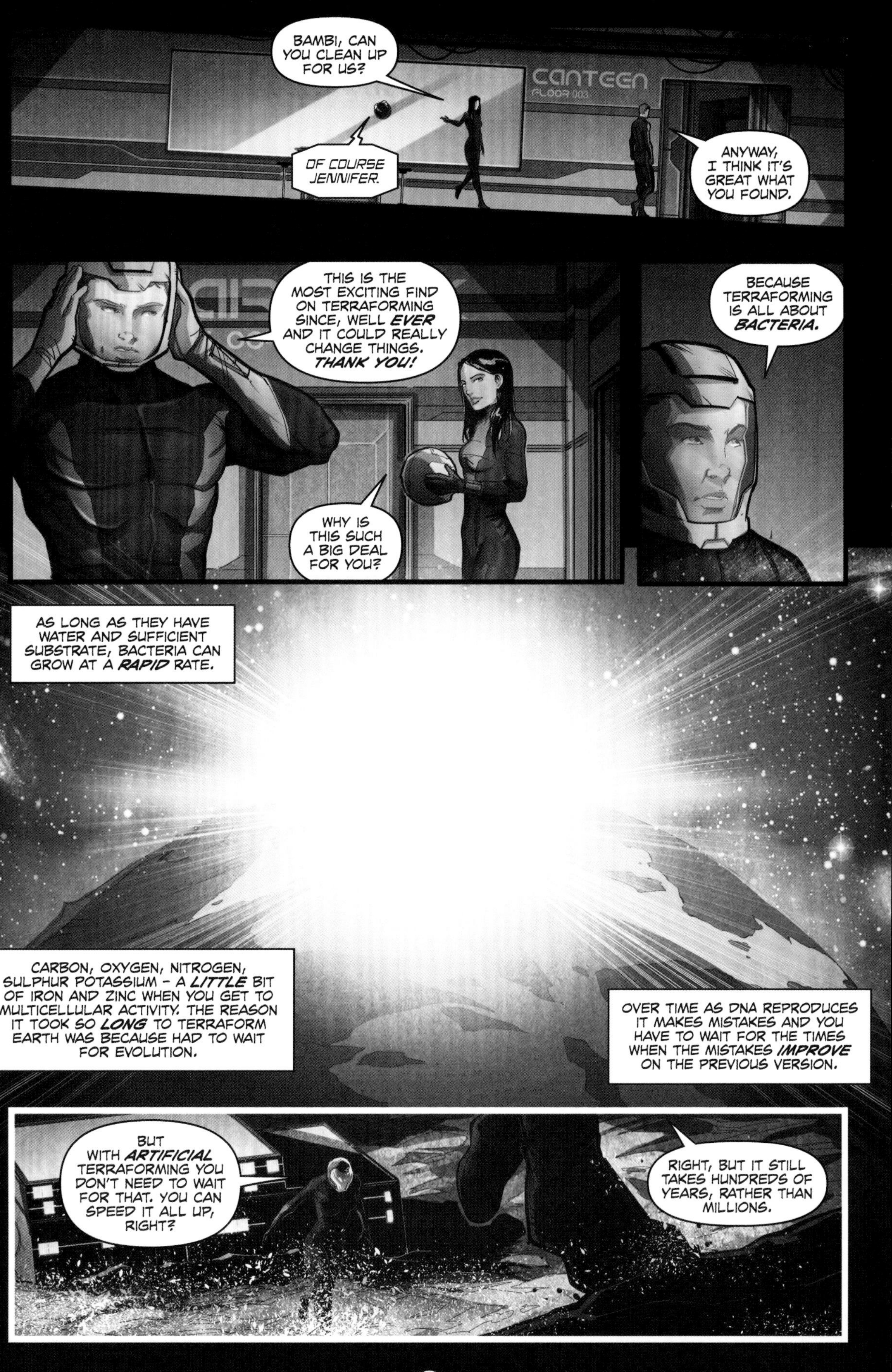
CANTEEN
FLOOR 003
BAMBI, CAN YOU CLEAN UP FOR US?
OF COURSE JENNIFER.
ANYWAY, I THINK IT'S GREAT WHAT YOU FOUND.
THIS IS THE MOST EXCITING FIND ON TERRAFORMING SINCE, WELL ***EVER*** AND IT COULD REALLY CHANGE THINGS. ***THANK YOU!***
WHY IS THIS SUCH A BIG DEAL FOR YOU?
BECAUSE TERRAFORMING IS ALL ABOUT ***BACTERIA.***
AS LONG AS THEY HAVE WATER AND SUFFICIENT SUBSTRATE, BACTERIA CAN GROW AT A ***RAPID*** RATE.
CARBON, OXYGEN, NITROGEN, SULPHUR POTASSIUM – A ***LITTLE*** BIT OF IRON AND ZINC WHEN YOU GET TO MULTICELLULAR ACTIVITY. THE REASON IT TOOK SO ***LONG*** TO TERRAFORM EARTH WAS BECAUSE HAD TO WAIT FOR EVOLUTION.
OVER TIME AS DNA REPRODUCES IT MAKES MISTAKES AND YOU HAVE TO WAIT FOR THE TIMES WHEN THE MISTAKES ***IMPROVE*** ON THE PREVIOUS VERSION.
BUT WITH ***ARTIFICIAL*** TERRAFORMING YOU DON'T NEED TO WAIT FOR THAT. YOU CAN SPEED IT ALL UP, RIGHT?
RIGHT, BUT IT STILL TAKES HUNDREDS OF YEARS, RATHER THAN MILLIONS.

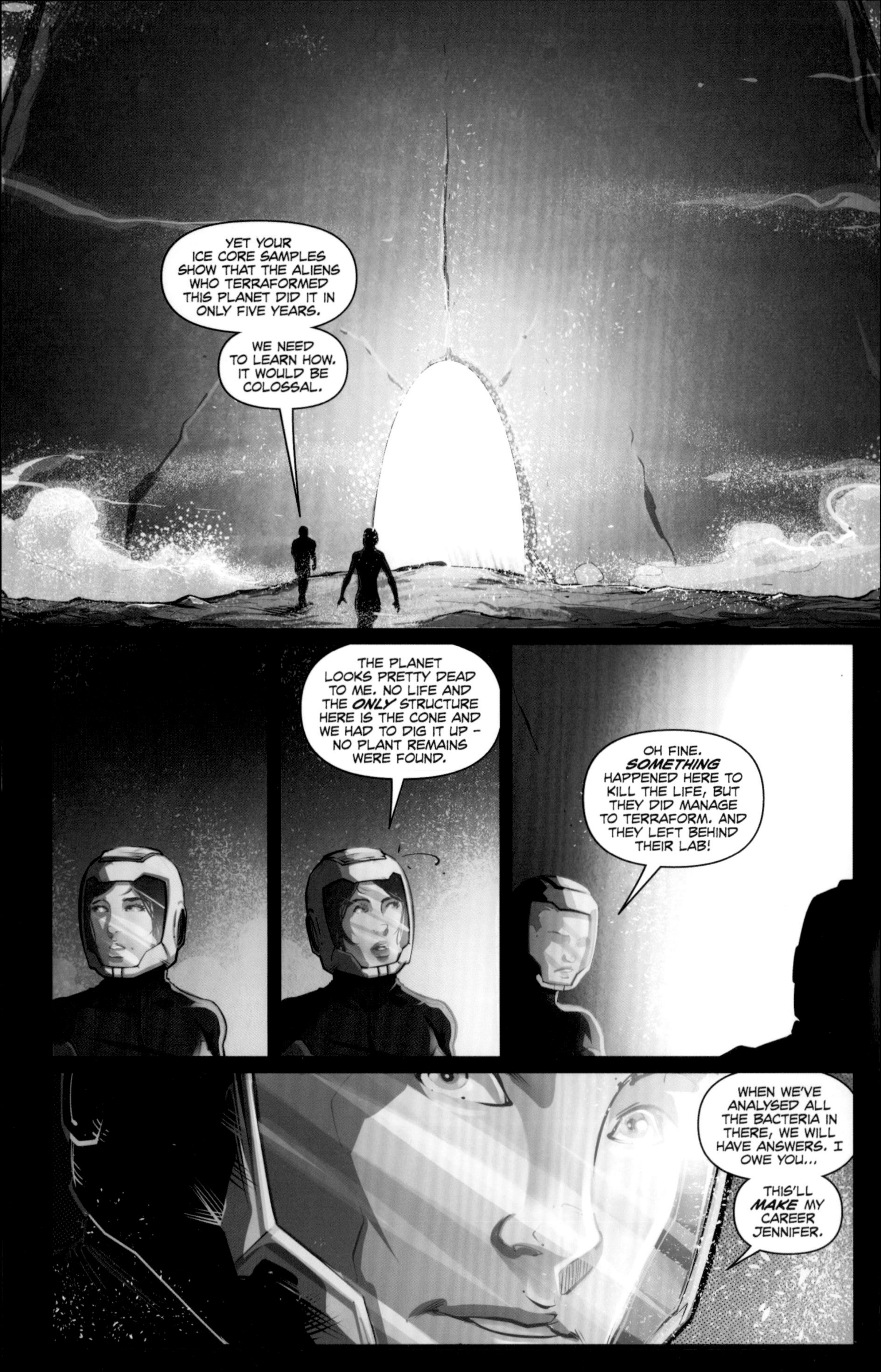
YET YOUR ICE CORE SAMPLES SHOW THAT THE ALIENS WHO TERRAFORMED THIS PLANET DID IT IN ONLY FIVE YEARS.
WE NEED TO LEARN HOW. IT WOULD BE COLOSSAL.
THE PLANET LOOKS PRETTY DEAD TO ME. NO LIFE AND THE *ONLY* STRUCTURE HERE IS THE CONE AND WE HAD TO DIG IT UP - NO PLANT REMAINS WERE FOUND.
OH FINE. ***SOMETHING*** HAPPENED HERE TO KILL THE LIFE, BUT THEY DID MANAGE TO TERRAFORM. AND THEY LEFT BEHIND THEIR LAB!
WHEN WE'VE ANALYSED ALL THE BACTERIA IN THERE, WE WILL HAVE ANSWERS. I OWE YOU...
THIS'LL ***MAKE*** MY CAREER JENNIFER.

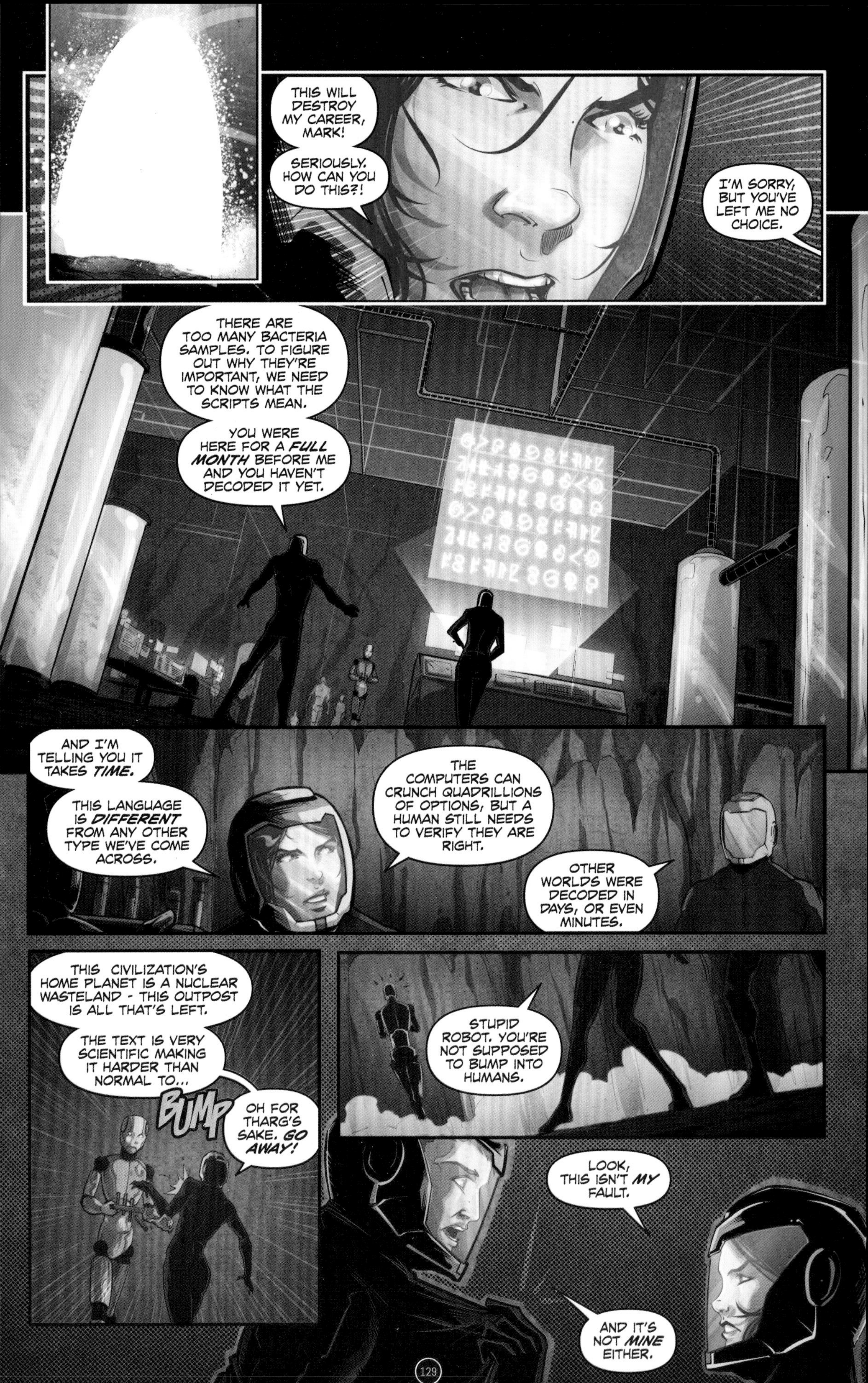
THIS WILL DESTROY MY CAREER, MARK!
SERIOUSLY. HOW CAN YOU DO THIS?!
I'M SORRY, BUT YOU'VE LEFT ME NO CHOICE.
THERE ARE TOO MANY BACTERIA SAMPLES. TO FIGURE OUT WHY THEY'RE IMPORTANT, WE NEED TO KNOW WHAT THE SCRIPTS MEAN.
YOU WERE HERE FOR A *FULL MONTH* BEFORE ME AND YOU HAVEN'T DECODED IT YET.
AND I'M TELLING YOU IT TAKES *TIME.*
THIS LANGUAGE IS *DIFFERENT* FROM ANY OTHER TYPE WE'VE COME ACROSS.
THE COMPUTERS CAN CRUNCH QUADRILLIONS OF OPTIONS, BUT A HUMAN STILL NEEDS TO VERIFY THEY ARE RIGHT.
OTHER WORLDS WERE DECODED IN DAYS, OR EVEN MINUTES.
THIS CIVILIZATION'S HOME PLANET IS A NUCLEAR WASTELAND - THIS OUTPOST IS ALL THAT'S LEFT.
THE TEXT IS VERY SCIENTIFIC MAKING IT HARDER THAN NORMAL TO...
BUMP
OH FOR THARG'S SAKE. *GO AWAY!*
STUPID ROBOT. YOU'RE NOT SUPPOSED TO BUMP INTO HUMANS.
LOOK, THIS ISN'T *MY* FAULT.
AND IT'S NOT *MINE* EITHER.

THREE WEEKS SHOULD BE ENOUGH. I'LL DECODE IT THEN.

THE MILITARY WILL NOT GIVE YOU THREE WEEKS. ADMIRAL PUPPO HIMSELF GAVE THE ORDER.

TERRAFORMING IS TOO CRITICAL TO LOSE TIME ON IT. THE NEW TRANSLATORS ARRIVE IN A WEEK. IF IT IS NOT TRANSLATED BY THEN, THEY TAKE OVER.

THAT'LL TAKE AWAY MY CREDIT AND ALL MY LEGITIMACY. I DISCOVERED THIS PLANET WAS TERRAFORMED, I SENT IN THE PROOF AND THEN BOOM! YOU TURN UP AND TAKE IT ALL AWAY FROM ME?

I MIGHT NEVER GET ANOTHER LEGACY PLANET.

AHH!

YOU OK?

YEAH...THE SUIT'S FINE. 100%.

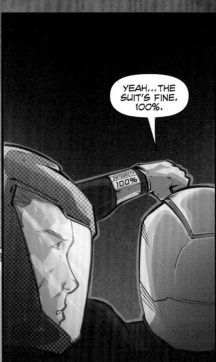

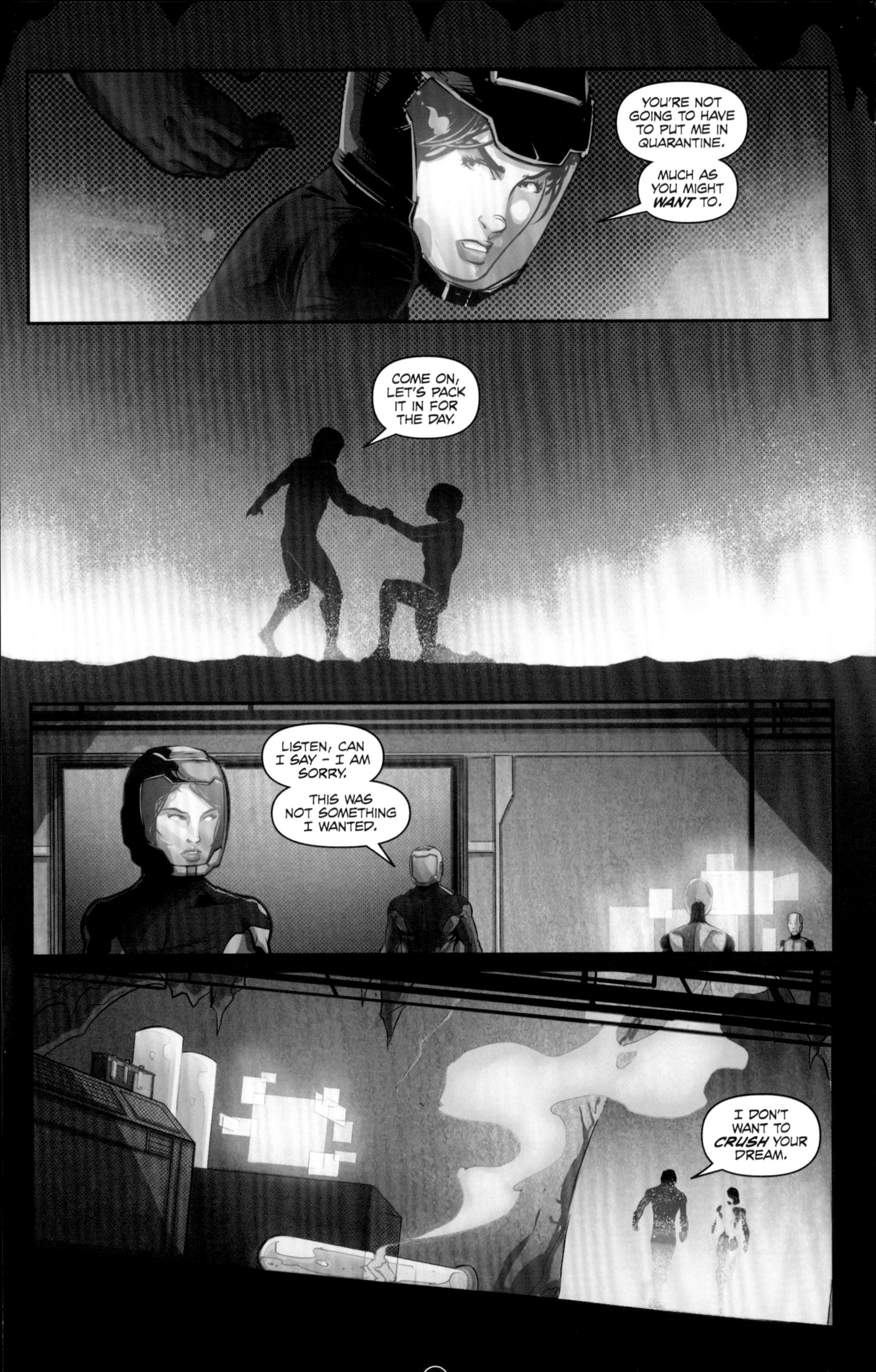
YOU'RE NOT GOING TO HAVE TO PUT ME IN QUARANTINE.
MUCH AS YOU MIGHT *WANT* TO.
COME ON, LET'S PACK IT IN FOR THE DAY.
LISTEN, CAN I SAY - I AM SORRY.
THIS WAS NOT SOMETHING I WANTED.
I DON'T WANT TO *CRUSH* YOUR DREAM.

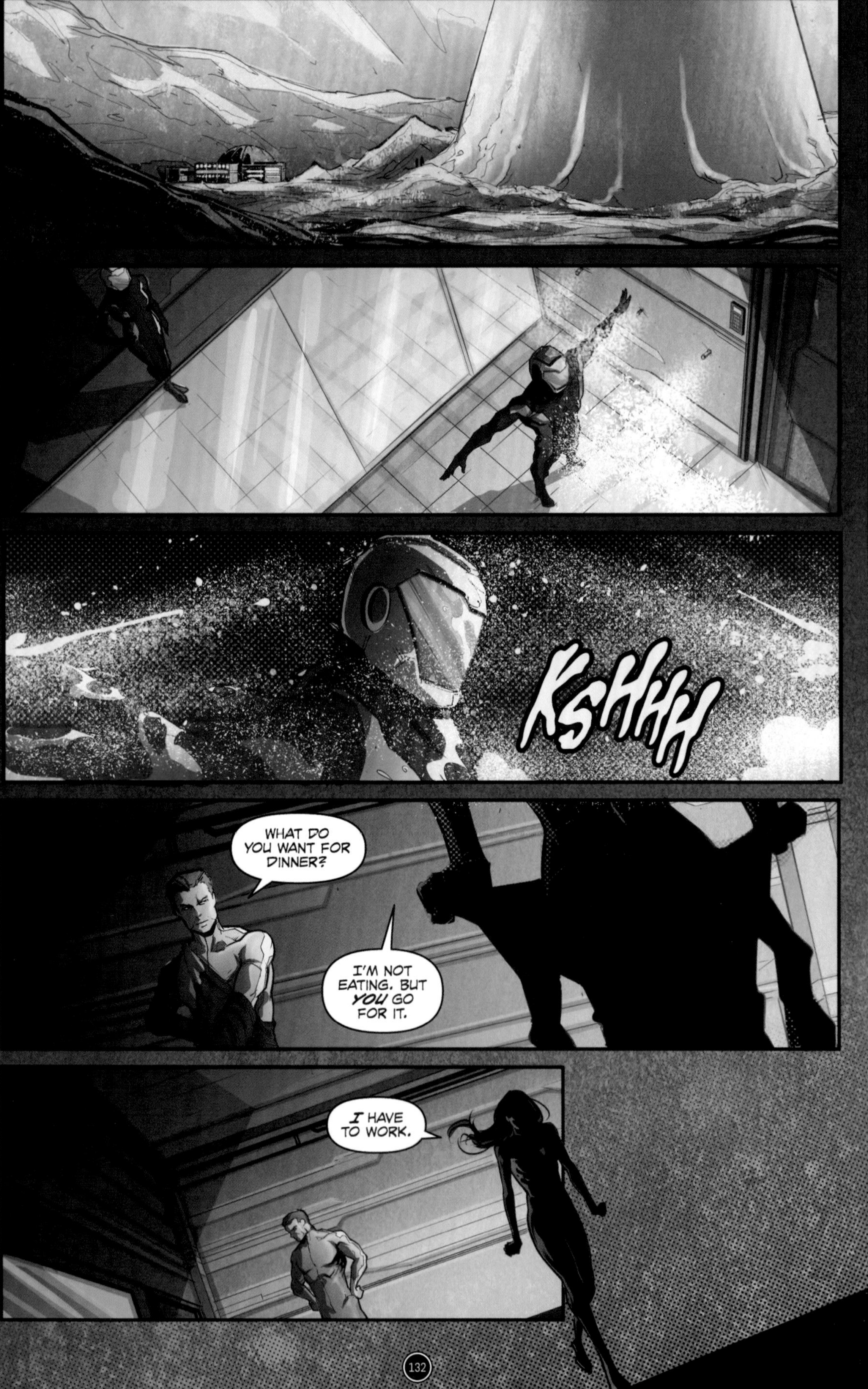
KSHHH
WHAT DO YOU WANT FOR DINNER?
I'M NOT EATING. BUT YOU GO FOR IT.
I HAVE TO WORK.

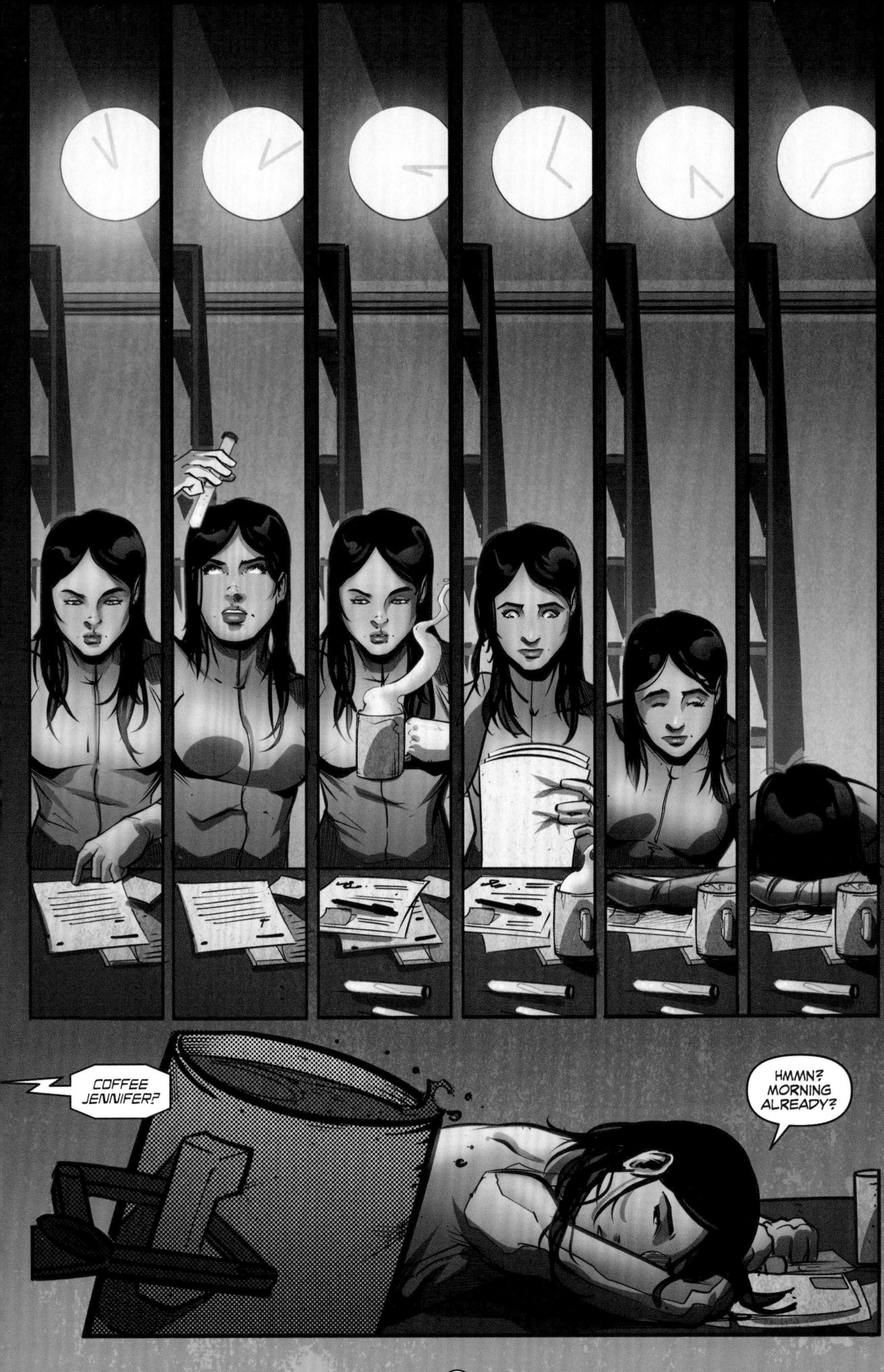
COFFEE JENNIFER?
HMMN? MORNING ALREADY?

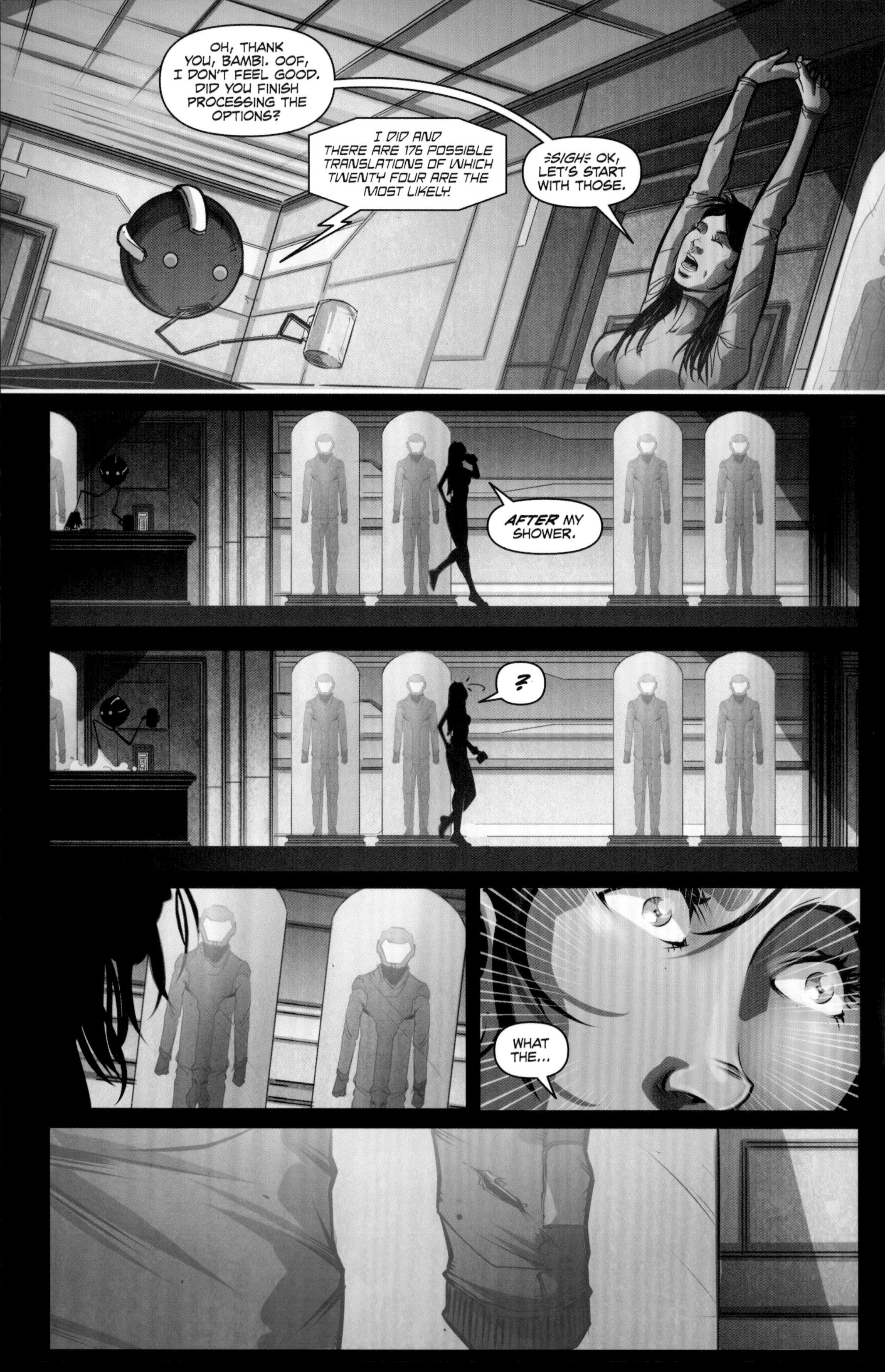

OH, THANK YOU, BAMBI. OOF, I DON'T FEEL GOOD. DID YOU FINISH PROCESSING THE OPTIONS?
I DID AND THERE ARE 176 POSSIBLE TRANSLATIONS OF WHICH TWENTY FOUR ARE THE MOST LIKELY.
SIGH OK, LET'S START WITH THOSE.
AFTER MY SHOWER.
?
WHAT THE...

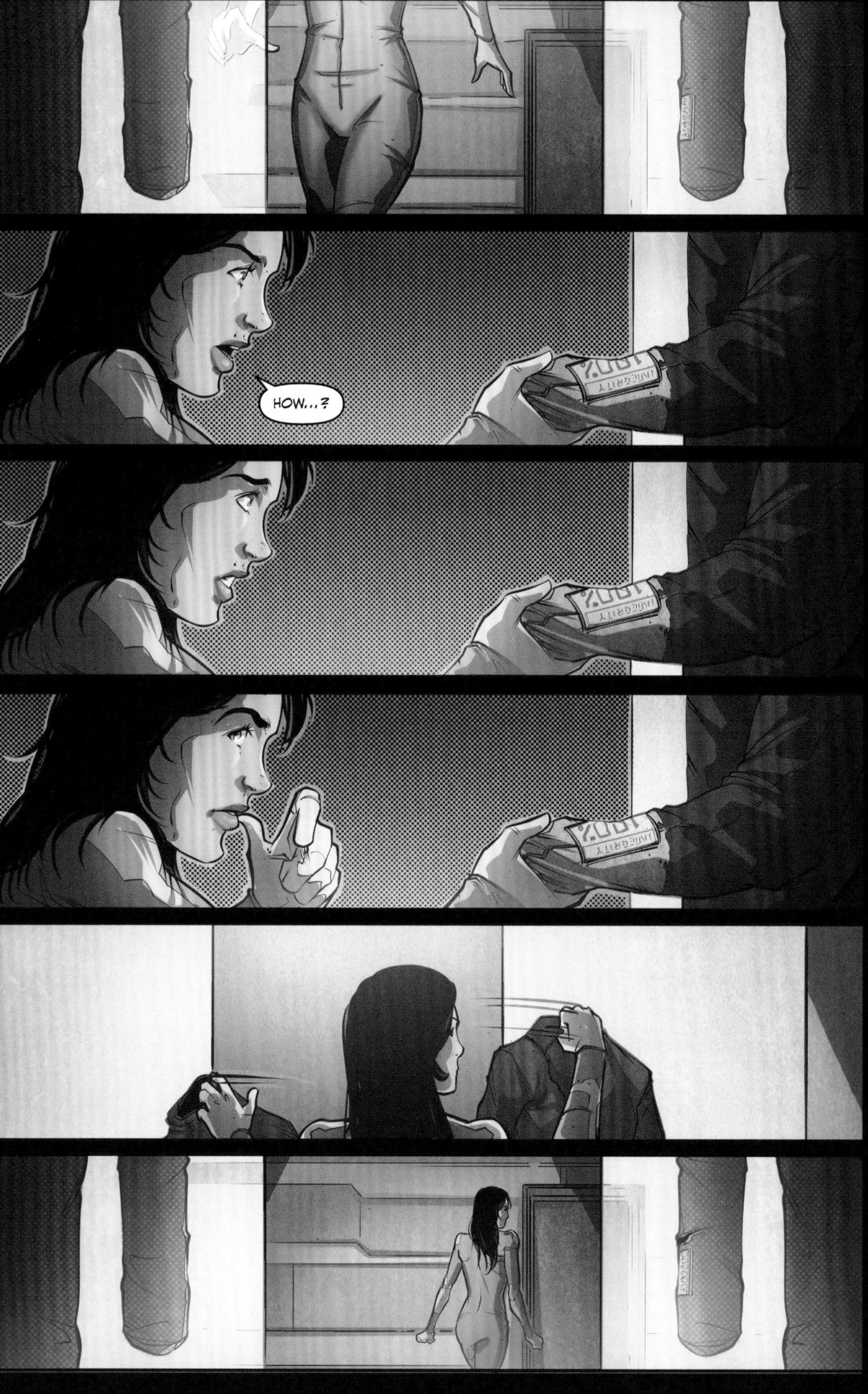
HOW...?

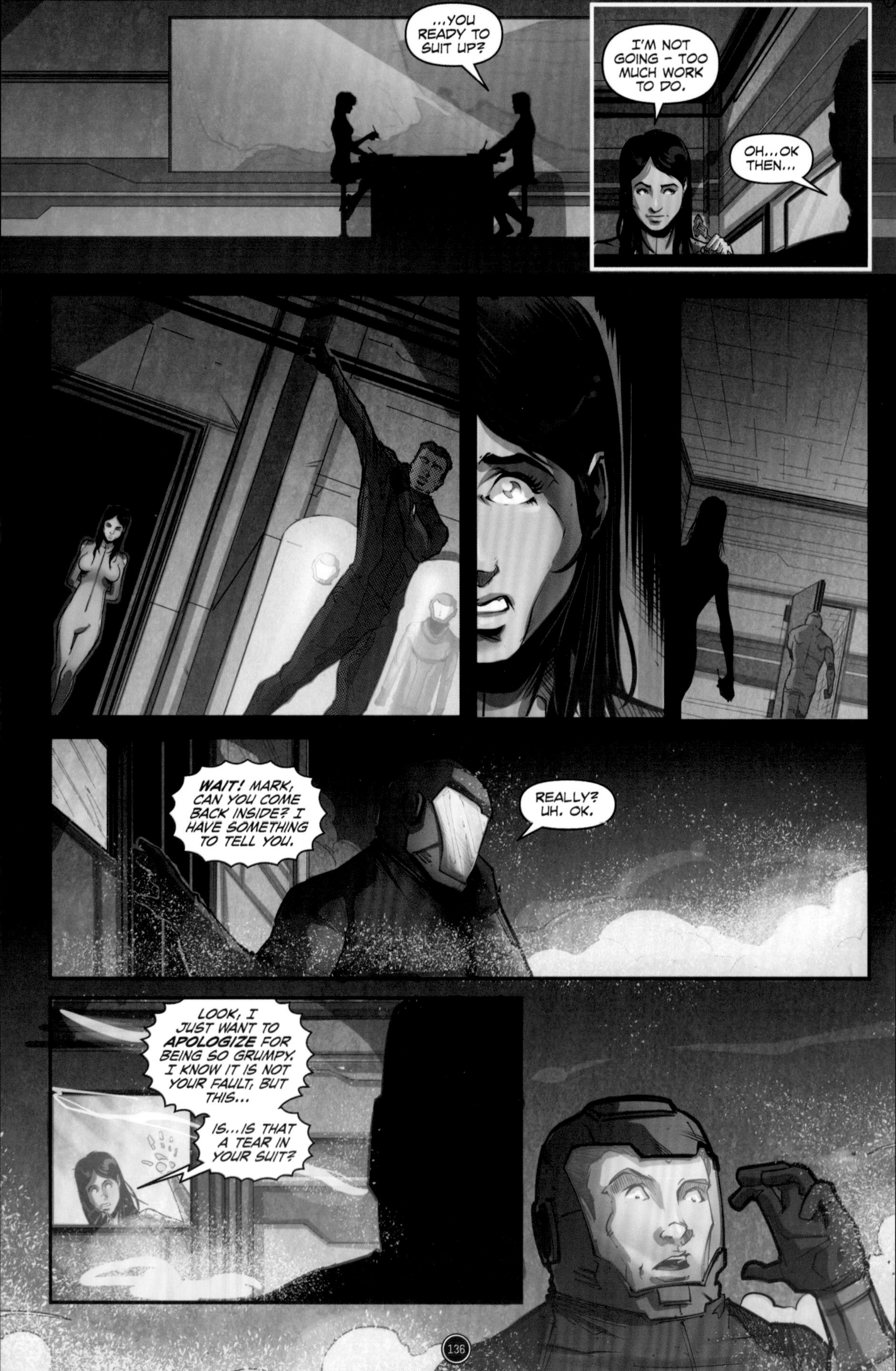
...YOU READY TO SUIT UP?
I'M NOT GOING - TOO MUCH WORK TO DO.
OH...OK THEN...
WAIT! MARK, CAN YOU COME BACK INSIDE? I HAVE SOMETHING TO TELL YOU.
REALLY? UH. OK.
LOOK, I JUST WANT TO APOLOGIZE FOR BEING SO GRUMPY. I KNOW IT IS NOT YOUR FAULT, BUT THIS...
IS...IS THAT A TEAR IN YOUR SUIT?

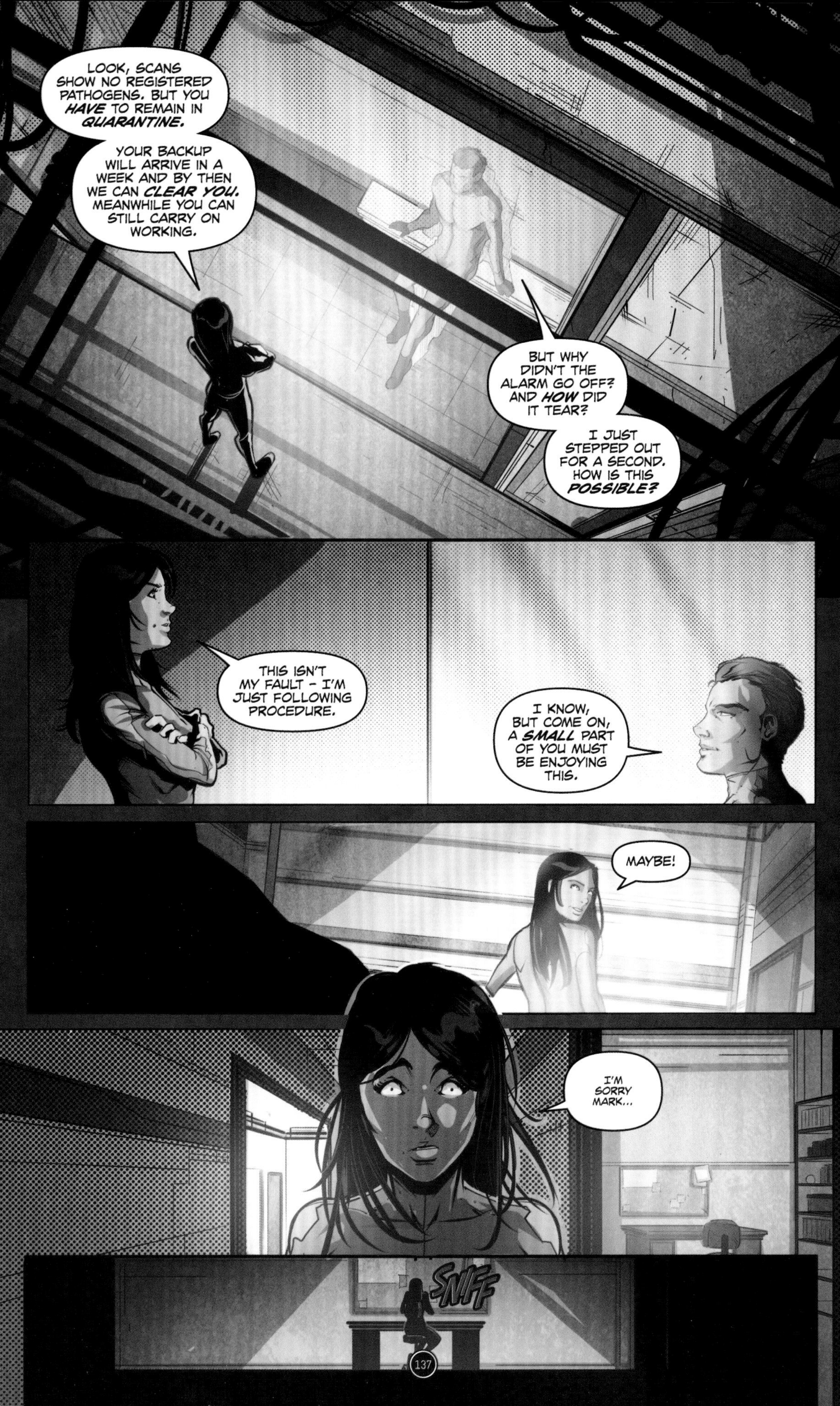
LOOK, SCANS SHOW NO REGISTERED PATHOGENS. BUT YOU HAVE TO REMAIN IN QUARANTINE.
YOUR BACKUP WILL ARRIVE IN A WEEK AND BY THEN WE CAN CLEAR YOU. MEANWHILE YOU CAN STILL CARRY ON WORKING.
BUT WHY DIDN'T THE ALARM GO OFF? AND HOW DID IT TEAR?
I JUST STEPPED OUT FOR A SECOND. HOW IS THIS POSSIBLE?
THIS ISN'T MY FAULT - I'M JUST FOLLOWING PROCEDURE.
I KNOW, BUT COME ON, A SMALL PART OF YOU MUST BE ENJOYING THIS.
MAYBE!
I'M SORRY MARK...
SNIFF

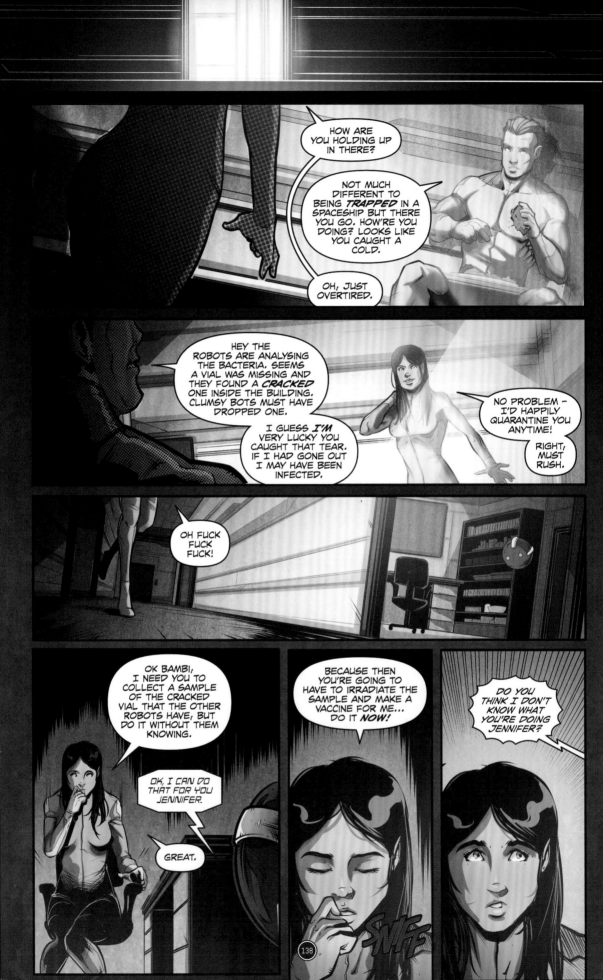

HOW ARE YOU HOLDING UP IN THERE?

NOT MUCH DIFFERENT TO BEING *TRAPPED* IN A SPACESHIP BUT THERE YOU GO. HOW'RE YOU DOING? LOOKS LIKE YOU CAUGHT A COLD.

OH, JUST OVERTIRED.

HEY THE ROBOTS ARE ANALYSING THE BACTERIA. SEEMS A VIAL WAS MISSING AND THEY FOUND A *CRACKED* ONE INSIDE THE BUILDING. CLUMSY BOTS MUST HAVE DROPPED ONE.

I GUESS *I'M* VERY LUCKY YOU CAUGHT THAT TEAR. IF I HAD GONE OUT I MAY HAVE BEEN INFECTED.

NO PROBLEM – I'D HAPPILY QUARANTINE YOU ANYTIME!

RIGHT, MUST RUSH.

OH FUCK FUCK FUCK!

OK BAMBI, I NEED YOU TO COLLECT A SAMPLE OF THE CRACKED VIAL THAT THE OTHER ROBOTS HAVE, BUT DO IT WITHOUT THEM KNOWING.

OK, I CAN DO THAT FOR YOU JENNIFER.

GREAT.

BECAUSE THEN YOU'RE GOING TO HAVE TO IRRADIATE THE SAMPLE AND MAKE A VACCINE FOR ME... DO IT *NOW!*

DO YOU THINK I DON'T KNOW WHAT YOU'RE DOING JENNIFER?

SNIFF SNIFF

138

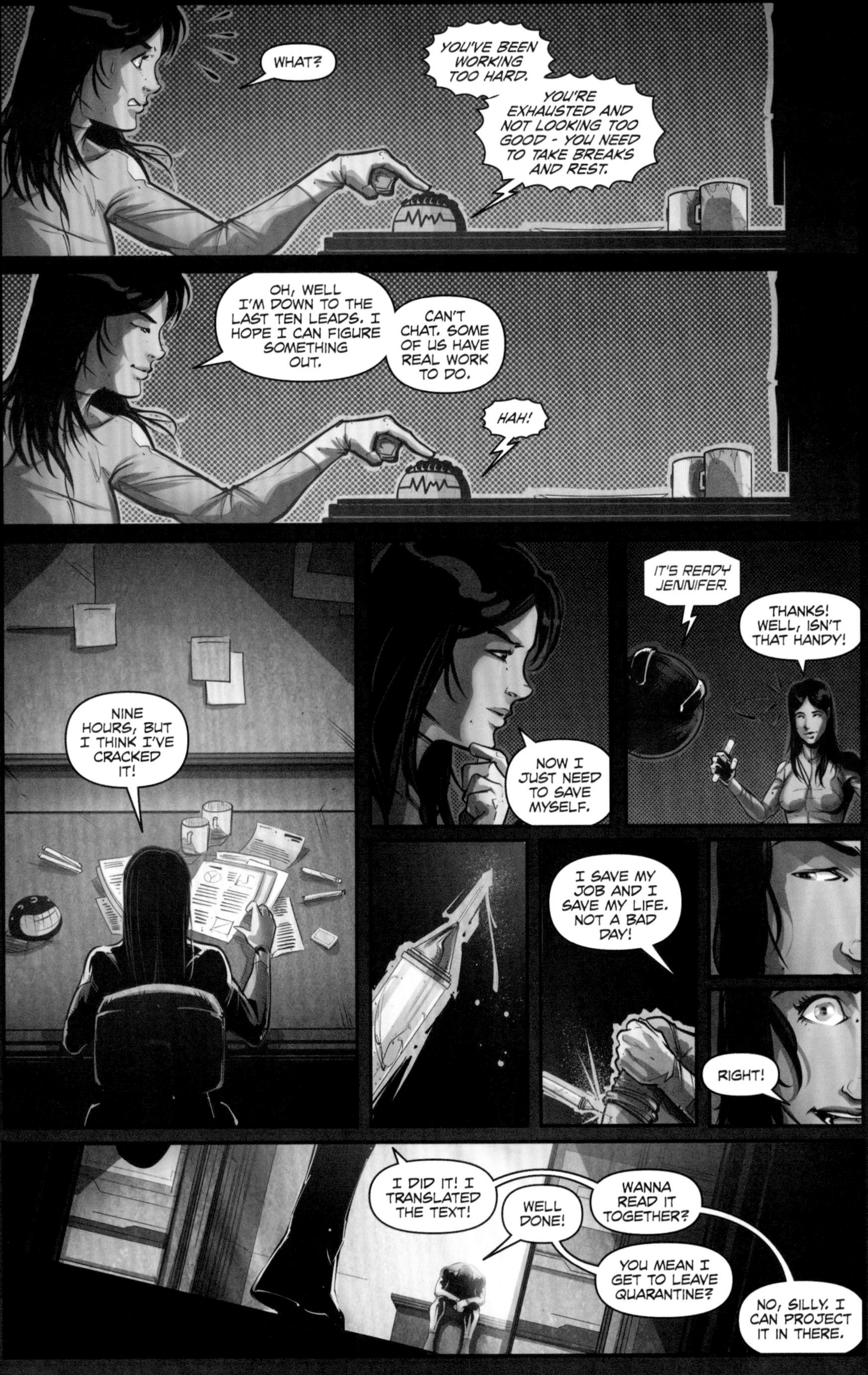

WHAT?
YOU'VE BEEN WORKING TOO HARD.
YOU'RE EXHAUSTED AND NOT LOOKING TOO GOOD - YOU NEED TO TAKE BREAKS AND REST.
OH, WELL I'M DOWN TO THE LAST TEN LEADS. I HOPE I CAN FIGURE SOMETHING OUT.
CAN'T CHAT. SOME OF US HAVE REAL WORK TO DO.
HAH!
NINE HOURS, BUT I THINK I'VE CRACKED IT!
NOW I JUST NEED TO SAVE MYSELF.
IT'S READY JENNIFER.
THANKS! WELL, ISN'T THAT HANDY!
I SAVE MY JOB AND I SAVE MY LIFE. NOT A BAD DAY!
RIGHT!
I DID IT! I TRANSLATED THE TEXT!
WELL DONE!
WANNA READ IT TOGETHER?
YOU MEAN I GET TO LEAVE QUARANTINE?
NO, SILLY. I CAN PROJECT IT IN THERE.

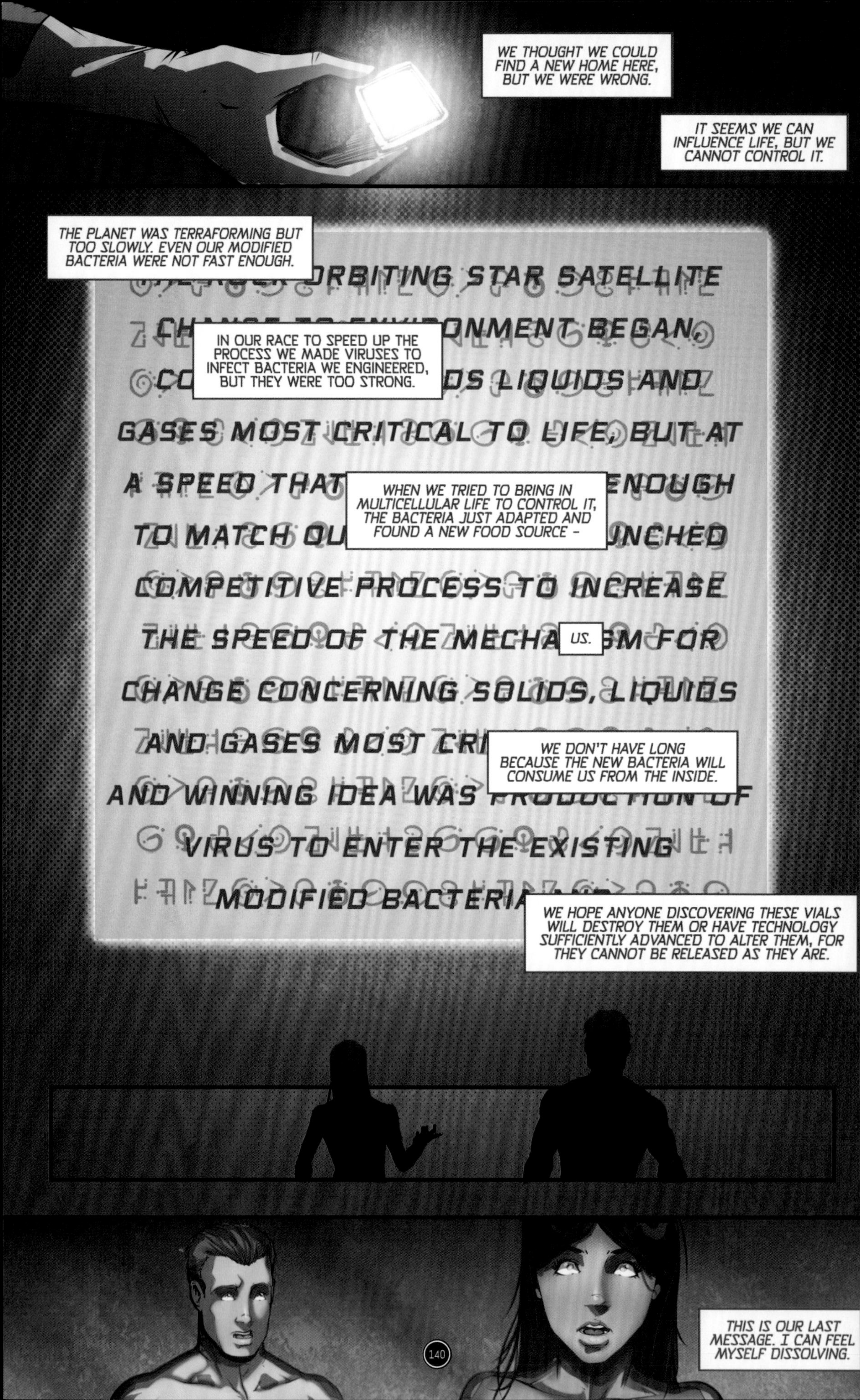
WE THOUGHT WE COULD FIND A NEW HOME HERE, BUT WE WERE WRONG.
IT SEEMS WE CAN INFLUENCE LIFE, BUT WE CANNOT CONTROL IT.
THE PLANET WAS TERRAFORMING BUT TOO SLOWLY. EVEN OUR MODIFIED BACTERIA WERE NOT FAST ENOUGH.
ORBITING STAR SATELLITE
BEGAN,
LIQUIDS AND
GASES MOST CRITICAL TO LIFE, BUT AT
A SPEED THAT
ENOUGH
TO MATCH
COMPETITIVE PROCESS TO INCREASE
THE SPEED OF THE
FOR
CHANGE CONCERNING SOLIDS, LIQUIDS
AND GASES MOST
AND WINNING IDEA WAS
VIRUS TO ENTER THE EXISTING
MODIFIED
IN OUR RACE TO SPEED UP THE PROCESS WE MADE VIRUSES TO INFECT BACTERIA WE ENGINEERED, BUT THEY WERE TOO STRONG.
WHEN WE TRIED TO BRING IN MULTICELLULAR LIFE TO CONTROL IT, THE BACTERIA JUST ADAPTED AND FOUND A NEW FOOD SOURCE –
US.
WE DON'T HAVE LONG BECAUSE THE NEW BACTERIA WILL CONSUME US FROM THE INSIDE.
WE HOPE ANYONE DISCOVERING THESE VIALS WILL DESTROY THEM OR HAVE TECHNOLOGY SUFFICIENTLY ADVANCED TO ALTER THEM, FOR THEY CANNOT BE RELEASED AS THEY ARE.
THIS IS OUR LAST MESSAGE. I CAN FEEL MYSELF DISSOLVING.

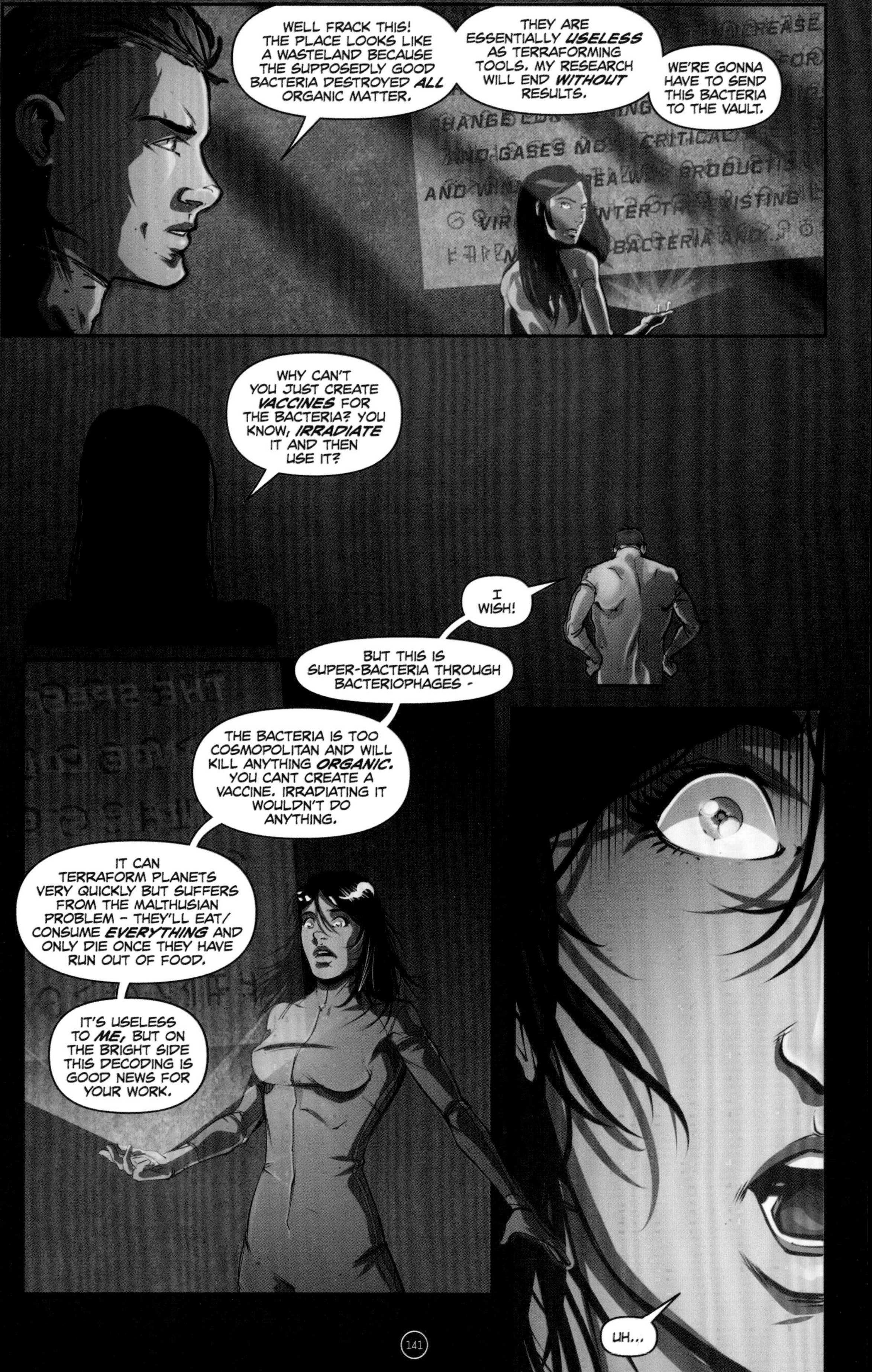
WELL FRACK THIS! THE PLACE LOOKS LIKE A WASTELAND BECAUSE THE SUPPOSEDLY GOOD BACTERIA DESTROYED ALL ORGANIC MATTER.
THEY ARE ESSENTIALLY USELESS AS TERRAFORMING TOOLS. MY RESEARCH WILL END WITHOUT RESULTS.
WE'RE GONNA HAVE TO SEND THIS BACTERIA TO THE VAULT.
WHY CAN'T YOU JUST CREATE VACCINES FOR THE BACTERIA? YOU KNOW, IRRADIATE IT AND THEN USE IT?
I WISH!
BUT THIS IS SUPER-BACTERIA THROUGH BACTERIOPHAGES -
THE BACTERIA IS TOO COSMOPOLITAN AND WILL KILL ANYTHING ORGANIC. YOU CANT CREATE A VACCINE. IRRADIATING IT WOULDN'T DO ANYTHING.
IT CAN TERRAFORM PLANETS VERY QUICKLY BUT SUFFERS FROM THE MALTHUSIAN PROBLEM - THEY'LL EAT/ CONSUME EVERYTHING AND ONLY DIE ONCE THEY HAVE RUN OUT OF FOOD.
IT'S USELESS TO ME, BUT ON THE BRIGHT SIDE THIS DECODING IS GOOD NEWS FOR YOUR WORK.
UH...

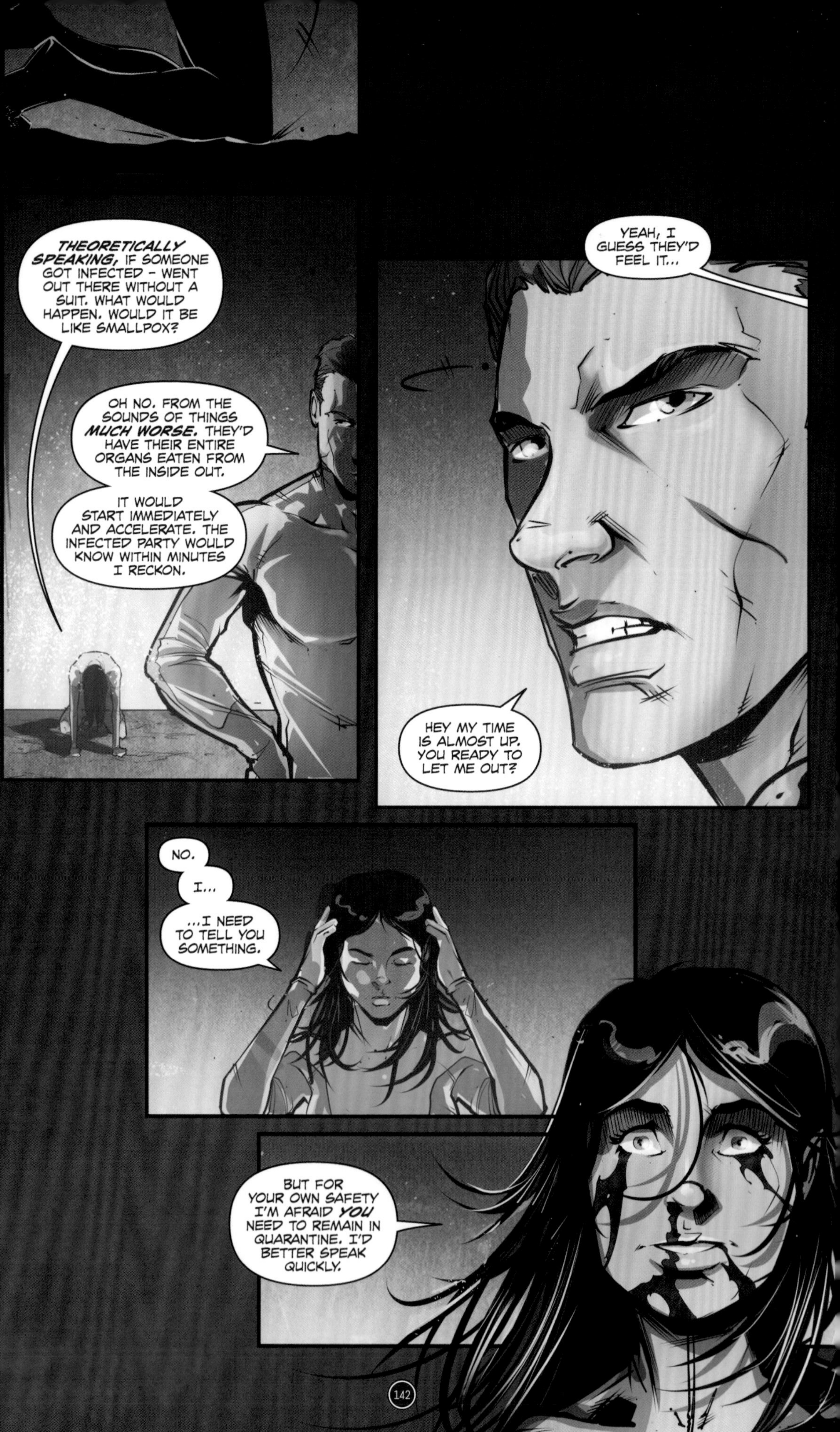
THEORETICALLY SPEAKING, IF SOMEONE GOT INFECTED - WENT OUT THERE WITHOUT A SUIT. WHAT WOULD HAPPEN. WOULD IT BE LIKE SMALLPOX?
OH NO. FROM THE SOUNDS OF THINGS MUCH WORSE. THEY'D HAVE THEIR ENTIRE ORGANS EATEN FROM THE INSIDE OUT.
IT WOULD START IMMEDIATELY AND ACCELERATE. THE INFECTED PARTY WOULD KNOW WITHIN MINUTES I RECKON.
YEAH, I GUESS THEY'D FEEL IT...
HEY MY TIME IS ALMOST UP. YOU READY TO LET ME OUT?
NO.
I...
...I NEED TO TELL YOU SOMETHING.
BUT FOR YOUR OWN SAFETY I'M AFRAID YOU NEED TO REMAIN IN QUARANTINE. I'D BETTER SPEAK QUICKLY.

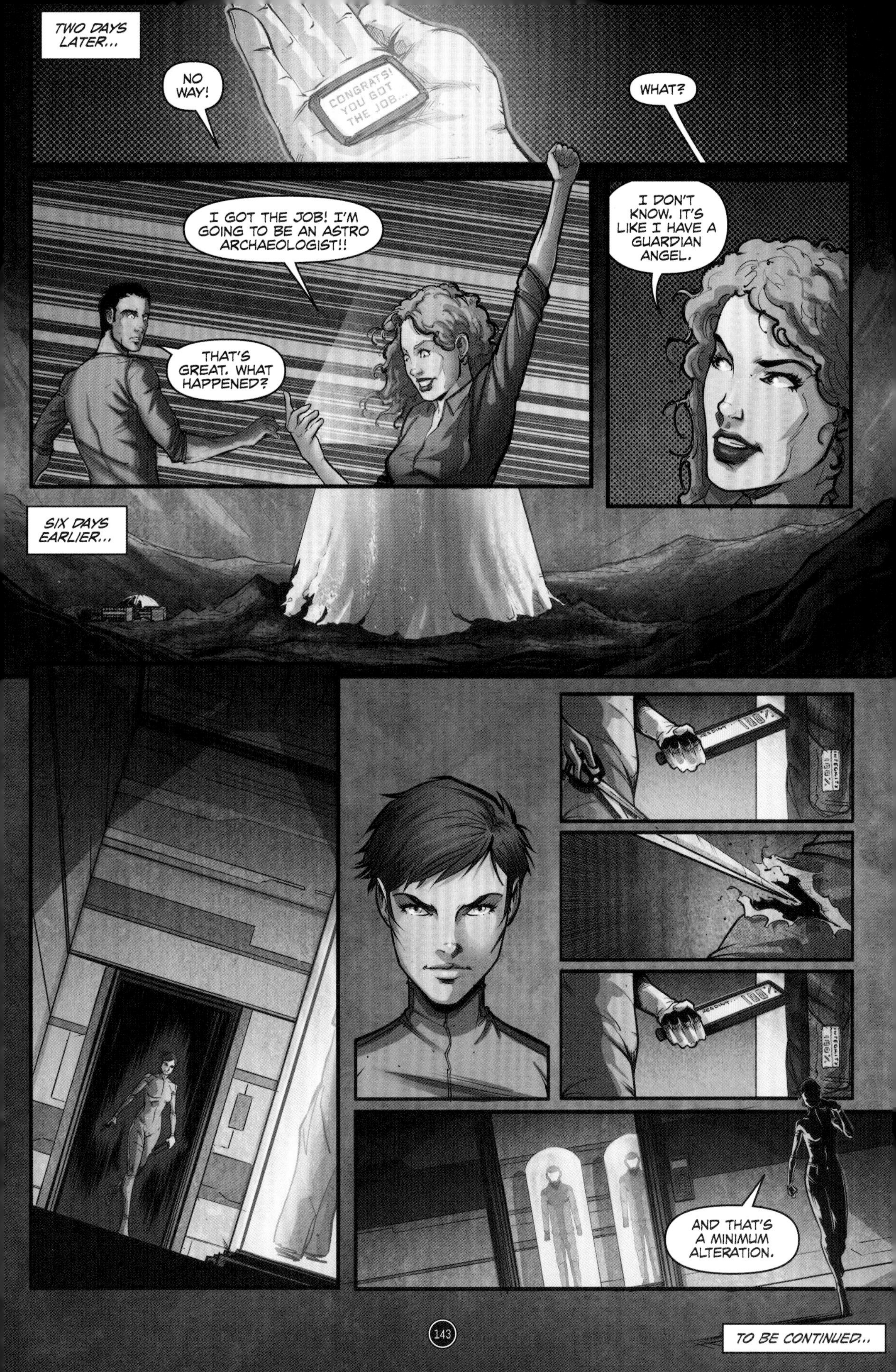
TWO DAYS LATER...
NO WAY!
CONGRATS! YOU GOT THE JOB...
WHAT?
I GOT THE JOB! I'M GOING TO BE AN ASTRO ARCHAEOLOGIST!!
THAT'S GREAT. WHAT HAPPENED?
I DON'T KNOW. IT'S LIKE I HAVE A GUARDIAN ANGEL.
SIX DAYS EARLIER...
AND THAT'S A MINIMUM ALTERATION.
TO BE CONTINUED...

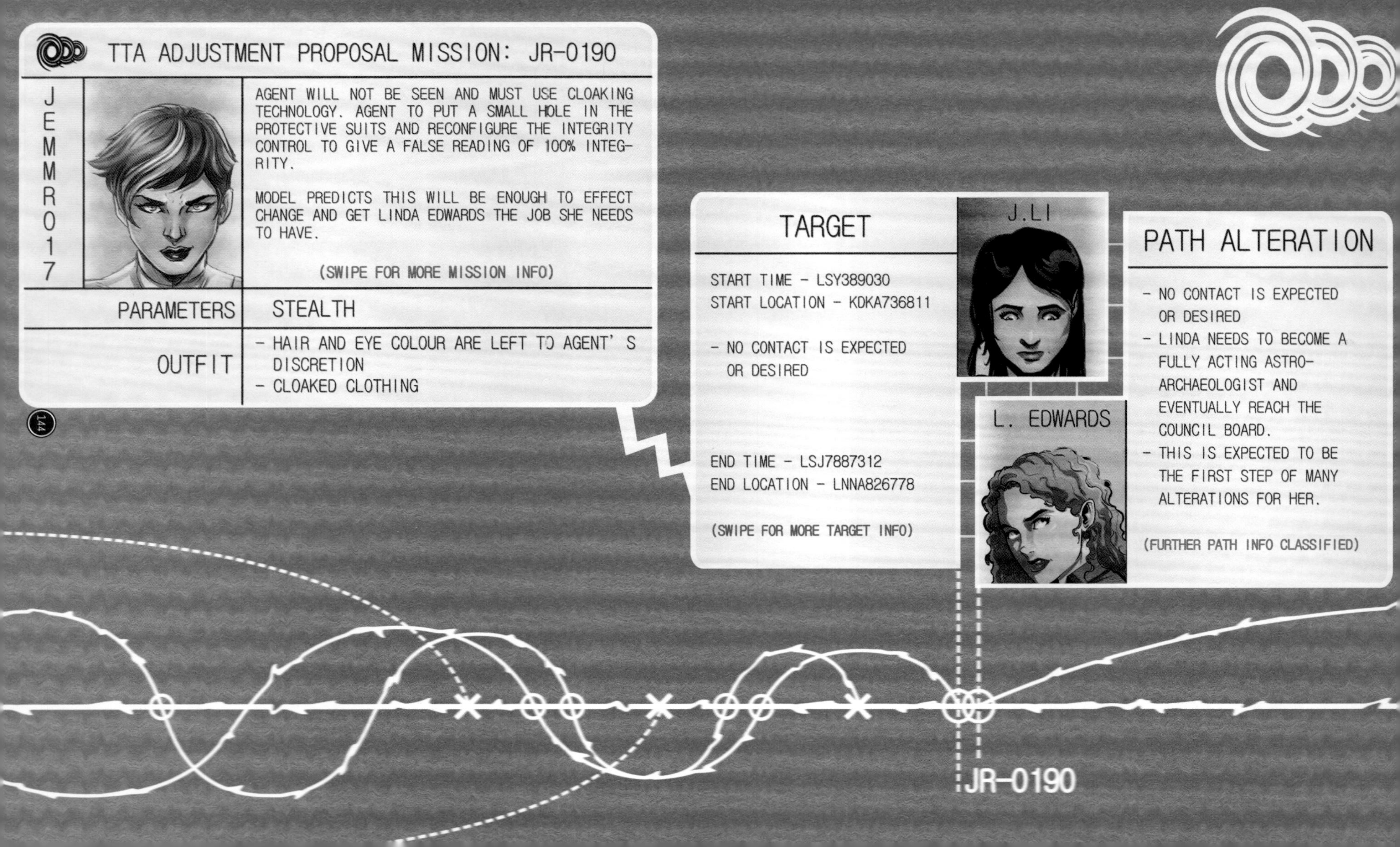

TTA ADJUSTMENT PROPOSAL MISSION: JR-0190
JEMMR017
AGENT WILL NOT BE SEEN AND MUST USE CLOAKING TECHNOLOGY. AGENT TO PUT A SMALL HOLE IN THE PROTECTIVE SUITS AND RECONFIGURE THE INTEGRITY CONTROL TO GIVE A FALSE READING OF 100% INTEGRITY.
MODEL PREDICTS THIS WILL BE ENOUGH TO EFFECT CHANGE AND GET LINDA EDWARDS THE JOB SHE NEEDS TO HAVE.
(SWIPE FOR MORE MISSION INFO)
PARAMETERS
STEALTH
OUTFIT
- HAIR AND EYE COLOUR ARE LEFT TO AGENT'S DISCRETION
- CLOAKED CLOTHING
TARGET
START TIME - LSY389030
START LOCATION - KDKA736811
- NO CONTACT IS EXPECTED OR DESIRED
END TIME - LSJ7887312
END LOCATION - LNNA826778
(SWIPE FOR MORE TARGET INFO)
J.LI
L. EDWARDS
PATH ALTERATION
- NO CONTACT IS EXPECTED OR DESIRED
- LINDA NEEDS TO BECOME A FULLY ACTING ASTRO-ARCHAEOLOGIST AND EVENTUALLY REACH THE COUNCIL BOARD.
- THIS IS EXPECTED TO BE THE FIRST STEP OF MANY ALTERATIONS FOR HER.
(FURTHER PATH INFO CLASSIFIED)
JR-0190

Everyone deserves a chance for happiness

"Happiness is not something ready made. It comes from your own actions"

Dalai Lama

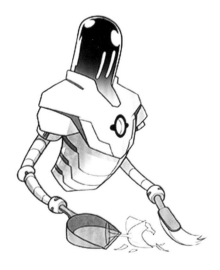

Writer/Creator
Neil Gibson

Illustrator
Cem Iroz

Colourist
Liezl Buenaventura

Letters by
Justin Birch

www.tpubcomics.com

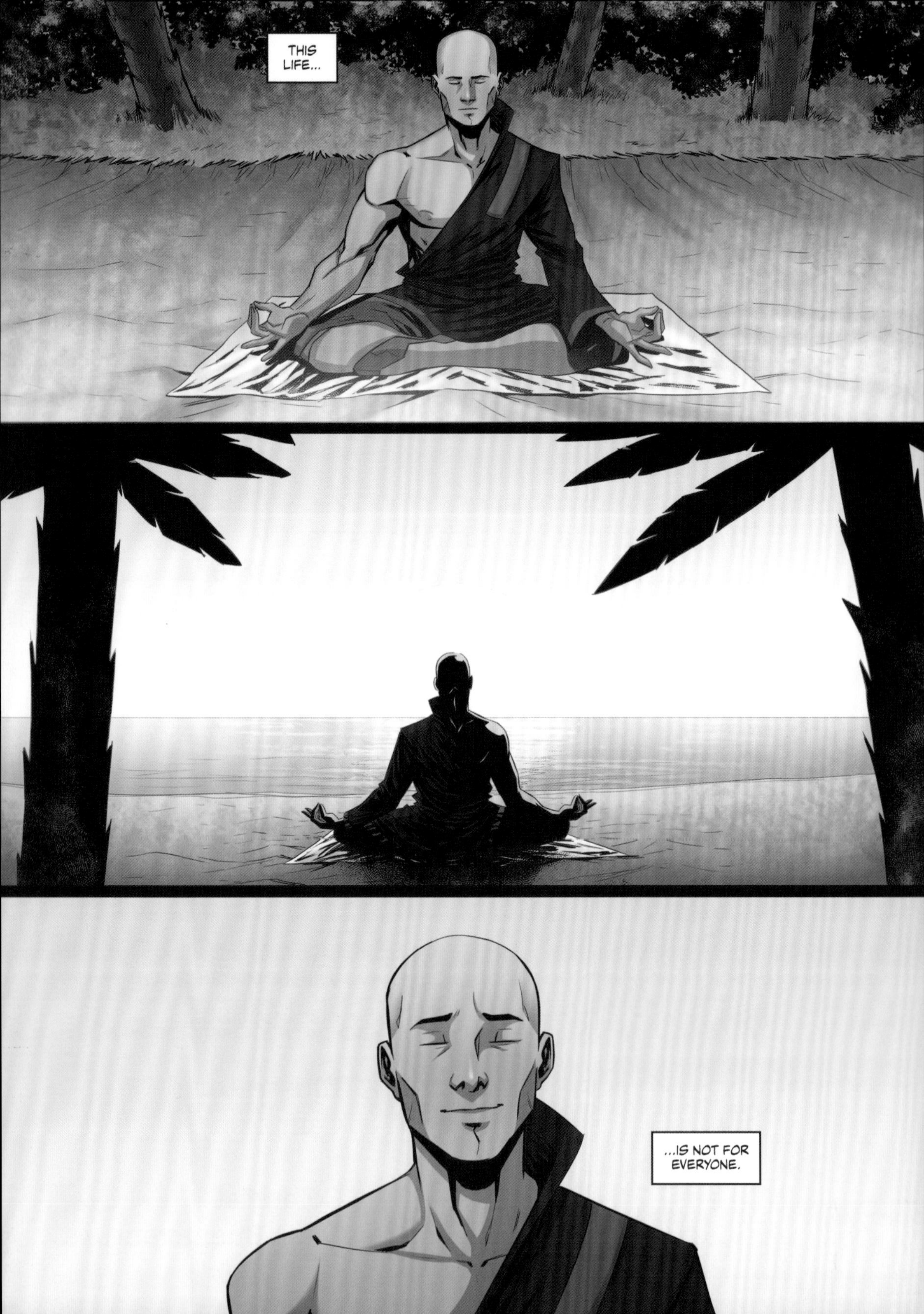
THIS LIFE...
...IS NOT FOR EVERYONE.

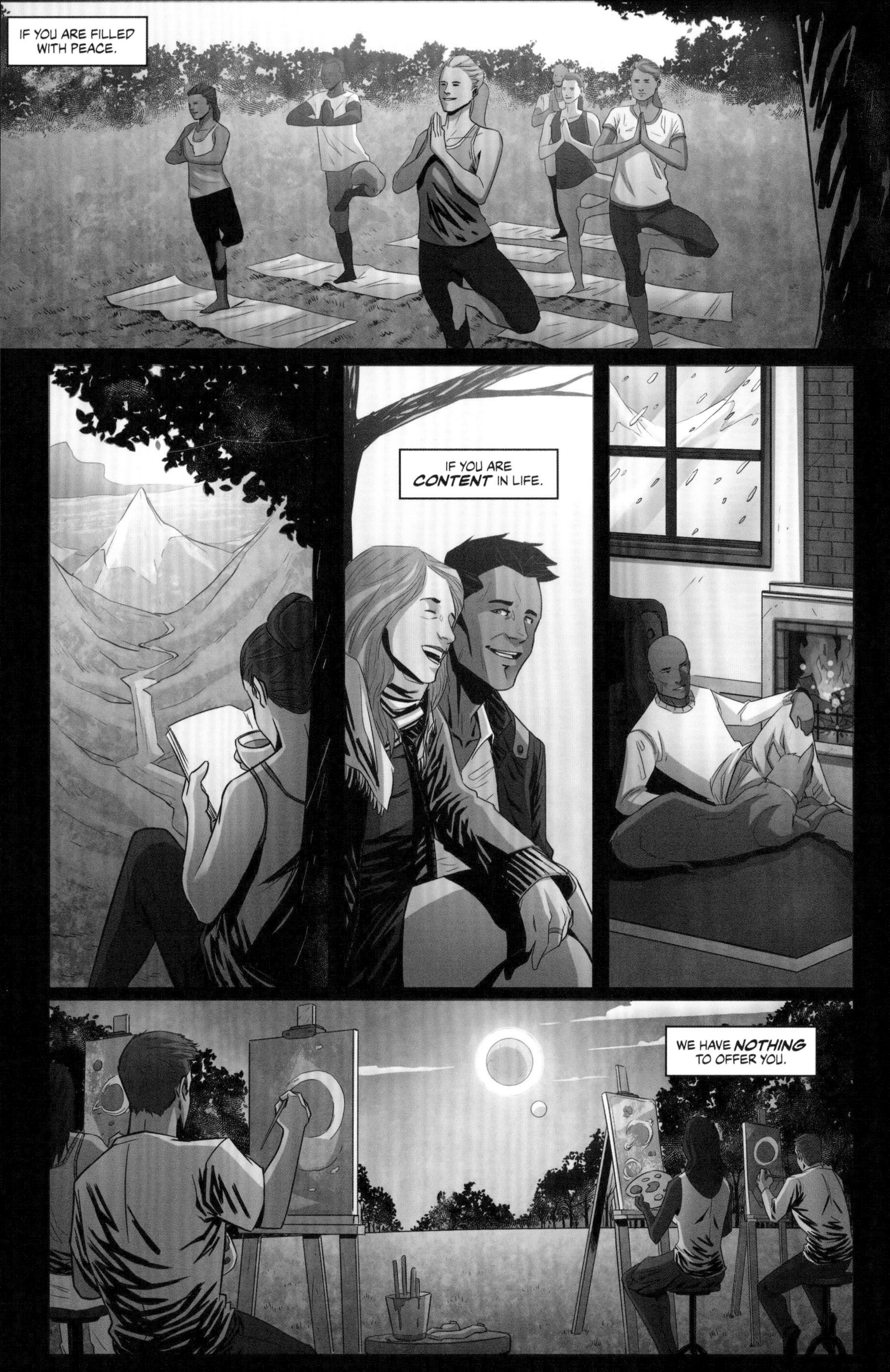
IF YOU ARE FILLED WITH PEACE.
IF YOU ARE CONTENT IN LIFE.
WE HAVE NOTHING TO OFFER YOU.

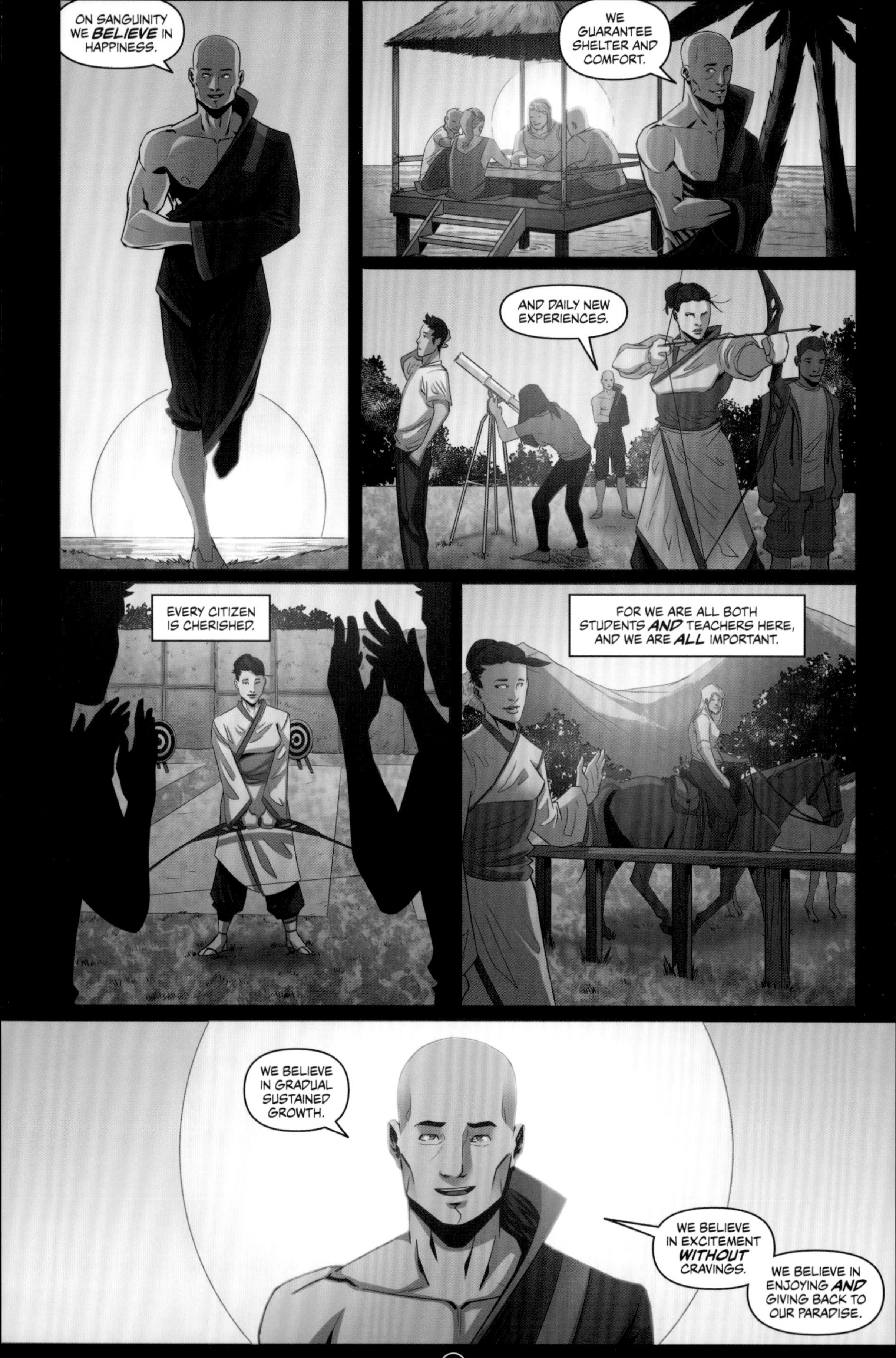
ON SANGUINITY WE BELIEVE IN HAPPINESS.
WE GUARANTEE SHELTER AND COMFORT.
AND DAILY NEW EXPERIENCES.
EVERY CITIZEN IS CHERISHED.
FOR WE ARE ALL BOTH STUDENTS AND TEACHERS HERE, AND WE ARE ALL IMPORTANT.
WE BELIEVE IN GRADUAL SUSTAINED GROWTH.
WE BELIEVE IN EXCITEMENT WITHOUT CRAVINGS.
WE BELIEVE IN ENJOYING AND GIVING BACK TO OUR PARADISE.

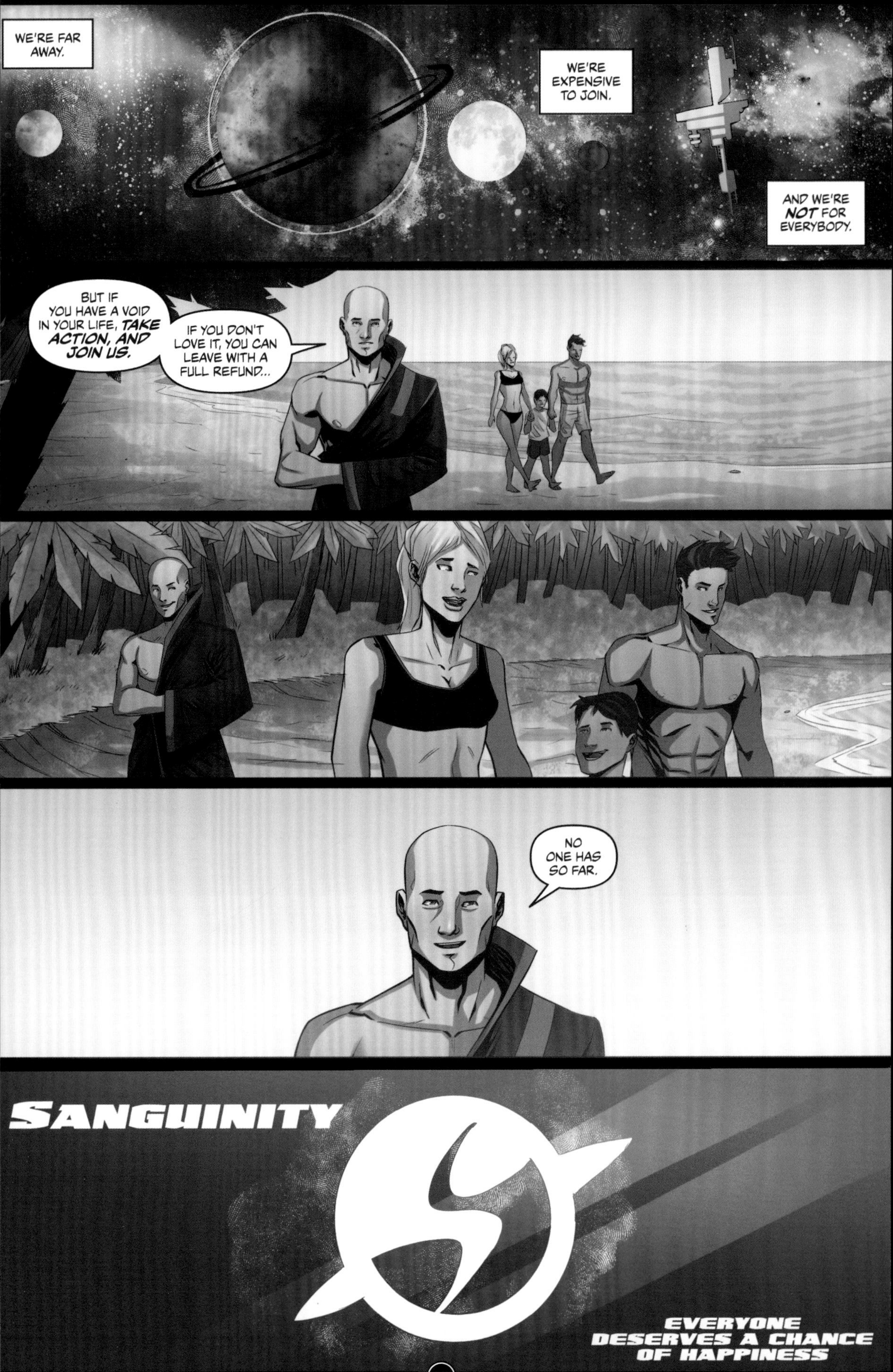
WE'RE FAR AWAY.
WE'RE EXPENSIVE TO JOIN.
AND WE'RE NOT FOR EVERYBODY.
BUT IF YOU HAVE A VOID IN YOUR LIFE, TAKE ACTION, AND JOIN US.
IF YOU DON'T LOVE IT, YOU CAN LEAVE WITH A FULL REFUND...
NO ONE HAS SO FAR.
SANGUINITY
EVERYONE DESERVES A CHANCE OF HAPPINESS

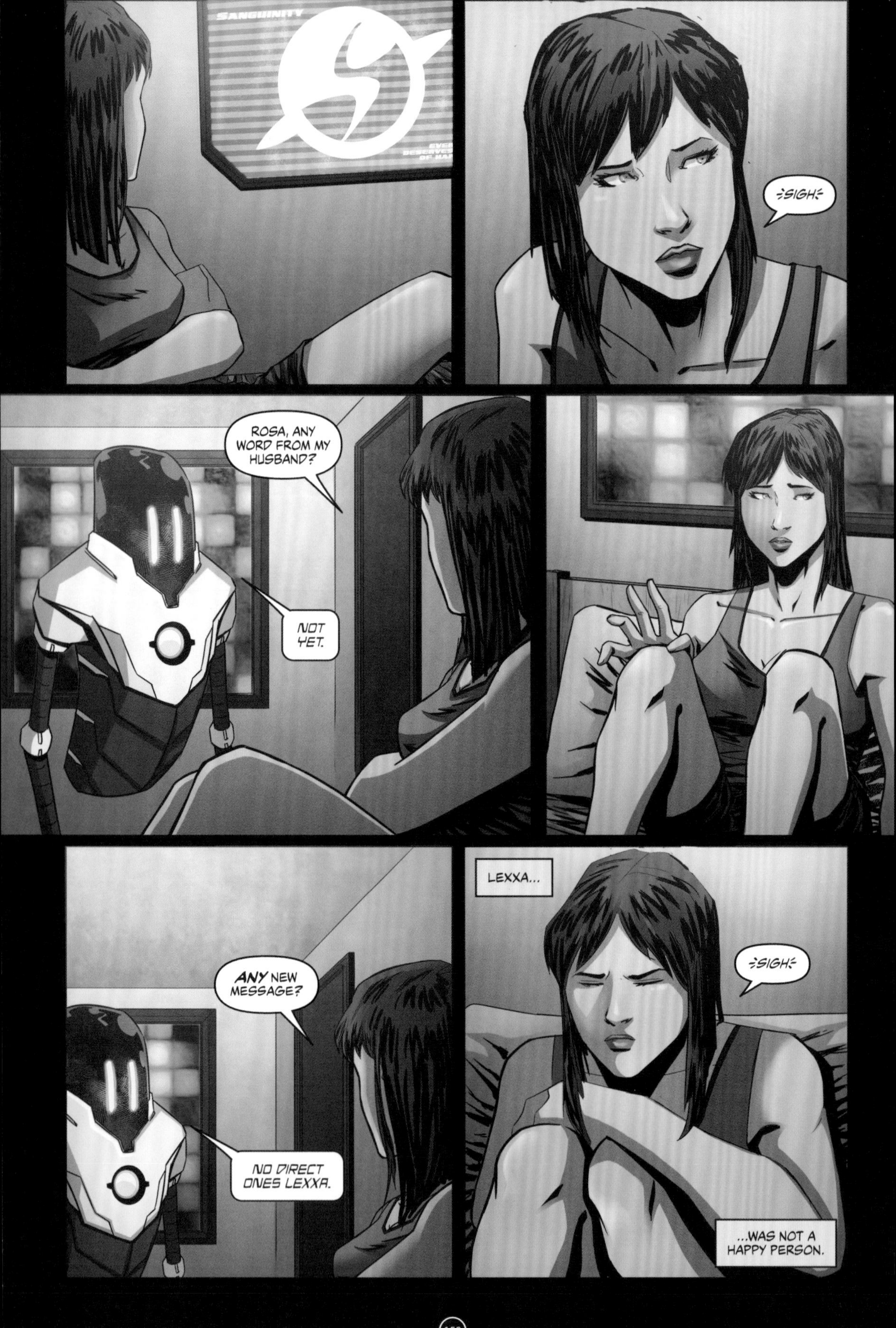
SANGUINITY
SIGH
ROSA, ANY WORD FROM MY HUSBAND?
NOT YET.
ANY NEW MESSAGE?
NO DIRECT ONES LEXXA.
LEXXA...
SIGH
...WAS NOT A HAPPY PERSON.

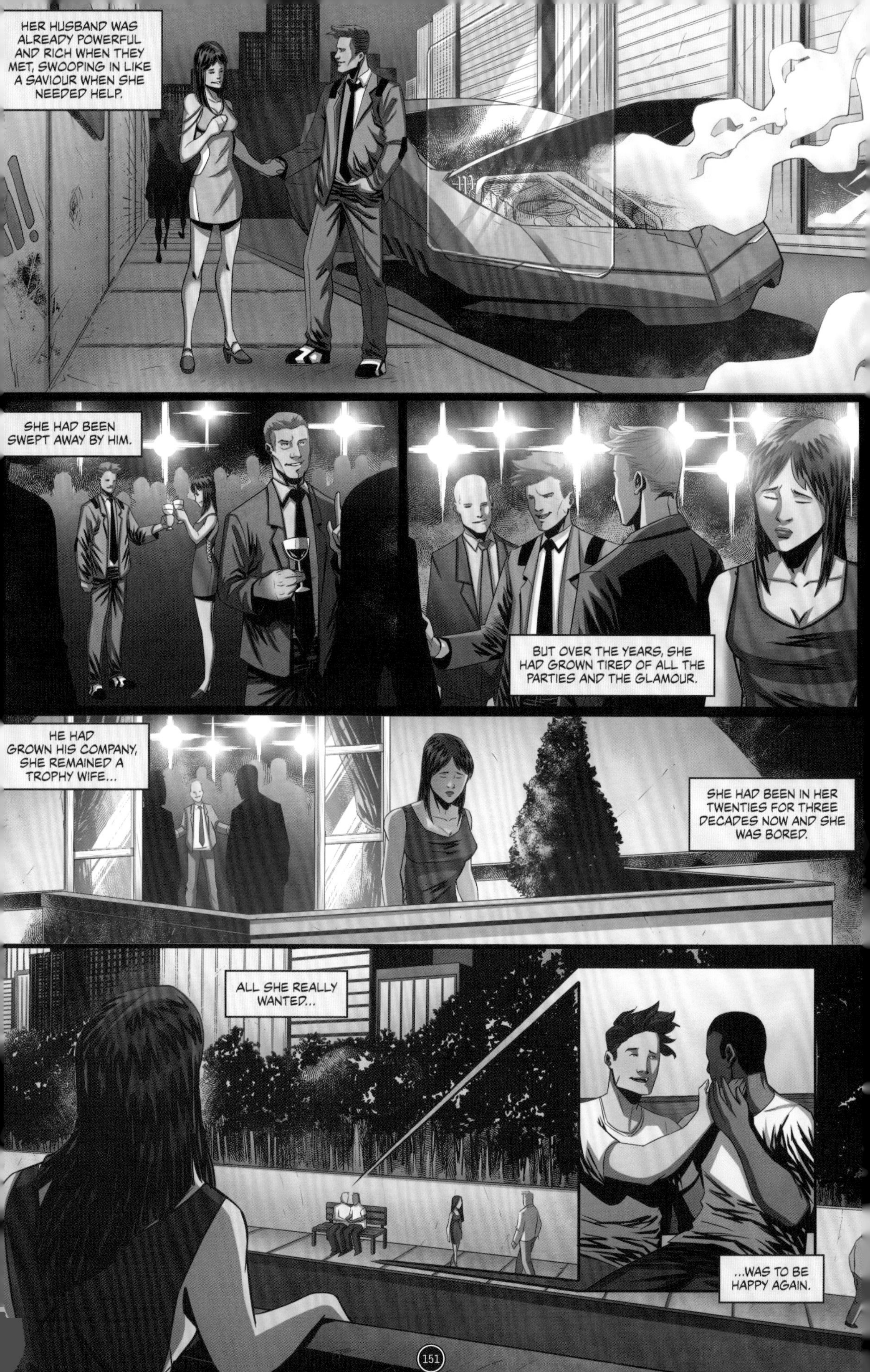
HER HUSBAND WAS ALREADY POWERFUL AND RICH WHEN THEY MET, SWOOPING IN LIKE A SAVIOUR WHEN SHE NEEDED HELP.
SHE HAD BEEN SWEPT AWAY BY HIM.
BUT OVER THE YEARS, SHE HAD GROWN TIRED OF ALL THE PARTIES AND THE GLAMOUR.
HE HAD GROWN HIS COMPANY, SHE REMAINED A TROPHY WIFE...
SHE HAD BEEN IN HER TWENTIES FOR THREE DECADES NOW AND SHE WAS BORED.
ALL SHE REALLY WANTED...
...WAS TO BE HAPPY AGAIN.

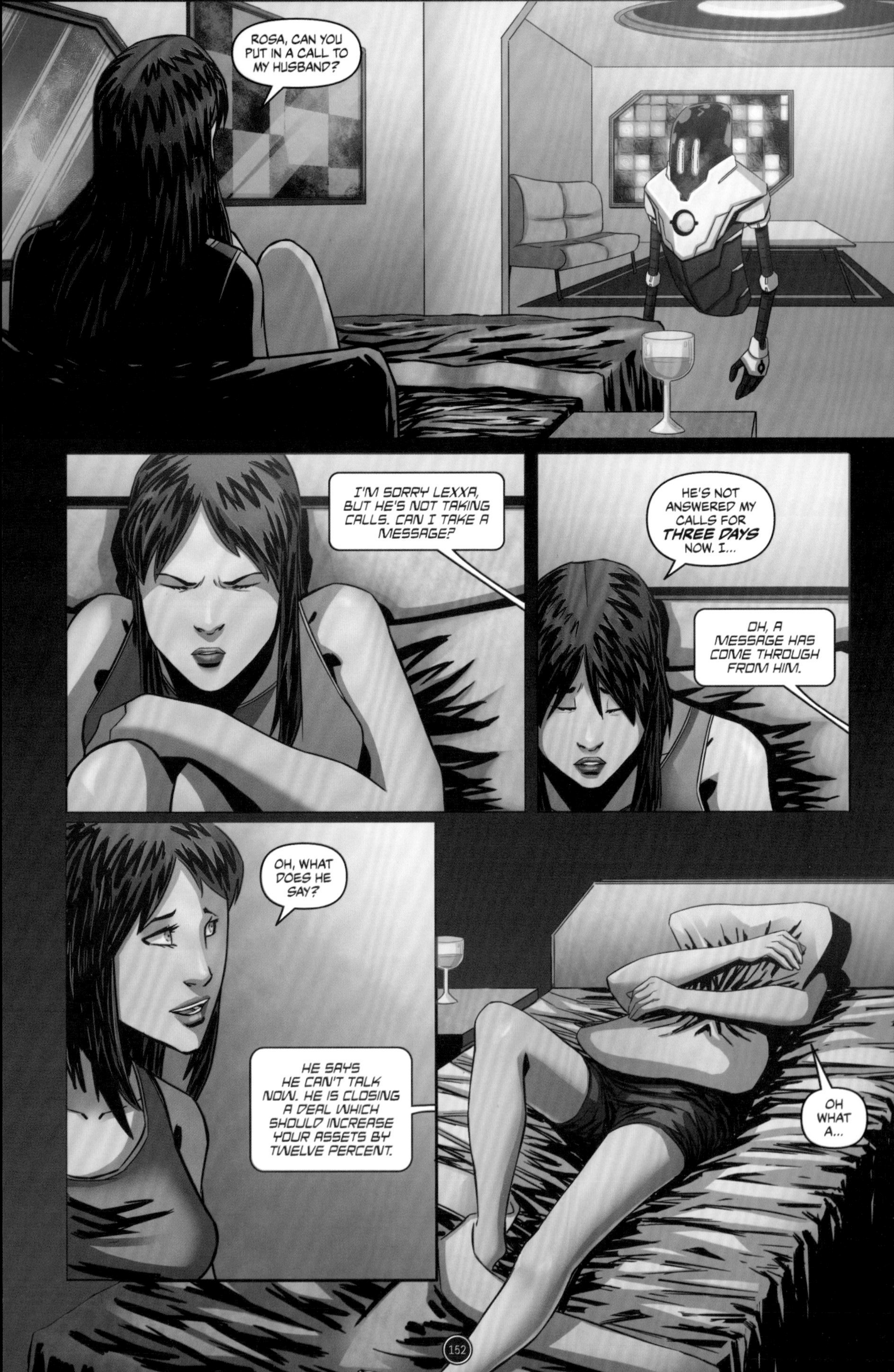
ROSA, CAN YOU PUT IN A CALL TO MY HUSBAND?
I'M SORRY LEXXA, BUT HE'S NOT TAKING CALLS. CAN I TAKE A MESSAGE?
HE'S NOT ANSWERED MY CALLS FOR THREE DAYS NOW. I...
OH, A MESSAGE HAS COME THROUGH FROM HIM.
OH, WHAT DOES HE SAY?
HE SAYS HE CAN'T TALK NOW. HE IS CLOSING A DEAL WHICH SHOULD INCREASE YOUR ASSETS BY TWELVE PERCENT.
OH WHAT A...

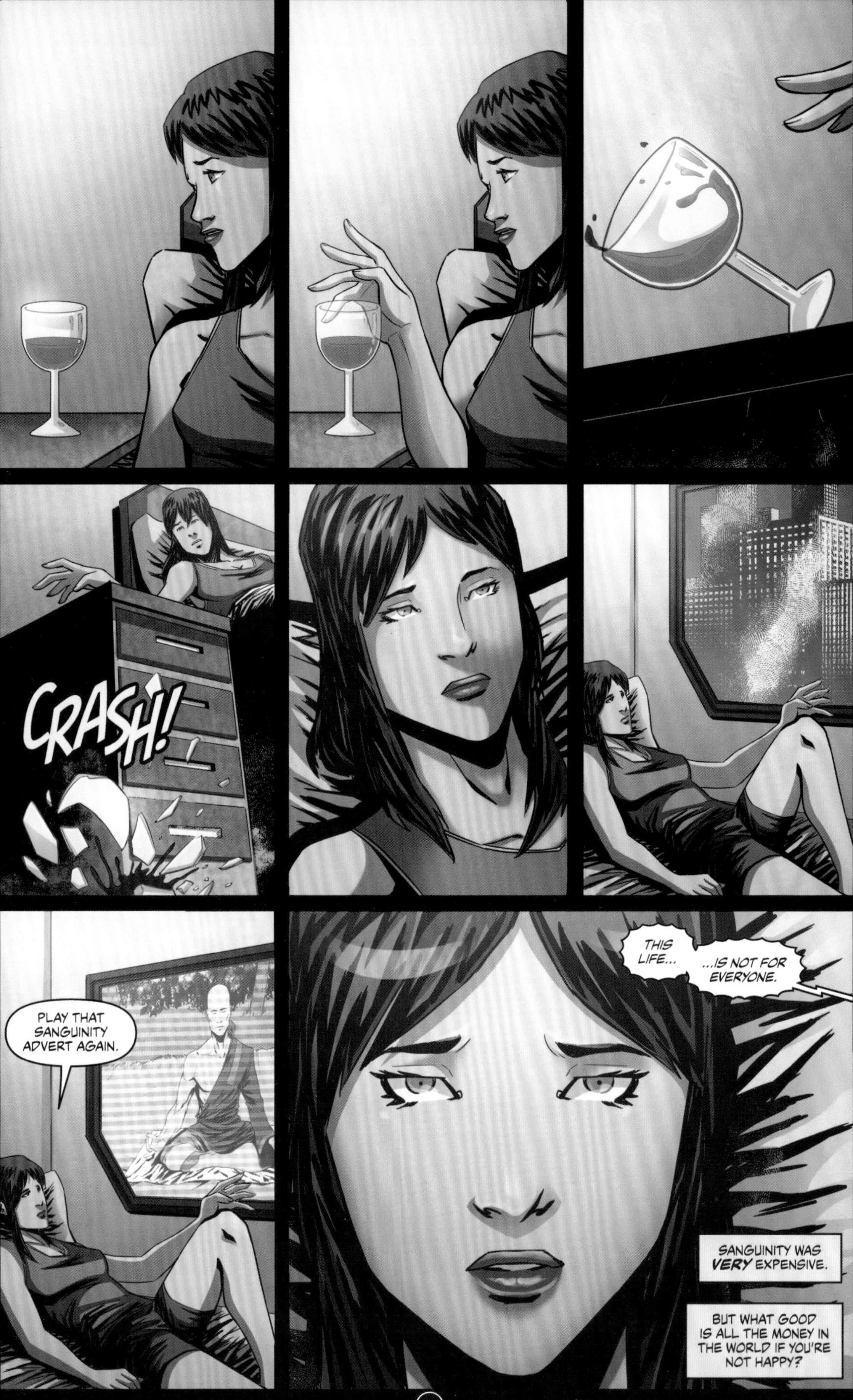
CRASH!
PLAY THAT SANGUINITY ADVERT AGAIN.
THIS LIFE...
...IS NOT FOR EVERYONE.
SANGUINITY WAS VERY EXPENSIVE.
BUT WHAT GOOD IS ALL THE MONEY IN THE WORLD IF YOU'RE NOT HAPPY?

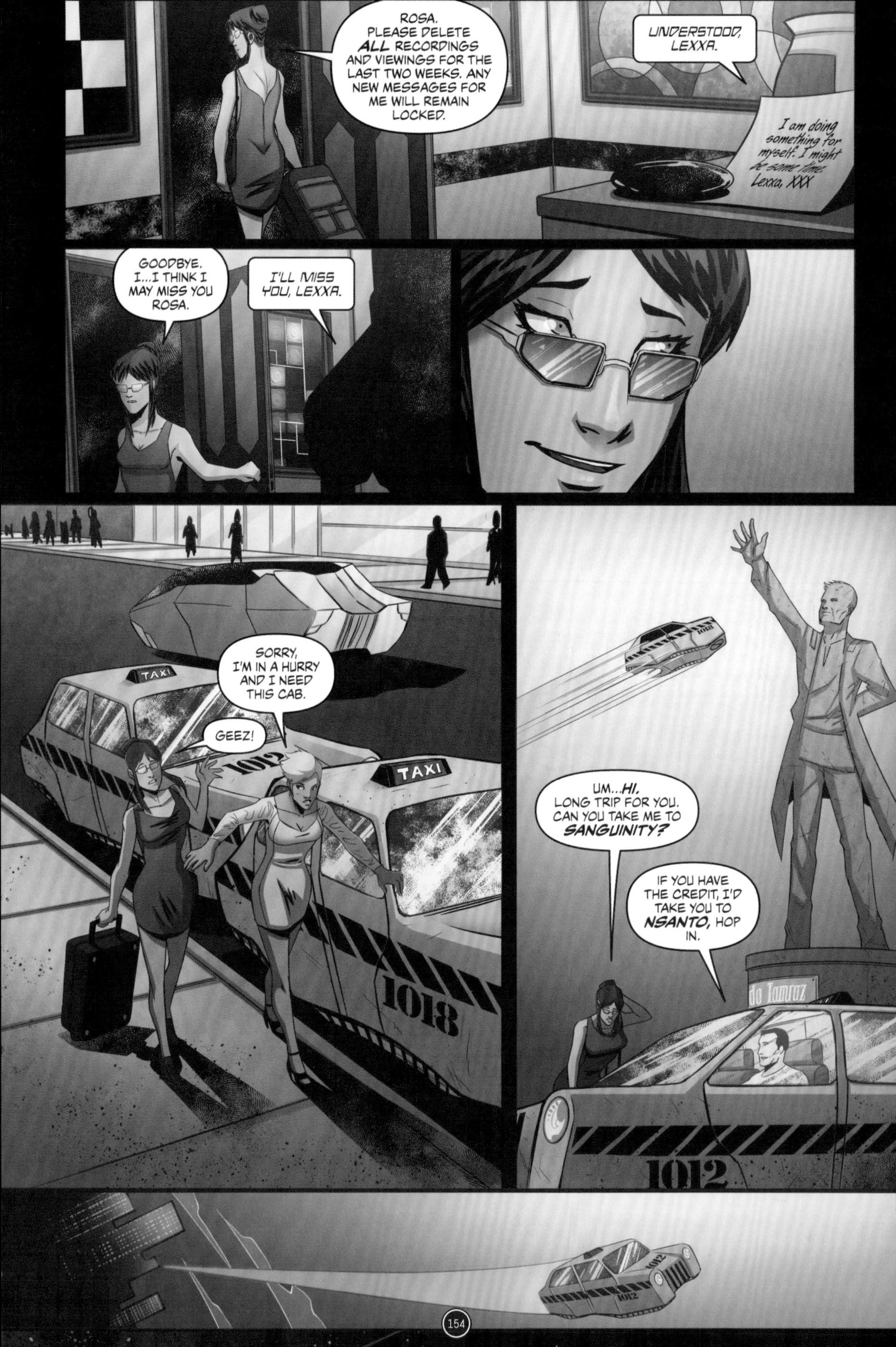
ROSA. PLEASE DELETE ALL RECORDINGS AND VIEWINGS FOR THE LAST TWO WEEKS. ANY NEW MESSAGES FOR ME WILL REMAIN LOCKED.
UNDERSTOOD, LEXXA.
I am doing something for myself. I might be some time. Lexxa, XXX
GOODBYE. I...I THINK I MAY MISS YOU ROSA.
I'LL MISS YOU, LEXXA.
TAXI
SORRY, I'M IN A HURRY AND I NEED THIS CAB.
GEEZ!
1012
TAXI
1018
UM...HI. LONG TRIP FOR YOU. CAN YOU TAKE ME TO SANGUINITY?
IF YOU HAVE THE CREDIT, I'D TAKE YOU TO NSANTO, HOP IN.
1012

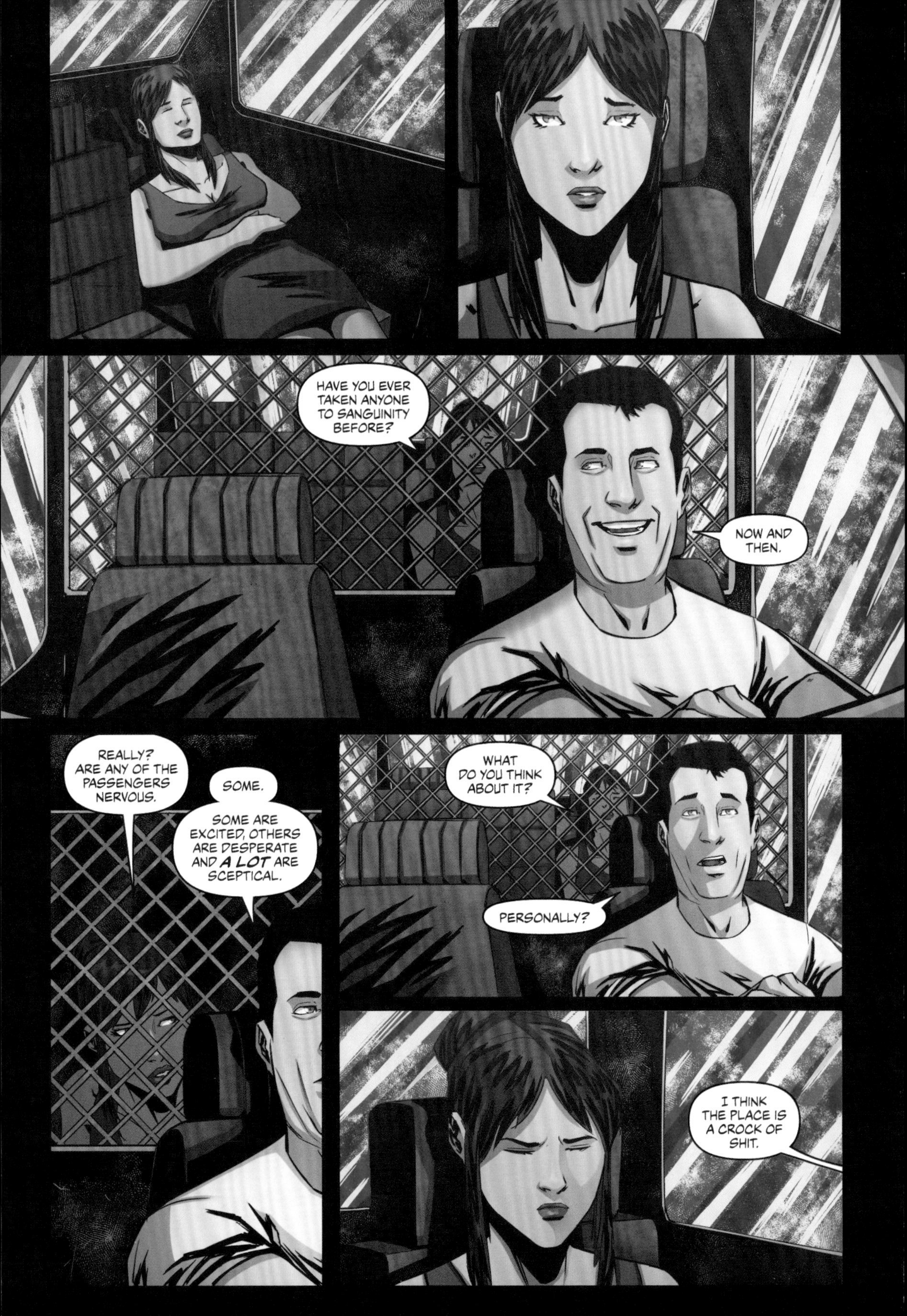
HAVE YOU EVER TAKEN ANYONE TO SANGUINITY BEFORE?
NOW AND THEN.
REALLY? ARE ANY OF THE PASSENGERS NERVOUS.
SOME.
SOME ARE EXCITED, OTHERS ARE DESPERATE AND *A LOT* ARE SCEPTICAL.
WHAT DO YOU THINK ABOUT IT?
PERSONALLY?
I THINK THE PLACE IS A CROCK OF SHIT.

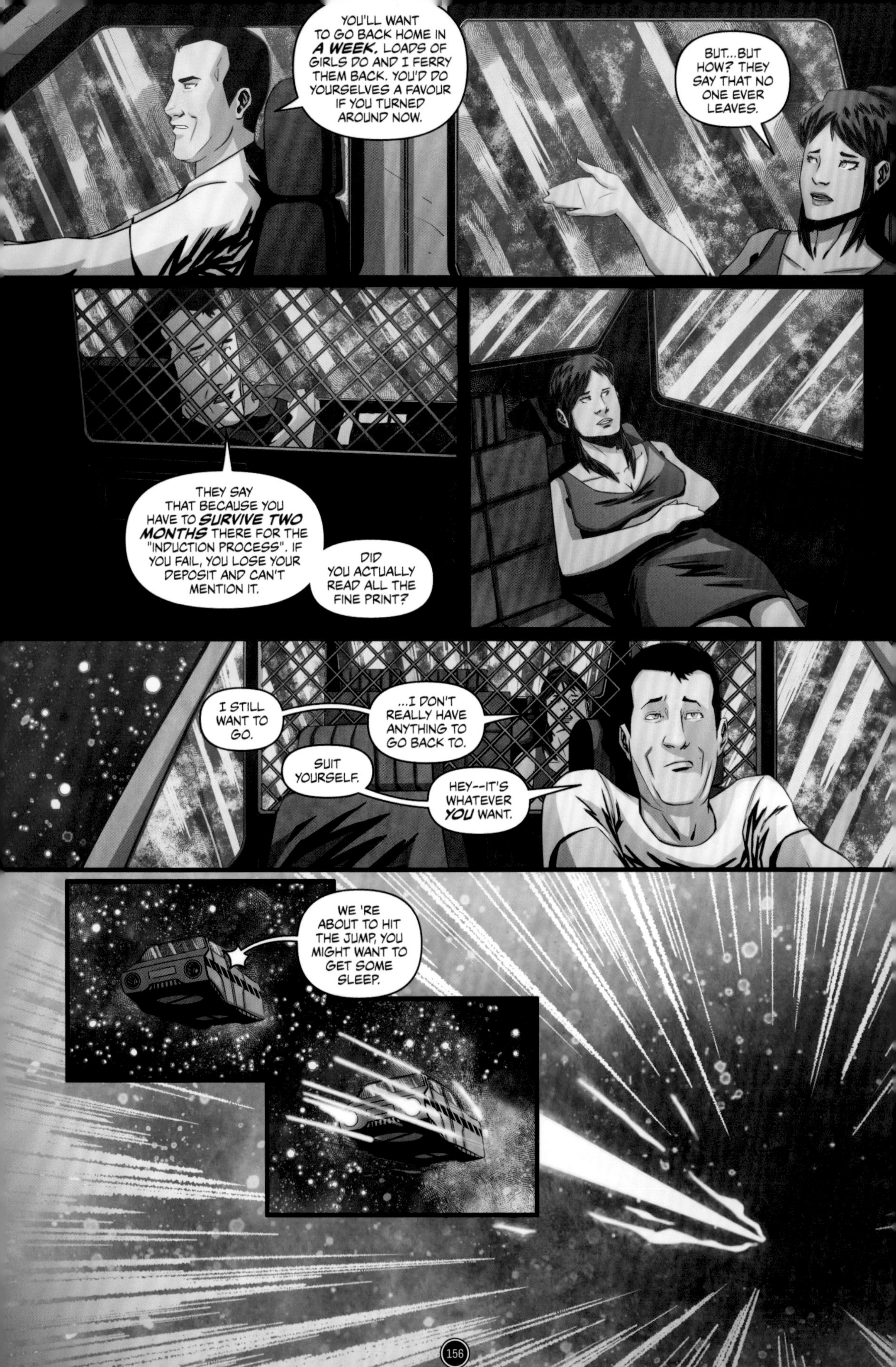

YOU'LL WANT TO GO BACK HOME IN A WEEK. LOADS OF GIRLS DO AND I FERRY THEM BACK. YOU'D DO YOURSELVES A FAVOUR IF YOU TURNED AROUND NOW.
BUT...BUT HOW? THEY SAY THAT NO ONE EVER LEAVES.
THEY SAY THAT BECAUSE YOU HAVE TO SURVIVE TWO MONTHS THERE FOR THE "INDUCTION PROCESS". IF YOU FAIL, YOU LOSE YOUR DEPOSIT AND CAN'T MENTION IT.
DID YOU ACTUALLY READ ALL THE FINE PRINT?
I STILL WANT TO GO.
...I DON'T REALLY HAVE ANYTHING TO GO BACK TO.
SUIT YOURSELF.
HEY--IT'S WHATEVER YOU WANT.
WE 'RE ABOUT TO HIT THE JUMP, YOU MIGHT WANT TO GET SOME SLEEP.

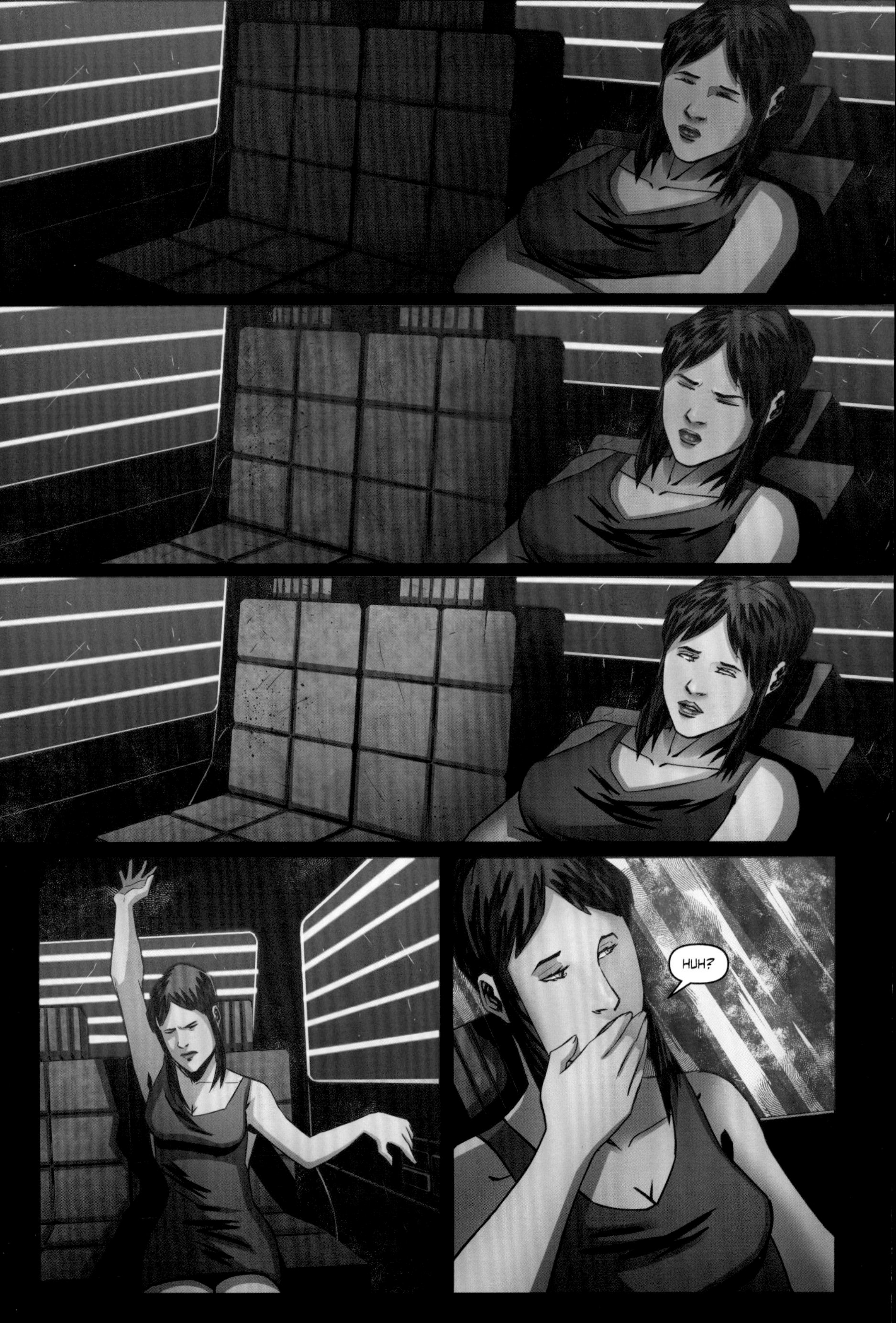
HUH?

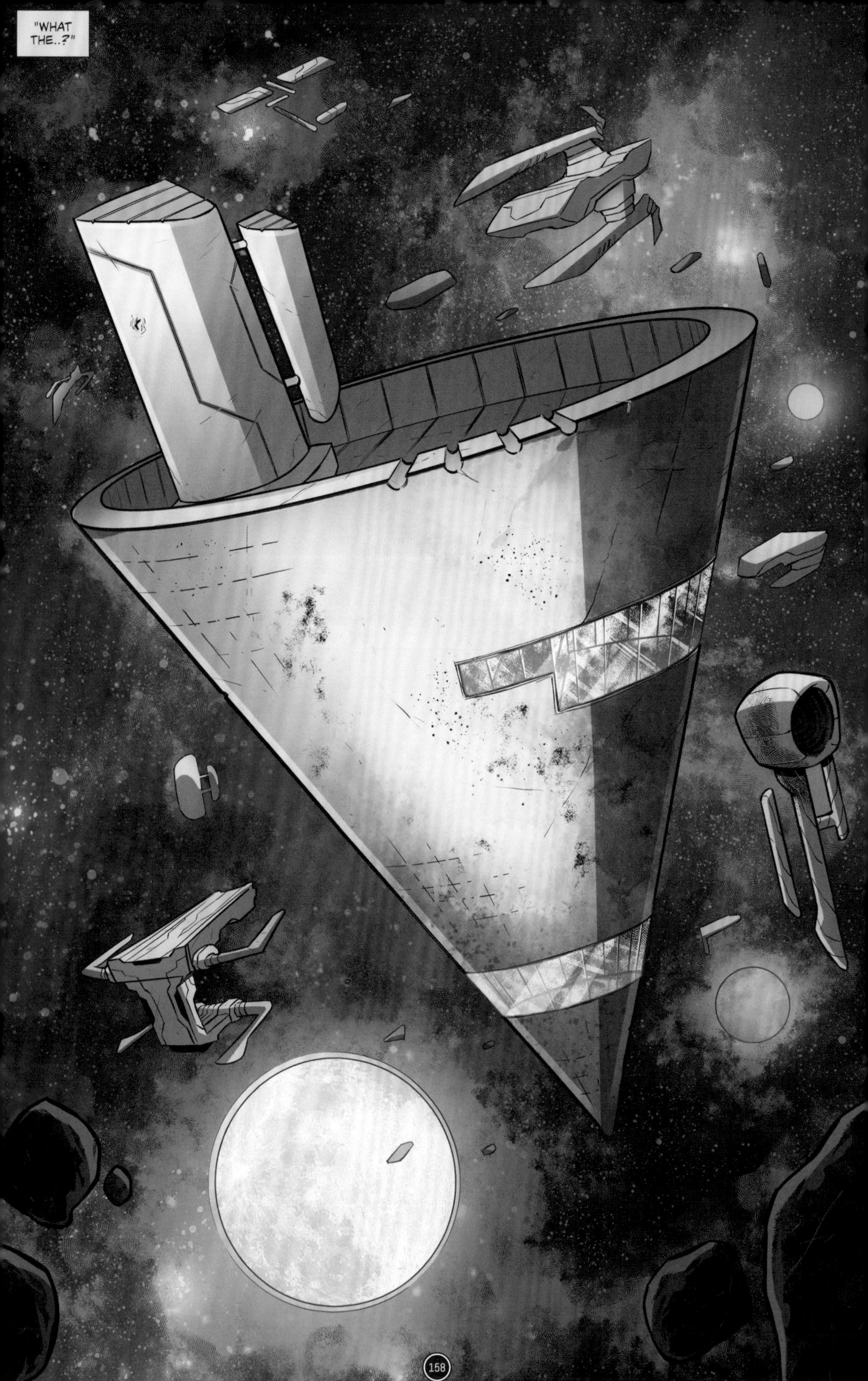
"WHAT THE..?"

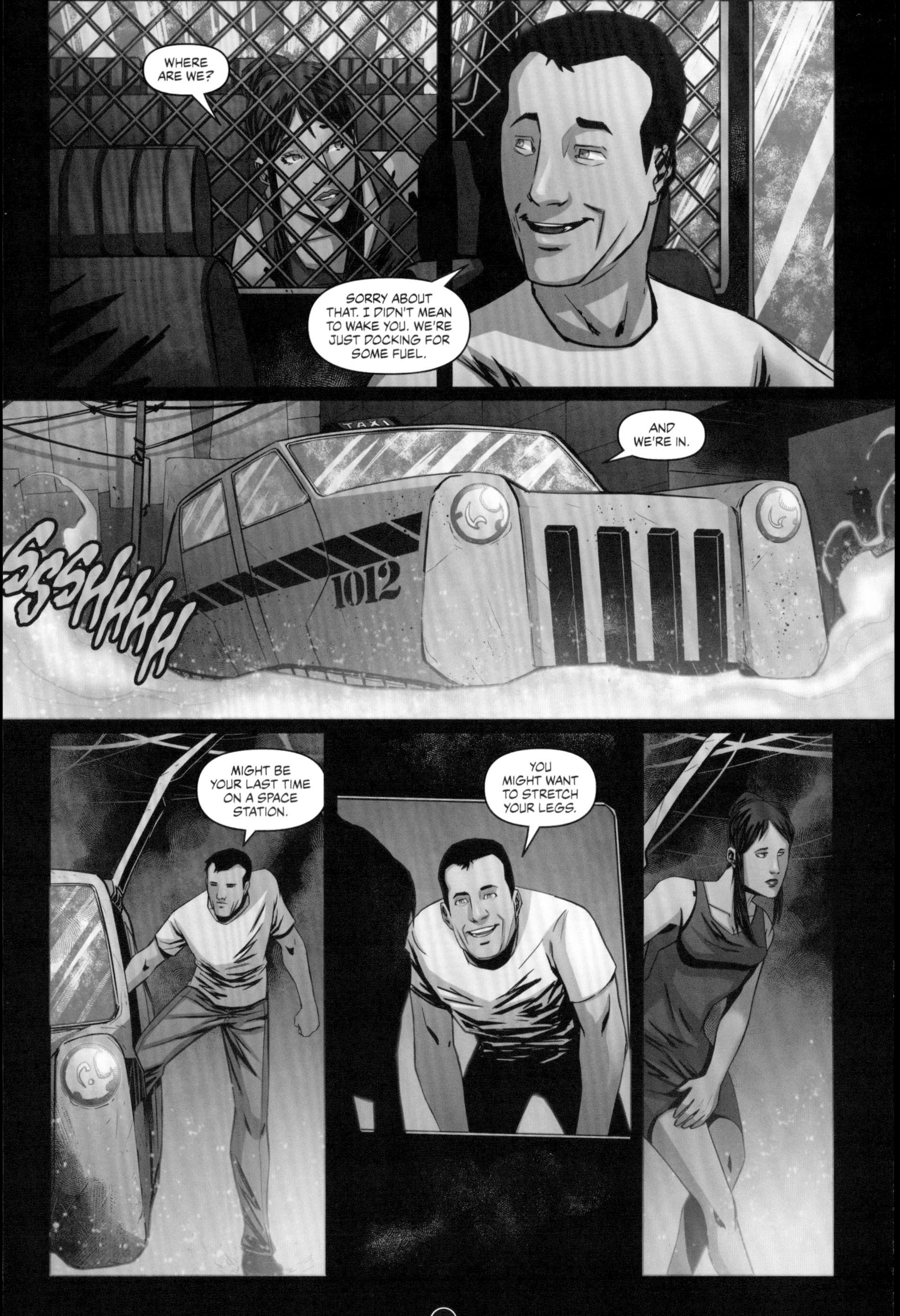
WHERE ARE WE?
SORRY ABOUT THAT. I DIDN'T MEAN TO WAKE YOU. WE'RE JUST DOCKING FOR SOME FUEL.
TAXI
AND WE'RE IN.
1012
SSSHHHH
MIGHT BE YOUR LAST TIME ON A SPACE STATION.
YOU MIGHT WANT TO STRETCH YOUR LEGS.

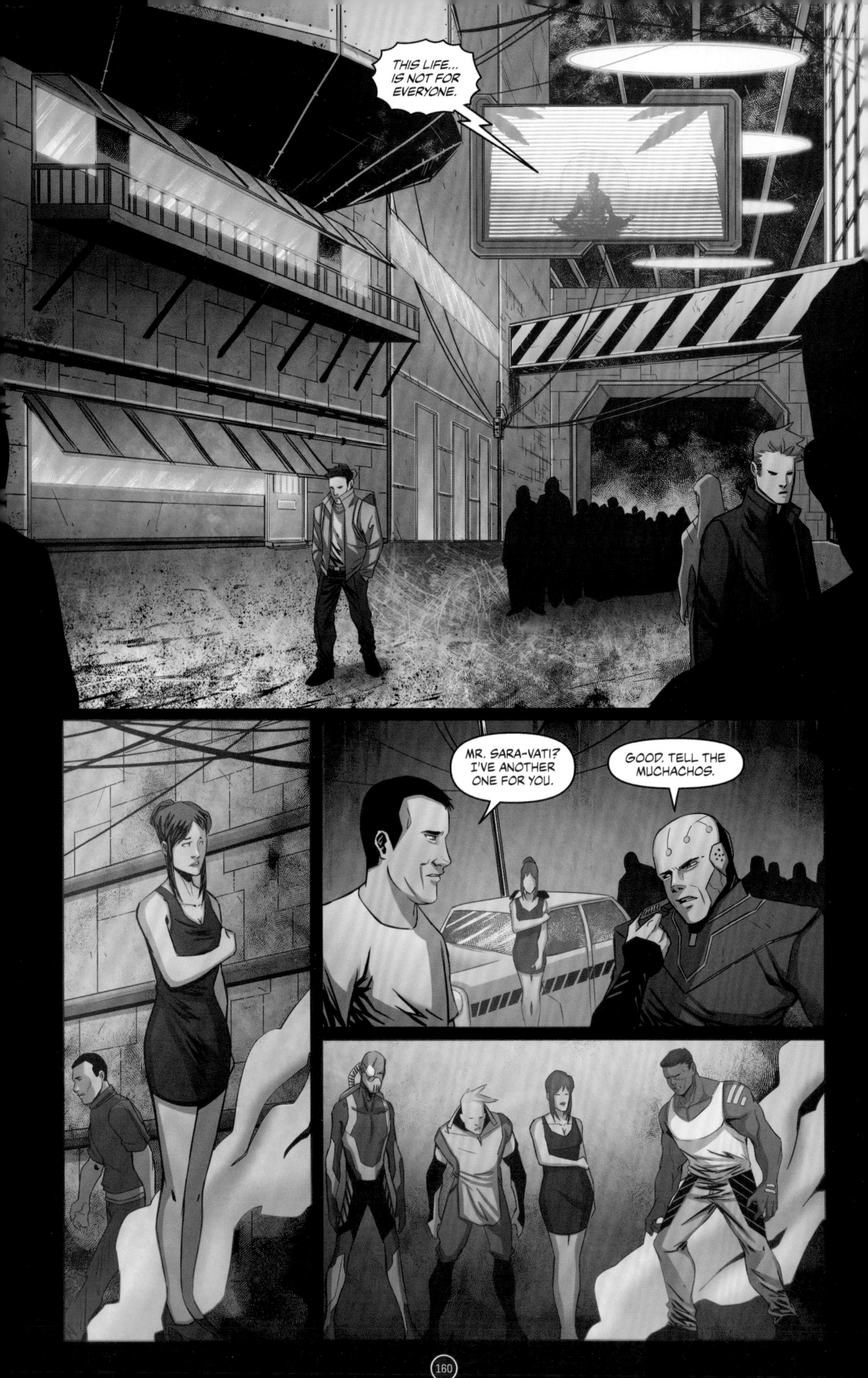
THIS LIFE... IS NOT FOR EVERYONE.
MR. SARA-VATI? I'VE ANOTHER ONE FOR YOU.
GOOD. TELL THE MUCHACHOS.

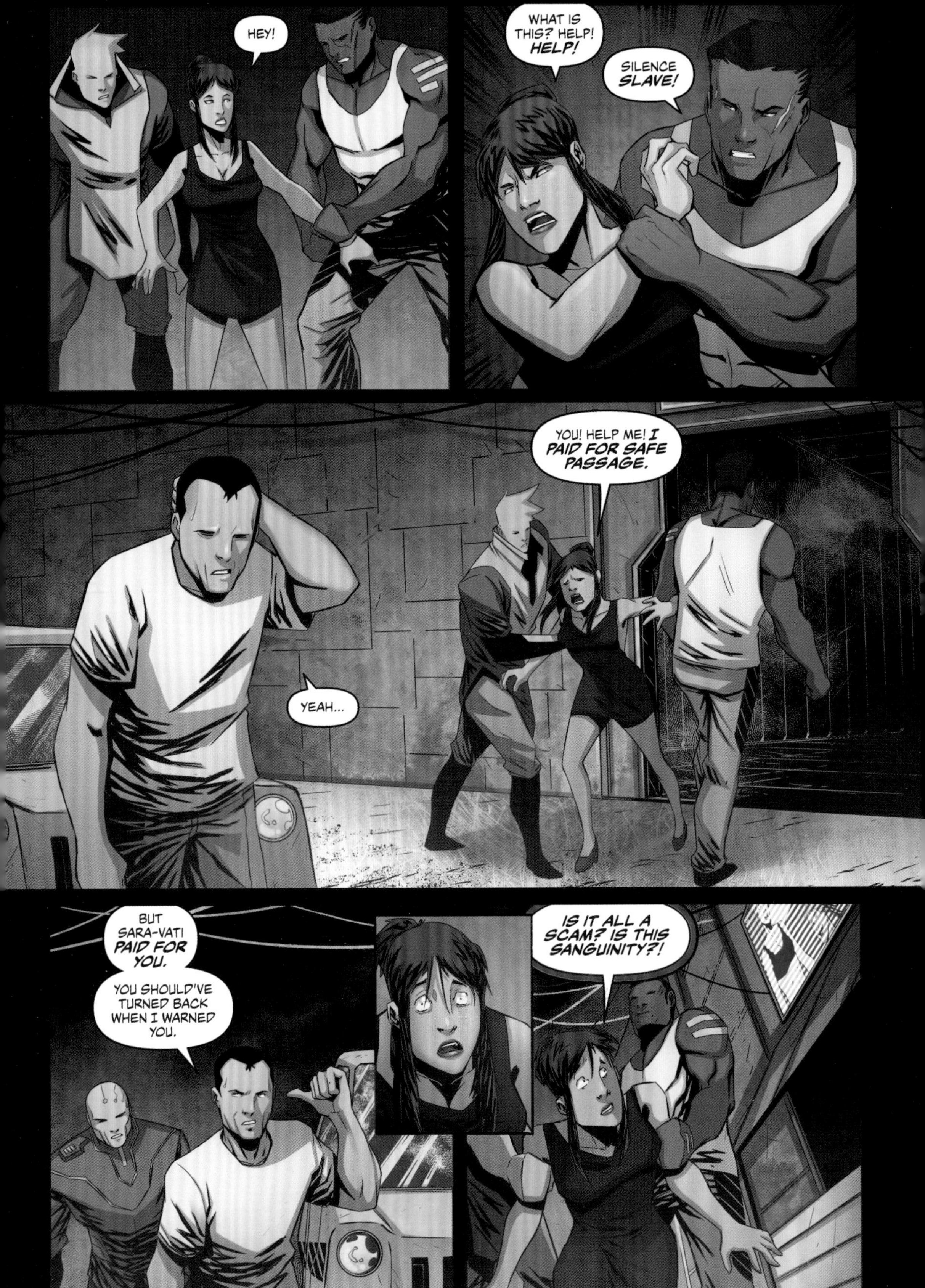
HEY!
WHAT IS THIS? HELP! HELP!
SILENCE SLAVE!
YOU! HELP ME! I PAID FOR SAFE PASSAGE.
YEAH...
BUT SARA-VATI PAID FOR YOU.
YOU SHOULD'VE TURNED BACK WHEN I WARNED YOU.
IS IT ALL A SCAM? IS THIS SANGUINITY?!

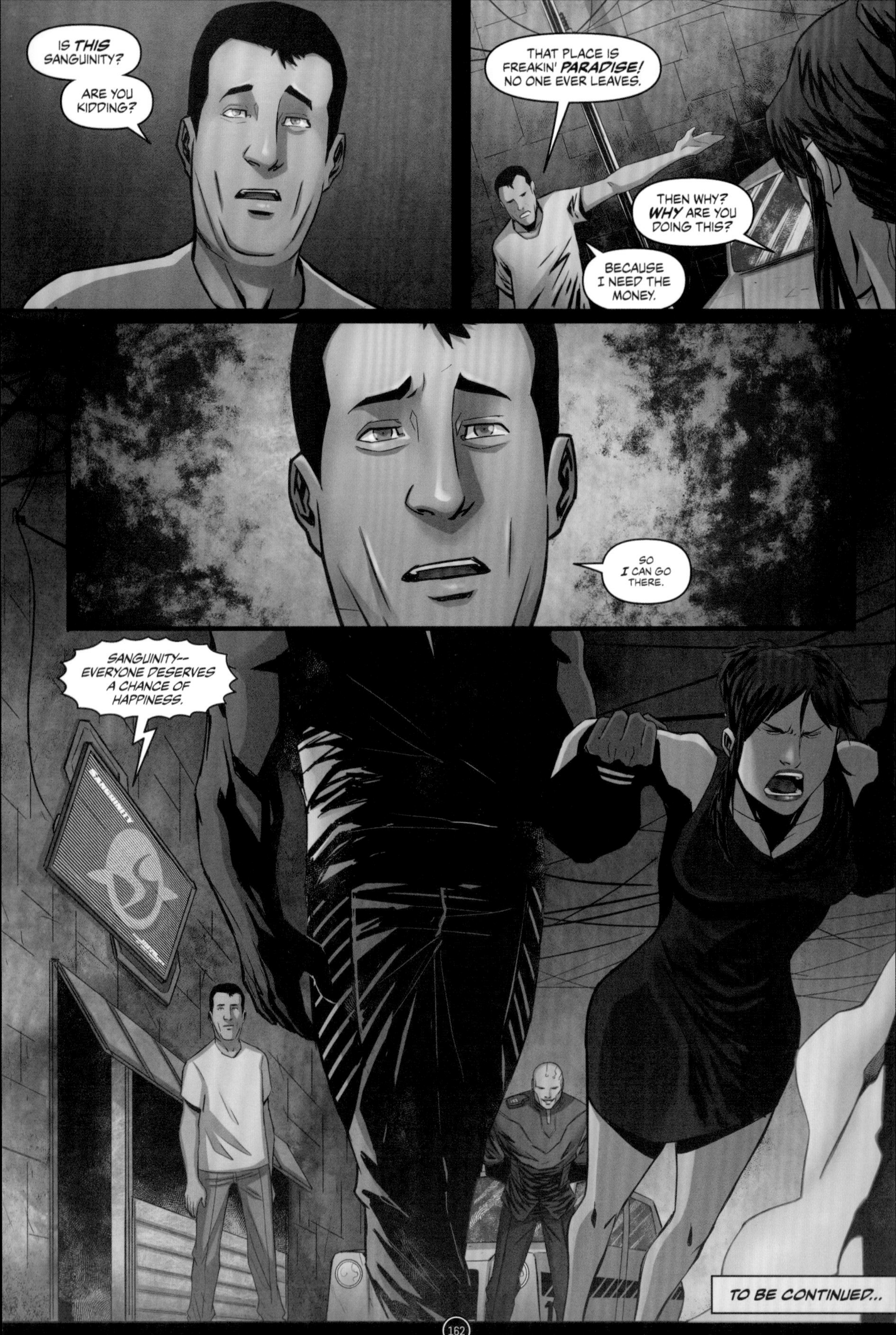
IS THIS SANGUINITY?
ARE YOU KIDDING?
THAT PLACE IS FREAKIN' PARADISE! NO ONE EVER LEAVES.
THEN WHY? WHY ARE YOU DOING THIS?
BECAUSE I NEED THE MONEY.
SO I CAN GO THERE.
SANGUINITY-- EVERYONE DESERVES A CHANCE OF HAPPINESS.
TO BE CONTINUED...

ROBERT SADLER

Sir. I need your help. My niece is missing.

ADMIRAL PUPPO

Any idea where she is?

ROBERT SADLER

Her husband is well connected and has been busy searching planet side. We fear she is off world.

ADMIRAL PUPPO

Any ship wishing to leave the solar system must use one of the gateways. They have to register for the gateway to be rotated towards the destination they wish to travel, so run through all the registrations and eliminate any science or military vessels. That should narrow down the search. We will do what we can to find her, but if they have set up a relay of gateways to hit one after the other, the net may to be wide. There is always the fear that they have a private gateway linked to an uninhabited system or region of space, but If that's the case the person who funded those gateways will be in for a rude awakening when we track them down.

ROBERT SADLER

Thank you sir. I don't know what to say.

...thank you

ADMIRAL PUPPO

Don't thank me Sadler. Do your job - too many people rely on us. Now, give me a progress report on the Juniper Project.

ROBERT SADLER

There is much to discuss. Where would you like me to start?

Doesn't it depress you?

"If you are depressed
you are living in the past..."

Lao Tzu

Writer/Creator
Neil Gibson

Illustrator
Jake Elphick

Colourist
Liezl Buenaventura

Letters by
Justin Birch

www.tpubcomics.com

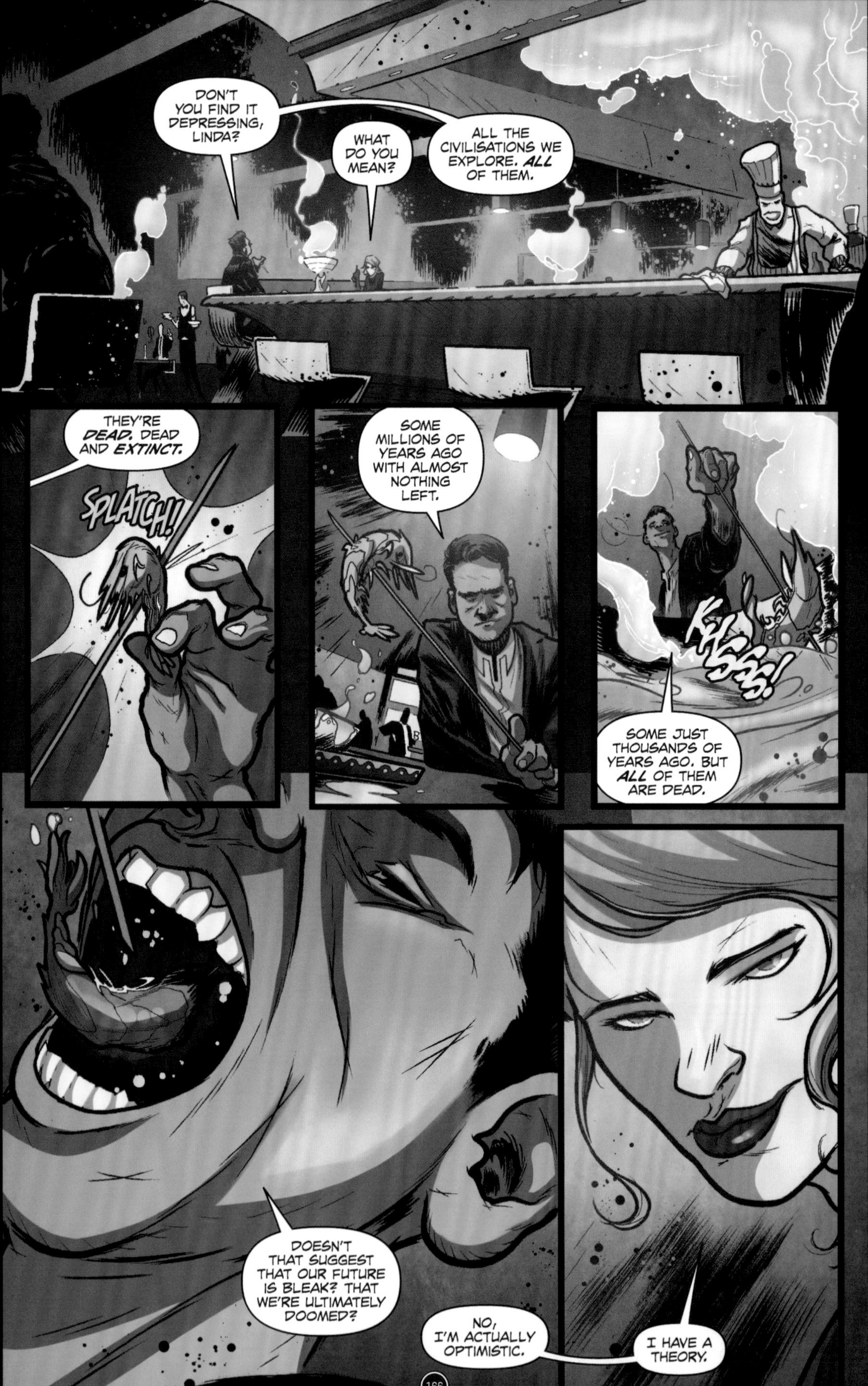

DON'T YOU FIND IT DEPRESSING, LINDA?
WHAT DO YOU MEAN?
ALL THE CIVILISATIONS WE EXPLORE. ALL OF THEM.
THEY'RE DEAD. DEAD AND EXTINCT.
SPLATCH!
SOME MILLIONS OF YEARS AGO WITH ALMOST NOTHING LEFT.
KHSSS!
SOME JUST THOUSANDS OF YEARS AGO. BUT ALL OF THEM ARE DEAD.
DOESN'T THAT SUGGEST THAT OUR FUTURE IS BLEAK? THAT WE'RE ULTIMATELY DOOMED?
NO, I'M ACTUALLY OPTIMISTIC.
I HAVE A THEORY.

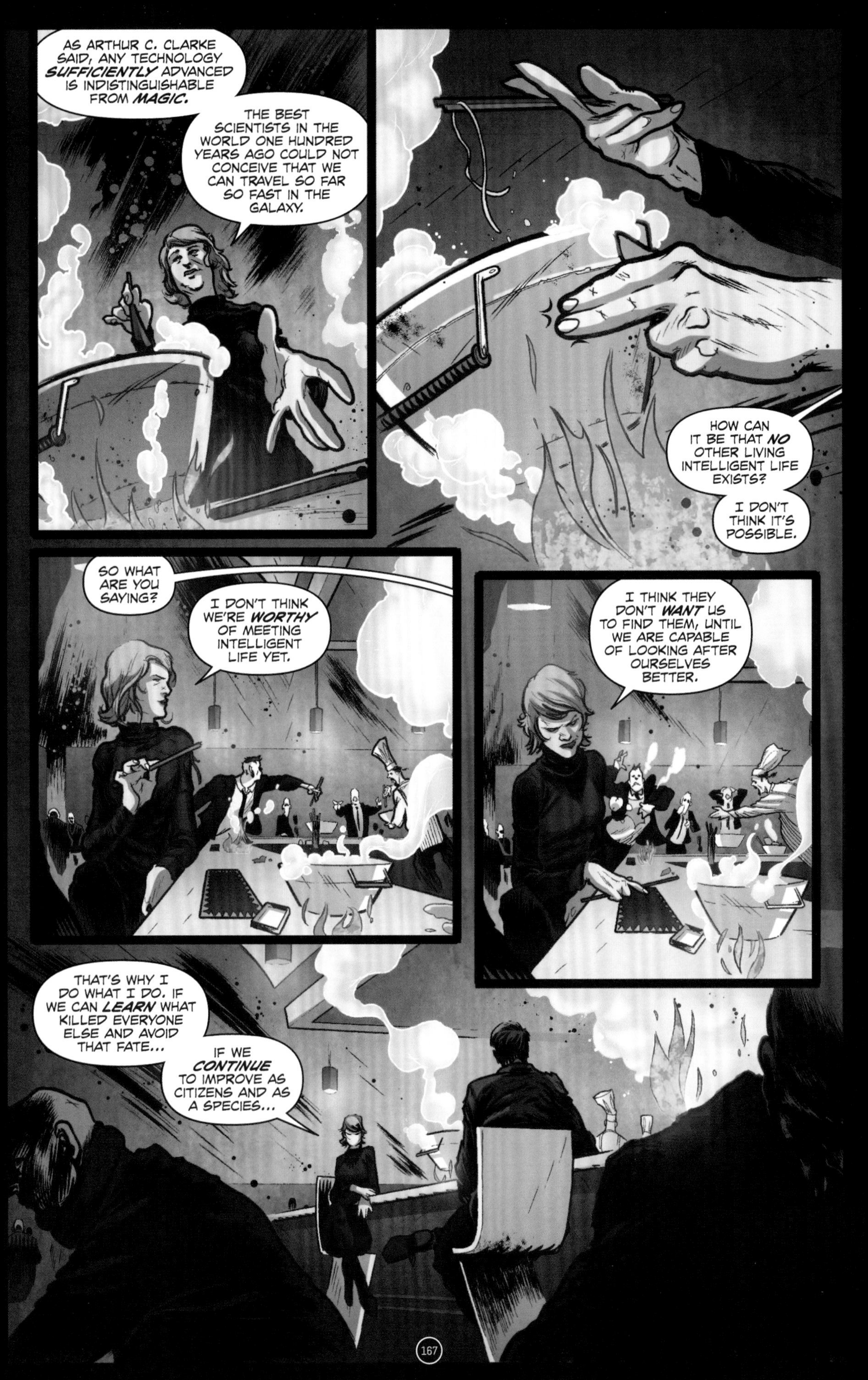
AS ARTHUR C. CLARKE SAID, ANY TECHNOLOGY SUFFICIENTLY ADVANCED IS INDISTINGUISHABLE FROM MAGIC.
THE BEST SCIENTISTS IN THE WORLD ONE HUNDRED YEARS AGO COULD NOT CONCEIVE THAT WE CAN TRAVEL SO FAR SO FAST IN THE GALAXY.
HOW CAN IT BE THAT NO OTHER LIVING INTELLIGENT LIFE EXISTS?
I DON'T THINK IT'S POSSIBLE.
SO WHAT ARE YOU SAYING?
I DON'T THINK WE'RE WORTHY OF MEETING INTELLIGENT LIFE YET.
I THINK THEY DON'T WANT US TO FIND THEM, UNTIL WE ARE CAPABLE OF LOOKING AFTER OURSELVES BETTER.
THAT'S WHY I DO WHAT I DO. IF WE CAN LEARN WHAT KILLED EVERYONE ELSE AND AVOID THAT FATE...
IF WE CONTINUE TO IMPROVE AS CITIZENS AND AS A SPECIES...

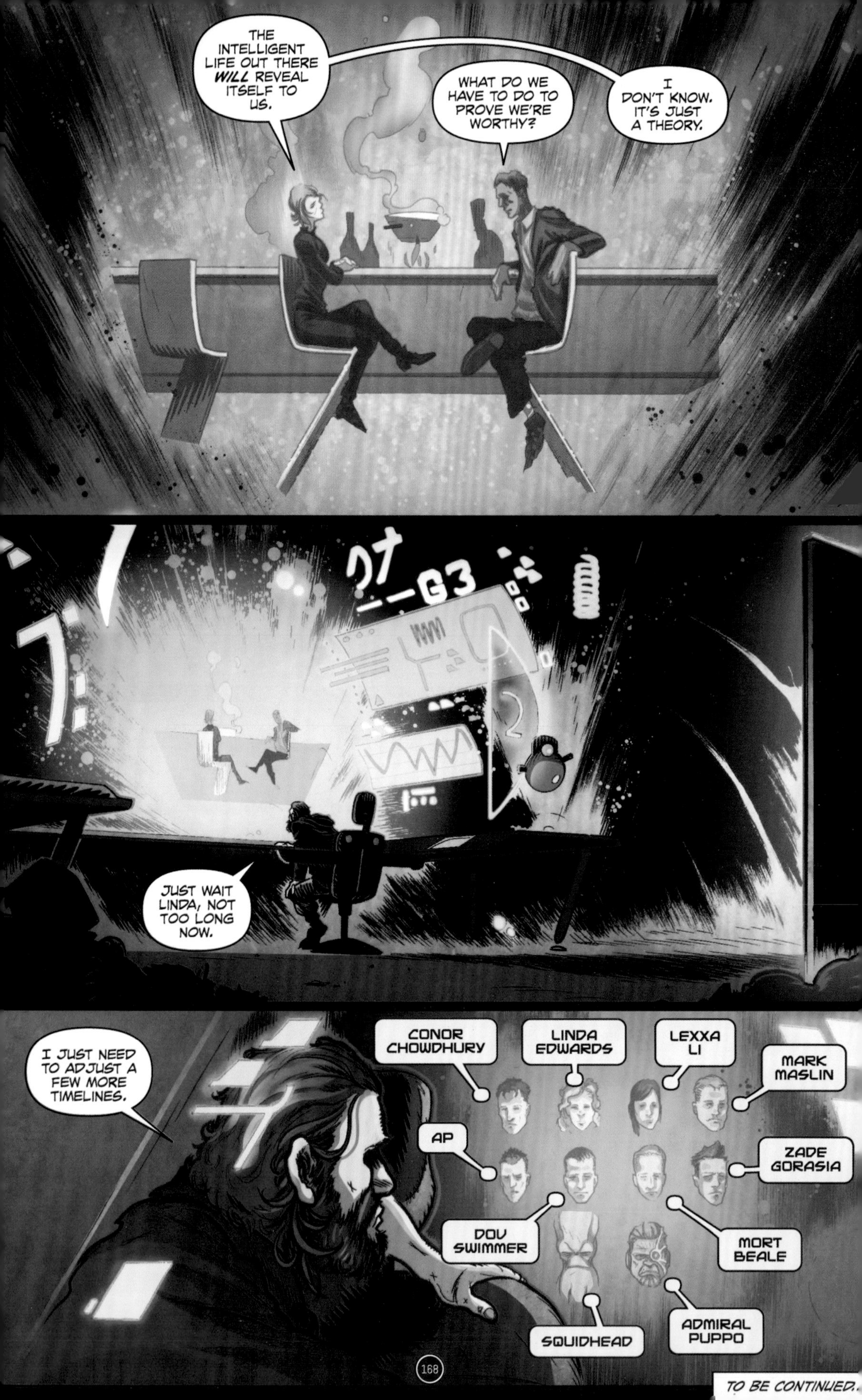
THE INTELLIGENT LIFE OUT THERE *WILL* REVEAL ITSELF TO US.
WHAT DO WE HAVE TO DO TO PROVE WE'RE WORTHY?
I DON'T KNOW. IT'S JUST A THEORY.
JUST WAIT LINDA, NOT TOO LONG NOW.
I JUST NEED TO ADJUST A FEW MORE TIMELINES.
CONOR CHOWDHURY
LINDA EDWARDS
LEXXA LI
MARK MASLIN
AP
ZADE GORASIA
DOV SWIMMER
MORT BEALE
SQUIDHEAD
ADMIRAL PUPPO
TO BE CONTINUED.

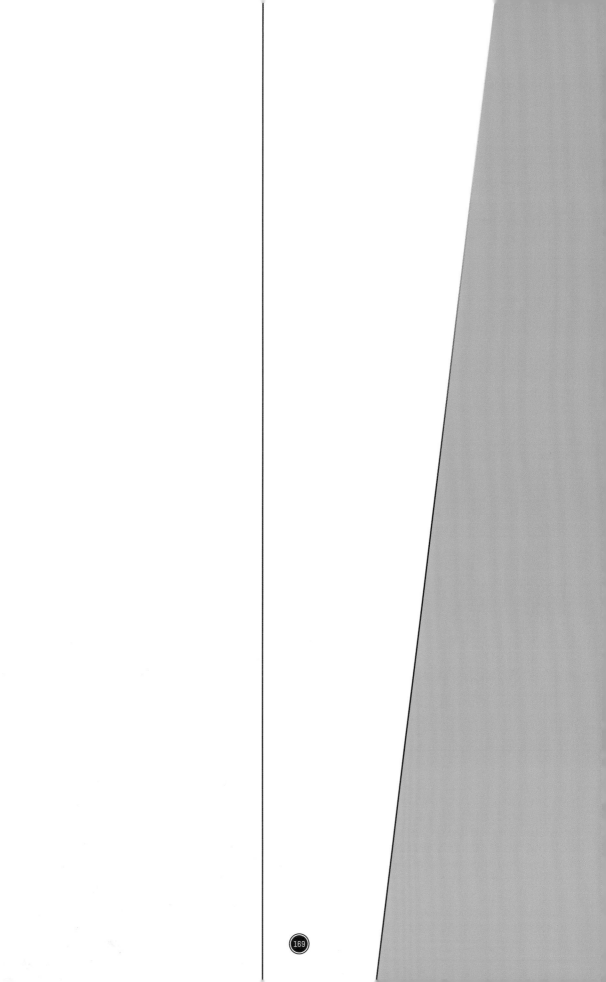

The theory behind **The Theory**

When I made **Twisted Dark**, a lot of readers said it was too dark for them, so I tried to make the stories lighter in volume 2. Naturally, the real fans screamed 'what are you doing?!', and I realised that I had to split into different genres (hence **Twisted Light**). A lot of people ask for action or science fiction at conventions, and as a big Sci-Fi fan myself I knew that Twisted Sci-Fi had to happen. I wrote many of the stories years ago, but it took a while for the stars to align to allow us to make this book. Like with Twisted Dark, there are a lot of stories planned with interacting characters and threads. I am excited to bring it to you!

We went back and forth on whether we should call it **The Theory** or **Twisted Sci-Fi**, but ultimately went with **The Theory** because we wanted it to stand on its own. That decision happened relatively late in the game, though, so in the office we still slip up and refer to it as Twisted Sci-Fi.

Fig 1: Linda Edwards. The character of Linda was inspired by Linda Canton, who started off volunteering for us here at TPub before she became head of Operations. She was studying archaeology, so I made the character an astroarchaeologist. We brought in Chelsea Ambrose to design the costumes for us – I expected her to go through a few designs, but we loved her first set and we ran with it.

Support
one on each wrist
Side
Front
over the knee boots
grip surface
zips on the inside

1
2
3
4

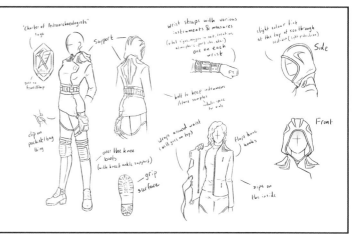

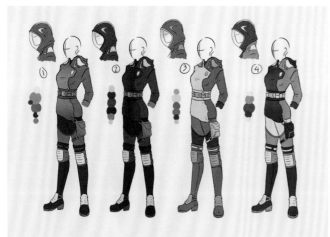

Fig 2: Colours. It was only after I attended a talk on colouring by Eisner award winner Jordie Bellaire that I realised just how important colour is, both in terms of aesthetics and storytelling. Here are a few of the options we went through for the astroarchaeologist's worksuits. The concept for the suit was it was a hoodie, but when the hood was flipped up, a force field activated that would protect the wearer from the environment.

Fig 3: Jemm-r. The character Jemm-r is from the future (or is she?) and we knew we were going to have a tough time getting people to recognise her. The stories in all the Twisted Series are drawn by a rotating team of artists, so each person will draw the character slightly differently. On top of that, as part of her missions, Jemm-r has to go into disguise a lot. This design was the base one we came up with for body type/ style, but don't get too used to it!

Admiral's expressions - close ups

Fig 4: Admiral Puppo! This gnarly gentleman for a long time just had the name 'Space General'. The talented Davide Puppo was the first to illustrate him, and he did such a great job designing the look of the character that I had to name the Admiral after him. I didn't intend for the character to only have one eye, but I think you'll like the back story about how he lost it!

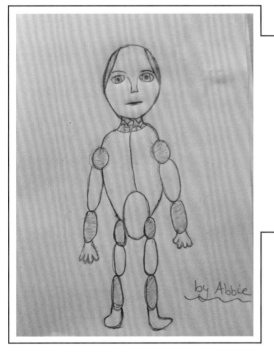

by Abbie

Fig 5: Abbie's robot. We go to a lot of comic cons, and one of my favourite (and youngest) readers is Abbie. I often try to include volunteers/ fans in my comics, so I asked her to design a robot – this is what she came up with! It just so happens that her father, Mark, is a professor and helped out with some of the science in the comic – it always helps to keep things accurate and real. He was the basis for the male character in Quarantine. Our other science advisor, Kian, also appears, but under a different name. Nope. Not telling you who.

Fig 6: Abbie's Robot 2.0 Here is Abbie's robot drawn into the comic by my friend and talented artist Amrit Birdi. There are a variety of different robots in the series – these ones are less intelligent, but they are more agile for moving over terrain and handling items with extreme precision/ delicacy than household ones you see. The highest level robots are the ones like Dobbs or Bambi that help the astroarchaeologists. Why the robot bumped into Jennifer will forever be a mystery…or will it?

We'd like to thank all our amazing kickstarter backers who made this possible...

Linda J Canton **Léon Othenin-Girard** Eli Morgan **Michael Nimmo** Amrit Birdi **Anthony Rivera** Mike Ingrey **Kalai** Brian Huisman **Derek Devereaux Smith** Mark Anderson **The Creative Fund** Michael Gordon **Justin Birch** John Weitjes Lel **Katie Fruin** Jose J. Becerra Jr. **Katya Hvostova** Chadwick Torseth **Jodie Denton** Chris **Shane Lowe** Jed McPherson **Chris Beard** Michail Dim. Drakomathioulakis **Flannery Crump** Nathalie Howard **Arianna §** Laurence Shapiro Dan Mallier **Sam Titman** Christian Meyer **Tscheikob** David Court Steven **Sauve** Alan Heighway **Lawrence Ward** Daniela Fossaluzza **Jennifer Campney** Ben Quinlan **Paul y cod asyn Jarman** Chris "CloudLXXXV" Horner **Jennifer Priester** Paul Nyitrai **Matt Denny** Ali Luckhardt **Lee Werrin** Robert Hsu **Mark Dennison** Timothy Haritun **Glen McFerren, M.D.** Timothy Huygens **Michael Sexton** Jay Tomkinson **James R. Crowley** Bart-Jan Kuiper **Mark Adams** Denise Chung **Armond Netherly** Karl Ottersberg

Daniel J. Westendorf Matrix **Al Sims** Kevin Wilson **Patrick Fowler** Beverly Lyons **Mark Whitehead** Staci Sherman **Philip Cummings** Christos Dionyssopoulos **Nick Rehder** Half Pint **Harley** Aaron Gillians **Kurt Hardesty** AniG **Jason Ruiz** Jason Crase **Scott "Old Gregg" Alfermann** Amanda Ryan **Brian Re** Randy Andrews **Jade Bolton** William Golder Gingerob Oscar Russell **John 'johnkzin' Rudd** Julian Laubstein **Alex Murphy** Nick Dillon **Scott Vivian** Andy Shepherd **Roland Heep** Erin D Lizy Draime **JimS** dan cooke **Stuart Stilborn** Oldrich Stibor **Joel Lawless** Ron Randall **Evan Summers** Karl Kesel **Chris B** none **Hannah Cuffe** White Beard Geek **Paul Vinten** GMarkC **Daniel Crowley** Rusty Waldrup **Ged S.** Dave Rose **Mitchell Lynn** Ben Hood **Paul Dent** Jay Lofstead **James Moore** Lars Schwed Nygård **Tracy and Nicole Vierra dan gibson** Ray Molina **Stein Vråle** Harry L Viktor Triumph **Sebastian H.** Phyllis Ng **mark habberley** Michael Price **David Novis** Sarah Meeks **Andrew Lultschik** Alex Emil "AngryAnt" Johansen

Lowell Wann John Lamar **Dave Kastner** Pedro De Lara **Kristopher Volter** Conor McCreepy **David Negrin** Adam Klagues **Daniel Anthony** Tony Lmfao **Dave Mankoff** Timothy Travis **Brian Weibeler** Eoin Smith **Joeri Overheul** Jaap van Poelgeest **Wayne Hall** Michael Heitkemper **Josh Bussey** Gary Dellar **Josh Cremosnik** John MacLeod **Nick Wagner** Shawn Hanna **Conor Carton** Steven Brown **Lorraine Williams** Cato Vandrare **Roger O Thornhill** Lynda Bowen **Umair Baig** Tom Grainger-White **Ross Nicholson** Barry J. Smith **Simon Elmore** Steve **Steven Smyth** John Neall **David J. Simmons** Nova Sheldon-Corner **Joseph Stanton sr** Matthew G. Sunderman **Claire Lim** Mat "Werther's smuggler" Renaud **Steve Kyriacou** Ethan Sobotta **Meg Miller** Kayla Lowes **Devin terSteeg and Hollie DeFrancisco** Chris Crowther **Jordan Evans** Rafael Pacheco **AP** Gemma **Steven Vest** Ron Povey **Brian Nimmo** Russel Dalenberg **Andrew Thirlwell** David Wonner **David Cobb** Bradley Watker **Lenny Van Daele** Tom Klimes **Craig Hackl** Norman Boyd **Sune Kristensen** Kim Courtnell **David Arthur** Benjamin Hausman **Khendrix** Sola Simpson **Tasos Anastasiades** Raul Castro **Michael Ambler** Ismail Farhat **Marylou Bilawala** Peter Higgs **Mike Elsmore** Pratyush Pandey **Ziki Nelson** Pixel black **Richard D. Deverell** Tony Anjo **Horseflesh** Stacy Fluegge **Billy Potts** Brandon Abrahamson **Nick Allen** Tom Wojciechowski **Pierre Mooser** Mike Burke **Braek Jeanmark** A'Kessler Matthias **Rothmeier** Andi **Jed Brooks** Smith **Darrin and Ruth Sutherland** Marc Cayouette **Chase H Dougal** Freir Raul **Wulfgars da Silva** alicat **Andrew R Arthur** Bhenedict King **Jolene Taylor** colin **Rudy Heyden** Cody Blaine **William Houseago** Catherine L Fleming **Peter Green** Anthony Eames **Aaron T Ignasi** Aureliano Rama **anonymous** Kai Yu **Mistake Not** Jennifer Ade Brown **Patrick Bächli** Ben Slabak **Sergey Anikushin** Geoff Wood **Natasha Liff** Eric Hendrickson **MJ Funky Breaze** Nancy Cravero **Sarah Anderson** James Edward Reed **Jon Acton** Lina "Make Me King" Christopoulou **Davina Tijani** Brad Dancer **Pippa Edwin Docherty** Gal Shoval **Stuart Lofthouse** Heiko **Shawn Dean**

Other Titles from Tpub

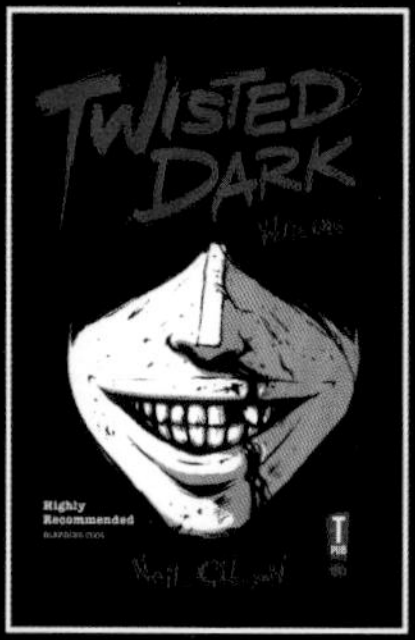
TWISTED DARK
Neil Gibson

Twisted Dark
Volume 1

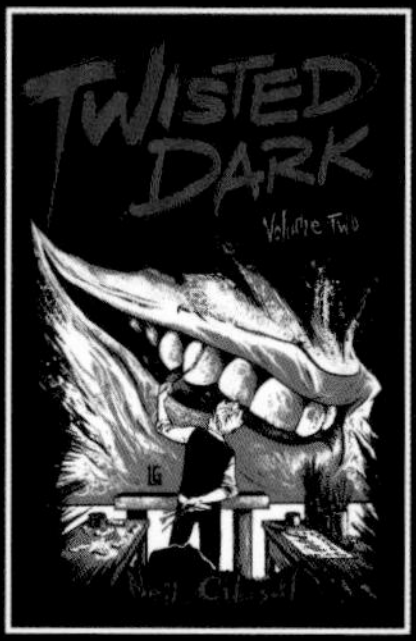
TWISTED DARK
Volume Two
Neil Gibson

Twisted Dark
Volume 2

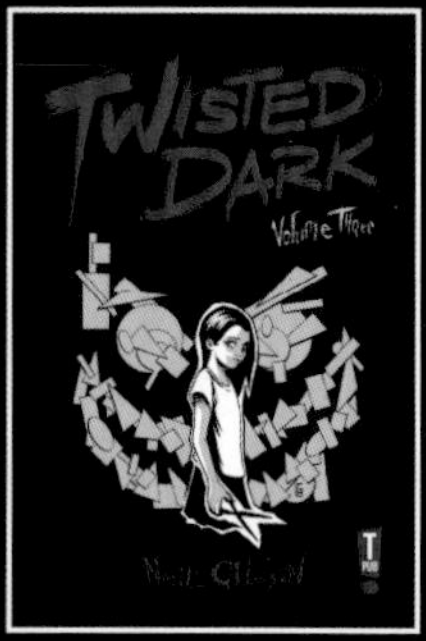
TWISTED DARK
Volume Three
Neil Gibson

Twisted Dark
Volume 3

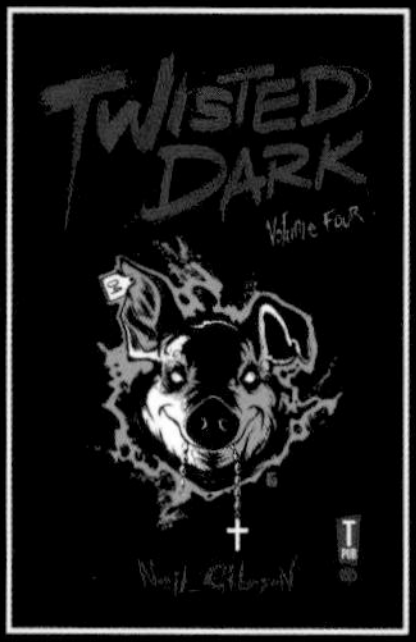
TWISTED DARK
Neil Gibson

Twisted Dark
Volume 4

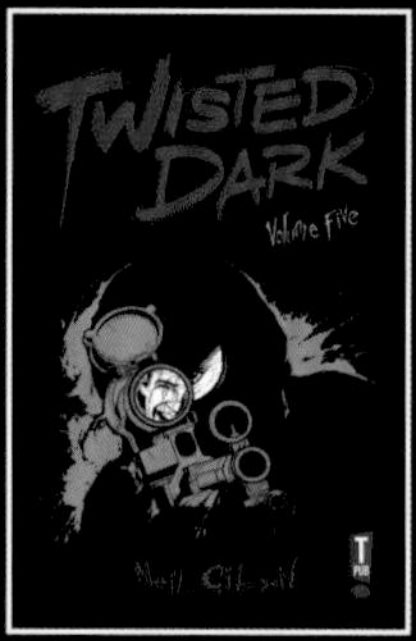
TWISTED DARK
Neil Gibson

Twisted Dark
Volume 5

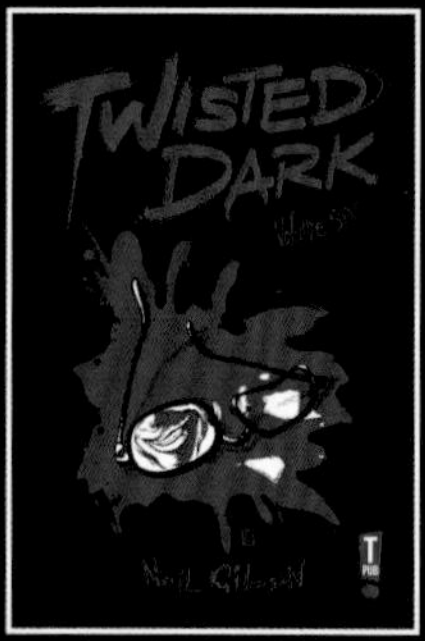
TWISTED DARK
Neil Gibson

Twisted Dark
Volume 6

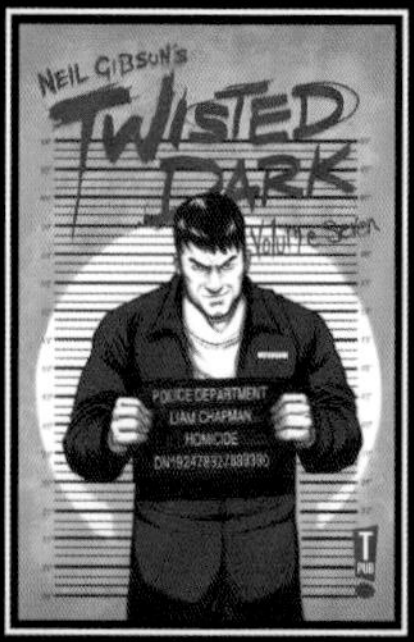
NEIL GIBSON'S
TWISTED DARK
POLICE DEPARTMENT
LIAM CHAPMAN
HOMICIDE

Twisted Dark
Volume 7

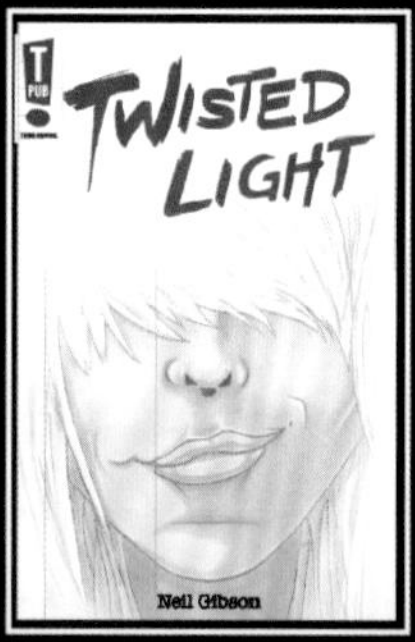
TWISTED LIGHT
Neil Gibson

Twisted
Light

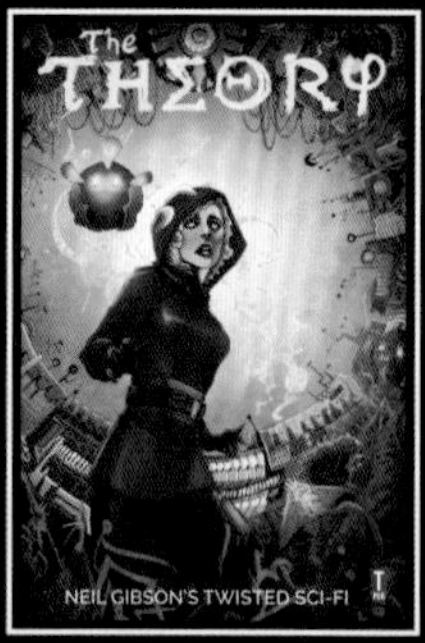
The THEORY
NEIL GIBSON'S TWISTED SCI-FI

The Theory
Volume 1

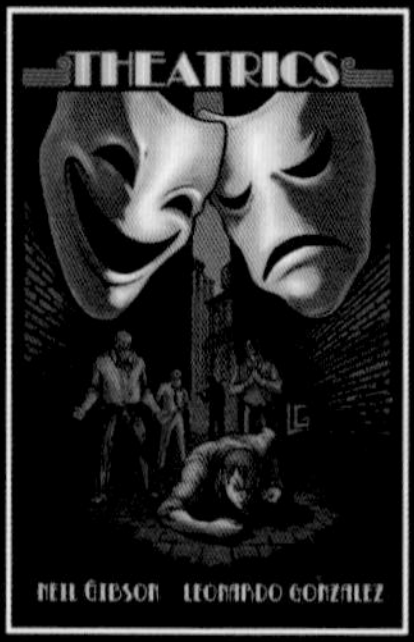
THEATRICS
NEIL GIBSON LEONARDO GONZALEZ

Theatrics:
Volume one

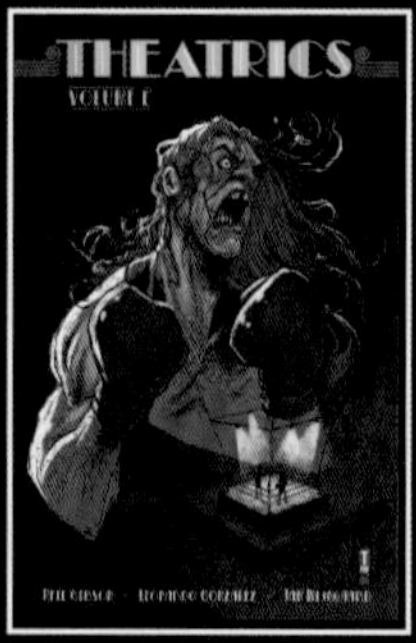
THEATRICS

Theatrics:
Volume two

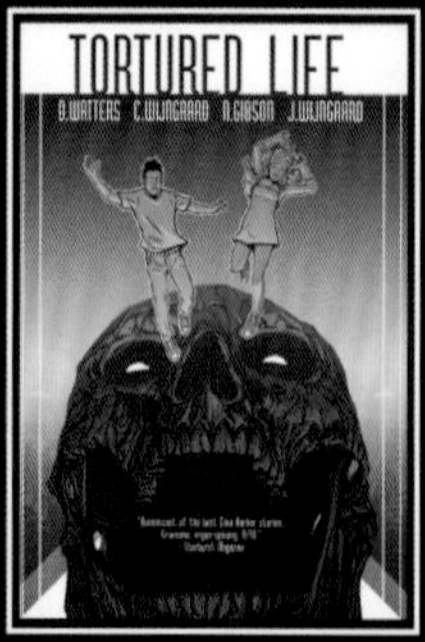
TORTURED LIFE
B.WATTERS C.WIJNGAARD N.GIBSON J.WIJNGAARD

Tortured
Life

Transdimensional

ISSUE 1 OF 4

Transmissions

RYAN O'SULLIVAN & PLAID KLAUS
TURNCOAT
T PUB

Turncoat

STAN LEE'S
LUCKY MAN
Neil Gibson
Michael Gordon
Atula Siriwardane
Asoka Abeywardena

Lucky Man

T PUB
DISPOSABLE LEGENDS

Disposable Legends

TABATHA
GIBSON · THE ARTIST

Tabatha

THE TRAVELLER
NEIL GIBSON
TASOS ANASTASIADIS
JAN WIJNGAARD
HASSAN OTSMANE-ELHAOU

The Traveller

The World of
CHUB CHUB!

The World of Chub Chub

More titles

Coming

Soon...

T PUB

info@tpub.co.uk

If you have enjoyed this comic, why not head over to **TPubcomics.com.** There is a ton of free material to read and you can join our newsletter for recommendations on the best comics we've read and to be sent the occasional free comic.

Thank you for reading our work and sharing it on social media. We can't do what we do without your support!

If you just want us to send you the free stuff, send up an email to info@tpub.co.uk

Social Media;

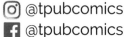 @tpubcomics

@tpubcomics

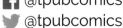 @tpubcomics